CW00516223

Secured Credit under English and American Law

Secured credit drives economic activity. Under English law it is possible to create security over almost any asset, but the law is widely considered to be unsatisfactory for several reasons, including a cumbersome registration system, a preoccupation with formalistic distinctions and the lack of clear and rationally determined priority rules. Gerard McCormack examines the current state of English law, highlighting its weaknesses. He uses Article 9 of the American Uniform Commercial Code as a reference point: this article has successfully serviced the world's largest economy for over forty years and is increasingly used as the basis for legislation by Commonwealth jurisdictions including Canada and New Zealand. The Law Commission has suggested the enactment of similar legislation in England. In addition, McCormack considers whether there really is a case for the priority of secured credit, as well as whether there are other international models to draw upon. The appendix contains the text of Article 9.

GERARD McCORMACK is Baker and McKenzie Professor of Corporate Law at the University of Manchester. His recent publications include *Registration of Company Charges* (1994), *Reservation of Title* (2nd edn 1995) and *Proprietary Claims and Insolvency* (1997).

Cambridge Studies in Corporate Law

Series Editor
Professor Barry Rider,
University of London

Corporate or Company Law encompasses the law relating to the creation, operation and management of corporations and their relationships with other legal persons. **Cambridge Studies in Corporate Law** offers an academic platform for discussion of these issues. The series is international in its choice of both authors and subjects, and aims to publish the best original scholarship on topics ranging from labour law to capital regulation.

Jane Dine
The Governance of Corporate Groups
0 521 66070 X

A. J. Boyle
Minority Shareholders' Remedies
0 521 79106 5

Gerard McCormack
Secured Credit under English and American Law
0 521 82670 5

Secured Credit under English and American Law

Gerard McCormack

CAMBRIDGE
UNIVERSITY PRESS

PUBLISHED BY THE PRESS SYNDICATE OF THE UNIVERSITY OF CAMBRIDGE
The Pitt Building, Trumpington Street, Cambridge, United Kingdom

CAMBRIDGE UNIVERSITY PRESS
The Edinburgh Building, Cambridge, CB2 2RU, UK
40 West 20th Street, New York, NY 10011–4211, USA
477 Williamstown Road, Port Melbourne, VIC 3207, Australia
Ruiz de Alarcón 13, 28014 Madrid, Spain
Dock House, The Waterfront, Cape Town 8001, South Africa

http://www.cambridge.org

© Gerard McCormack 2004

This book is in copyright. Subject to statutory exception
and to the provisions of relevant collective licensing agreements,
no reproduction of any part may take place without
the written permission of Cambridge University Press.

First published 2004

Printed in the United Kingdom at the University Press, Cambridge

Typeface Plantin 10/12 pt.   *System* LᴬTEX 2$_\varepsilon$ [TB]

A catalogue record for this book is available from the British Library

Library of Congress Cataloguing in Publication data
McCormack, G. (Gerard)
Secured credit under English and American law / Gerard McCormack
    p. cm. – (Cambridge studies in corporate law)
Includes bibliographical references and index.
ISBN 0 521 82670 5 (hbk.)
1. Security (Law) – England.   2. Security (Law) – United States.   I. Title.   II. Series.
K1100.M33 2003
346.07′4–dc21   2003053182

ISBN 0 521 82670 5 hardback

The publisher has used its best endeavours to ensure that URLs for external websites
referred to in this book are correct and active at the time of going to press. However, the
publisher has no responsibility for the websites and can make no guarantee that a site will
remain live or that the content is or will remain appropriate.

Contents

Preface

One of the characters created by a famous Irish playwright said that the world is in a state of 'chassis', by which was meant 'chaos'. This may or may not be true but, whatever the broader geopolitical developments, the English law of security interests is in a state of some upheaval. We are possibly at the threshold of major reform heralded by the Company Law Steering Group in their final report on *Modern Company Law for a Competitive Economy* and by the Law Commission in their consultation paper on *Registration of Security Interests*.

Given that corporate rescue law has recently been streamlined is there not a case now for streamlining the law of secured credit? Why is the present law on secured credit considered to be unsatisfactory? Is reform really needed? Would the cure be worse than the disease? Is Article 9 of the American Uniform Commercial Code really a suitable legislative guide? Are there other international models to draw upon? Is there really a case for the priority of secured credit?

This book attempts to address these questions. The focus is on the law of secured credit rather than on corporate and insolvency law more generally. Corporate rescue law only gets a look-in as an adjunct to secured credit law. English law and the alleged deficiencies of the same are analysed against the backdrop of Article 9 of the Uniform Commercial Code. Article 9 moves away from the formalistic preoccupations of current English law and combines a more comprehensive filing system with clearer and more rationally determined rules for determining priorities between competing security interests in the same property. For good pragmatic reasons, however, reform in England may be slow and piecemeal. Practitioners might say, 'half a loaf is better than no bread at all' and even, 'if it is not broke why fix it?' On the other hand, the fact that a system works very successfully in the largest economy in the world is not a reason for saying that it could not work very well here.

Why use Article 9 as a direct comparator rather than New Zealand and the Canadian province of Saskatchewan as the Law Commission has done? Two reasons spring to mind. Firstly, Article 9 is the catalyst that inspired the others; and secondly, the English business community might find the American comparison more appropriate. The jurisdictions relied upon by the Law Commission do not have developed financial markets on the English scale.

The focus is on English law as compared with Article 9. I recognise that Scots law is different in some significant respects though Scottish lawyers may find the more general analysis to be of some use. This is not a comprehensive treatise. Some topics receive more attention than others. Certain topics warrant much more extended treatment, as they have received elsewhere from other writers on the subject. I would single out in this regard the issue of security over intellectual property and the whole area of financial collateral, which is the subject of a recent EU directive.

The relevant provisions of the Enterprise Act came into force on 15 September 2003. The Insolvency Act 1986 (Prescribed Part) Order 2003 sets aside a proportion of floating-charge recoveries for the benefit of unsecured creditors of a company. The proportion is based on a sliding scale and calculated as 50% of the first £10,000, then 20% of a remainder but subject to a ceiling so that the fund for unsecured creditors shall not exceed £600,000.

The draft Financial Collateral Regulations 2003 came too late for discussion in this text.

In the writing of the book I have incurred many debts. Special thanks are due to the British Academy and the Leverhulme Trust for facilitating some of the research on which the book is based as well as to the University of Manchester and the National University of Singapore. Hugh Beale, John De Lacy, Janet Dine, David Milman, Agasha Mugasha, Tan Cheng Han, Alan Ward and many others have also helped me in various ways. Finally, I would like to thank Presy y Amelia por todo.

Gerard McCormack
Manchester
September 2003

Abbreviations

AJIL	*American Journal of International Law*
Ark LR	*Arkansas Law Review*
Can Bus LJ	*Canadian Business Law Journal*
CFILR	*Company, Financial and Insolvency Law Review*
Chicago-Kent Law Rev	*Chicago-Kent Law Review*
CLJ	*Cambridge Law Journal*
CLP	*Current Legal Problems*
Co Law	*Company Lawyer*
Colum Bus L Rev	*Columbia Business Law Review*
Colum L Rev	*Columbia Law Review*
Conn L Rev	*Connecticut Law Review*
Conv	*Conveyancer*
Cornell L Rev	*Cornell Law Review*
Duke LJ	*Duke Law Journal*
DULJ	*Dublin University Law Journal*
EBLR	*European Business Law Review*
Ga L Rev	*Georgia Law Review*
Harv L Rev	*Harvard Law Review*
ICLQ	*International and Comparative Law Quarterly*
Idaho LR	*Idaho Law Review*
Int Bus Lawyer	*International Business Lawyer*
Int'l Rev L & Econ	*International Review of Law and Economics*
JBL	*Journal of Business Law*
JIBL	*Journal of International Banking Law*
J Legal Stud	*Journal of Legal Studies*
Kan LR	*Kansas Law Review*
LMCLQ	*Lloyds Maritime and Commercial Law Quarterly*
LQR	*Law Quarterly Review*
McGill LJ	*McGill Law Journal*
Minn LR	*Minnesota Law Review*

MLR	Modern Law Review
Nebraska LR	Nebraska Law Review
NILQ	Northern Ireland Legal Quarterly
NLJ	New Law Journal
NYULR	New York University Law Review
NZBLQ	New Zealand Business Law Quarterly
NZLJ	New Zealand Law Journal
NZULR	New Zealand Universities Law Review
OJLS	Oxford Journal of Legal Studies
Rutgers L Rev	Rutgers Law Review
Tenn L Rev	Tennessee Law Review
Tex Int'l LJ	Texas International Law Journal
Texas L Rev	Texas Law Review
UCC LJ	Uniform Commercial Code Law Journal
U Ch L Rev	University of Chicago Law Review
U Pa J Int'l Econ L	University of Pennsylvania Journal of International Economic Law
U Pa L Rev	University of Pennsylvania Law Review
UWALR	University of Western Australia Law Review
Va L Rev	Virginia Law Review
Vand L Rev	Vanderbilt Law Review
Yale LJ	Yale Law Journal

1   The essence and importance of security

This book compares and contrasts American and English approaches towards the recognition and enforcement of security interests in personal property. United States law is found almost exclusively in the Uniform Commercial Code (UCC), whereas English law is derived from a variety of sources, both statutory and non-statutory. If one could compare the two systems in a word, one might say that the US approach is functional whereas the English approach is pragmatic though the overall tendency is to be facilitative and enabling. There are almost no limits on the category of assets that may be used as security, and the procedures for the creation of security interests are quite flexible and informal. The law is pragmatic rather than functional, as transactions that serve the same economic ends are often visited with different legal consequences. The latter state of affairs has attracted criticism but so far the legislature has resisted efforts to recast English law along the lines of Article 9 of the US UCC. Article 9 attempts to apply similar rules to all transactions that in economic terms are intended to serve as security. Moreover, Article 9 embodies a near-comprehensive registration obligation, i.e. public notice of security interests must be given. Under English law, by contrast, certain transactions that in economic terms might be regarded as creating a security interest are not subject to any public registration or filing requirements that might alert other potential creditors – or, indeed, the world at large – to the existence of the security interest.

The definition of security interests

The contrasting approaches between England and the US are even manifest when one considers a necessary starting-point for any analysis: the definition of security. The term 'security interest' is defined in Article 1(37) of the UCC as meaning an interest in personal property that secures either payment of money or the performance of an obligation and also the interest of a buyer of accounts. By contrast, there is no statutory definition of 'security interest' in England and so one must fall back on judicial interpretations that, necessarily, are conditioned and qualified by the circumstances of a particular case.[1] A notable example is provided in the judgment of Browne-Wilkinson V-C in *Re Paramount Airways Ltd*,[2] where the following definition of security was accepted: 'Security is created where a person (the creditor) obtains rights exercisable against some property in which the debtor has an interest in order to enforce the discharge of the debtor's obligation to the creditor.'

Clearly this is not a comprehensive definition, for it does not recognise the fact that security may be granted to secure the obligations of somebody other than the grantee. Professor Sir Roy Goode, acknowledging the 'third party' issue, has defined a security interest as a right given to one party in the asset(s) of another party to secure payment or performance by that other party or by a third party.[3] On his analysis a security interest:[4]

(1) arises from a transaction intended as security;
(2) is a right in rem;
(3) is created by a grant or declaration, not by reservation;
(4) if fixed, or specific, implies a restriction on the debtor's dominion over the asset;
(5) cannot be taken by the creditor over his own obligation to the debtor.

These characteristics ascribed to a security interest cannot be accepted in their entirety – in particular point 5, which suggests that it is a conceptual impossibility for a bank to be granted a charge over its own indebtedness to a customer.[5] There is a strong contrary view that a debt is simply an item of property and, like any other item of property, it may be charged to anybody that the creditor wishes.[6] This pragmatic approach appealed to Lord Hoffmann in *Re BCCI (No. 8)*,[7] who spoke for a unanimous House of Lords in categorically rejecting the doctrine that it was conceptually

---

[1] See the statement in P. Ali *The Law of Secured Finance* (Oxford University Press, 2002) at p. 15: 'Despite the obvious importance of the concept of "security interest" to the law of secured transactions, the concept continues to evade precise definition.'

[2] [1990] BCC 130 at 149. See also the comments of Lord Scott in *Smith v. Bridgend County Borough Council* [2002] 1 AC 336 at 355 that 'a contractual right enabling a creditor to sell his debtor's goods and apply the proceeds in or towards satisfaction of the debt is a right of a security character'.

[3] See R. Goode *Legal Problems of Credit and Security* (Sweet & Maxwell, 2nd edn. 1988) at p. 1. See generally for a definitional exposition of security Fidelis Oditah *Legal Aspects of Receivables Financing* (Sweet & Maxwell, 1991) chap. 1.

[4] Goode *Legal Problems* at pp. 1–2.

[5] As was held by Millett J in *Re Charge Card Services Ltd* [1987] 1 Ch 150.

[6] See e.g. William Blair 'Cash Deposits as a Form of Security' in [1987] *Butterworths Banking and Financial Law Review* at pp. 163, 173–4; P. Wood 'Three Problems of Set-off: Contingencies, Build-Ups and Charge-Backs' (1987) 8 *Co Law* 262.

[7] [1998] AC 214.

impossible for a security interest to be taken by a creditor over his own obligations to the debtor. In Lord Hoffmann's view, the law should be slow to declare a practice of the commercial community to be conceptually impossible given the fact that the law was fashioned to suit the practicalities of life. He added that legal concepts such as 'proprietary interest' and 'charge' were no more than labels given to clusters of related and self-consistent rules of law. Such concepts did not have a life of their own from which the rules were inexorably derived. In fact, English law has long taken a non-doctrinaire view towards the recognition and enforcement of security interests in property. Lord Hoffmann highlighted the example of the charge which, as he pointed out, is a security interest created without any transfer of title or possession to the beneficiary. An equitable charge could be created by an informal transaction for value and over any kind of property.[8] The workhorse of the secured credit industry in England has traditionally been the charge, particularly the floating charge,[9] but there are many different types of security right recognised under English law. The law on both sides of the Atlantic is similar in generally granting secured creditors priority over unsecured creditors. Priority over other creditors in the event of debtor insolvency is commonly identified as the most important reason behind the taking of security, but there are other important reasons why a creditor might wish to take security. The rest of the chapter will look at these reasons and also ask why the law permits the taking of security as well as whether the recognition of security is economically efficient.[10]

---

[8] See also the definition of security in *Edwards* v. *Flightline Ltd* [2003] 1 WLR at 1200, where the Court of Appeal accepted the proposition that

> an agreement between a debtor and a creditor that the debt owing shall be paid out of a specific fund coming to the debtor, or an order given by a debtor to his creditor upon a person owing money or holding funds belonging to the giver or the order, directing such person to pay such funds to the creditor, will create a valid equitable charge upon such fund, in other words, will operate as an equitable assignment of the debts or fund to which the order refers. An agreement for valuable consideration that a fund shall be applied in a particular way may found an injunction to restrain its application in another way. But if there is nothing more, such a stipulation will not amount to an equitable assignment. It is necessary to find, further, that an obligation has been imposed in favour of the creditor to pay the debt out of the fund.

This proposition is derived from the judgment of the Privy Council in *Palmer* v. *Carey* [1926] AC 703 at 706–7, and was also approved by the House of Lords in *Swiss Bank Corporation* v. *Lloyds Bank Ltd* [1982] AC 584 at 613.

[9] A floating charge is a charge which permits the grantor to carry on business in the normal way until some event occurs which causes this management freedom to terminate.

[10] The 'efficiency of secured credit' debate has become something of a veritable cottage industry in the US. The literature is truly enormous and a lot of contributions seem to consist of assertions or attempts to demonstrate that most previous contributions to the debate have been flawed: see J. White 'The Politics of Article 9: Work and Play

Finally the chapter will consider the fate of proposals, in both England and the United States, to limit the full priority of secured credit.

Reasons for the taking of security

An important point to note in this connection is that security is pervasive. The law does not require the taking of security but nevertheless as one American commentator puts it, banks pursue the taking of security with apostolic zeal.[11] Commonly banks argue for stronger, broader and more effective security rights but not for narrower and weaker ones. The controversy over security rights in deposit accounts provides a good example. In both England and the US courts recognised banks as having rights of set-off in situations of mutual indebtedness, i.e. a bank could set off a

in Revising Article 9' (1994) 80 *Va L Rev* 2089, 'a game with no purpose other than to satisfy and stimulate one's intellect'. For just a flavour of the available literature see T. Jackson and A. Kronman 'Secured Financing and Priorities among Creditors' (1979) 88 *Yale LJ* 1143; S. Levmore 'Monitors and Freeriders in Commercial and Corporate Settings' (1982) 92 *Yale LJ* 49; A. Schwartz 'A Theory of Loan Priorities' (1989) *J Legal Stud* 209; A. Schwartz 'Security Interests and Bankruptcy Priorities: A Review of Current Theories' (1981) 10 *J Legal Stud* 1; A. Schwartz 'The Continuing Puzzle of Secured Debt' (1984) 37 *Vand L Rev* 1051; R. Scott 'A Relational Theory of Secured Financing' (1986) 86 *Colum L Rev* 901; P. Shupack 'Solving the Puzzle of Secured Transactions' (1989) 41 *Rutgers L Rev* 1067; J. White 'Efficiency Justifications for Personal Property Security' (1984) 37 *Vand L Rev* 473; B. Adler 'An Equity-Agency Solution to the Bankruptcy-Priority Puzzle' (1993) 22 *J Legal Stud* 73; J. Bowers 'Whither What Hits the Fan?: Murphy's Law, Bankruptcy Theory, and the Elementary Economics of Loss Distribution' (1991) 26 *Ga L Rev* 27; S. L. Harris and C. W. Mooney 'A Property-Based Theory of Security Interests: Taking Debtors' Choices Seriously' (1994) 80 *Va L Rev* 2021; H. Kanda and S. Levmore 'Explaining Creditor Priorities' (1994) 80 *Va L Rev* 2103; L. LoPucki 'The Unsecured Creditor's Bargain' (1994) 80 *Va L Rev* 1887; R. Picker 'Security Interests, Misbehavior, and Common Pools' (1992) 59 *U Ch L Rev* 645; G. Triantis 'Secured Debt under Conditions of Imperfect Information' (1992) 21 *J Legal Stud* 225. There are also symposia on the issue of the efficiency of secured credit in the 1994 *Virginia Law Review* and the 1997 *Cornell Law Review*. For slightly more general but specifically English contributions see R. Mokal 'The Authentic Consent Model: Contractarianism, Creditors' Bargain and Corporate Liquidation' (2001) 21 *Legal Studies* 400; R. Mokal 'Priority as Pathology: The Pari Passu Myth' [2001] *CLJ* 581; R. Mokal 'The Seach for Someone to Save: A Defensive Case for the Priority of Secured Credit' (2002) 22 *OJLS* 687; V. Finch, 'Security, Insolvency and Risk: Who Pays the Price?' (1999) 62 *MLR* 633; V. Finch 'Is Pari Passu Passe' [2000] *Insolvency Lawyer* 194; V. Finch *Corporate Insolvency Law: Perspectives and Principles* (Cambridge University Press, 2002) at pp. 75–105.

[11] See White 'Work and Play' at 2091. White says:

> Unless these secured creditors can be convinced that it is in their interest to have Article 9 abolished, Article 9 will continue and the debates about its efficiency will be limited to academics. At most, we academics might snatch a small morsel off the table while the banks' attention is diverted; we will not be seated at the main course.

customer's deficit on its loan account with credit balances on other accounts the customer might have with the bank.[12] Nevertheless, because of possible weaknesses in set-off rights vis-à-vis third parties banks in both countries pressed for legislative or judicial recognition of full-blown security interests in deposit accounts and their wishes were realised with the decision in *Re BCCI (No. 8)*[13] and the revision of Article 9.[14] It seems that the appetite of banks for secured credit has expanded over the years. One leading US commentator has spoken[15] of a

dramatic increase in the number and size of firms that rely on secured credit as their principal means of financing both ongoing operations and growth opportunities. Previously, with a few exceptions . . . , secured financing principally had served second-class markets as the 'poor man's' means of obtaining credit. Now, it has become the linchpin of private financing, prompting even large firms to employ leveraged buyouts as a means of fleeing public equity markets for the safe harbors of Article 9.

Put simply, the taking of security maximises the creditor's prospects of recovery in the event of the debtor's insolvency. This is commonly identified as the first, and most important, reason for the taking of security. When a company or other debtor declines into insolvency there is, by definition, insufficient money in the corporate kitty to satisfy everybody. The basic principle of insolvency law is one of 'equality of misery' or equality of treatment of creditors, i.e. *pari passu* distribution of available assets amongst creditors.[16] This hallowed principle of insolvency law is, however, in fact somewhat hollow.[17] Amongst other things, the law of insolvency in some jurisdictions – England included – privileges certain categories of claims by according them preferential status. The categories of preferential debt are set out in Schedule 6 to the Insolvency Act 1986 and, until the reforms introduced by the Enterprise Act 2002,

---

[12] *Re Charge Card Services Ltd* [1987] Ch 150; on which see Goode *Legal Problems* at pp 124–9. For the position in the United States see the detailed report *Use of Deposit Accounts as Original Collateral* by the UCC Permanent Editorial Study Board (1992).

[13] [1998] AC 214.

[14] The revised Article 9 in so far as deposit accounts as original collateral is concerned departs fairly radically from traditional perfection and priority rules with the only permissible method of perfecting such a security interest being by 'control' rather than by 'filing': see generally on this area G. McCormack 'Security Interests in Deposit Accounts: An Anglo-American Perspective' [2002] *Insolvency Lawyer* 7.

[15] R. Scott 'The Politics of Article 9' (1994) 80 *Va L Rev* 1783 at 1784–5.

[16] Section 107 Insolvency Act 1986 which applies to voluntary liquidations and rule 4.181(1) Insolvency Rules 1986 applicable to compulsory liquidations.

[17] See generally Mokal 'Priority as Pathology', who argues that the *pari passu* principle is rather less important than it is sometimes made out to be, and does not fulfil any of the functions often attributed to it.

have basically comprised certain tax and employee claims.[18] A variety of arguments have been advanced for recognising claims by particular categories of creditors to preferential status.[19] As far as claims by governmental entities are concerned, such creditors are said to be involuntary and not consciously to have assumed the risk of the debtor's insolvency.[20] It is also arguable that they are not in a position effectively to monitor the debtor's behaviour and to assess the risk of default or insolvency. The main justification for according employees preferential status centres on inequality of bargaining power and rests on the fact that employees lack the economic strength to bargain for security rights and, consequently, may lose out in their employer's insolvency. The Enterprise Act 2002[21] abolishes Crown preference (but not employee preference[22]) as part of an 'integrated package of measures' whereby in return secured creditors lose some of their existing entitlements.[23]

Preferential creditors are paid ahead of general creditors and also one type of secured creditor – the floating-charge holder – but not other secured creditors. Financially distressed firms commonly use the Revenue as effectively an additional source of credit and an expansion in the volume of preferential debts has led secured lenders to push forward the frontiers of the fixed-charge security into territory that has traditionally been occupied by the floating charge.[24] These efforts may have been

---

[18] Section 251 Enterprise Act 2002 removes paras. 1 and 2 (debts due to Inland Revenue), paras. 3–5C (debts due to Customs and Excise) and paras. 6 and 7 (social security contributions) from Schedule 6 to the Insolvency Act 1986 and thereby puts into effect the abolition of Crown preference.

[19] See generally A. Keay and P. Walton 'The Preferential Debts Regime in Liquidation Law: In the Public Interest? [1999] *CFILR* 84; and see also, for a Canadian perspective, S. Cantlie 'Preferred Priority in Bankruptcy' in J. Ziegel ed. *Current Developments in International and Comparative Corporate Insolvency Law* (Clarendon Press, 1994) at p. 413.

[20] See generally the report by the Department of Trade and Industry and HM Treasury review group *A Review of Company Rescue and Business Reconstruction Mechanisms* (London, 2000).

[21] The philosophy underlying the Enterprise Act is explained in the White Paper *Insolvency: A Second Chance* (2001) Cm 5234 (London, TSO, 2001) though as the legislation was in the process of gestation the banks won some significant concessions from the government.

[22] For a succinct statement of the position see the White Paper *Insolvency: A Second Chance* at para. 2.20: 'The preferential status of certain claims by employees in insolvency proceedings, such as wages and holiday pay within certain limits, will remain, as will the rights of those subrogated to them.'

[23] Holders of existing floating charges, however, enjoy significant short-term benefits from the Enterprise Act, for they benefit from the immediate abolition of Crown preference but are not subject to any requirement to set aside a proportion of floating-charge recoveries for the benefit of unsecured creditors. The latter requirement applies only with respect to floating charges created after certain prescribed dates.

[24] See the comments of Lord Millett in the *Brumark* case [2001] 2 AC 710 at para. 17: 'By the 1970s, however, the banks had become disillusioned with the floating charge. The

stymied by the decision of the Privy Council in the *Brumark* case.[25] Be that as it may, the failure on the part of a bank to take security will not only reduce the bank to the category of unsecured creditor but also means that its claim will rank after preferential creditors.

The taking of security maximises a creditor's possibilities of recovery, whereas placement in the ranks of the ordinary unsecured creditor may leave a person with little hope of recovering anything. Judicial utterances to this effect are well borne out by the empirical evidence. According to data from the Society of Practitioners of Insolvency, on average 75 per cent of cases return nothing to unsecured creditors and in only 2 per cent of cases can they expect to receive 100 per cent returns.[26] More recent findings suggest recovery rates for banks in the order of 77 per cent, and this compares with 27 per cent for preference creditors and negligible returns for unsecured trade creditors.[27]

Security serves a raft of other functions as well as maximising the prospect of recovery in a debtor's insolvency.[28] The second reason for taking security focuses on control. If a lender takes security over a specific asset of the borrower then the borrower relinquishes exclusive control over that asset. The borrower may be more likely to pay the lender than general creditors because failure to pay may result in the loss of an asset that is essential to the conduct of the borrower's business. In certain circumstances this factor may be the primary reason behind the taking of security by the lender. In the American legal literature this point has been highlighted in the setting of equipment financing. As Professor Baird puts the matter:[29]

In other contexts, the primary purpose of a security interest may be to give a secured creditor a priority over a firm's other creditors in the event that the firm encounters financial distress and cannot meet its fixed obligations. In the case

---

growth in the extent and amount of the preferential debts, due in part to increases in taxation and in part to higher wages and greater financial obligations to employees, led banks to explore ways of extending the scope of their fixed charges.'

[25] The case is reported as *Agnew* v. *Commissioner of Inland Revenue* [2001] 2 AC 710; on which see F. Oditah 'Fixed charges over Book Debts after *Brumark*' (2001) 14 *Insolvency Intelligence* 49; G. McCormack 'The Nature of Security over Receivables' (2002) 23 *Co Law* 84.

[26] *Eighth Survey of Company Insolvency by Society of Practitioners of Insolvency* (1997–8) at p. 20. The survey is referred to in the preface to D. Milman and D. Mond *Security and Corporate Rescue* (Hodgsons, 1999).

[27] See DTI *Company Rescue and Business Reconstruction Mechanisms* at para. 57. The information is drawn from research carried out by Professor Julian Franks and Dr Oren Sussman 'The Cycle of Corporate Distress, Rescue and Dissolution: A Study of Small and Medium Sized UK Companies' (April 2000).

[28] See generally Scott 'Relational Theory'; Schwartz 'Theory of Loan Priorities'.

[29] D. Baird 'Security Interests Reconsidered' (1994) 80 *Va L Rev* 2249 at 2252.

of the equipment financier, however, the security interest may serve a different purpose. A lender may lend because it is confident that the procedures available to it in the event of default will allow it to realise much of the amount of the loan in the event of default. Thus, the lender may take a security interest in large part because its rights upon default against the debtor are greater than they would be if it did not take security.

Thirdly, security over specific assets may enable the lender to sell off or take possession of the assets without having to seek judicial or other official intervention. This basically remains the position under the Enterprise Act 2002. Under existing law before the reforms introduced by the Enterprise Act 2002 take effect, the holder of a floating charge over the whole or substantially the whole of a company's assets may appoint an administrative receiver who may carry on the running of the business of the company with a view to optimal realisation of assets.[30] Although designated by statute as an agent of the company,[31] the basic function of the receiver is to realise the assets of the company for the benefit of the secured lender who made the appointment. The Enterprise Act abolishes administrative receivership in the generality of cases[32] but still allows a floating-charge holder to make an out-of-court appointment of an administrator.[33] An administrator has somewhat wider duties than an old-style administrative receiver, including a duty to rescue the business of the company if at all viable.[34] Nevertheless, the essential point remains that even under the new regime a secured lender will retain a substantial

---

[30] Section 29(2) Insolvency Act 1986. For a defence of receivership as traditionally understood see J. Armour and S. Frisby 'Rethinking Receivership' (2001) 21 *OJLS* 73. They examine two proposals for the reform of insolvency law: firstly, the idea of a debtor-in-possession reorganisation regime; and secondly, the imposition of more expansive duties of care and/or loyalty on administrative receivers and suggest that the case for reform is not made out.

[31] Section 44 Insolvency Act 1986.

[32] Section 250 and Schedule 16 of the Enterprise Act; but nevertheless, there are a substantial number of cases where the holder of a qualifying floating charge may still appoint an administrative receiver. Moreover, holders of existing floating charges continue to enjoy the right to appoint administrative receivers. The legislative restriction on the appointment of administrative receivers only applies with respect to floating charges created after 15 September 2003.

[33] Section 248 and Schedule 16 of the Enterprise Act.

[34] According to Schedule 16 para. 3(1) of the Enterprise Act, the administrator of a company must perform his functions – (a) with the objective of rescuing the company, or (b) where it is not reasonably practicable to rescue the company, with the objective of achieving a better result for the company's creditors as a whole than would be likely if the company were wound up (without first being in administration), or (c) where it is not reasonably practicable to rescue the company or achieve the result mentioned in paragraph (b), with the objective of realising property in order to make a distribution to one or more secured or preferential creditors. Furthermore, even in cases where rescue is not reasonably practicable, an administrator must not unnecessarily harm the interests of the creditors of the company as a whole.

measure of control over realising the assets of financially distressed firms. Timing the sale of secured assets is important from the point of view of increasing recoveries and it also avoids giving the appearance of a 'forced sale'. If the lender can control the time and manner of realisation of secured assets, then this strengthens his hand greatly both from a nego- tiating position vis-à-vis the borrower and in terms of optimising value from the security. As one US observer has noted aptly:[35] 'Security is desir- able because it makes available summary legal procedures that bypass the slowness with which the mills of justice sometimes grind.' 'Self-help' and other extra-judicial remedies remain controversial in many jurisdictions, however, and England appears to be something of an exception, up to now, in allowing out-of-court enforcement of security by a secured lender.

Fourthly, there is an argument that the taking of security obviates the need to conduct a possibly detailed and expensive investigation into the financial circumstances of the borrower. In theory, all that the lender need do is to check the value of the secured property so as to ensure that it serves as adequate security for the loan. Of course, the prudent lender will allow for a certain excess in the value of the security over the amount of the loan to cover for legal and practical obstacles to enforcement as well as unfavourable enforcement timing and conditions. In the words of one commentator, secured lending substitutes information about the secured property offered by the borrower for information about the borrower himself:[36]

At its extreme, secured lending makes a nearly total substitution: a pawnshop, for example, asks no more information about the borrower than is necessary to identify the borrower in the event that the borrower has stolen the pawned good. Rather, the pawnshop operator must know the value of the collateral and the price than can be realised from selling that collateral. The history of the borrower and the purpose of the loan are immaterial.

During the government review of company rescue and business recon- struction mechanisms that preceded the Enterprise Act, banks, however,

---

[35] H. Kripke 'Law and Economics: Measuring the Economic Efficiency of Commercial Law in a Vacuum of Fact' (1985) 133 *U Pa L Rev* 929 at 948.

[36] Heywood Fleisig 'Economic Functions of Security in a Market Economy' in J. Norton and M. Andenas eds. *Emerging Financial Markets and Secured Transactions* (Kluwer, 1998) p. 15, at 19. Fleisig examines legal deficiencies in the framework governing secured trans- actions over movable property in Argentina. Theoretical and empirical perspectives are presented and the author concludes that 'three-quarters of the problem of high interest rates facing borrowers who do not use real estate as collateral is a problem that arises from the laws and legal procedures that govern lending against immovable property'. According to the author (at p. 34): 'In most transitional and developing economies, in- stituting a modern system of secured transactions would probably reduce the cost of financing movable equipment to a few hundred basis points over the government dollar borrowing rate.'

were concerned to emphasise that they advanced funds based on an assessment of the viability of the borrower's business plans rather than on a simple calculation of the value of the property offered as collateral. The British Bankers' Association (BBA) said:[37] 'There is a perception . . . that banks are effectively pawnbrokers, lending only against security; or collateral. The truth is that banks principally lend against viability and cashflow. Collateral is taken as a contingency if things do not work out as planned.' Numerous respondents to the DTI consultation exercise stressed that the real worth of security rights, and in particular the floating charge, was the control rights it gave the holder in the event of a default by the borrower.

While the achievement of priority over other creditors in the event of the debtor's insolvency is often identified as the single driving force behind the taking of security, it certainly seems that the focus on force and liquidation outcomes is to present too simplistic a picture. An important empirical study that highlights the cycle of corporate distress with a concentration on small and medium-sized UK companies suggests a more complex pattern of lender behaviour.[38] In short, the variety of security devices available to a bank lender place it in a powerful position from where it can exert pressure over the company in financial distress, both within formal insolvency procedures, and in informal rescue contexts. This study demonstrates the existence, even in the case of small and medium-sized companies, of an elaborate rescue process outside formal procedures:

About 75% of firms emerge from rescue and avoid formal insolvency procedures altogether (after 7.5 months, on average). Either they are turned-around or they repay their debt by finding alternative banking sources. . . . Turnarounds are often accompanied by management changes, asset sales, and new finance or directors' guarantees. There is evidence that these changes significantly influence the bank's response and the likelihood of a successful outcome.[39]

Banks, it appears, use their control rights to encourage or force financially distressed firms to undergo restructuring that would include downsizing and management replacement.

As far as larger quoted companies in the UK are concerned, a well-established but informal rescue procedure exists: the so-called 'London

---

[37] See the quotation at p. 50 of DTI *Company Rescue and Business Reconstruction Mechanisms*.
[38] See Franks and Sussman 'The Cycle of Corporate Distress'. This study was sponsored by the DTI/Treasury Working Group on Company Rescue and Business Reconstruction Mechanisms. See also G. Cook, N. Pandit and D. Milman 'Formal Rehabilitation Procedures and Insolvent Firms: Empirical Evidence on the British Company Voluntary Arrangement Procedure' (2001) 17 *Small Business Economics* 255.
[39] Franks and Sussman 'The Cycle of Corporate Distress' at 2.

Approach'.[40] The details of the procedure will vary from case to case but the basic outline remains the same. Essentially the 'London Approach' applies to multi-banked companies which are experiencing financial difficulties. The respective lenders agree to facilitate an attempt for a non-statutory resolution of the company's difficulties. The lenders will commission an independent review that addresses the issue of the company's long-term viability, with the review team making use of all the relevant information made available by all the lenders. During this review period, the lenders agree to maintain existing lending agreements in place and a moratorium on the enforcement of claims against the company. The second phase of the 'London Approach' involves agreement upon and implementation of a restructuring plan. Typically, the restructuring will involve either an element of debt forgiveness and/or a debt-for-equity swap. Moreover, new loans are accorded priority over existing debt but in so far as lenders have to share losses then generally the pre-existing entitlements of secured creditors will be respected. Again, while the company does not proceed to the stage of administration or liquidation a lender's security rights will enable it to exert an element of control over the terms of the corporate workout.

Why the law permits the taking of security

Recognition of security interests appears to clash with a basic fairness principle – namely, equality of treatment of creditors in the debtor's insolvency or, in other words, the principle that losses among company creditors are apportioned on a pro rata basis. As one writer says:[41] 'The normal rule in a corporate insolvency is that all creditors are treated on an equal footing – pari passu – and share in insolvency assets pro rata according to their pre-insolvency entitlements or the sums they are owed. Security avoids the effects of pari passu distribution by creating rights that have priority over the claims of unsecured creditors.' Others have argued that before a creditor is entitled to claim a preferred position it must be demonstrated that deviation from the inveterate and equitable *pari passu* principle is warranted. Of course, the *pari passu* principle is not as extensive, pervasive and all-embracing in practice as it appears to be in theory since empirical evidence suggests that the vast bulk of a company's

---

[40] On the 'London Approach' see generally P. Brierley and G. Vlieghe 'Corporate Workouts, the London Approach and Financial Stability' [1999] *Financial Stability Review* 168; P. Kent 'Corporate Workouts – a UK Perspective' (1997) 6 *International Insolvency Review* 165; J. Armour and S. Deakin 'Norms in Private Bankruptcy: The "London Approach" to the Resolution of Financial Distress' [2001] *Journal of Corporate Law Studies* 21.

[41] See Finch 'Security, Insolvency and Risk' at 634.

assets are distributed other than on a *pari passu* basis.[42] The hallowed
principle of *pari passu* distribution is fundamentally hollow since all it
seems to mean in practice is that creditors within a particular class must
be treated equally and the law recognises different classes of creditors.
Pari passu distribution across the board is very much the rule rather than
the exception, but the atypicality of *pari passu* is partly a consequence
of the recognition of security. The question arises why the law should
permit the taking of security. Three justifications are usually offered.

The first reason is based on freedom of contract: security is seen as representing a fair exchange for the loan. In other words, the secured creditor
has bargained for rights of a proprietary nature over the debtor's property
whereas the general creditors have not. This kind of 'bargain' approach
resides comfortably with traditional English legal and judicial thinking.
Debtor and creditor have made a contract and, absent overwhelming considerations of public policy, others should respect that contract. Strong
echoes of 'freedom of contract' reasoning are found in some of the leading
floating charge cases. In *Re Brightlife Ltd* Hoffmann J said:[43]

I do not think that it is open to the courts to restrict the contractual freedom of
parties to a floating charge on [grounds of public policy]. The floating charge was
invented by Victorian lawyers to enable manufacturing and trading companies to
raise loan capital on debentures. It could offer the security of a charge over the
whole of the company's undertaking without inhibiting its ability to trade. But
the mirror image of these advantages was the potential prejudice to the general
body of creditors, who might know nothing of the floating charge but find that all
the company's assets, including the very goods which they had just delivered on
credit, had been swept up by the debenture holder. The public interest requires a
balancing of the advantages to the economy of facilitating the borrowing of money
against the possibility of injustice to unsecured creditors. These arguments for
and against the floating charge are matters for Parliament rather than the courts
and have been the subject of public debate in and out of Parliament for more than
a century.

The same 'freedom of contract' notions appealed to Nourse LJ in *Re
New Bullas Trading Ltd*,[44] who said that just as it is open to contracting
parties to provide for a fixed charge on future book debts, so it is open to
them to provide that they shall be subject to a fixed charge while they are
uncollected and a floating charge on realisation. The principle is an old
one and was articulated by Lord Macnaghten in the seminal company law
case *Salomon* v. *A. Salomon & Co.*[45] He said: 'Every creditor is entitled
to get and to hold the best security the law allows him to take.'

---

[42] See generally Mokal 'Priority as Pathology'.
[43] [1987] Ch 200 at 209.   [44] [1994] 1 BCLC 485.   [45] [1897] AC 22 at 52.

A variant of the freedom of contract argument is the 'property rights' or freedom of alienation argument, i.e. a debtor should be free to sell or alienate his property. This argument has been developed by those responsible for the drafting of the revised version of Article 9 of the US UCC, Professors Steven Harris and Charles Mooney, to justify the institution of secured credit and the Article 9 priority scheme.[46] They point out that security is often indistinguishable in its economic effects from other transactions such as sales contracts and the repayment of debts that the state generally facilitates. The creditor is providing value and in return is taking security, and to deny the creditor that security to its full extent would be to deprive the creditor of something for which it has paid. Moreover, a debtor that grants security is merely alienating its property and since capitalist societies encourage freedom of alienation this strengthens the normative presumption that society should encourage the issuance of security. This property-rights justification for security only goes so far, however. Many jurisdictions have a closed list or '*numerus clausus*' of property rights, and non-possessory security does not come within the list. If the law, on a prospective basis, forbade the taking of security then priority over other creditors is not something that a particular creditor could lawfully have exacted as the price of its loan.

The 'bargain theory' of security rights is open to the objection that if a debtor grants a creditor a security interest in the debtor's property this will potentially affect the interests of third parties who are unsecured creditors, whether voluntary or involuntary, of the debtor. The question arises to what extent A and B may make a contract that might potentially harm C. Ordinarily when two parties try to alter the rights of third parties who are absent from the negotiations and who are unable to refuse such altered treatment, the law does not permit this. Parties are free to barter away their own rights but are not free to give away the rights of those who did not consent to such treatment. One may ask why the law should take the extraordinary step of permitting two parties to negotiate away the rights of a third party who was not present at the negotiation table.[47] Making the same point in different language, other commentators have argued that the priority of secured claims is actually inconsistent with an

---

[46] 'A Property-Based Theory' at 2103.
[47] See E. Warren 'Making Policy with Imperfect Information: The Article 9 Full Priority Debates' (1997) 82 *Cornell L Rev* 1373 at 1376. Professor Warren adds: 'The justification for contractual priority remains, at best disputed, and at worst, thoroughly debunked. Nonetheless, the real-world aspect of the debate rears its head from time to time, and the world of reform and modernisation efforts does not leave time for the luxury of waiting for a resolution of the theoretical debate.'

important general principle of commercial law against non-consensual subordination.[48] According to this principle a borrower may not subordinate one creditor's claim to that of another without the consent of the subordinated creditor.

Proponents of the bargain theory would accept that when a debtor grants a creditor a security interest this will increase the risks faced by other creditors because it reduces the value they receive in an insolvency. On the other hand, in their view, the other creditors are aware of this risk and will make appropriate adjustments either by altering the rates on their loans or by taking security or quasi-security. In other words, it is said that the other creditors impliedly consent to their claims having subordinated status by lending on an unsecured basis, but this implicit consent rationalisation only goes so far. There are certain non-adjusting creditors, such as tort claimants, as well as those whose claims against the debtor's estate are comparatively small so as to make it uneconomic to adjust the terms of the extension of credit to reflect the fact that others are taking security. It may not be worthwhile for creditors with small claims to determine whether a borrower has created security interests that would subordinate their claims in the event of bankruptcy. Moreover, many creditors with small claims are not sophisticated enough to adjust the implicit interest rate they charge a borrower on advances to take into account the existence, or non-existence, of secured debt in the borrower's financial structure.

The property-rights justification for security interests could also be attacked on the basis that the bankruptcy estate belongs to the borrower's creditors as a group rather than to the borrower. The law does not permit the borrower directly to transfer or allocate its insolvency assets to third parties or to give certain creditors advantages over others and it should not be required to do so indirectly through the use of a security interest giving the secured creditor full priority.[49] One could object to this line of analysis, however, by saying that the agreement conferring advantages on the creditor has been made outside and before bankruptcy and, generally speaking, the policy of the law should be to respect non-bankruptcy entitlements.

By way of conclusion, the 'freedom of contract' or 'contract' theories provide some justifications for the recognition of security interests but are

---

[48] L. Bebchuk and J. Fried 'The Uneasy Case for the Priority of Secured Claims in Bankruptcy: Further Thoughts and a Reply to Critics' (1997) 82 *Cornell L Rev* 1279 at 1286–90.

[49] For an American perspective on this point see J. Rogers 'The Impairment of Secured Creditors' Rights in Corporate Reorganizations: A Study of the Relationship between the Fifth Amendment and the Bankruptcy Clause' (1983) 96 *Harv L Rev* 973.

ultimately inconclusive largely because of the existence of third parties who may be harmed by legislative or judicial acceptance of the security interest. The third parties are either involuntary creditors such as tort claimants or else other creditors who are not in a position effectively to alter the terms on which they advance credit to take into account the existence of secured debt in the borrower's capital structure.

Secured credit and the promotion of economic activity

There are other, more instrumentalist and consequentialist, reasons why the law might permit the taking of security. These are bound up with the promotion of economic growth and the facilitation of economic activity.[50] Secured credit is variously said to be the oil of the economy and the engine of economic growth. Firstly, the availability of security is said to encourage lenders to make loans that would not otherwise be available and, in this way, economic activity is stimulated. In other words, the risk of debtor insolvency is one of the factors that determines whether a particular credit transaction will be seen as profitable for the creditor. Default on a particular loan will not only make that individual transaction unprofitable but will offset the gains from other lending transactions. If the risk of default within a particular category of loans is seen as high then the lender may shy away from this class of borrowing because losses on loans within that class may outweigh the corresponding gains from other loans within the class. Extending interest charges across the board to compensate for projected losses may not work, as one analysis points out:[51]

It might appear that the creditor can ameliorate the problem of losses from debtor default simply by raising the interest rate so that the profits from the transactions in which the debtors pay are high enough to outweigh the losses from those in which the debtors default. This solution can work only in a narrow range, though. After all, raising the interest rate makes it less likely that the credit transaction will be profitable for the borrower. If the borrower does not see the transaction as profitable, it will not take place. Thus, when the risk of loss from debtor insolvency is high, it will be difficult to construct a credit transaction in which both parties foresee profits.

---

[50] See generally D. Banowsky and J. Norton 'Secured Financing Issues for International Lenders: Bridging the Gap between the Civil and Common Law through Asset-Backed Securitisation – Lessons from and Respecting Argentina and Mexico' in Norton and Andenas eds. *Emerging Financial Markets* at p. 307. World Bank report *How Legal Restrictions on Collateral Limit Access to Credit in Argentina* (World Bank, 1993).

[51] See N. Cohen 'Internationalising the Law of Secured Credit: Perspectives from the US Experience' (1999) 20 *U Pa J Int'l Econ L* 423 at 429.

According to the World Bank, the widespread insistence on security for payment indicates that credit extension is not simply a function of price and, in many cases, a prospective borrower who is unable to furnish adequate security will be refused credit altogether rather than being charged a higher rate of interest than a borrower offering security.[52] In the World Bank's view, credit expansion and the facilitation of economic activity require not only an orderly system for the collection of debts but also a legal regime which recognises and accommodates security rights in both real property and personal property. The taking of security protects the lender's downside with the lender being protected, at least to some extent, against the loss of his investment. This is particularly important with loan transactions where the 'upside' in terms of interest rate return, if not fixed absolutely at the outset, is almost certainly capped in some way. The availability of security enables the lender to assess the investment risk differently. If the borrower defaults on the loan then the lender will have rights against the specific property that forms the subject matter of the security. If the borrower declines into insolvency then the lender has the right to be paid out of the secured assets in priority to the borrower's general creditors.[53]

Secondly, security is also said to lower the cost of credit, and again this serves as a stimulus for economic activity. It is often asserted in the literature that secured loans attract a lower interest payment than unsecured loans: 'Secured creditors, for example, would have paid for their priority position by accepting a lower rate of return and, should therefore be allowed to retain the benefits of their initial bargain by receiving an equivalent value for their collateral in bankruptcy.'[54]

The argument is that if security rights are available to the lender, this will affect the assessment of the credit risk and lead to a reduction in the

[52] See World Bank *Building Effective Insolvency Systems* (World Bank, 1999) – a report from the Working Group on Debtor–Creditor Regimes at p. 3.

[53] See the comments by L. Mistelis 'The EBRD Model Law on Secured Transactions and its Impact on Collateral Law Reform in Central and Eastern Europe and the Former Soviet Union' (1998) 5 *Parker School Journal of East European Law* 455 at 456–7:

> A jurisdiction which protects property and proprietary rights provides for an adequate regulation of secured transactions and is further seen to give practical protection and remedies in the case of non-payment of a debt, a jurisdiction where security is guaranteed is attractive both to local and international investors. If the investor is not persuaded that the law gives real protection and remedies, then it becomes irrelevant and he will not invest. The establishment of secured transactions legislation is fundamental for the construction of a market economy and is a precondition for a sustainable flow of foreign capital in the region. In short, the practice of granting collateral to secure loans is one of the most dominant features of commerce in any country.

[54] See T. Jackson and R. Scott 'On the Nature of Bankruptcy: An Essay on Bankruptcy Sharing and the Creditors' Bargain' (1989) 75 *Va L Rev* 155 at 161.

amount of interest that is charged on the loan. On the other hand, there is a view that this argument makes idealised assumptions as to creditor behaviour that are not mirrored by real-life experience. Banks are in the business of making profits. The banks charge whatever rate of interest they think they will be able to get away with; in other words, whatever rate of interest the market will bear. If a company is perceived as a bad credit risk then not only will the banks request security, but moreover they may demand a higher interest payment to compensate for the greater risk premium. By contrast, if the borrower is a blue-chip company, not only may the company be able to resist demands for the grant of security but the competition among banks to lend to that company may have the effect of forcing down the company's cost of borrowing.

These points, amongst others, are brought home in a valuable empirical study undertaken by Professor Ronald Mann that demonstrates the complexity of the issues.[55] On Mann's analysis of the data, secured credit offers benefits but also imposes burdens on both the borrower and the lender.[56] The advantages for the lender include the direct legal rights to bring about repayment of the loan by recourse against the secured property, whether this is done via judicial intervention or by means of self-help remedies where such remedies are available and appropriate. There are, however, also indirect advantages in taking security, which operate before the lender tries to obtain payment of the secured debt. Firstly, subsequent borrowings may be limited since the borrower's ability to grant valuable security interests to subsequent lenders will be reduced. Secondly, the lender possesses leverage that increases the borrower's incentive to repay the loan. Finally, the lender is able, often through specific covenants in the loan agreement, to restrain the borrower from engaging in risky conduct that might reduce its ability to repay the loan.[57] The advantages are, of course, counterbalanced by costs and these costs may, in turn, explain

---

[55] Ronald J. Mann 'Explaining the Pattern of Secured Credit' (1997) 110 *Harv L Rev* 626.
[56] *Ibid.* at 668:

> The possible benefits include not only the direct enhancement of the lender's ability to collect its debt forcibly, but also indirect effects that substantially increase the likelihood that the borrower will be in a position to, and choose to, repay the debt without forcible collection. All of these benefits work together to lower the lender's pre-loan perception of the risk of non-payment, allowing the lender to make a profitable loan at a lower interest rate or on more lenient terms. On the downside, the parties also must consider the corresponding burdens. For large companies, secured credit is likely to carry with it a significant increase in the information costs of the lending transaction. More generally, secured credit imposes costs on all borrowers – large and small – by diminishing their operating flexibility.

[57] Of course clauses in an unsecured loan agreement may also impose restrictions on the conduct of the borrower.

why debts are not always secured. Filing fees represent a distinct element of expenditure in respect of secured transactions, though the level of filing fees is quite low in the Anglo-American world. The category of costs also includes the cost of closing the transaction; in particular, information costs concerning the value of the secured property and the borrower's title thereto. By comparison, in an unsecured transaction, creditors focus on the creditworthiness of the borrower as a whole and, if the borrower is a quoted company, the information will be readily available to the creditor at low cost. It is arguable that this factor produces a significant bias in favour of unsecured credit for public companies.[58] On the other hand, the costs of documenting the bargain, i.e. formalising the arrangement and reducing it to a set of loan documents that specify the terms of the transactions, do not vary greatly depending on the presence or absence of security in the transaction.

This analysis demonstrates that the financial strength of the borrowing company, whether large or small, has an impact on the incidence of secured credit. When a company has a strong balance sheet, the lender may take the view that the risk of non-payment is insignificant. Moreover, the ready availability of information about public companies enhances the relative advantage of unsecured credit. As a borrower's financial strength increases, secured credit becomes a less attractive alternative: its benefits decrease and its costs, at best, remain constant.[59] This explains why a lot of the lending to large public companies is done on an unsecured basis.

The international consensus on secured credit

There seems to be a growing international consensus that secured credit is a general social and economic good. The instrumental factors behind the law's facilitation of secured credit are evident when one considers the experience of the transitional economies in Central and Eastern Europe.[60] When the former socialist economies in Central and Eastern Europe were undergoing the transition to a more free-market-oriented system, various international financial institutions identified the importance of effectively functioning laws on secured credit in the commercial legal system. Organisations such as the European Bank for Reconstruction and Development (EBRD) considered that such laws were critical in fostering market-based

---

[58] *Ibid.* at 661.   [59] *Ibid.* at 674.

[60] On 8 February 2002, the Organisation of American States (OAS) also produced a model law on secured transactions – the Model Inter-American Law on Secured Transactions. This is available on the OAS website: www.oas.org/ and see generally B. Kozolchyk and J. Wilson 'The New Model Inter-American Law on Secured Transactions' (2002) 7 *Uniform Law Review* 69.

decision making and crucially impacted on the pace of private-sector investment activity. Consequently, partly as a result of pressure from these organisations, the task of reforming such laws assumed a high priority on the legislative agenda in the transitional economies.[61] As a general proposition, the transitional economies did not permit non-possessory security, and international financial institutions felt that the possibility of taking security over such property might encourage lenders to advance credit that would not otherwise be extended.[62]

The belief that a far-reaching and comprehensive law facilitating secured credit is an essential tool for economic development represents not only the views of those advising on the transition process in Eastern Europe but also an international consensus more generally. The doyen of English commercial lawyers, Professor Sir Roy Goode, for example, argues that without an adequate legal regime for personal property security rights, it is almost impossible for a national economy to develop.[63] He points to the fact that the World Bank considers the role of security so central in promoting economic growth that before making a loan to a developing country it will normally seek to establish to what extent a sound legal system for the creation and protection of security interests is or will be in place. Moreover, the distinguished German commentator Professor Ulrich Drobnig has developed the same point, arguing that the more advanced a market economy is, the greater the demand for credit and, correspondingly, the greater the pressure on legislatures and courts to find ways effectively to use non-possessory security interests.[64] Drobnig repeats the accepted wisdom that since the debtor offering security decreases the creditor's risk of not being paid, the latter's price for the utilisation of his money, i.e. his interest rate, is lower for a secured than for an unsecured credit.

The economic upheavals among the former 'Tiger' economies of East Asia in the late 1990s was the spark that led to reports from the G22 Working Group on Financial Crises which stressed both the importance

---

[61] See G. McCormack and F. Dahan 'The EBRD Model Law on Secured Transactions: Comparisons and Convergence' [1999] *CFILR* 65; Mistelis 'EBRD Model Law' and also A. Garro 'Difficulties in Obtaining Secured Lending in Latin America: Why Law Reform Really Matters' in Norton and Andenas eds. *Emerging Financial Markets and Secured Transactions* at p. 251.

[62] On 'conditionality' in international loan agreements see J. Head 'Evolution of the Governing Law for Loan Agreements of the World Bank and Other Multilateral Development Banks' (1996) 90 *AJIL* 214.

[63] See R. Goode 'Security in Cross-Border Transactions' (1998) 33 *Tex Int'l LJ* 47.

[64] See U. Drobnig 'Secured Credit in International Insolvency Proceedings' (1998) 33 *Tex Int'l LJ* 53 at 54. Professor Drobnig points to the example of the transitional economies of Eastern Europe and suggests that their economic development under market conditions requires vast financial means that must be raised largely by secured credits.

and the desirable features of insolvency and debtor/creditor regimes. The G22 report said:[65]

The law should permit: property to serve as collateral with a legal framework for mortgages (for immovable property) and a legal framework for secured transactions (for movable property); all economically important assets to serve as collateral for a loan: and security interests in tangible property (such as inventory, equipment and livestock) and in intangible property (such as accounts receivable) to be created. All economically important agents should be able to act as lenders and as borrowers in secured transactions and all economically important secured transactions should be permitted. The creation of security interests should be inexpensive relative to the amounts lent.

The same perspective emerges from the work of the United Nations Commission on International Trade Law (UNCITRAL). UNCITRAL has recently begun the task of preparing a draft legislative guide on secured transactions.[66] UNCITRAL had previously done work on this general area in the 1970s, commissioning Professor Drobnig to produce a comprehensive report detailing the legal treatment of security interests in many jurisdictions.[67] Professor Drobnig's report also looked at the fate of previous international harmonisation efforts but the limited precedents, such as they were, did not engender optimism on his part about the likelihood of framing international rules governing security interests. Even with respect to model laws Drobnig considered that moral persuasion or intellectual insight into the virtues of the laws would persuade some states to adopt them but in case of other states it would only be insistence on the part of international financing institutions that would lead to the enactment of such model laws. Eventually, however, UNCITRAL concluded that worldwide unification of the law of security interests in goods was in all likelihood unattainable.[68] After working on the specific area of receivables financing in the 1990s UNCITRAL returned to more general work on secured credit in the new millennium. UNCITRAL, conscious of its own remit, stressed the connections between secured financing and international trade, suggesting that modern secured-credit laws could have a significant impact on the availability and the cost of

---

[65] G22 Working Group on International Financial Crises, 'Key Principles and Features of Effective Insolvency Regimes' (1998), at p. 47, available at www.imf.org/external/np/g22/index.htm.

[66] Up-to-date information on the progress of the work may be found on the UNCITRAL website: www.uncitral.org/. See also Spiros Bazinas 'UNCITRAL's Work in the Field of Secured Transactions' in Norton and Andenas eds. *Emerging Financial Markets and Secured Transactions* at p. 211.

[67] 'Study on Security Interests' (1997) 8 *UNCITRAL Yearbook* 171; UN Doc.A/CN.9/SER.A/1977.

[68] See generally Cohen 'Internationalising the Law of Secured Credit'.

credit and thus on international trade.[69] In the Commission's view, the creation of a legal system that promoted secured credit not only aided in the cultivation and growth of individual businesses but also in general economic prosperity. It suggested that countries with inadequate secured transactions regimes suffered significant losses in gross domestic product (GDP). The Commission observed:[70]

The key to the effectiveness of secured credit is that it allows borrowers to use the value inherent in their assets as a means of reducing credit risk for the creditor. Risk is mitigated because loans secured by the property of a borrower give lenders recourse to the property in the event of non-payment. Studies have shown that as the risk of non-payment is reduced, the availability of credit increases and the cost of credit falls. Studies have also shown that in States where lenders perceive the risks associated with transactions to be high, the cost of credit increases as lenders require increased compensation to evaluate and assume the increased risk. In some countries, the absence of an effective secured transactions regime has resulted in the virtual elimination of credit for consumers or commercial enterprises.

While the views articulated above represent the general international consensus,[71] something of an alternative perspective is possible. For example, it could be that there are other factors that limit bank lending in developing countries apart from the absence of a comprehensive legal regime protecting secured transactions.[72] It has been argued that banks are under pressure to make potentially non-performing loans to social or political elites, and politically motivated pressure may make it difficult – if not impossible – to foreclose on such loans when they turn out to be non-performing. There may also be a concern about fraudulent transfer of assets by debtors on the verge of bankruptcy which creditors are powerless to prevent. This point has been made by US commentators Professors Bebchuk and Fried, who suggest[73] that

---

[69] Draft Legislative Guide on Secured Transactions – Report of the Secretary General – Background Remarks A/CN.9/WG.VI/WP.2 (12 February 2002) at para. 2.

[70] *Ibid.* at p. 2, and see also the report by the Asian Development Bank *Secured Transactions Law Reform in Asia: Unleashing the Potential of Collateral* (Asian Development Bank, 2002).

[71] See also Garro 'Secured Lending in Latin America'.

[72] In other words, that law is a tool and not a foundation. See generally E. Ferran 'Corporate Law, Codes and Social Norms – Finding the Right Regulatory Combination and Institutional Structure' (2001) 1 *Journal of Corporate Law Studies* 381 at 388 and footnotes accompanying the same. Compare the 'law matters' analysis of the 'Gang of Four': R. La Porta, F. Lopez-de-Silanes, A. Shleifer and R. W. Vishny 'Legal Determinants of External Finance' (1997) 52 *Journal of Finance* 1131.

[73] 'Uneasy Case: Further Thoughts' at 1330; and see also R. Cranston 'Credit Security and Debt Recovery: Law's Role in Reform in Asia and the Pacific' in Norton and Andenas eds. *Emerging Financial Markets* at p. 219.

creditors in these countries might restrict their lending not because they lack priority in their collateral over the claims of unsecured creditors in bankruptcy, but because in the absence of a functional security system, they cannot prevent a borrower on the verge of failure from liquidating its assets and transferring the proceeds to its owners or related parties (or transferring the collateral directly to these parties). We suspect that the primary reason that lenders in these countries are reluctant to lend is their inability to prevent such fraudulent transfers.

The efficiency of secured lending

There has been an extensive debate, going back over twenty years, among legal academics in the US about whether secured credit is efficient, and this debate has gained particular momentum in the context of the revision of Article 9. The prevailing legal norm, still reflected in Article 9, is based on full priority for secured credit over unsecured credit,[74] but there have been critics of this orthodoxy both from 'right' and 'left' perspectives. Those from the right generally hail from the 'law and economics' camp and essentially argue that secured credit is not economically efficient, or at least has not been proved to be economically efficient. Those from the left have been dubbed 'Symps', or Sympathetic Legal Scholars, and these legal scholars argue against secured credit, or at least full priority for secured credit, because of concerns that this might be unfair or damaging to the interests of unsecured – particularly non-adjusting or involuntary – creditors.[75]

The outlawing of secured credit would not seem to be a realistic political proposition in the US, and more recently, secured credit critics, especially those in the 'Symp' camp, have suggested the denial of full credit for collateral by creating a 'carve-out' for unsecured creditors.[76] While the details of the various proposals differ, the basic tenor is that a secured creditor would not enjoy the full value of its collateral but that a certain proportion of its value would be set aside for the benefit of unsecured creditors.[77] The 'carve-out' proposal has, however, fallen on deaf ears among the councils and counsels of the American Law Institute and the National Conference of Commissioners on Uniform State Laws, the bodies responsible for the revision of Article 9.

---

[74] See the comment by W. Woodward 'The Realist and Secured Credit: Grant Gilmore, Common-Law Courts, and the Article 9 Reform Process' (1997) 82 *Cornell L Rev* 1511 that 'one of the central, defining features of secured debt is its priority'.

[75] There is a full debate on this issue at a symposium reported at 82 *Cornell L Rev* (1997).

[76] For spirited advocacy along these lines see Warren 'Making Policy'.

[77] See also J. Hudson 'The Case against Secured Lending' (1995) 15 *Int'l Rev L & Econ* 47.

In judging economic efficiency, 'law and economics' scholars commonly use two standards – the Kaldor–Hicks test and the Pareto test.[78] According to the Kaldor–Hicks definition of economic efficiency, an arrangement, activity or rule is efficient to the extent that it maximises total social wealth, even if the arrangement, activity or rule reduces the wealth of some parties.[79] In other words, in the secured credit context the benefits to the secured creditor and the debtor need only outweigh the harm to unsecured creditors. To be Pareto superior, on the other hand, an extension of secured credit must make a secured creditor better off without making unsecured creditors worse off. This has the consequence that while a reallocation of resources which leaves someone worse off will not be Pareto efficient, it can meet the Kaldor–Hicks standard of efficiency.

The whole efficiency of secured credit debate was started by Professors Jackson and Kronman in an article in 1979 in the *Yale Law Journal*.[80] On their analysis, the economic utility of secured credit rests upon the perhaps questionable assumption that the total costs of monitoring the debtor's behaviour can sometimes be reduced by giving certain creditors priority over others. The debate was taken a stage further by Professors Bebchuk and Fried in the same journal[81] who have striven to demonstrate that the principle of 'full' priority for secured credit over unsecured claims causes excessive use of security interests as well as reducing the incentives for firms to take adequate precautions and to choose appropriate investment. Moreover, in their view, the full priority principle distorted the monitoring arrangements chosen by firms and their creditors. Perhaps the most vocal critic of secured credit from a law and economics perspective has however been Professor Alan Schwartz.[82] Professor Schwartz has argued strongly that the favourable treatment by the law of secured credit is without a plausible economic rationale and he rejects several efficiency justifications commonly offered for security. These include the reduction of overall costs incurred in monitoring the debtor; the fact that secured credit may serve as a signal to other creditors; the proposition that properly staggered debt enhances profits; reduction in levels of creditor

---

[78] See generally B. Cheffins *Company Law: Theory, Structure and Operation* (Oxford University Press, 1997) at pp. 14–15.

[79] See K. Klee 'Barbarians at the Trough: Riposte in Defense of the Warren Carve-Out Proposal' (1997) 82 *Cornell L Rev* 1466 at n. 19.

[80] 'Secured Financing'.

[81] See L. Bebchuk and J. Fried 'The Uneasy Case for the Priority of Secured Claims in Bankruptcy' (1996) 105 *Yale LJ* 857.

[82] See Schwartz 'Theory of Loan Priorities'; Schwartz 'Security Interests and Bankruptcy Priorities'; A. Schwartz 'Taking the Analysis of Security Seriously' (1994) 80 *Va L Rev* 2073; Schwartz 'Continuing Puzzle'.

uncertainty; and the fact that security interests may serve to shift risk from more to less risk-averse creditors.

Essentially, the law and economics critics such as Schwartz argue that secured credit is a zero-sum game and make use of the Modigliani and Miller irrelevance hypothesis in this connection.[83] The Modigliani–Miller (MM) theory holds that the value of a company is unaffected by changes in capital structure, i.e. the particular combination of debt and equity is irrelevant in the overall assessment of the value of the company. The point has been developed pithily as follows:[84]

The value of a firm is the value of the claims to the firm's cash flow. The famous Modigliani and Miller ('MM') result holds that, on the assumptions they make, a firm cannot increase the present value of its cash flow by altering its capital structure. As a consequence, firm value will remain the same whether the firm finances the projects that generate its cash flow with debt, with equity, with a combination of the two, or with instruments more exotic than simple debt or equity. The MM result thus predicts that capital structure is a matter of indifference to firms.

On the other hand, it is fair to point out that the Modigliani–Miller theorem

was developed on the basis of certain restrictive assumptions, including the absence of taxes and insolvency and transaction costs and the existence of perfect capital markets in which all investors have equal access to information . . . The upshot of these competing considerations is that the addition of debt to a company's capital structure will be beneficial up to the point where the tax savings resulting from debt are eclipsed by insolvency costs. On that basis, the focus then shifts to determining the proportion of debt within a company's capital structure that represents its optimal gearing level.[85]

In fact, companies spend considerable time and money creating the financial instruments that constitute their capital structure and the question arises why would expensively advised companies spend money on economically unproductive activities like this? These companies can afford to hire high-powered lawyers and accountants and why would they waste money? The most obvious answer is to focus on the extremely restrictive set of assumptions on which the MM theory is based, which do not seem to be replicated in real-life experience.

---

[83] See F. Modigliani and M. Miller 'The Cost of Capital, Corporation Finance and the Theory of Investment' (1958) 48 *American Economic Review* 433. There is a collection of papers devoted to reviewing the theorem after thirty years in (1988) 2 *Journal of Economic Perspectives* 99 and see generally on the theorem R. Brealey and S. Myers *Principles of Corporate Finance* (McGraw-Hill, 5th edn. 1996) chaps. 17 and 18.

[84] See Schwartz 'Analysis of Security' at 2079.

[85] See E. Ferran *Company Law and Corporate Finance* (Oxford University Press, 1999) at p. 61.

Nevertheless, the MM theory has been developed to support the proposition that secured credit is arguably inefficient because it does not increase the overall wealth of a company.[86] By increasing its debt, a firm makes its cost of equity cheaper, but at the same time raises its cost of debt by an equal and offsetting amount.[87] The creation of a leveraged capital structure, on this analysis, is not more efficient because the reduced cost of capital to investors who are accorded a higher priority increases the riskiness of the capital provided by others, who will correspondingly demand a higher return for their capital.[88] In other words, while secured creditors might reduce the rate of interest to reflect the fact that they are assuming less risk, unsecured creditors will compensate for their own greater risks by charging correspondingly higher interest rates. As Professor Schwartz explains:[89]

[T]he existence of later secured debt would commonly reduce the value of earlier unsecured debt . . . Initial creditors then would either bar later security (so it would not be seen) or raise their interest rates to make up for the loss in value of their loans. On my assumptions, the rise in interest rates would exactly offset the decline in value of the unsecured debt, so security could not create gains for the firm. Because it was costly to issue security, again no secured debt should be observed. This led to an MM-like puzzle: If secured debt generates costs but does not increase the revenues from the projects it finances, why is so much security seen? I then considered whether security could reduce a firm's financing or production costs or increase its gross revenues. Either effect would increase firm value and thus justify incurring the costs of issuing security. The various possibilities of how security could reduce costs or increase revenues did not seem promising. Thus, for me, the security interest puzzle remained.

In response to Schwartz one might argue that other creditors are either involuntary or not sufficiently sophisticated to alter their patterns of behaviour to take into account the existence of secured debt in the company's capital structure. A more frontal assault on 'law-and-economics'

---

[86] See generally Warren 'Making Policy' 1373 at n. 5 and accompanying text.

[87] See D. Baird 'The Importance of Priority' (1997) 82 *Cornell L Rev* 1420 at 1422.

[88] See Kripke 'Law and Economics' at 965–6. Professor Kripke is, however, particularly critical of the Schwartz thesis, saying:

> His method . . . is built on a weak reed. Not only does stratification theory not reign undisputed in economic circles, but also it fails Milton Friedman's test of accurate prediction for failing to predict the almost universal presence of stratified capital structures among corporations, and the wide use of security. Stratification theory overlooks numerous practical considerations that lead real firms to prefer different capital structures. There is a whole body of finance theory on optimal capital structures and the appropriate leveraging of corporations. It is a failure to let the facts distract him from his preconceptions that sends Professor Schwartz out on his fruitless quest through abstractions of economics.

[89] See Schwartz 'Analysis of Security' at 2079–80.

theorising in this sphere was launched by Professor Homer Kripke, the drafter of the previous version of Article 9.[90] In his view, analysis of the kind typified by Schwartz and by Jackson and Kronman is notable for its use entirely of examples made up to illustrate their theories and for the absence of any attempt to determine whether these factual assumptions are typical of real world events. Professor Kripke suggests that while economic analysis may have something to contribute to commercial law, there is a great danger in hypotheses neither premised on nor tested by facts, even in situations where getting the facts may not be easy. He adds that the study of abstract concepts developed in other contexts for other purposes cannot, in any way, contribute to an understanding of practical commercial law or policy.[91]

At the end of the day the 'efficiency' debate had little impact on the Article 9 revision processes. It seems there were three reasons for this.[92] Firstly, the gist of the thesis raised by law and economics scholars was merely to raise doubts about the efficiency of secured credit; to say that it presented a puzzle. These sceptics did not affirmatively establish that secured credit was inefficient but merely asked questions, and an inefficiency conclusion would go against the grain of history. Security devices are widespread and pervasive not only in the modern industrialised world but also in ancient societies, and one might ask the rhetorical question: why does secured credit persist for so long if it is inefficient? Secondly, banks and others with influence on the political process continuously press for more effective and comprehensive security rights rather than weaker ones or no security rights at all. It may be, of course, that banks are acting in a manner that is inimical to their own interests, but this thesis is difficult to credit. Pro-Article 9 adherents add a *coup de grâce*:[93] 'There is a final reason to favour Article 9 even if it is inefficient; the state of affairs that would arise upon the abolition of Article 9 would be almost certainly less efficient, more costly and more wasteful than the current regime. Those costs and that inefficiency outweigh any inefficiencies caused by Article 9.'

The effect of the Article 9 revision process was to extend the scope of secured credit and to broaden the range of permissible collateral. In

---

[90] 'Law and Economics'.
[91] See Kripke's comment in *ibid.* at 931:

> These articles proceed in a world of academic reasoning reminiscent of the cloister and unfounded on any discussion of the factual world of commerce. They do not display an understanding of the role played by the system of secured financial credit in developing a distribution system for the great outpouring of goods that has occurred in the past century.

[92] See White 'Work and Play'.
[93] *Ibid.* at 2091; and see also Kanda and Levmore 'Explaining Creditor Priorities'.

short, the new Article 9 expanded the reach of secured creditors. The most spirited objection to this outcome came not from the law and economics school but from the ranks of 'Symps', who sought to set aside a portion of the secured creditor's cake for the benefit of unsecured creditors. The arguments advanced by these opponents of 'full' priority for secured credit, and the fate of their efforts, will now be considered.

The Article 9 'full priority of secured credit' debate

The most forceful proponent of the view that secured credit should not enjoy full priority under the Article 9 regime has perhaps been Professor Elisabeth Warren of the Harvard Law School. Professor Warren made two important points. Firstly, law and economics analysis only tells us certain things; and secondly, considerations of fairness and distributional balance are also important. She states:[94]

Economic analysis is well-suited to contribute to debates over allocative efficiency, but the tools of economic analysis are not nearly as useful in dealing with questions of distributive efficiency. Methods to produce expansion or contraction of credit are good subjects for deductive debates: decisions to prefer banks over utility companies or tort victims are not. Economic analysis can help inform debates about distributive issues by pointing out, for example, that commercial lenders are able to spread risks in a way utility companies or tort victims cannot, or that reallocation would be unworkable. Nonetheless, the ultimate normative question about preference for one group over another in the distribution of limited assets is beyond the expertise these tools provide.

The import of these remarks is that the priority of secured credit is at least as much a question of distributional fairness as of efficiency. In other words, distributional consequences are a major determinant in the setting of sound policy in the insolvency sphere, and rank – at least on a par – with efficiency considerations. Professor Warren argues persuasively that where a security device promotes lending there may be reasons not to adopt it. The sole goal of a commercial law system should not, in her view, be the expansion of credit because there are questions of community sensibilities and fairness to consider. She asks rhetorically,[95] 'Why not permit security interests in body parts? Any debtor who promised her

---

[94] Warren 'Making Policy' at 1377.
[95] *Ibid.* at 1386. She also says:

> If the only test of any part of a commercial law system were whether it promoted or constricted credit, then our system would look very different. Why not return to the days of debt servitude? There were efficiency concerns about servitude, but the bottom line was that servitude made credit available to people who otherwise could not obtain it. Nonetheless, it was gone by the early 1800s.

liver or her heart would surely have strong incentives to perform on the loan. It would be possible to restrict security interests to body parts that leave the debtor diminished, but alive, such as offering a kidney, skin for a graft, a womb, or a cornea as collateral.'

Professor Warren also castigates the actions of economists who spend a great deal of time explaining why any rule that aims to redistribute wealth to the underdog would actually reduce wealth to everyone and raises the question that, if the point of secured lending is to control the post-lending, risk-taking decisions of debtors then there is no justification for the last place treatment of the victims of that risky behaviour, i.e. tort victims.[96]

Supporters of the Warren carve-out proposal saw it as preserving some value for the debtor's unsecured creditors by counteracting the secured creditor's all-embracing security.[97] Moreover, the proposal increased the secured creditor's incentive to help the debtor avoid bankruptcy, as the se-cured creditor was certain to lose 20 per cent of the value of the collateral in a bankruptcy case. Because part of the secured creditor's claim would become unsecured, the secured creditor would become incentivised to act efficiently and monitor the debtor more closely than under current law. By exposing the secured creditor to the risk of holding an unsecured deficiency claim, on this analysis, it was also encouraged to act in the in-terests of all creditors. It could be argued that the carve-out for unsecured creditors was warranted precisely because tort and other non-adjusting creditors lacked the legal capacity or practical ability to protect them-selves and were not present at the negotiating table when the secured credit contract was negotiated. Supporters also dismissed constitutional objections to the carve-out suggesting that to the extent that implementa-tion of the proposal would be prospective there was no question of taking of the secured creditor's property without compensation. Moreover, all future secured loans would be extended on the basis of a law that allowed only for partial priority.

A developed version of the carve-out proposal was advanced by Professors Bebchuk and Fried who made the valuable point that, to a certain extent, secured credit in the US already operated in a world of partial priority.[98] While the principle of full priority is reflected in the US Bankruptcy Code, there are nevertheless a number of rules, doctrines and practices that have the effect of eroding the priority of secured claims

---

[96] *Ibid.* at 1378–9; and see also the comment by LoPucki, 'Ah, to be exquisitely cruel but at the same time efficient – what more could an economist ask of an institution?' in 'The Unsecured Creditor's Bargain' at 1889.

[97] See generally Klee 'Barbarians at the Trough'.

[98] See Bebchuk and Fried 'Uneasy Case' and 'Uneasy Case: Further Thoughts'.

in bankruptcy. Most notable is Chapter 11 of the US Bankruptcy Code governing corporate reorganisation proceedings which imposed restrictions on the enforcement of security interests, during which time the value of the collateral may fall.[99] Moreover, state legislatures, over the years, had increased the number of statutory lienholders with priority over the claims of secured creditors.[100] Bebchuk and Fried also voiced scepticism at claims that the supply of secured credit would materially decrease under a bankruptcy regime that contained an explicit carve-out for unsecured creditors, pointing out that a system of partial priority already operated to a degree and suggesting that, ultimately, the matter would depend on the percentage of collateral set aside.

Essentially the criticism directed at the carve-out proposal centred on the proposition that secured creditors would extend less secured credit to the debtor because the carve-out for unsecured creditors would be factored into the borrowing base. The net effect would be a net decrease in the amount of credit extended to the borrower, and this would hurt marginal businesses and cause more bankruptcies.[101] Commercial lenders vigorously propounded the proposition that a shift away from full priority would cause their clients to alter their lending practices and to constrict credit and thereby to inflict losses on all businesses. This case was also advanced by academic supporters, such as the Article 9 reporters Professors Harris and Mooney, who fell back on the old proposition that security can facilitate extensions of credit that creditors would not otherwise make and debtors can use the credit extended to create wealth.[102] Harris and Mooney suggested that the institution of secured credit was not necessarily harmful to unsecured creditors as a class and gave the example of secured credit that enabled a debtor to pay unsecured creditors for goods and services or that reduced a debtor's risk on insolvency. In their view, even a partial subordination of secured debt regime would

---

[99] See D. Baird and T. Jackson 'Corporate Reorganizations and the Treatment of Diverse Ownership Interests: A Comment on Adequate Protection of Secured Creditors in Bankruptcy' (1984) 51 *U Ch L Rev* 97 at 112–14.

[100] See Klee 'Barbarians at the Trough' at 1474–5.

[101] See, *ibid.* at 1472:

> For example, where the debtor is in a risky start-up venture or on the verge of insolvency, the risk to unsecured creditors might be so great that instead of seeking a high interest to compensate for increased risk, they simply will not extend new credit. The resulting liquidity crisis will force the debtor into bankruptcy, where unsecured creditors will recover less than if the debtor had not filed.

[102] See Harris and Mooney 'A Property-Based Theory; S. L. Harris and C. W. Mooney 'Measuring the Social Costs and Benefits and Identifying the Victims of Subordinating Security Interests in Bankruptcy' (1997) 82 *Cornell L Rev* 1349; and see also Steven L. Schwarcz 'The Easy Case for the Priority of Secured Claims in Bankruptcy' (1997) 47 *Duke LJ* 425.

create an economic disincentive that would cause many potential lenders to refuse to make loans to debtors. Caution was urged in tampering with the old Article 9 priority regime since the social and economic benefits of priority rights were indirect.[103] The denial of full priority might impinge on the ability of entrepreneurs to locate investors, but it was impossible to identify particular companies that never came into existence as the result of a particular change in priority rights. It was easier to spot an unpaid worker than one who was never able to find a job because a particular project did not receive start-up financing.[104] Harris and Mooney added:[105] 'The conventional wisdom in the credit markets supports our hypothesis that the contraction of credit is likely to be material, inasmuch as subordination of a security interest would diminish the collateral value on which a secured lender could rely.' They suggest that secured creditors who can credit profitably under current law might lose profits under a new regime but the biggest losers would be debtors, who would receive less funding, and potential contracting parties with such debtors.

Harris and Mooney mustered support from the federal government to support their rejection of subordination or carve-out proposals citing a letter from the Attorney General's office to the effect that:[106]

The proposal could have detrimental effects on many highly leveraged sectors of the economy, such as small businesses and agriculture. Secured lenders . . . might either reduce lines of credit, demand greater security, exact higher rates of interest or impose a combination of all three. To the extent that lenders react by demanding greater collateral, even more property of a borrower might become encumbered . . . Ironically, unsecured creditors could be harmed to the extent that businesses that could otherwise survive and generate profits with the help of secured credit are forced out of business or into bankruptcy.

The Article 9 reporters concluded their summation of the arguments with a rhetorical flourish, stating:[107]

As a political matter, the subordination proposals have no realistic prospects for widespread support and adoption. Entrepreneurship is an indelible feature of the

---

[103] Professor Warren even accuses Harris and Mooney of playing a race card in the debates. She says ('Making Policy' n. 62):

> Harris and Mooney state: 'For example, data may confirm that small businesses (and, accordingly, minority-owned businesses) would disproportionately comprise that group [that would face constriction of credit]' . . . Their support? Anecdotal evidence. This argument can be rephrased to say that banks want full priority to help their minority friends. Some critics may demand more than anecdotes to support this proposition.

[104] See Baird 'The Importance of Priority' at 1421.
[105] Harris and Mooney 'Social Costs and Benefits' at 1357.
[106] *Ibid.* n. 49.   [107] *Ibid.* at 1371–72.

American social fabric. Even assuming that hiking the price of admission to the business marketplace would promote efficiency, so that only those with substantial unleveraged capital could afford to participate (a dubious assumption), many – perhaps most – would shrink from the prospect. In the end, the needs and aspirations of the market participants – from the small businesses on Main Street to the economic engines on Wall Street – will prevail.

The Harris and Mooney assessment of political realities turned out to be correct and the subordination or carve-out proposals fell by the wayside in the US. Political realities turned out to be different in Britain and a 'carve-out' provision for unsecured creditors was included in the Enterprise Act.[108] The fate of the 'carve-out' provisions in the two countries should not be viewed in isolation, however. The US Bankruptcy Code has traditionally been seen as very 'pro-debtor' compared with the UK position which, by contrast, is seen as 'pro-creditor'.[109] In the US corporate reorganisation proceedings are governed by Chapter 11 of the Bankruptcy Code[110] and are almost always begun by a voluntary petition filed by the corporate debtor. The filing brings about a moratorium on enforcement proceedings against the debtor or its property and the incumbent management normally remain in place – during the early stages at least – of the reorganisation proceedings. As the DTI review of company rescue and business reconstruction mechanisms points out, on the standard tests, the US should be classed as pro-debtor rather than pro-creditor: it allows an automatic stay on assets; allows unimpeded petition for reorganisation; and allows the company's board to remain in control during reorganisation.[111] One distinguished American commentator has observed:[112]

[108] Section 252 Enterprise Act 2002, which inserts a new section 176A into the Insolvency Act 1986.

[109] See generally D. Milman 'Reforming Corporate Rescue Mechanisms' in J. De Lacy ed. *The Reform of United Kingdom Company Law* (Cavendish, 2002) at p. 415.

[110] See generally on Chapter 11 R. Broude 'How the Rescue Culture Came to the United States and the Myths that Surround Chapter 11' (2000) 16 *Insolvency Law and Practice* 194. The economic efficiency etc. of Chapter 11 is discussed in M. Bradley and M. Rozenweig 'The Untenable Case for Chapter 11' (1992) 101 *Yale LJ* 1043; E. Warren 'The Untenable Case for Repeal of Chapter 11' (1992) 102 *Yale LJ* 437; T. Eisenberg 'Baseline Problems in Assessing Chapter 11' (1993) 43 *University of Toronto Law Journal* 633; K. Kordana and E. Posner 'A Positive Theory of Chapter 11' (1999) 74 *NYULR* 161.

[111] *DTI Company Rescue and Business Reconstruction Mechanisms* at pp. 38–41. At p. 33 the review group however observes that 'it would be wholly inappropriate to attempt to replicate Chapter 11 in the UK, where the business culture and economic environment are quite different'.

[112] See J. Westbrook 'A Comparison of Bankruptcy Reorganisation in the US with the Administration Procedure in the UK' (1990) 6 *Insolvency Law and Practice* 86 at 87; and see also J. Franks and W. Torous 'Lessons from a Comparison of US and UK Insolvency Codes' (1993) 8 *Oxford Review of Economic Policy* 70.

If an American banker is very, very good, when he dies he will go to the United Kingdom. British banks have far more control than an American secured lender could ever hope to have. Receiverships on the British model are unknown and almost unthinkable in the US. A US banker could barely imagine a banker's Valhalla in which a bank could veto a reorganisation as a UK bank may effectively veto an administration by appointing an administrative receiver.

The broad thrust of the Enterprise Act is to redress the balance somewhat in favour of the debtor and unsecured creditors in the UK. A 'carve-out' or 'set aside' for unsecured creditors is part of that redressing of the balance.

The 'carve-out' for unsecured creditors in England

The Enterprise Act proposes that a certain percentage of floating-charge realisations should be set aside for the benefit of unsecured creditors.[113] That percentage is not settled in the legislation but remains to be prescribed by statutory instrument.[114] The idea is an old one, which can be traced back to the Cork Committee Report on Insolvency Law and Practice in 1982 which recommended that 10 per cent of floating-charge realisations should be set aside for distribution to unsecured creditors.[115] Like the provisions of the Enterprise Act the proposal was part of a package, as the chairman of the committee, Sir Kenneth Cork, a noted insolvency practitioner, himself explained:[116]

First, the almost total abolition of preferences; secondly, restrictions on the reservation of title; thirdly, creditors having fixed charges to be restrained from realising their security for 12 months after the appointment of a receiver . . . Therefore it seems fair to some of us . . . to give the unsecured creditors a stake, say 10 per cent, in the net realisations of the receiver.

Banks, however, saw the so-called 10 per cent fund as the thin end of the wedge and concerns were expressed that, on subsequent occasions,

---

[113] Section 252 Enterprise Act 2002, which inserts a new section 176A into the Insolvency Act 1986. On the reforms to insolvency procedure introduced by the Enterprise Act see generally A. McKnight 'The Reform of Corporate Insolvency Law in Great Britain – the Enterprise Bill 2002' [2002] *JIBL* 324.

[114] For suggestions that a single percentage might not be applied across the board but rather that a sliding scale could be adopted see HL Official Report (Enterprise Bill), col. 768, 29 July 2002; on which see generally McKnight 'Corporate Insolvency Law in Great Britain' at 334–5.

[115] Cmnd 8588; on which see generally D. Milman 'The Ten Per Cent Fund' [1999] *Insolvency Lawyer* 47.

[116] *Minutes of the Cork Committee*, 24 Nov. 1980 at pp. 2–3, quoted in B. Carruthers and T. Halliday, *Rescuing Businesses: The Making of Corporate Bankruptcy Law in England and the United States* (Oxford University Press, 1998) at p. 200.

the 10 per cent figure might be increased substantially. Moreover, it was suggested that, on implementation of the proposal, banks would only be willing to advance less funds and on more stringent terms. When the Insolvency Act that resulted from the Cork report was eventually published in 1984 it did not include provision for the 10 per cent fund and the government successfully resisted opposition amendments that would have led to the inclusion of such a provision.[117] The government expressed a deep solicitude for the views of the banking community and a concern not to reduce the operating flexibility of banks. Those pressing for the creation of the 10 per cent fund advanced two lines of reasoning. The first focused on the redistributive function of the fund, seeing it is as a compensation measure for the benefit of economically weak unsecured creditors. The second saw the fund as a fighting fund used to meet the expenses of insolvency practitioners who were contemplating the institution of proceedings, such as improper preference or wrongful trading actions, to recover misdirected company monies.[118] In other words, establishment of the fund would reinforce other measures designed to secure proper standards of corporate behaviour. In the words of one opposition member: 'There have been too many scandals . . . we are trying to stop people hiding behind limited liability and carrying on nefarious activities that no decent businessman would countenance.'[119]

On a cynical level, one might observe that banks feared the loss of control that a 10 per cent 'fighting fund' would entail. Insolvency practitioners would move out of the ambit of the banks and not only would the banks lose 10 per cent, the insolvency practitioners could use this money to take away even more of what the banks perceived to be as 'their' money. The government saw the proposal as hindering rather than helping business. Money would be tied up in specialist insolvency accounts, and in its view, an expensive bureaucracy would be needed to police such accounts. Not surprisingly, a Conservative government, committed to parsimony with the public purse, baulked at such a suggested increase in expenditure. More generally, the point was made that the 10 per cent fund would lead banks to lend less, charge higher rates of interest and take other defensive measures that would work to the detriment of small business. Not all interested parties were persuaded, however, by this line of analysis. Lord Denning, for example, said:[120]

---

[117] See generally Carruthers and Halliday *Rescuing Businesses* at pp. 339–46.
[118] See the comments at HC debates vol. 78, cols. 156, 157–8 (30 April 1985), by the opposition spokesperson, Mr Brian Gould.
[119] HL debates vol. 458, cols. 912–13 (15 Jan. 1985).
[120] See Carruthers and Halliday *Rescuing Businesses* at p. 346.

I am afraid the Government must have been much influenced by those big bankers . . . The banking community want every penny. They want the last 10 percent . . . They always want their interest, right to the very top rate. The banking community do not need this 10 percent . . . They ought to allow the unsecured creditors a little but, just 10 percent, that is all.

The Cork 10 per cent fund proposal would reduce some of the priority that secured creditors enjoy over other creditors. It was opposed by lenders for this reason and also on the more general basis that it would cause a diminution in the supply and quality of credit offered. The whole debate begs the more general question of why lenders wish to take security and, indeed, why the law permits the taking of security.

The Enterprise Act provisions

Under the provisions of the Enterprise Act a prescribed part of floating-charge recoveries shall be made available for the satisfaction of unsecured debts.[121] The provision operates once claims secured by a fixed charge or preferential debts on the same property have been discharged. The provision does not apply, however, if the company's net property is less than a prescribed minimum and where the liquidator, administrator or receiver thinks that the cost of making a distribution to unsecured creditors would be disproportionate to the benefits. The basic reform provision has long been advocated in the writings of academic, and other, commentators. For instance, Milman and Mond suggest[122] that it 'seems a fair concession to unsecured creditors without destroying the notion of security in its entirety'. Likewise Finch recognises that the proposal is 'no complete answer but it does have the merit of reducing the possibility that unsecured creditors will be faced with empty coffers'.[123] Finch concedes that the establishment of a fund for the payment of unsecured debts is a blunt instrument since it benefits all unsecured creditors and not just those creditors who are unable to adjust the terms (implicit or explicit) on which they lend in order to take into account the fact that the borrower has granted security. On the other hand, in her view, 'it is a known quantity that allows attendant risks to be calculated and which is unlikely to reduce the availability of secured credit. It would accordingly not impede trading materially.' Commentators seem relatively sanguine about the prospect of such a fund impinging on the availability

---

[121] Section 252 Enterprise Act 2002, which introduces a new section 176A into the Insolvency Act 1986. The prescribed part has been fixed by the Insolvency Act 1986 (Prescribed Part) Order 2003.

[122] *Security and Corporate Rescue*, at p. 52.

[123] 'Security, Insolvency and Risk' at 665.

of credit for the corporate sector.[124] The Cork Committee specifically rejected the proposition that any such diminution of credit would occur, stating:[125]

There is no evidence that any such diminution occurred in 1897 following the intervention of statute to subordinate the floating charge to the claims of preferential creditors, or in 1975 following the substantial increase in the monetary limits on the preferential claims of employees: yet each involved a far greater erosion of the priority accorded to the floating charge than anything we now propose.

Milman and Mond are even blunter in their discounting of the risks of the supply of credit drying up stating that similar arguments were raised in the early nineteenth century when proposals were made to 'abolish imprisonment for debt: creditors survived that change in the law and there is no reason to doubt that they would adapt to an era of reduced security rights'.[126] Moreover, any possibility of a hike in interest rates as a result is offset by the fact that lending is often an extremely profitable venture and the increasingly competitive market can be expected to mitigate any unreasonable reactions by particular lenders.

It has been suggested that the cutback on floating-charge priorities is constitutionally questionable in the light of the provisions of the Human Rights Act and Article 1 of Protocol 1 to the European Convention on Human Rights, which provides:[127] 'Every natural or legal person is entitled to the peaceful enjoyment of his possessions. No one shall be deprived of his possessions except in the public interest and subject to the conditions provided for by law and by the general principles of international law.' Article 1 goes on to provide, however, that the preceding prescriptions do not in any way impair the right of a state to enforce such laws as it deems necessary to control the use of property in accordance with the general interest or to secure the payment of taxes or other contributions of penalties.[128] The European Court has declared that Article 1 is made up of three distinct rules. Firstly, there is a statement of the principle of the peaceful enjoyment of property. Secondly, there is a regulation of the conditions relating to the deprivation of possessions. Thirdly, there is a recognition that states are entitled to control the use of property in accordance with the general interest.

---

[124] See *ibid.* at 652.   [125] Cmnd 8558 (1982) at para. 1535.

[126] *Security and Corporate Rescue* at p. 53.

[127] See generally for an assessment of the implications of these provisions in the commercial law sphere A. Dignam and J. Allen *Company Law and Human Rights* (Butterworths, 2000) at pp. 263–85.

[128] For a discussion of the position in the United States under the Fifth Amendment ('no taking without due process') see Rogers 'Impairment of Secured Creditors' Rights'; Baird and Jackson 'Corporate Reorganizations'.

It is submitted that the jurisprudence of the European Court offers little prospect of a challenge to the 'carve-out' provisions contained in the Enterprise Act succeeding. The provision is designed to protect the interests of third parties, and legislatures have been accorded a wide discretion in framing provisions to safeguard third-party rights. A case in point is *James* v. *United Kingdom*[129] where it was said: 'The Court, finding it natural that the margin of appreciation available to the legislature in implementing social and economic policies should be a wide one, will respect the legislature's judgment as to what is "in the public interest" unless that judgment be manifestly without reasonable foundation.'

The possibility remains, however, that banks might attempt to circumvent a change in the law by altering their lending behaviour either by taking fixed rather than floating security or else by making use of devices such as factoring, title retention, sale and lease-back or agency sales financing.[130] To a certain extent, however, the most far-reaching and potentially profitable possibility – that of taking a fixed charge over receivables owing to the company – has been foreclosed by the decision of the Privy Council in the *Brumark* case – *Agnew* v. *Commissioner of Inland Revenue*.[131] The Privy Council make it clear that it would only be in rare cases where a fixed-charge characterisation of security over receivables would be upheld. According to Lord Millett the critical feature which distinguished a floating from a fixed charge was the security giver's ability, freely and without the security taker's consent, to control and manage the charged assets and withdraw them from the security. In the court's view, since alienation and collection merely signified different ways of realising a debt, a restriction on disposal which permitted collection and free use of the proceeds enabled a debt to be withdrawn from the security by the security giver's act and was inconsistent with the nature of a fixed charge.

In other words, the chargor must be required to pay the debt proceeds into a bank account under the control of the lender before the lender's security can be designated as a fixed charge. In the wake of *Brumark* it has been suggested that banks might channel business to factoring subsidiaries, and again, factoring arrangements could be a mechanism

---

[129] (1986) 8 EHRR 123; and see also *Lithgow* v. *United Kingdom* (1986) 8 EHRR 329 and *Pine Valley Developments Ltd* v. *Ireland* (1992) 14 EHRR 319. See also now the decision of the House of Lords in *Wilson* v. *Secretary of State for Trade and Industry* [2003] UKHL 40 (10 July 2003).

[130] It may be noted that the Cork 10 per cent fund concept was rejected in the 1984 White Paper, *A Revised Framework for Insolvency Law* (Cmnd 9175) at paras. 26–27 on the basis that it would not work because of the proliferation of fixed charges over future assets.

[131] [2001] 2 AC 710.

employed by banks to overcome restrictions on floating-charge recoveries.[132] In fact, in legal terms the distinction between a fixed charge over receivables and an undisclosed factoring arrangement whereby the 'borrower' continues to collect the receivables is quite a narrow one.[133] Factoring, however, offers less flexibility to the parties and more information has to be disclosed by the 'borrower' to the bank. It may be that, for these reasons, factoring will not be widely employed in practice notwithstanding the avoidance possibilities that it presents.

Conclusion

In its consultation paper *Registration of Security Interests*,[134] the Law Commission suggested that the system of public notice of security interests was here to stay. The same may be said about the institution of secured credit, which is a long-established part of Anglo-American legal culture as well as other legal cultures. Judicial recognition of security devices usually proceeds on the basis that such recognition is but a manifestation of freedom of contract and, moreover, that it contributes to the promotion of economic activity. The 'helping to stimulate economic activity' line of argument has been given a more contemporary spin by American commentators, particularly of the law-and-economics ilk, but the traffic is not all one way. Some observers have questioned the efficiency of secured credit, and even some from an economic perspective. But the proposals of such observers for limiting the effectiveness of security interests, while interesting and challenging on a theoretical level, failed singularly to penetrate into the realm of political acceptability.[135] The theoretical discussion has been less advanced and detailed in England, but nevertheless, proposals for limiting the 'full' priority of secured credit found

---

[132] See generally on *Brumark* McCormack 'The Nature of Security over Receivables'; P. Watts 'The Rending of Charges' (2002) 118 *LQR* 1; A. Berg 'Brumark Investments Ltd and the Innominate Charge' [2001] *JBL* 532; P. Wood 'Fixed and Floating Charges' [2001] *CLJ* 472.

[133] See *Lloyds and Scottish Finance* v. *Cyril Lord (Carpet Sales) Ltd* [1992] BCLC 609.

[134] July 2002 at para. 3.2.

[135] See the comment by the Article 9 reporters Professors S. L. Harris and C. W. Mooney in 'How Successful was the Revision of UCC Article 9?: Reflections of the Reporters' (1999) 74 *Chicago-Kent L Rev* 1357 at 1359 n. 6:

> The task force, comprised largely of bankruptcy specialists, devoted particular attention to proposals by academics for restricting the effectiveness of security interests . . . Having received hardly any support among members of the task force and no support whatsoever from anyone who ever attended a meeting of the Drafting Committee, these proposals were rejected. The proposals were advocated also before the Council of the ALI and at a NCCUSL Annual Meeting, where they met with almost unanimous disapproval.

greater political resonance. The Enterprise Act contains a 'carve-out' in favour of unsecured creditors with an as yet unspecified proportion of floating-charge recoveries being set aside for their benefit. There are at least two views on this provision.

One view sees it as redressing the balance somewhat in favour of the unsecured creditor and as a valuable measure that might forestall the domino effect of a chain of insolvencies following on from the failure of a business that leaves its trade creditors and suppliers unpaid. Another view sees the measure as interfering with the contractual freedom and property rights of banks and one which will hurt business by making banks more reluctant to lend, or only willing to do so on harsher terms. On this analysis, a proposal designed to help small businesses will end up damaging them. It may be that these fears are exaggerated and that implementation of the proposal will not have a significant impact on bank lending activity. Banks are in the business of lending money and the informed view of industry professionals suggests that they are unlikely to stop doing so because of partial loss of priority rights. Banks, however, fear that the scope and size of the carve-out could be increased over time and a different pattern could emerge if the attack on security runs deep. Certainly the provisions should be kept under review with a view to mitigating any untoward changes in bank lending strategies. On the more technical level, the provision is not 'avoidance-proof' and it may be that banks will make greater use of fixed charges, factoring and a plethora of 'artificial' security devices to counteract its effects. Such tactics, if successfully employed, might completely deprive the provision of force. The courts and legislature must be alert to such attempts and be prepared to recharacterise transactions if necessary.

2   Security rights under English law

There are many different types of security right recognised under English law but the workhorse of the secured credit industry has traditionally been the charge and, in particular, the floating charge.[1] The different kinds of security right under English law will be examined in this chapter. The chapter then examines the pressure points for reform of the law and makes some basic comparisons with the functional approach under Article 9 of the American Uniform Commercial Code.

Basic distinctions

There are three basic distinctions: firstly, between legal and equitable security interests; secondly between possessory and non-possessory security interests; and thirdly, between consensual and non-consensual security interests. These various distinctions cut across one another. The main types of security interest are mortgages, charges, pledges and liens – both common-law and equitable liens.

The distinction between legal and equitable security interests is perhaps most confusing to a non-common-law lawyer but it is easy to exaggerate the importance of the distinction in practice. The distinction stems from the historical separation between law and equity and the fact that certain kinds of security right were only recognised in courts of equity, as distinct from courts of common law, prior to the unification of the court structure in the 1870s. For example, a mortgage of future property was void at common law, and consequently any security interest in future personalty must necessarily be equitable in nature.[2] The distinction retains some importance in the context of priorities. Legal interests are said to bind the whole world whereas equitable interests are said to bind all, save

---

[1] See generally chap. 15, 'Secured debt', in Eilis Ferran *Company Law and Corporate Finance* (Oxford University Press, 1999).

[2] See e.g. *Lunn* v. *Thornton* (1845) I CB 379; *Tailby* v. *Official Receiver* (1888) 13 App Cas 523.

for a bona fide purchaser of a legal interest in the same property for value without notice of the prior equitable interest. The priority issue is, however, affected by the question of registration because, generally speaking, a charge created by a corporate debtor is invalid in the event of the debtor going into liquidation.[3] Moreover, if an equitable security interest on property requires registration then the fact of registration should infect the holders of subsequent legal security interests in the same property with notice.

The distinction between possessory and non-possessory security interests is highly significant in practical terms. Mortgages, charges and equitable liens are non-possessory security interests – in other words, the lender does not have possession of the items used as security – whereas the pledge and the common-law lien are possessory in nature, i.e. the lender is entrusted with possession of the items used as security. Finally, mortgages, charges and pledges are consensual security interests, in other words they are created by agreement between the parties. Liens, on the other hand, are non-consensual, i.e. they arise by operation of law, irrespective of the agreement of the parties, in certain defined circumstances. A brief description of each of these types of security right is appropriate.

Mortgages and charges

In many contexts the phrases 'mortgage' and 'charge' are used interchangeably whereas in other settings 'charge' is defined so as to encompass a 'mortgage'. There is, however, a distinction between the two concepts. As Slade J explained in *Re Bond Worth Ltd*,[4] the technical difference between a 'mortgage' and a 'charge' lies in the fact that a mortgage involves a conveyance of property subject to a right of redemption, whereas a charge conveys nothing and merely gives the chargee certain rights over the property as security for the loan.[5] In other words, a mortgage involves the transfer of rights of ownership whereas 'charge' is a general umbrella expression to cover a right of recourse to property for security

---

[3] Section 395 Companies Act 1985. See also the comments of Lord Hoffmann in *Smith* v. *Bridgend County Borough Council* [2002] 1 AC 336 at 347–8:

> Section 395 . . . was intended for the protection of the creditors of an insolvent company. It was intended to give persons dealing with a company the opportunity to discover, by consulting the register, whether its assets were burdened by floating and certain fixed charges which would reduce the amount available for unsecured creditors in a liquidation. Whether this was a realistic form of protection and whether the choice of registrable charges was entirely logical is not presently relevant.

[4] [1980] Ch 228.   [5] *Ibid.* at 250.

purposes.[6] The chargee has certain rights over the property of the chargor to ensure the payment of money due or the performance of some other obligation. The chargee is entitled to resort to the property only for the purpose of satisfying some liability due to him, and, whatever the form of the transaction, the chargor has an equity of redemption to have the property restored to him once the liability has been discharged.

In *Re BCCI (No. 8)*[7] Lord Hoffmann described an equitable charge as

a species of charge, which is a proprietary interest granted by way of security. Proprietary interests confer rights in rem which, subject to questions of registration and the equitable doctrine of purchaser for value without notice, will be binding upon third parties and unaffected by the insolvency of the owner of the property charged. A proprietary interest provided by way of security entitles the holder to resort to the property only for the purpose of satisfying some liability due to him (whether from the person providing the security or a third party) and, whatever the form of the transaction, the owner of the property retains an equity of redemption to have the property restored to him when the liability has been discharged.

Pledges

A pledge has been described as the actual or constructive delivery of possession of an asset to a creditor by way of security.[8] In the case of a pledge the pledgee (lender) is given possession of the items pledged whereas ownership of the items remains with the pledgor (borrower). As possessor, the pledgee is said to enjoy a 'special property' in the goods but the general property, however, or what might be termed 'ownership', still belongs to the pledgor.[9] To constitute a pledge, delivery of possession need not be contemporaneous with the making of a loan but it

---

[6] See also the comments of Buckley LJ in *Swiss Bank Corporation* v. *Lloyds Bank Ltd* [1982] AC 584 at 595:

> An equitable charge which is not an equitable mortgage is said to be created when property is expressly or constructively made liable or specifically appropriated, to the discharge of a debt or some other obligation, and confers on the chargee a right of realisation by judicial process, that is to say, by the appointment of a receiver or an order for sale.

[7] [1998] AC 214.

[8] See generally R. Goode *Legal Problems of Credit and Security* (Sweet & Maxwell, 2nd edn. 1988) at p. 10; and see also E. Sykes and S. Walker *The Law of Securities* (Law Book Company, 5th edn. 1993) at pp. 734–7 and N. Palmer *Bailment* (Law Book Company, 2nd edn. 1991) chap. 22.

[9] The pledgee has an inherent right to sell unredeemed chattels after the loan period has expired. In *Matthew* v. *TM Sutton Ltd* [1994] 4 All ER 793 it was held that a pledgee who sells unredeemed chattels for more than the sum owed by the pledgor holds the surplus as a fiduciary on trust for the pledgor.

should be stressed that the actual or constructive delivery of possession is indispensable. The requirement of delivery means that the class of assets capable of forming the subject matter of a pledge is confined to goods and to documentary intangibles which are 'documents embodying title to goods, money or securities such that the right to these assets is vested in the holder of the document for the time being and can be transferred by delivery with any necessary indorsement'.[10] Consequently pledges may be created in respect of bills of lading and other documents of title to goods but not over common commercial contracts. The fact that a bill of lading may be pledged signifies the usefulness of pledges for the financing of international trade. The requirement, however, that a creditor takes a pledge over a document which is actually a document of title suggests the limitations of the pledge as a security vehicle. Bills of lading are documents of title and so too are bearer share certificates but not warehouse receipts or certificates relating to registered shares.[11] On the other hand, the usefulness of the pledge mechanism has been extended by judicial validation of three techniques. The first is that of 'constructive delivery of possession'.[12] The second is that of attornment and the third technique is the 'trust receipt'.

The concepts of 'constructive delivery of possession' and attornment were explained by the Privy Council in *Official Assignee of Madras* v. *Mercantile Bank of India Ltd*:[13]

At common law a pledge could not be created except by a delivery of possession of the thing pledged, either actual or constructive. It involved a bailment. If the pledgor had the actual goods in his physical possession, he could effect the pledge by physical delivery; in other cases he could give possession by some symbolic act, such as handing over the key of the store in which they were. If, however, the goods were in the custody of a third person, who held for the bailor so that in law his possession was that of the bailor, the pledge could be effected by a change of the possession of the third party, that is by an order to him from the pledgor to hold for the pledgee, the change being perfected by the third party attorning to the pledgee, that is acknowledging that he thereupon held for him; there was thus a change of possession and a constructive delivery; the goods in the hands of the third party became by this process in the possession constructively of the pledgee.

[10] Goode *Legal Problems* at p. 11. Professor Goode in *Commercial Law* (Penguin, 2nd edn. 1996) at pp. 52–5 makes a distinction between 'pure' and 'documentary' intangibles. A pure intangible is 'a right which is not in law considered to be represented by a document', while in the case of the latter the obligation 'is considered in law to be locked up in the document such that the delivery of the document will transfer ownership of the intangible without the need for any separate formal assignment'.
[11] *Harrold* v. *Plenty* [1901] 2 Ch 314.
[12] The example was given in *Hilton* v. *Tucker* (1888) 39 Ch D 669 of delivery of a key as the symbol of possession where the transfer of possession itself was practically impossible.
[13] [1935] AC 53 at 58–9.

As the judicial statement shows, where goods are in the possession of a third party rather than the debtor, the third party can 'attorn' to the creditor, i.e. undertake to hold the goods for the benefit of the creditor. Attornment is a technique that is often used in the art world:[14]

If, for instance, the debtor is an art dealer who has deposited works of art with an auction house, the auction house can, by attorning in favour of the creditor (ie by confirming, at the request of the debtor, that it holds the works of art on behalf of the creditor), transfer constructive possession in the works of art to the creditor.

On the third technique the 'trust receipt' is a document which permits a pledgee to release goods to his pledgor as agent for sale and trustee of the proceeds but simultaneously maintaining his pledge interest.[15] The fact that goods are released back by the 'pledgee' to the 'pledgor' will not prejudice the claim to a pledge where the release takes place under the auspices of a trust receipt. Trust receipts received the approval of the House of Lords in *North Western Bank Ltd* v. *Poynter, Son and Macdonalds*.[16] It was held that a pledgee may redeliver the goods to the pledgor for a limited purpose without thereby losing his rights under the contract of pledge. Pledgees of a bill of lading representing a specific cargo returned the bill of lading to the pledgors to obtain delivery of the merchandise and sell on the pledgees' behalf and account for the proceeds towards satisfaction of the debt. The House of Lords took the view that the pledgees' security was not affected and that they were entitled to the proceeds of the cargo as against the general creditors of the pledgors.

The same principle was applied in *Re David Allester Ltd*.[17] Here a company pledged bills of lading with a bank to secure an overdraft but when it came to sell the goods the company, in accordance with long-standing mercantile practice, obtained the bills of lading from the bank. Realisation was on the terms stated in the usual letter of trust given by the company to the bank, i.e. that the company received the bills of lading in trust on the bank's account and undertook to hold the goods when received and the proceeds when sold as the bank's trustees and to remit the entire net proceeds as realised. The court held that the bank's previous rights as pledgee remained unaffected by this common and convenient mode of realisation.

---

[14] Richard Calnan 'Taking Security in England' in Michael Bridge and Robert Stevens eds. *Cross-Border Security and Insolvency* (Oxford University Press, 2001) 17 at p. 19.

[15] See generally *North Western Bank Ltd* v. *Poynter, Son and Macdonalds* [1895] AC 56; *Re David Allester Ltd* [1922] 2 Ch 211.

[16] [1895] AC 56.   [17] [1922] 2 Ch 211.

Reference has occasionally been made to another form of possessory security right based on contract: the contractual lien.[18] It is clear that contractual liens and pledges are akin. Certainly they share many of the same characteristics; in particular they both depend on delivery of possession to the creditor. Millett LJ, however, distinguished between them in *Re Cosslett (Contractors) Ltd*,[19] saying that in the case of a pledge the owner delivers possession to the creditor as security, whereas in the case of a lien the creditor retains possession of goods previously delivered to him for some other purpose.

Liens: common-law liens

A common-law lien is a right to retain possession of an asset until discharge of an outstanding debt and is to be distinguished from an equitable lien which is essentially a form of non-possessory security interest arising by operation of law. The distinction between the two concepts has been expounded in the following terms:[20] 'An equitable lien differs from a common-law lien in that a common law lien is founded on possession and, except as modified by statute, merely confers a right to detain until payment, whereas an equitable lien, which exists quite irrespective of possession, confers on the holder the right to a judicial sale.'

In *Tappenden* v. *Artus*[21] Diplock LJ compared the common-law remedy of a possessory lien with other 'primitive remedies' such as abatement of nuisance, self-defence or ejection of trespassers to land. The remedy was a self-help one. Diplock LJ said the possessory lien was a remedy *in rem* exercisable on the goods and its exercise required no intervention by the courts, for it was exercisable only by a person who had actual possession of the goods subject to the lien. A common-law lien afforded a defence to an action for recovery of the goods by a person who, but for the lien, would be entitled to immediate possession.

Common-law liens are non-consensual in nature and are confined to historically determined situations.[22] Statute, however, has sometimes

---

[18] *George Barker Ltd* v. *Eynon* [1974] 1 WLR 462.

[19] [1998] Ch 495. It was also held by the Court of Appeal in *Re Hamlet International plc* [1999] 2 BCLC 506 that the existence of a power of sale in the relevant contract did not turn a contractual possessory lien into an equitable charge.

[20] *Halsbury's Laws of England* (4th edn. reissue 1997) vol. XXVIII, para. 754. The relevant chapter is by Professor Norman Palmer and Sir Anthony Mason, former Chief Justice of Australia.

[21] [1964] 2 QB 185.

[22] See M. Bridge *Personal Property Law* (Oxford University Press, 3rd edn. 2002) at pp. 170–1. Professor Bridge points to a general confluence between the conferment of a lien and the exercise of a common calling. See also A. Bell *Modern Law of Personal Property in England and Ireland* (Butterworths, 1989) at pp. 138–9.

recognised or created lien-type rights. Section 88 Civil Aviation Act 1982 which was considered in *Bristol Airport plc* v. *Powdrill*[23] serves as a case in point. The section conferred on airport authorities the right to detain aircraft to force payment of unpaid airport charges. The Court of Appeal took the view that the statutory right of detention was a 'lien or security' over property within the meaning of section 248 of the Insolvency Act 1986. In general a common-law lien equals a passive power of detention. The lienee may, however, have a power of sale in the case of a statutorily conferred lien as is the situation with section 88 Civil Aviation Act 1982. Moreover, statute sometimes invests a lienee with a power of sale in other circumstances.[24]

Liens: equitable liens

Equitable liens are more expansive in nature than common-law liens in that they are not dependent on possession.[25] It has even been suggested that 'the equitable lien is a dangerous and elusive enemy of the law of [*pari passu* distribution of a debtor's assets in an insolvency]' and that as 'applied to some bankruptcy cases, it seems as well named as the Holy Roman Empire, for it is neither equitable nor a lien'.[26] An equitable lien is a form of equitable charge arising by operation of law. In other words, it[27] is a right against property which arises automatically by implication of equity to secure the discharge of an actual or potential indebtedness.[28] An equitable lien may be enforced by obtaining an order of sale from the court.[29] The best-known equitable liens are the vendor's lien for unpaid

---

[23] [1990] Ch 744.

[24] See, for example, Torts (Interference with Goods) Act 1977, ss 12 and 13. Moreover, under the Civil Procedure Rules 1998, r 25.1(1)(c)(v) the court has power on the application of any party to a cause or matter to order the sale of any property which is the subject of a claim or as to which any question may arise on a claim and which is of a perishable nature or which for any other good reason it is desirable to sell quickly.

[25] Adopting the words of Lord Mersey in *Kreglinger* v. *New Patagonia Meat and Cold Storage Co Ltd* [1914] AC 25 at 46. See generally on equitable liens the decision of the High Court of Australia in *Hewett* v. *Court* (1983) 149 CLR 639 which case is extensively discussed by I. Hardingham 'Equitable Liens for the Recovery of Purchase Money' (1985) 15 *Melbourne University Law Review* 65.

[26] M. McLaughlin 'Amendment of the Bankruptcy Act' (1927) 60 *Harv L Rev* 341 at 389, referred to by J. Phillips 'Equitable Liens – a Search for a Unifying Principle' in N. Palmer and E. McKendrick eds. *Interests in Goods* (Lloyds of London Press, 2nd edn. 1998) chap. 39 at pp. 992–3.

[27] See *Hewett* v. *Court* (1983) 149 CLR 639; on which see Hardingham 'Equitable Liens'.

[28] See also *Re Bernstein* [1925] Ch 12 at 17–18 and *Re Bond Worth Ltd* [1980] Ch 228 at 251.

[29] *Bowles* v. *Rogers* (1800) 31 ER 957; *Re Stucley* [1906] 1 Ch 67.

purchase money and the purchaser's lien, both arising in the case of contracts for the sale of land.[30] The former is founded on the principle that 'a person, having got the estate of another, shall not, as between them, keep it, and not pay the consideration'.[31] The purchaser's lien rests on the converse principle that he who has agreed to convey property in return for a purchase price will not be allowed to keep the price if he fails to convey the property as agreed.[32]

English law and the essentials of a modern law of security interests

It is widely believed, at least among the international lending community, that a modern law of security interests must be founded on five key elements.[33] Firstly, the security right must adhere to the essential qualities of a property right (right *in rem*). Secondly, the law should provide for the granting of security in the widest possible range of circumstances. Thirdly, the existence of a security right over property must be effectively publicised. Fourthly, there should be a rapid and cost-effective means of recovering the debt from the secured asset. Fifthly, the cost of creating, maintaining and exercising the right should be kept at a reasonable level.[34]

Adopting a broad-brush approach, English law essentially implements these principles.[35] Firstly, security rights in English law are rights *in rem*. In other words, they are enforceable against third parties and not just *inter partes*, i.e. between debtor and creditor. Secondly, English law does provide for the granting of security in the widest possible range of circumstances. Through the floating charge it is possible to create security over the entirety of a company's business operations by simply charging the company's undertaking. It is also possible to create a fixed charge over almost any asset provided that the company debtor is restricted in

---

[30] Under sections 41–43 Sale of Goods Act 1979 an unpaid seller of goods has a possessory lien and also a right to stop goods in transit but the courts have refused to recognise equitable liens in sale of goods transactions that operate independently of the legislation: *Re Wait* [1927] 1 Ch 606.

[31] *Mackreth* v. *Symmons* (1808) 15 Ves 329 at 340; 33 ER 778 at 782.

[32] See *Rose* v. *Watson* (1864) 10 HL Cas 672 at 684.

[33] See D. Fairgrieve 'Reforming Secured Transactions Laws in Central and Eastern Europe' [1998] *EBLR* 254.

[34] See also the preface to the *Model Law on Secured Transactions* (1994) published by the EBRD.

[35] See for a comparison between the model law and English law G. McCormack and F. Dahan 'The EBRD Model Law on Secured Transactions: Comparisons and Convergence' [1999] *CFILR* 65; and more generally J. Norton and M. Andenas eds. *Emerging Financial Markets and Secured Transactions* (Kluwer, 1998).

the manner that it can deal with the assets that form the subject matter of the security. For instance, the courts have acknowledged the possibility of creating a fixed charge over future receivables provided that the chargee pays the proceeds of the receivables into a special bank account under the control of the chargor.[36]

It is in this area of extensiveness of possible security interests that English law scores most highly and earned its reputation for being favourably disposed towards the secured creditor.[37] In the nineteenth century legal practitioners and the courts responded to the growing needs of commerce by the development of an all-encompassing form of security – the floating charge. The transition from an agricultural to an industrial economy brought about by the Industrial Revolution meant that only a small proportion of a company's wealth might be tied up in buildings and fixed equipment. The bulk of a company's assets could now be in the form of raw materials, manufactured goods or goods in the process of manufacture, stock-in-trade and debts owed to the company by trade customers. The existing fixed forms of security could not capture these assets. Moreover, the advent of the limited liability company meant that bank lending on a totally unsecured basis was an even more hazardous proposition.[38] Judicial reaction to this state of affairs was twofold. The validity of mortgages on after-acquired property – both goods and receivables – was recognised[39] and also the floating charge was given the judicial imprimatur. The floating charge made it possible to create a security interest over the entire existing and future assets of an undertaking.[40] A floating charge is essentially a charge on a class of assets, both present and future, which permits the company creating the charge to dispose of a clean title to the assets which form the subject matter of the charge until some event occurs which causes the charge holder to intervene.[41] Such an event is called a 'crystallising' event. Put another way, the corporate debtor has management autonomy with respect to the category of assets

---

[36] *Siebe Gorman* v. *Barclays Bank* [1979] 2 Lloyd's Rep 142; *Re Brightlife Ltd* [1987] Ch 200; *Agnew* v. *Commissioner of Inland Revenue* [2001] 2 AC 710.

[37] See generally on the history and development of the floating charge R. Pennington 'The Genesis of the Floating Charge' (1960) 23 *MLR* 630.

[38] Limited Liability Act 1855.

[39] *Holroyd* v. *Marshall* (1862) 10 HL Cas 191.

[40] *Re Panama, New Zealand and Australian Royal Mail Co.* (1870) 5 Ch App 318.

[41] For an account of the juridical basis of the floating charge see J. Farrar 'World Economic Stagnation Puts the Floating Charge on Trial' (1980) 1 *Co Law* 83; E. Ferran 'Floating Charges – the Nature of the Security' [1988] *CLJ* 213; S. Worthington 'Floating Charges – an Alternative Theory' [1994] *CLJ* 81; R. Gregory and P. Walton 'Fixed Charges over Changing Assets – the Possession and Control Heresy' [1998] *CFILR* 68; and see generally P. Ali *The Law of Secured Finance* (Oxford University Press, 2002) 114–31.

covered by the floating charge.[42] The centrality of the floating charge in English lending practice was acknowledged by the Privy Council in *Agnew* v. *Commissioner of Inland Revenue*.[43] Lord Millett said:[44]

The floating charge is capable of affording the creditor, by a single instrument, an effective and comprehensive security upon the entire undertaking of the debtor company and its assets from time to time, while at the same time leaving the company free to deal with its assets and pay its trade creditors in the ordinary course of business without reference to the holder. Such a form of security is particularly attractive to banks, and it rapidly acquired an importance in English commercial life which . . . should not be underestimated.

Thirdly, in the main, English law publicises the existence of security interests over property through the registration of company charges regime. There is general legislative and judicial hostility to the recognition and enforcement of secret security interests, and this hostility is based on the avoidance of detriment to other creditors. Such creditors may advance credit to a company on the basis that its assets are unencumbered, and are prejudiced if it later emerges that the company has in fact given security for some or all of its existing debts. Part 12 Companies Act 1985 sets out specifically the categories of charge that necessitate registration for effectiveness in the event of a corporate debtor's liquidation. Not all charges require registration but the most common categories of charge are within the scope of the registration requirement including floating charges and fixed charges over land, goods and debts.[45] The register is open to public inspection and, in this way, third parties are alerted to the scope of a company's secured borrowings.

There is no requirement of registration in the case of pledges and common-law liens but the fact that the creditor has possession of the items used as security may be taken as the functional equivalent of notice. There are no notification or registration requirements in the case of security interests arising by operation of law, i.e. equitable liens. This

---

[42] See the comments of Millett LJ (as he then was) in *Re Coslett (Contractors) Ltd* [1998] Ch 495 at 510:

The essence of a floating charge is that it is a charge, not on any particular asset, but on a fluctuating body of assets which remain under the management and control of the chargor, and which the chargor has the right to withdraw from the security despite the existence of the charge. The essence of a fixed charge is that the charge is on a particular asset or class of assets which the chargor cannot deal with free from the charge without the consent of the chargee. The question is not whether the chargor has complete freedom to carry out his business as he chooses, but whether the chargee is in complete control of the charged assets.

[43] [2001] 2 AC 710.   [44] *Ibid.* at 717–18.
[45] For example, charges over goods, land, book debts and floating charges.

is a gap in the system and is, perhaps, the main reason why the judiciary have set their face against any extension of the category of equitable liens. There is, however, an even larger gap in the system in that English law adopts a narrow conception of security interests. In economic terms, there are many strategies for taking what would be regarded as the functional equivalent of security but which do not, in a legal sense, involve the creation of a security interest. In other words, there are various ways, outside the creation of a charge, in which a creditor may improve its position in the event of the debtor's insolvency.[46]

Fourthly, English law provides for a rapid and cost-effective means of recovering secured debts from the secured asset. From the point of view of a charge holder there has been an especially efficacious method of enforcing security rights in England through the appointment of a receiver.[47] Traditionally, the holder of a charge may appoint a receiver out of court pursuant to a facility contained in the instrument of charge. Although nominally the agent of the borrowing company to which he was appointed, the basic function of the receiver is to realise the secured assets for the benefit of the secured creditor. The Enterprise Act changes the procedure by removing the power to appoint an administrative receiver in the generality of cases as far as 'new' floating charges are concerned. The holder of a qualifying floating charge may, however, appoint an administrator out of court though the administrator must perform his functions with the objective of rescuing the company as a going concern where this is reasonably practicable – and even in circumstances where it is not, the administrator must not unnecessarily harm the interests of company creditors as a whole. Fifthly and finally, under English law the cost of creating, maintaining and exercising security interests appear to be at reasonable levels in that there are no notarisation fees or other levies payable on instruments of charge. Registering a charge and searching the register are subject to payment of a small fee but there are no other transaction costs apart of course from lawyer's remuneration.

In so far as English law is judged against the benchmark of these principles, it scores quite well. The main pluses are the freedom to create security interests in almost all classes of assets and the general absence of procedural barriers in respect of the creation of security interests. The

---

[46] See generally on the company charge registration system W. J. Gough *Company Charges* (Butterworths, 2nd edn. 1996); G. McCormack *Registration of Company Charges* (Sweet & Maxwell, 1994).

[47] As far as floating charges created after 15 September 2003, the Enterprise Act 2002, in the generality of cases but subject to certain exceptions, removes the power of a floating-charge holder to appoint an administrative receiver over a company's assets. Section 250 Enterprise Act inserts a new section 72A into the Insolvency Act 1986 to this effect.

minuses, on the other hand, centre around the relatively formalistic preoccupations of the law and the lack of a comprehensive registration obligation.

Viewing the law through the lens of the secured creditor, the development of the floating charge is a 'definite' plus as far as the English position is concerned. In this respect, English law compares very favourably with pre-Article 9 US law which did not recognise any equivalent of the floating charge on the basis that it was incompatible with the nature of a security interest that the debtor should have dominion over the assets used as security.[48] This state of affairs was transformed by Article 9.[49] Article 9, however, also goes beyond current English law by adopting a wider conception of security interests, e.g. by embracing reservation of title or factoring agreements that in English eyes would be viewed as 'quasi-security' rather than security strictly so-called. The Company Law Review Steering Group in its final report, *Modern Company Law for a Competitive Economy*, drew attention to the English legal treatment of 'quasi-security interests', i.e. functionally equivalent legal devices and the possibility of enacting a comprehensive register of security interests along North American lines.[50] The Law Commission in the consultation paper *Registration of Security Interests* endorsed this approach of moving away from the formalistic preoccupations of existing law to a greater emphasis on functionalism.[51] The formalistic distinctions of English law will now be examined in some detail.[52]

[48] *Benedict v. Ratner* (1925) 268 US 354; *Zartman v. First National Bank* (1907) 189 NY 267. There is also something of a feeling expressed in the pre-Article 9 American cases that all the debtor's property should not be swept away by security-interest holders and that the debtor should have a 'cushion' of free assets that is available for payment of debts owing to unsecured creditors.

[49] Article 9 was most recently revised in 1998, with the revision coming into force on 1 July 2001; for access to the revised version of Article 9 see the National Conference of Commissioners on Uniform State Laws website, www.nccusl.org.

[50] *Modern Company Law for a Competitive Economy: Final Report Volume 1* (July 2001) at p. 247:

> Although charges created by companies over their assets other than land must far outnumber similar charges created by other debtors, it would not be sensible to consider a notice-filing system for company charges without at the same time considering a similar system for all charges over property other than land and for functionally-equivalent legal devices (often termed 'quasi-security' devices).

[51] July 2002.

[52] Professor Grant Gilmore, one of the principal drafters of Article 9 of the UCC, has said that 'pre-Code personal property security law may be described as closely resembling that obscure wood in which Dante discovered the gates of hell': see 'The Good Faith Purchase Idea and the Uniform Commercial Code: Confessions of a Repentant Draftsman' (1981) 15 *Ga L Rev* 605 at 620. See generally on quasi-security under English

Formalism of the English law of security interests

In *Chow Yoong Hong* v. *Choong Fah Rubber Manufactory*[53] Lord Devlin observed that there are many ways of raising cash besides borrowing. To adjust the statement slightly, there are many ways in which a person who has 'advanced' money might enhance its prospects of recovery in the event of the debtor's insolvency besides being party to the creation of a charge. These methods include the following: (1) sale and lease-back/hire purchase; (2) title retention/conditional sale; (3) factoring/assignment of receivables; (4) agency sales financing; (5) Quistclose trusts. These are all 'quasi-security' devices and will now be considered.[54]

Quasi-security: sale and lease-back/hire purchase

A not uncommon financing technique involves the sale of goods or land followed by a lease-back. In all probability, the vendor will never have parted with possession and, in practice, it may be difficult to distinguish a genuine sale and lease-back from the creation of a charge over the property in question. In a leading case, *Re George Inglefield Ltd*,[55] Romer LJ attempted to explain the essential differences. He said:[56]

In a transaction of sale the vendor is not entitled to get back the subject-matter of the sale by returning to the purchaser the money that has passed between them. In the case of a mortgage or charge the mortgagor is entitled, until he has been foreclosed, to get back the subject-matter of the mortgage or charge by returning to the mortgagee the money that has passed between them. The second essential difference is that if the mortgagee realises the subject-matter of the mortgage for a sum more than sufficient to repay him, with interest and the costs, the money that has passed between him and the mortgagor he has to account to the mortgagor for the surplus. If the purchaser sells the subject-matter of the purchase, and realises a profit, of course he has not got to account to the vendor for the profit. Thirdly, if the mortgagee realises the mortgage property for a sum that is insufficient to

---

law V. Finch *Corporate Insolvency Law: Perspectives and Principles* (Cambridge University Press, 2002) chap. 13; A. Belcher and W. Beglan 'Jumping the Queue' [1997] *JBL* 1; J. Ulph 'Equitable Priority Rights in Insolvency: The Ebbing Tide' [1996] *JBL* 482; J. Ulph 'Sale and Lease-Back Agreements in a World of Title Relativity' (2001) 64 *MLR* 481.

[53] [1962] AC 209 at 216.

[54] See generally S. Worthington *Proprietary Interests in Commercial Transactions* (Oxford University Press, 1996).

[55] [1933] Ch 1.

[56] *Ibid.* at 26–7. It was made clear in *Durham Bros* v. *Robertson* [1898] 1 QB 765, however, that once the security nature of a transaction is established, equity will imply a right of redemption: see at 772 per Chitty LJ. Having regard to this fact Fidelis Oditah 'Financing Trade Credit: *Welsh Development Agency* v. *Exfinco*' [1992] *JBL* 541 at 546 argues that the speech of Romer LJ gives very little, if any, useful guidance.

repay him the money that he has paid to the mortgagor, together with interest and costs, then the mortgagee is entitled to recover from the mortgagor the balance of the money . . . If the purchaser were to resell the purchased property at a price which was insufficient to recoup him the money that he has paid to the vendor, of course he would not be entitled to recover the balance from the vendor.

These distinctions, while easy to state on paper, may become blurred in practice. For example, sale agreements may include options to repurchase and also profit-sharing clauses under which the original vendor shares in profits from resales as well as provisions whereby the vendor agrees to indemnify the buyer in respect of any losses incurred on a resale. As Millett LJ pointed out in *Orion Finance Ltd* v. *Crown Financial Management Ltd*,[57] no single one of the features enumerated by Romer LJ in *Re George Inglefield Ltd* may be determinative. He added:[58]

The absence of any right in the transferor to recover the property transferred is inconsistent with the transaction being by way of security; but its existence may be inferred, and its presence is not conclusive. The transaction may take the form of a sale with an option to repurchase, and this is not to be equated with a right of redemption merely because the repurchase price is calculated by reference to the original price together with interest since the date of the sale. On the other hand, the presence of a right of recourse by the transferee against the transferor to recover a shortfall may be inconsistent with a sale; but it is not necessarily so, and its absence is not conclusive. A security may be without recourse. Moreover, the nature of the property may be such that it is impossible or at least very unlikely that it will be realised at either a profit or loss. Many financing arrangements possess this feature. The fact that the transferee may have to make adjustments and payments to the transferor after the debts have been got in from the debtors does not prevent the transaction from being by way of sale.

The modern form of hire-purchase agreement in relation to goods builds on the clear theoretical distinction between a sale and a lease or hire of goods. Hire purchase entails a hiring coupled with an option to purchase. In legal terms, however, there is a lot to be said for the view that this description is, in reality, a legal fiction that bears little or no relation to reality.[59] In legal terms there is a contract for the hiring of goods coupled with an option on the part of the hirer to purchase the goods.[60] While the agreement subsists, the property in the goods remains in the owner and the hirer has no power to dispose of them. Moreover, although the hirer

---

[57] [1996] BCC 621.   [58] *Ibid.* at 626.
[59] See generally, Crowther Committee report *Consumer Credit* (1971) Cmnd 4569, pp. 175–6.
[60] For a modern analysis see *Forthright Finance Ltd* v. *Carlyle Finance Ltd* [1997] 4 All ER 90.

has an option to purchase the goods it is not under a binding obligation to do so.[61]

Normally a hire-purchase transaction involves three parties, namely, a dealer, finance house and hirer. Goods are sold by the dealer to the finance house who then lets them on hire-purchase terms to a hirer who had no prior interest in the goods. The tripartite nature of the transaction makes it difficult to argue that in reality it constitutes a loan. But the essential principle remains the same, irrespective of the fact that there are only two parties as when the owner of goods sells them to a finance house and takes a lease-back under a hire-purchase agreement.

Quasi-security: retention-of-title clauses

Title-retention clauses may take many forms but basically the clause refers to a situation where the seller of goods retains title to those goods until they have been paid for.[62] This is the simplest and perhaps the most common form of title-retention clause, but more complicated variants are possible. Under a 'current account' clause the seller retains title until all debts owing by the buyer to the seller have been paid and not just indebtedness arising under the particular contract of sale. A 'proceeds' or 'tracing' retention-of-title clause permits the buyer to resell the goods in the ordinary course of business before the original debt has been discharged but transfers the seller's claim to the proceeds generated by the resale. 'Products' clauses are used in quite complex factual scenarios where the goods supplied have formed all or part of the raw materials in a process of manufacture. With such a clause the supplier of the raw materials is claiming all or part of the finished article.

English law holds that security interests created by grant, but not by way of reservation, in the main require registration.[63] Part 12 Companies Act 1985 requires that certain charges created by companies must be registered to be valid in the event of the company going into liquidation. How does this charge analysis apply to retention-of-title clauses? Basically, 'simple' retention-of-title clauses and current-account clauses – have been given the judicial imprimatur but the more complex variants – namely,

---

[61] On hire purchase see generally R. Goode, *Consumer Credit Legislation* (Butterworths, looseleaf publication); A. Guest, *The Law of Hire-Purchase* (Sweet & Maxwell, 1966); R. Goode, *Hire-Purchase Law and Practice* (Butterworths, 2nd edn. 1970).

[62] For a comprehensive analysis see McCormack *Reservation of Title* (Sweet & Maxwell, 2nd edn. 1995).

[63] Browne-Wilkinson V-C (as he then was) adopted the following definition of security in *Re Paramount Airways Ltd* [1990] BCC 130 at 149: 'Security is created where a person (the creditor) obtains rights exercisable against some property in which the debtor has an interest in order to enforce the discharge of the debtor's obligations to the creditor.'

'proceeds' and 'products' clauses – have met with judicial disfavour.[64] The analysis goes like this: with a simple clause and a current clause the seller is merely retaining ownership of the goods until satisfaction of some condition. Until this condition is fulfilled the buyer does not acquire any bit of ownership which he can hand back to the seller by way of a security interest.[65] On the other hand, where goods have been sold, the seller's claim does not translate readily into the resale proceeds. Originally the courts were prepared to recognise the seller's claim on the basis that in reselling the seller was acting in a dual capacity, i.e. as an agent vis-à-vis the original seller but as a principal as far as the resale buyers were concerned so that the latter were not brought into direct contractual relations with the original seller.[66] More recently, however, the courts have moved away from this analysis, holding that the seller's entitlement to resale proceeds is a limited interest by way of charge since it comes to an end upon the discharge of the original purchase price.[67] Likewise 'product claims' have attracted the disapproval of the courts. The dominant view is that where there is a mixture of heterogeneous goods in the manufacturing process a new product – *nova species* – is created which belongs, initially at least, to the manufacturer, so to speak.[68]

Quasi-security: assignment of receivables

In England receivables financing may take one of two forms: either the creation of charges, whether fixed or floating, on receivables (debts); or else the outright assignment of receivables, which is referred to as factoring.[69] Factoring, or the absolute assignment of receivables, serves as the functional economic equivalent of taking a charge over the receivables. Factoring of debts is a well-recognised and established economic activity, with many of the major financial institutions having factoring subsidiaries. A factoring transaction does not have to be registered but where a company creates a charge over its debts, registration is a necessity.[70] Of course the factoring of debts equates to a loan of money on

---

[64] See generally McCormack *Reservation of Title*.

[65] See *Clough Mill Ltd* v. *Martin* [1985] 1 WLR 111; *Armour* v. *Thyssen Edelstahlwerke AG* [1991] 2 AC 339.

[66] *Aluminium Industrie Vaassen BV* v. *Romalpa Aluminium Ltd* [1976] 1 WLR 676.

[67] See, for example, *Pfeiffer Weinkellerei-Weineinkauf GmbH Co* v. *Arbuthnot Factors Ltd* [1988] 1 WLR 150; *Compaq Computer Ltd* v. *Abercorn Group Ltd* [1991] BCC 484.

[68] *Borden* v. *Scottish Timber Products Ltd* [1981] Ch 25; *Re Peachdart Ltd* [1984] Ch 131.

[69] See generally F. Salinger *Factoring Law and Practice* (Sweet & Maxwell, 3rd edn. 1999); F. Oditah *Legal Aspects of Receivables Financing* (Sweet & Maxwell, 1991).

[70] The distinction between factoring and the creation of a charge over debts was explored at length by the House of Lords, in *Lloyds & Scottish Finance* v. *Cyril Lord Carpet Sales Ltd* [1992] BCLC 609.

the security of debts to the extent that ready cash is released to the assignor. The latter receives money up front rather than having to wait for the debts to mature, or to be collected. Factoring, however, can serve functions other than the immediate release of funds. For instance, if it is done on a notification basis then the assignor is relieved of the responsibility of collecting the debts. The factor may also take over the burden of accounts administration. Factoring may also take on some of the features of credit insurance if the factor assumes the responsibility for the debtor failing to pay as distinct from the assignor being under an obligation to accept a reassignment of bad debts.

Receivables financing is often carried out in a manner that blurs the distinction between the outright sale of receivables and their transfer by way of security.[71] In English law, it is possible to mortgage a debt by an assignment of the debt to the mortgagee coupled with a provision for reassignment of the debt once the obligation to which the mortgage relates has been discharged. The formalities for legal assignments of debts are laid down in section 136 Law of Property Act 1925. One of the requirements is that an assignment be 'absolute' and 'not purporting to be by way of charge only'.[72] It is perfectly possible, nevertheless, that an assignment is 'absolute' for purposes of section 136 and still operate by way of security. The test for the application of section 136 is whether for the time being the assignor has unconditionally transferred to the assignee the right to receive payment from the debtor. On the other hand, if the assignor is a corporate body, the transaction will require registration under Part 12, Companies Act 1985 where the assignor retains an equity of redemption, i.e. if the transaction is by way of mortgage. With a mortgage the assignee has ownership of the debt transferred subject to the assignor's right of redemption. A charge of a debt, however, gives the chargee not ownership of the debt but rather preferential rights thereto.[73] Professor Goode has

---

[71] See M. Bridge, R. Macdonald, R. Simmonds and C. Walsh 'Formalism, Functionalism and Understanding the Law of Secured Transactions' (1999) 44 *McGill LJ* 567 at n. 46. In *Orion Finance Ltd* v. *Crown Financial Management Ltd* [1996] BCC 621 at 622 Millett LJ commented: 'This appeal raises a familiar question which has caused problems before and no doubt will cause problems again. It is whether an assignment of book debts forming part of complex financing arrangements is by way of security or should be characterised as an outright sale with an option to repurchase.'

[72] *Burlinson* v. *Hall* (1884) 12 QBD 347. See also *Bovis International Inc* v. *Circle Ltd Partnership* (1995) 49 Con LR 12 at 29 where Millett LJ said: 'An assignment does not cease to be absolute merely because it is given by way of security and is subject to an express or implied obligation to reassign on redemption.'

[73] Denman J stated in *Tancred* v. *Delagoa Bay and East Africa Railway Co* (1889) 23 QBD 239 at 242 that 'a document given by way of charge is not one which absolutely transfers the property with a condition for reconveyance, but is a document which only gives a right to payment out of a particular fund or particular property, without transferring that fund or property'.

suggested that to facilitate a transfer of the legal title to the debt in case
the chargee wishes to dispose of it, the default provisions in the charge
should (1) confer a power of attorney on the chargee to collect or dispose
of the debt and (2) convert the charge into a mortgage by executing an
assignment in the name of the chargor.[74] It has been argued that these
powers diminish to vanishing point any remaining distinctions between a
mortgage and a charge.[75] Be that as it may, the distinction, in legal terms,
clearly remains between an outright transfer of debts, on the one hand,
and the transfer subject to an equity of redemption, i.e. a mortgage or
charge, on the other. In other words, there is still a fundamental distinction between factoring of debts and the creation of a security interest in
the same.

Quasi-security: agency sales financing

Agency sales financing is a fairly complicated form of financing technique
that was employed in *Welsh Development Agency* v. *Export Finance Co. Ltd*[76]
and the technique is perhaps best explained by looking at the facts of the
case. These basically involved an exporter of computer software gaining
finance for its export trade transactions by selling the software in question to a financier and then fulfilling the overseas orders as the financier's
agent. The financier acted as an undisclosed principal with the foreign
buyers dealing at all times with the software supplier. The buyers made
payment into a bank account that was in the name of the software supplier
but which was under the complete control of the financier. The price that
the financier paid the software supplier for the goods was not fixed at the
outset but was subject to variation depending on the speed with which the
foreign buyers paid for the goods. The financing arrangement also had a
termination clause under which, on cessation of the agreement, the supplier would satisfy all claims owing to the financier by the foreign buyers
and, when this payment had been made, the financier would transfer all
interests it had in the goods to the supplier. It is important to note that
the financing technique purported to involve a sale of goods rather than
an assignment of debts.

It seems that, in the particular case, this form of financing arrangement
was used because of a clause in a prior lending agreement under which
the supplier covenanted not to factor, discount or assign its debts. Breach

---

[74] R. Goode 'The Effect of a Fixed charge on a Debt' [1984] *JBL* 172 at 174.
[75] See Oditah *Receivables Financing* at p. 96.
[76] [1992] BCLC 148. The case is analysed by Oditah 'Financing Trade Credit'. Contrast
Re Curtain Dream plc [1990] BCLC 925.

of this undertaking would entitle the lender to appoint a receiver. Unfortunately, the software supplier experienced financial difficulties and it was argued that the financing arrangement was invalid for non-registration on the basis that, in reality, it represented a charge over goods rather than an absolute sale.[77] The Court of Appeal rejected this proposition. The transaction was not a sham because there was no evidence that the parties intended rights and obligations to apply *inter se* other than those set out in the agreement. Moreover, looking at the internal workings of the transaction, there was nothing therein that was necessarily incompatible with the transaction being one of sale. The termination clause was like a repurchase agreement and options to repurchase were not uncommon in sales transactions. Furthermore, price variation clauses were often found in sales contracts.

Quasi-security: Quistclose/conditional-purpose trusts

Some trusts may be regarded as serving a security-type function and, in particular, the conditional-purpose or 'Quistclose' trust.[78] Under a Quistclose trust money is advanced subject to the condition that it is applied for a particular purpose. If this purpose is not fulfilled or is no longer capable of accomplishment the money is said to be held on a secondary trust for the payer rather than being part of the debtor's assets available for payment to the debtor's general creditors.[79] The courts have

---

[77] See also the comments of Lawrence LJ in *Re George Inglefield Ltd* [1933] Ch 1 at 23:

> As the law stands at present, there is nothing to prevent a limited company from selling its assets without giving notice of that sale to the public or to anyone else, remaining in possession of the assets so sold, with the consent of the buyer, and obtaining credit on the faith of that possession. If such a state of things ought to be remedied it is for Parliament to supply the remedy. All that the Court has to do . . . is to ascertain whether there has, in fact, been a sale of the assets and to give effect to the transaction if that be the case.

[78] See the leading case *Barclays Bank Ltd* v. *Quistclose Investments Ltd* [1970] AC 567; and see now *Twinsectra Ltd* v. *Yardley* [2002] 2 All ER 377. See generally on the 'Quistclose' trust L. Priestley 'The Romalpa Trust and the Quistclose Trust' in Paul Finn ed. *Equity in Commercial Relationships* (Law Book Company, 1987) at p. 217; W. Goodhart and G. Jones 'The Infiltration of Equitable Doctrine into English Commercial Law' (1980) 43 *MLR* 489; M. Bridge 'The Quistclose Trust in a World of Secured Transactions' (1992) 13 *OJLS* 333; C. Rickett 'Different Views on the Scope of the Quistclose Analysis: English and Antipodean Insights' (1991) 107 *LQR* 608; L. Ho and P. St J. Smart 'Reinterpreting the Quistclose Trust: A Critique of Chambers' (2001) 21 *OJLS* 267.

[79] This was the analysis adopted in the *Quistclose* case itself, but Lord Millett in *Twinsectra Ltd* v. *Yardley* [2002] 2 All ER 377 took a different approach. He said (at para. 100) that the Quistclose trust was

held that debt and trust can coexist – in other words that the same trans-action can give to the legal relationship of debt and also to a trust. It has been contended that a Quistclose trust constitutes a security interest in that the 'payer is to be protected from the claims of other creditors of the payee' on the latter's insolvency and thus 'clearly evinces an intention to seek and provide security'.[80] On this analysis, the Quistclose trust se-cures performance of the debtor's obligation to carry out the purpose of the advance.

Having said that, however, it must be recognised that the Quistclose trust is not a conventional security interest. In the typical advance the secured assets and the monies advanced are quite clearly separate and the former secures the latter. With a Quistclose trust the payer is asserting a de facto security interest in the advance itself and it is not the failure to repay that is secured but rather the execution of the purpose. If the purpose is carried out the payer is converted from a secured into an unsecured creditor.[81] Under a Quistclose trust the payee (debtor) never acquires beneficial ownership but is rather a trustee – a conduit for the transmission of funds. Doctrinal niceties, however, did not stop the House of Lords from holding in *Re BCCI (No. 8)*[82] that a bank could create a charge over its own customer's credit balances. There were theoretical obstacles to this conclusion premised on the assumption that since the banker–customer relationship was a debtor–creditor one, a charge would involve the bank as creditor having a security interest in the money it owed its customer (debtor). How, the argument went, could one own something that one owed? The House of Lords, however, took the view

---

an entirely orthodox example of the kind of default trust known as a resulting trust. The lender pays the money to the borrower by way of loan, but he does not part with the entire beneficial interest in the money, and in so far as he does not it is held on a resulting trust for the lender from the outset . . . When the purpose fails, the money is returnable to the lender, not under some new trust in his favour which only comes into being on the failure of the purpose, but because the resulting trust in his favour is no longer subject to any power on the part of the borrower to make use of the money. Whether the borrower is obliged to apply the money for the stated purpose or merely at liberty to do so, and whether the lender can countermand the borrower's mandate while it is still capable of being carried out, must depend on the circumstances of the particular case.

See also the article by P. Millett QC (as he then was) 'The *Quistclose* Trust: Who can Enforce it?' (1985) 101 *LQR* 269.

[80] See Bridge 'The Quistclose Trust' at 345–6 and 360–1.

[81] See Bridge et al. 'Formalism, Functionalism and Understanding' at n. 156. See the comments of Lord Millett in *Twinsectra Ltd* v. *Yardley* [2002] 2 All ER 377 at para. 72: 'Arrangements of this kind are not intended to provide security for repayment of the loan, but to prevent the money from being applied otherwise than in accordance with the lender's wishes. If the money is properly applied the loan is unsecured.'

[82] [1998] AC 214.

that theoretical points such as these were of no consequence in a practical, business context. Adopting a similar broad-brush approach in the sphere of special-purpose trusts, one of the objectives of a Quistclose trust is to give the provider of funds priority over other creditors in the event that the recipient of the funds becomes insolvent.[83] Therefore, it seems to fall within the functional definition of security though in the consultation paper *Registration of Security Interests* the Law Commission provisionally concluded that special-purpose trusts should be outside the requirement to register (either because no security arises, or alternatively any security arises through operation of law).[84]

Pressure for reform of the English law of security interests

It is possible to say that there are a number of pressure points for reform of the English law of security interests. These can be considered under various heads and, to mix metaphors, bottom up as follows: (1) dissatisfaction with the current priority regime; (2) the corporate rescue agenda and (3) the Article 9 agenda. These heads will now be addressed.

Dissatisfaction with the current priorities regime

A significant pressure point for reform comes from practitioner dissatisfaction with the existing priority rules. There is no single reference point for determining priorities between competing security interests in the same property. Unlike the position in the US under Article 9 of the UCC, registration is not per se a priority determinant. Under English law interests that involve the use of absolute title by way of security, such as interests under trusts and 'simple' retention of title clauses,[85] enjoy super-priority status. Moreover, they are not subject to any requirement of registration.[86] As far as charges, strictly so-called, are concerned, while failure to register a registrable charge will result in the invalidation of the charge in the event of the corporate debtor going into liquidation, once registration has been duly effected then priority among competing charges turns inter alia on the date of creation. Fixed charges rank amongst themselves according to the order of creation but, on the other

---

[83] See generally G. McCormack 'Personal Property Security Law Reform in England and Canada' [2002] *JBL* 113 at 125–6.

[84] Para 7.54.

[85] Put shortly, the property never comes into the beneficial ownership of the insolvent.

[86] The registration obligation contained in Part 12 Companies Act 1985 only applies to charges created by a company.

hand, a floating charge is postponed, priority-wise, to a fixed charge ir-respective of the order in which the two charges were created.[87]

If, however, a floating-charge instrument contains a 'negative pledge' or 'restrictive' clause, i.e. a clause forbidding the creation of any subse-quent security having priority to the floating charge and a subsequent fixed-charge holder has actual notice, not just constructive notice, of the restrictive clause, then the floating-charge holder will be paid out of the as-sets in question in priority to the floating-charge holder.[88] It appears that the practice of submitting details of a negative pledge clause among the particulars of a charge delivered for registration does not automatically fix the subsequent fixed chargee with notice of the negative pledge clause, though it is something from which notice may be inferred.[89] Registration of a negative pledge clause is not required by statute. In practice, though, a bank which is thinking about making a secured loan to a corporate borrower will consult the register of charges and, in this way, previous se-cured borrowings by the company will come to light.[90] The priority rules are further complicated by apparent judicial acceptance of the proposi-tion that where a second floating charge covers only part of the assets covered by a prior floating charge, then the second floating charge will have priority provided that the first instrument of charge authorises the creation of subsequent charges having this effect.[91]

---

[87] See G. McCormack 'Priority of Charges and Registration' [1994] *JBL* 587.

[88] In *G & T Earle Ltd* v. *Hemsworth Rural District Council* (1928) 44 TLR 605 Wright J said:

> The debentures having been duly registered . . . the plaintiffs, like all the world, are deemed to have constructive notice of the fact that there are debentures. But it has never been held that the mere fact that persons in the position of the plaintiffs have constructive notice of the existence of debentures also affects them with constructive notice of the actual terms of the debentures or that the debentures are subject to the restrictive condition to which these debentures were subject. No doubt it is quite common for debentures to be subject to this limiting condition as to further charges, but that fact is not enough in itself to operate as constructive notice of the actual terms of any particular set of debentures.

> See *also Re Standard Machine Co Ltd* (1906) 95 LT 829 *and Wilson* v. *Kelland* [1910] 2 Ch 306.

[89] But see J. Farrar 'The Crystallisation of the Floating Charge' (1976) 40 *Conv* (NS) 397 who argues for the existence of inferred actual knowledge rather than constructive knowledge. The argument seems inconsistent, however, with *Re Valletort Sanitary Steam Laundry Co.* [1903] 2 Ch 654 and *Welch* v. *Bowmaker (Ireland) Ltd* [1980] IR 251. For a discussion of the priority position in Australia in this context see Ali *Law of Secured Finance* at pp. 152–3.

[90] For possible circularity problems see *Re Portbase Clothing Ltd* [1993] Ch 388 and *Re Woodroffes (Musical Instruments) Ltd* [1986] Ch 366; and see generally Ali *Law of Secured Finance* at pp. 242–7.

[91] *Re Automatic Bottle Makers* [1926] Ch 412; *Re Benjamin Cope & Co.* [1914] 1 Ch 800. See also *Griffith* v. *Yorkshire Bank Ltd* [1994] 1 WLR 1427; *Re H & K Medway Ltd* [1997] 1 WLR 1422. Surely the question should be, however, whether the first floating

Where there is more than one assignment of the same debt, then priority among competing assignments is determined by the order in which notice of the assignments is given to the debtor save where a subsequent assignee has actual or constructive notice of an earlier assignment at the time that the subsequent assignment is made.[92] In the latter situation priority is governed by a simple 'first-in-time-has-priority' rule. The complexities in the law governing priorities has led to calls for clarificatory legislation or at least private law solutions negotiated amongst secured parties. As one commentator has said:[93]

The priority rules are a potential minefield for secured creditors. The rules vary depending on the nature of the assets concerned, floating charges are governed by a different set of rules altogether, and there is yet another set of rules for money lent after the creditor has received notice of a subsequent charge . . . For all these reasons, it is common practice for secured creditors to enter into a priority agreement with any other secured creditor of which they become aware.

There seems little doubt that new rules which make priority turn, in the first instance at least, on the date of registration (or perfection where it is possible to perfect by a method other than registration) would bring a necessary degree of simplicity and clarity to the law.

The corporate rescue agenda

The second major pressure point for reform of the English law of security interests stems from a desire on the part of government to promote the rescue or rehabilitation of ailing businesses.[94] The focus of insolvency law reform has increasingly been on the promotion of a rescue culture, and this has been part of a growing international trend to encourage a more collective approach to corporate rescue mechanisms. Moreover, there is a concern that the procedure of administrative receivership is insufficiently concerned with the goal of maximising economic value and, additionally,

charge authorises the creation of superior-ranking subsequent floating charges, and not whether the second floating charge is over part only of the assets covered by the first: see generally R. Goode *Principles of Corporate Insolvency Law* (Sweet & Maxwell, 2nd edn. 1997) at p. 208 n. 14.

[92] This is known as the rule in *Dearle v. Hall* and see generally J. De Lacy 'The Priority Rule of *Dearle v. Hall* Restated' [1999] *Conv* 311. For a discussion of whether the principle applies to competing fixed charges over receivables as distinct from competing assignments see L. Smith *The Law of Tracing* (Oxford University Press, 1997) at p. 359. See also the statement in the affirmative by Lord Hoffmann in *Colonial Mutual General Insurance Co. Ltd v. ANZ Banking Group* [1995] 1 WLR 1140 at 1144.

[93] Calnan 'Taking Security in England' at 33.

[94] See the White Paper *Insolvency: A Second Chance* (Cmnd 5234, July 2001). For a comprehensive study of this area with major theoretical underpinnings see Finch *Corporate Insolvency Law*.

is excessively oriented towards protecting the secured creditor's position to the neglect of other parties.[95] Under 'old' law, a secured creditor with a floating charge over the whole or substantially the whole of a company's assets may appoint an administrative receiver without having to seek court approval. The vast majority of receivership appointments are made on this basis. Although designated an agent of the corporate debtor, the primary task of an administrative receiver is to realise the charged assets for the benefit of the creditor by whom he was appointed.[96] The receiver owes only limited duties to the company and to other debtors.[97] In particular, the receiver is not obliged to delay a sale of the charged assets merely because delay is likely to result in a substantially higher value being obtained at a later stage.[98]

In the Insolvency Act 1986 a new procedure – 'administration' – was introduced to facilitate the objective of encouraging the continuation and disposal of a debtor's business as a going concern, wherever possible. Where a company is actually or potentially insolvent, the court may appoint an administrator if this is likely to result in the achievement of one or more of the statutory objectives. Once the order of appointment is made, the administrator takes charge of the company's affairs and formulates a plan with a view to achieving the objectives for which he was appointed. In carrying out his functions, an administrator owes his duties to all interested parties and not exclusively to secured creditors. The Insolvency Act 1986, however, permits a floating- – but not a fixed- – charge holder to block the appointment of an administrator to an ailing company. This power of veto enshrined in the insolvency legislation has led to the practice whereby lenders who are already secured up to the hilt by fixed charges over a company's most valuable assets will, nevertheless, take a floating charge over the same assets.[99] The instrument containing the floating charge will be shorn of the usual covenants – hence the expression 'lightweight' floating charge. The sole purpose of including

[95] See generally the DTI report *A Review of Company Rescue and Business Reconstruction Mechanisms* (November 2000).
[96] *Gomba Holdings (UK) Ltd* v. *Homan* [1986] 3 All ER 94; *American Express International Banking Corp* v. *Hurley* [1985] 3 All ER 564.
[97] *Cuckmere Brick Co. Ltd* v. *Mutual Finance Ltd* [1971] Ch 949; *Standard Chartered Bank Ltd* v. *Walker* [1982] 1 WLR 1410; *China and South Sea Bank Ltd* v. *Tan* [1990] 1 AC 536; *Downsview Nominees Ltd* v. *First City Corp Ltd* [1993] AC 295.
[98] *China and South Sea Bank Ltd* v. *Tan* [1990] 1 AC 536; *Medforth* v. *Blake* [1999] 2 BCLC 221. See generally G. McCormack 'Receiverships and the Rescue Culture' [2000] *CFILR* 229; and see also S. Frisby 'Making a Silk Purse out of a Pig's Ear' (2000) 63 *MLR* 413.
[99] Such floating charges were given the judicial imprimatur in *Re Croftbell Ltd* [1990] BCLC 844; on which see F. Oditah 'Lightweight Floating Charges' [1991] *JBL* 49.

the additional floating-charge security in these circumstances is for the secured lender to acquire the power of veto over the appointment of an administrator. This legislative provision strengthened the position of the floating charge in English lending practice.

The Enterprise Act 2002 removes the general right of floating-charge holders to appoint administrative receivers but leaves the power intact in some situations. The removal of the power only applies, however, to floating charges created after 15th September 2003 and, moreover, the holders of qualifying floating charges (basically a floating charge over the whole, or substantially the whole, of a company's assets) are given a new power to appoint administrators out of court. The new Act toughens time limits and streamlines the administration procedure.[100] An administrator is now obliged to perform his functions with the overarching objective of rescuing the company as a going concern where this is reasonably practicable. In effect there is a hierarchy of objectives which an administrator must strive to achieve and it is only in circumstances where attainment of the first objective is not reasonably practicable that the second objective comes into play, and likewise where achievement of the first two objectives are not reasonably practicable it is only then that the third objective may be carried out. The second objective is achieving a better result for the company's creditors as a whole than would be likely if the company were wound up (without first being in administration) and the third is realising property in order to make a distribution to one or more secured or preferential creditors. Even in the latter situation the administrator must not unnecessarily harm the interests of the creditors of the company as a whole.

As discussed in the previous chapter the Enterprise Act couples the abolition of Crown preference[101] (but not employee preference) with a proposal to ringfence a proportion of floating-charge recoveries for the

---

[100] A copy of the administrator's proposals must be sent to creditors along with an invitation to an initial creditors' meeting. The latter is required to be held within ten weeks of the administration commencing. Paragraph 76 lays down that the administrator will automatically vacate office one year after the date the administration commenced, though this may be extended for a further period with the consent of creditors or by the court, on application to it by the administrator. These time limits are not too tight. The facility for extensions, approved by the creditors or by the court, introduces an additional measure of flexibility but one hopes that they do not become the order of the day. Otherwise the objective of achieving a speedy resolution will be fatally undermined.

[101] Section 251 which removes paras. 1 and 2 (debts due to Inland Revenue), paras. 3–5C (debts due to Customs and Excise) and paras. 6 and 7 (social security contributions) from Schedule 6 to the Insolvency Act.

benefit of unsecured creditors.[102] As the White Paper *Insolvency: A Second Chance* points out the Enterprise Act is intended as a balancing act and the motivation behind ringfencing a portion of floating-charge recoveries for unsecured creditors is to ensure that the fruits of the abolition of Crown preference are enjoyed by all creditors.[103] The proportion set aside will be fixed by statutory instrument, but if it is very large then the measure has the potential seriously to detract from the status of the floating charge.

The Article 9 agenda

There have been many calls for fundamental reform of English law pertaining to security interests along North American lines.[104] Perhaps the most radical blueprint for reform was that contained in the 1989 report by Professor Aubrey Diamond commissioned by the Department of Trade and Industry. Diamond concluded his review of the law by stating that a security interest could be taken in almost anything provided that an appropriate method was used, but it was not always easy to decide which method was appropriate.[105] In his view, the English law suffered from three main defects: compartmentalisation, complexity and difficulty in determining priorities.[106] The compartmentalisation problem was overriding and stemmed from the fact that the law lacked a functional basis. The law was divided into rigid compartments making it fragmented and incoherent. Essentially similar transactions were treated by the law in very different ways, which had the effect of complicating the legal issues quite unnecessarily. Complexity and uncertainty were also compounded by the old division between common law and equity which loomed large in the security-law field. Common law and equity had been administered

---

[102] Section 252 Enterprise Act 2002 which inserts a new section 176A into the Insolvency Act 1986.

[103] See the statement at para 2.20 of the White Paper:

> Where there is no floating charge-holder, the benefit of abolition will be available for the unsecured creditors. Where there is a floating charge-holder (in relation to a floating charge created after the coming into force of the legislation), we would ensure that the benefit of the abolition of preferential status goes to unsecured creditors. We will achieve this through a mechanism that ringfences a proportion of the funds generated by the floating charge.

[104] See also Crowther Committee report *Consumer Credit*; Cork Committee report on *Insolvency Law and Practice* (Cmnd 8558, 1982).

[105] A. Diamond *A Review of Security Interests in Property* (HMSO, 1989) at p. 31.

[106] See generally *ibid.* at pp. 31–3.

in parallel but separate court systems before the 1870s and, while both sets of principles were now administered in the same courts, the different historical antecedents of similar security-law rights contributed to complexities in exposition and characterisation. For example, a purchaser of goods who bought, not knowing of any security interest in them, might be in a radically different position depending on whether the security interest was legal or equitable. Simply stated, there were difficulties in determining priorities, and priority problems were exacerbated by the fact that there were so many different ways of achieving similar economic ends. The Diamond prescription for England was comprehensive reform along the lines of Article 9 of the US UCC and the Canadian personal property security legislation.[107] More recently, the Company Law Review Steering Group in its final report made proposals in relation to company charges that are very much in line with Article 9, e.g. notice filing and the time of registration being used as a point of reference for determining priorities.[108] The Law Commission has now carried forward the work of the Company Law Review and recommended a three-pronged approach towards reform in England.[109] Firstly, a notice-filing system would be introduced in place of the current system of *ex post facto* company charge registration as contained in Part 12 Companies Act 1985.[110] This charge would be part of a general Companies Bill to implement the overall reforms suggested by the Company Law Review Steering Group. Secondly, the notice-filing system would be extended to 'quasi-securities', i.e. functionally equivalent legal devices such as retention of title clauses and the outright transfer of receivables that are presently outwith registration requirements. This measure would require a separate legislative initiative and finally, and also necessitating a distinct statute, there would be a comprehensive restatement of the law of security interests. The New Zealand Personal Property Securities Act 1999 and the Saskatchewan statute in Canada were suggested as appropriate models but these in turn have been heavily shaped by Article 9.[111]

Article 9 applies to any transaction, regardless of form, that in substance creates a security interest in personal property. Article 9 was first

---

[107] See generally on the reform agenda D. Prentice 'The Registration of Company Charges: Ripe for Reform' (1985) 101 *LQR* 330; I. Davies 'The Reform of English Personal Property Security Law' (1990) *30 Malaya Law Review* 88; M. Lawson 'The Reform of the Law Relating to Security Interests in Property' [1989] *JBL* 287.

[108] *Modern Company Law* at p. 247.

[109] Consultation Paper No. 164 *Registration of Security Interests* (July 2002).

[110] The Scottish Law Commission, however, has not embraced the idea of a notice-filing system in Scotland.

[111] See generally McCormack 'Personal Property Security Law Reform'.

promulgated in the 1950s and has since been revised on many occasions, most notably in 1998, with the 1998 revisions coming into force in 2001.[112] The original Article 9 has been described as the work of gifted generalists, particularly Professor Grant Gilmore, but the revised Article 9 is best viewed as the work of gifted specialists. Consequently it has grown very significantly in length and complexity, almost doubling in size and with many more detailed and particularised provisions, so much so that the initial goal of producing a simpler, more easily understood law may have been lost sight of.

Be that as it may, the great virtue of Article 9 was to produce a unified law of security interests with similar provisions applying to different transactions serving the same policy end unless there were good policy reasons for varying legislation. The old distinctions, which were based essentially on form rather than substance, were swept away. The taking of security was facilitated by the removal of formalistic distinctions. In considering the merits or otherwise of the American law, it is worth remembering that the pre-Article 9 history of personal property security law in the US differs significantly from the English experience. American courts were not so hospitable towards the secured creditor and state legislatures were not so eager to sweep away restrictions on the taking of security. Gradually, however, the tide turned and this has led one of the principal authors of Article 9, Grant Gilmore, to the conclusion that the article is not so much 'a new start or fresh approach as it is a reflection of work long since accomplished'.[113] In his view Article 9 can best be described as 'an anthological collection of the most celebrated security law controversies of the preceding forty years'.[114] Inventory (stock-in-trade) and receivables (book debts) financing are recognised. It is also possible to provide in an Article 9 security agreement that collateral, whenever acquired, shall secure all obligations covered by the security agreement and that obligations covered may include future advances. Moreover, 'Article 9 draftsmen argued from the premise that, under existing security law, a lender could take an enforceable interest in all of a debtor's present and future personal property to the conclusion that the new statute should provide for the accomplishment of this result in the simplest possible fashion'.[115]

---

[112] The revised version of Article 9 can be accessed through the National Conference of Commissioners on Uniform State Laws website: www.nccusl.org.
[113] Grant Gilmore *Security Interests in Personal Property* (Little Brown, 1965), vol. I at p. 290.
[114] Grant Gilmore 'Security Law, Formalism and Article 9' (1968) 47 *Nebraska L R* 659 at 671.
[115] *Ibid.* at 672.

Article 9 has been described as the most modern system of secured transactions law in the modern world.[116] It has successfully serviced the world's largest economy for over forty years and been the subject of authoritative judicial interpretation. In the early 1990s, however, the government decided not to accept the Diamond recommendations for fundamental reform along Article 9 lines, and it remains to be seen whether the passage of years will lead to a change of heart. The government's reluctance to embrace Diamond was based on three interlinked reasons.[117] Firstly, in its view there was no major constituency pressing for reform. Secondly, it was suggested that reform would be disruptive and, in view of proposed registration requirements, potentially costly to government and to business. Thirdly, there was the possibility of EU harmonisation measures in this sphere. This prospect was felt to preclude domestic legislative initiatives. There have not, however, been any general harmonisation measures in the security-law field, though it is worth highlighting Article 4 of the Directive on Late Payment in Commerical Transactions which contains provisions for the recognition of 'simple' retention-of-title clauses,[118] and also the Directive on Financial Collateral.[119]

While the government's case for not implementing Diamond may not be entirely convincing, it is certainly arguable that Diamond overstated the defects of the present system. Certainly banks and other users of the system are reasonably happy with its operation and remain to be convinced that reform would bring appreciable benefits without accompanying disadvantages. This point is made when one looks at the desirable features of a modern system of personal property security law as enunciated by bodies such as the EBRD. In large measure, English law complies with these desirable features. Moreover, while English law has recognised title-retention clauses without the need for registration such clauses do not intrude too greatly on a bank's security. In the main, the super-priority status enjoyed by trade creditors using title-retention clauses only extends to the original good supplied and does not embrace proceeds or products. In any reform of the law that might benefit lenders in certain respects there is the corresponding danger that these hard-won advantages might be lost. As one commentator has concluded:[120]

---

[116] See the comments by Professor Aubrey Diamond 'The Reform of the Law of Security Interests' (1989) 42 *CLP* 231 at 241.

[117] HC debates vol. 189, col. 482, 24 April 1991.

[118] The text of the directive can be viewed through the Europa website: http://www.europa.eu.int/ or in the official journal: OJ L 2000/35, 8.8.2000.

[119] Directive 2002/47/EC on financial collateral arrangements: OJ L 168 2002/47/EC, 27.06.2002.

[120] M. Bridge 'How Far is Article 9 Exportable? The English Experience' (1996) 27 *Can Bus LJ* 196 at 221.

The English bank has obtained all the freedom it needs to make its position ironclad. It is therefore hardly surprising that the banks are not pressing for a reform along the lines of Article 9. The position in English law is a world away from the strict line on accounts receivable financing by the United States Supreme Court in *Benedict* v. *Ratner*.[121] If England were to adopt an Article 9 statute, these hard-won gains would be surrendered for something new whose implications would take some time to be felt.

Nevertheless, the final report of the Company Law Review Steering Group and the Law Commission consultation paper on *Registration of Security Interests* has put the question of Article 9-type reforms in England back on the agenda.[122]

Conclusion

From the point of view of banks and other lending institutions the English law of security interests has much to commend it. It is possible to create security rights in the widest possible range of circumstances including security over intangible property and over property that is not yet owned by the debtor. Like industrialisation, sweeping security rights came early to England and the vehicle of much of the early development was the floating charge over circulating assets. The great beauty of the floating charge was that it permitted the creation of a security interest but at the same time left the debtor with managerial freedom in relation to the class of charged assets until what is known as a crystallising event occurs to bring that managerial freedom to an end. The floating charge, however, does not attach to any specific assets until crystallisation. Moreover, the floating charge occupies a relatively weak priority position, ranking as it does after fixed-charge holders over the same asset and also preferential creditors. Nevertheless, the floating-charge holder retains substantial enforcement powers.

The English law of security interests has been under attack from a number of quarters. For example, there appears to be considerable practitioner dissatisfaction with the existing priority rules, with many believing in the need for more rational principles for determining priorities between competing security interests in the same property. Secondly, there is the strong sentiment that the enforcement of security should not conflict with the goal of corporate rehabiliation. To this end, the Enterprise Act has watered down some of the enforcement rights of security interest holders. But the most far-reaching challenge to the present English regime comes

[121] (1925) 268 US 353.
[122] See also Roy Goode 'Insularity or Leadership? The Role of the United Kingdom in the Harmonisation of Commercial Law' (2001) 50 *ICLQ* 751 at 759–60.

from the Article 9 agenda, i.e. the pressure to reform English law pertaining to security interests along American Article 9 lines. Legal advisers, however, feel comfortable with the existing precepts, and the advantages of familiarity are not easily forsaken. Moreover, and more importantly, the credit industry as a whole – and banks in particular – see no obvious merits in moving over to a new system, and this reluctance seems well founded, at least from their point of view. Writing a new legislative blueprint risks reopening old controversies, long since resolved in favour of banks, on the scope of secured creditors' rights.[123] When the alternatives remain to be determined, the attractions of the 'tried and trusted' are obvious. As far as practitioners are concerned, and to use a colourful metaphor, one might safely sacrifice theoretical perfection at the altar of practical utility. While of course New Zealand has recently gone down the Article 9 route,[124] this is not necessarily any reason for England to follow suit; at least not without careful consideration of the consequences.[125] The next chapter will examine in more detail the fundamentals of the systems of secured transactions law in the US.

---

[123] See generally M. Bridge 'Form, Substance and Innovation in Personal Property Security Law' [1992] *JBL* 1.

[124] Personal Property Securities Act 1999. Up-to-date information on the legislation can be found on the following website: www.ppsr.govt.nz/ and for an unbridled attack on the New Zealand reforms see B. Dugan 'PPSA – the Price of Certainty' [2000] *NZLJ* 242. See generally on the philosophy animating the reforms D. Allan 'Personal Property Security – Rip Van Winkle Awakes in the Antipodes' [1998] *JIBL* 1.

[125] For the possibility of change in Ireland see M. Donnelly 'Reforming Personal Property Security Law: Is There a Case for a Single Securities Register?' [2000] *DULJ* 50.

3 An overview of Article 9 of the Uniform Commercial Code

This chapter looks at the basic features of Article 9 of the Uniform Commercial Code and compares it with the English law pertaining to security interests in personal property. According to received wisdom, it is a fundamental part of a modern system of secured-transactions law that public notice of the existence of a security interest in property must be given. For example, in the EBRD Principles of Secured Transactions Law it is stated that the existence of a security right over property must be effectively publicised.[1] Public notice and consequential registration requirements are a central feature of Article 9 of the UCC and also of the English system. It is fair to say, however, that the registration obligation under Article 9 is much more extensive and overarching. Moreover, Article 9 contains more superficially straightforward rules for determining priorities between competing security interests in the same collateral.[2] English law is often compared unflatteringly in this respect with the position in the United States.[3]

[1] For a discusssion of the EBRD principles see J. Simpson and J.-H. Rover 'General Principles of a Modern Secured Transactions Law' in J. Norton and M. Andenas eds. *Emerging Financial Markets and Secured Transactions* (Kluwer, 1998) at p. 143; D. Fairgrieve 'Reforming Secured Transactions Laws in Central and Eastern Europe' [1998] *EBLR* 245; L. Mistelis 'The EBRD Model Law on Secured Transactions and its Impact on Collateral Law Reform' (1998) 5 *Parker School Journal of East European Law* 455; G. McCormack and F. Dahan 'The EBRD Model Law on Secured Transactions: Comparisons and Convergence' [1999] *CFILR* 65; and see also the EBRD website: www.ebrd.com/. Publicity is also a feature of the Model Inter-American Law on Secured Transactions (2002) which may be accessed via the Organisation of American States website: www.oas.org/.

[2] Article 9 was first promulgated in the 1950s by two sponsoring organisations, the American Law Institute and the National Conference of Commissioners on Uniform State Laws. It has been revised on many occasions since, with the most recent revised version (1998) coming into force on 1 July 2001. For access to the text see http://www.nccusl.org. See also Corinne Cooper ed. *The New Article 9* (American Bar Association, 2nd edn. 2000); also J. Honnold, S. L. Harris and C. W. Mooney *Security Interests in Personal Property* (Foundation Press, 3rd edn. 2001). The new Article 9 is also discussed in a special issue of the *Chicago-Kent Law Review*: (1999) 74 *Chicago-Kent Law Review* no 3.

[3] Professor Sir Roy Goode has long propounded this view, arguing that 'a unified concept of security interests in which rules of attachment, perfection and priority are clearly

The general features of Article 9

The fundamental features of Article 9 and other systems modelled upon it such as those in the common-law provinces of Canada and now in New Zealand[4] are firstly, a bias in favour of functionalism rather then formalism and secondly, a registration obligation that is very extensive in its ambit. In other words, there is a general principle enshrined in the law that public notice of the security interest must be given.[5] In Article 9 in a sense substance emerges triumphant over form with the UCC abandoning the old distinctions, still prevalent in English law, between the different ways of securing a claim and also the use of absolute title as security.[6] Article 9 adopts the universal, generic concept of a security interest. All the old terminology of the law and the favourites beloved of lawyers such as pledge, mortgage, conditional sale, trust receipt etc. have been consigned to the corridors of legal history and replaced by the unitary concept of a security interest.[7] Article 9 does not make any distinction between legal and equitable security interests or between fixed and floating security interests.[8]

Article 9-109 states the scope of application of Article 9, with the article applying to any transaction, regardless of its form, that creates a security interest in personal property or fixtures by contract and to a sale of accounts, chattel paper, payment intangibles or promissory notes.[9]

---

laid out and are designed to produce results that are fair in the typical case is greatly preferable to the uncodified and unsystematised collocation of rules we have painfully developed in this country over the past century': see 'The Exodus of the Floating Charge' in D. Feldman and F. Meisel eds. *Corporate and Commercial Law: Modern Developments* (Lloyds of London Press, 1996) chap. 10 at pp. 202–3.

[4] Personal Property Securities Act 1999. For information on the New Zealand PPSA see the following website: http://www.ppsr.govt.nz/.

[5] For a detailed account of the Ontario PPSA see J. Ziegel and D. Denomme *The Ontario Personal Property Security Act: Commentary and Analysis* (Canada Law Book Inc., 2nd edn. 2000); R. McLaren *The Ontario Personal Property Security Act* (Carswell, 1994). See also more generally G. McCormack 'Personal Property Security Law Reform in England and Canada' [2002] *JBL* 113.

[6] But for criticisms of this approach see T. Plank 'Sacred Cows and Workhorses: The Sale of Accounts and Chattel Paper under the UCC and the Effects of Violating a Fundamental Drafting Principle' (1994) 26 *Conn L Rev* 397.

[7] Briefer descriptions of Article 9 that are particularly useful for English lawyers can be found in P. Winship 'Selected Security Interests in the United States' in Norton and Andenas eds. *Emerging Financial Markets* at p. 267 and Richard F. Broude 'Secured Transactions in Personal Property in the United States' in M. Bridge and R. Stevens eds. *Cross-Border Security and Insolvency* (Oxford University Press, 2001) at p. 45.

[8] See the decision of the Supreme Court of Canada in *Royal Bank of Canada* v. *Sparrow Electric Corp* (1997) 143 DLR (4th) 385, on which see K. Davis 'Priority of Crown Claims in Insolvency' (1997) 29 *Can Bus LJ* 145.

[9] Article 9, however, does not apply to a sale of accounts, chattel paper, payment intangibles or promissory notes as part of a sale of the business out of which they arose or

'Security interest' is defined in Article 1-201(37) as meaning an interest in personal property or fixtures that secures either payment or else the performance of an obligation. The term also includes any interest of a consignor and a buyer of accounts, chattel paper etc.[10] The special property interest of a buyer of goods on identification of those goods to a contract for sale[11] is not characterised as a 'security interest', but a buyer may also acquire a security interest by complying with Article 9. In other words, a retention-of-title clause in a sale-of-goods contract, even a 'simple' retention-of-title clause, is transformed by statutory fiat into the reservation of a security interest.[12] According to Article 9-202, the article applies irrespective of whether title to collateral is in the secured party or the debtor though there are special rules for sales of accounts, chattel paper and payment intangibles.[13]

The scope of Article 9 is broad enough to encompass what the Company Law Steering Group and the Law Commission have termed 'functionally equivalent legal devices', for example transactions such as factoring of debts and retention of title clauses in sale-of-goods contracts that in English legal terms do not involve the creation of security but nevertheless, in economic terms, serve the same financing purpose.[14] With the enactment of an Article 9-type law, all the old learning associated with the use of factoring or retention of title would largely disappear from the realm of practical utility in England.[15]

---

to an assignment of the same which is for the purpose of collection only. Neither does it apply to an assignment of a right to payment under a contract to an assignee that is also obligated to perform under the contract nor to an assignment of a single account, payment intangible or promissory note to an assignee in full or partial satisfaction of a pre-existing indebtedness.

[10] 'Chattel paper' is defined in Article 9-102(11) as meaning a record or records that evidence both a monetary obligation and a security interest in specific goods. Chattel-paper financing is a way of refinancing credits extended to hirers/buyers under hire-purchase or conditional-sale agreements. Article 9 distinguishes between chattel-paper financing and 'ordinary' accounts receivable financing for the purpose of awarding the chattel-paper financier certain enhanced priority rights: see Article 9-330.

[11] See section 2-401 of the UCC.

[12] For a description of the different forms of retention-of-title clause see G. McCormack *Reservation of Title* (Sweet & Maxwell, 2nd edn. 1995) at p. 2.

[13] A payment intangible is defined in Article 9-102(61) as meaning a general intangible under which the account debtor's principal obligation is a monetary obligation. General intangibles are the residual category of personal property.

[14] *Modern Company Law for a Competitive Economy: Final Report* (July 2001) at para. 12.8; Law Commission Consultation Paper No. 164 *Registration of Security Interests* (July 2002) at para. 1.26.

[15] See generally G. McCormack 'Rewriting the English Law of Personal Property Securities and Article 9 of the US Uniform Commercial Code' (2003) 24 *Co Law* 68.

Attachment of an Article 9 security interest

The central concepts of Article 9 are attachment and perfection. A security interest is said to attach when it becomes enforceable between creditor and debtor, i.e. it creates an obligation. It should be noted that the attachment of a security interest in (secured property) collateral gives a secured party the right to proceeds and is also regarded as attachment of a security interest in a supporting obligation for the collateral.[16] Perfection, on the other hand, refers to the process whereby the security interest becomes effective against third parties, i.e. it creates a property right.[17] Perfection generally occurs through filing.

Article 9-203 lays down that a security agreement attaches if value has been given; the debtor has rights in the collateral or the power to transfer rights in the collateral to a secured party and additionally one of a number of other alternative conditions are fulfilled, including that the debtor has authenticated a security agreement that provides a description of the collateral. The parties, however, may agree to postpone the time for attachment, in which case the security interest attaches at the agreed time. It is specifically stated in Article 9-204 that a security agreement may cover after-acquired property but, of course, the security agreement will not attach unless and until the debtor 'has rights in the collateral'. The concept of 'rights in the collateral' is not free from controversy, though it clearly connotes something less than full ownership.

While floating charges are not specifically referred to in Article 9-203 there is little doubt that they are made subject to the general rules on attachment.[18] Therefore, if the parties use language in the security agreement that is reminiscent of the English-style floating charge attachment will still occur at the time that the financing transaction is entered into, even if the collateral is floating and the debtor can carry on business in the ordinary way as far as the assets charged are concerned. In fact, pre-Article 9 US law did not recognise the equivalent of an English floating charge. The leading authority is *Benedict v. Ratner*,[19] where the Supreme Court had to decide on the legal implications of a purported assignment of account receivables under which the assignor went on collecting the receivables from the debtors, who had not been notified of the assignment.

---

[16] Articles 9-203(f) and 9-315.   [17] See generally Article 9-308.

[18] The fact that the parties have used the terminology of the floating charge is not enough to warrant the implication that they have thereby agreed to postpone the time for attachment: see *Canadian Imperial Bank of Commerce v. Otto Timm Enterprises* (1995) 130 DLR (4th) 91. See also the decision of the Supreme Court of Canada in *Royal Bank of Canada v. Sparrow Electric Corp.* (1997) 143 DLR (4th) 385.

[19] (1925) 268 US 353.

The assignors continued to use the proceeds in the ordinary course of business without accounting in any way to the assignee. In England, of course, an arrangement of this kind would be categorised as a floating charge and upheld on this basis but the US Supreme Court held that the transaction was void against the assignor's trustee in bankruptcy as a fraudulent conveyance under the state law of New York. The court said:[20] 'Under the law of New York a transfer of property as security which reserves to the transferor the right to dispose of the same, or to apply the proceeds thereof, for his own uses is, as to creditors, fraudulent in law and void.'

Benedict v. *Ratner* may also be rationalised on the basis of a supposed conceptual repugnancy between the nature of a security interest and a reserved power on the part of the debtor freely to dispose of assets in the ordinary course of business. It is perhaps not surprising that in a country as legally sophisticated and commercially pragmatic as the US legal professionals sought to circumvent the limitations of the decision and a sophisticated avoidance industry developed.[21] As a result of pre-Article 9 legislative developments in the US most types of personal property, whether tangible or intangible, became available as collateral to secure loans.[22] Often change came as the result of particular legislation passed at the behest of finance companies. Special interest groups might plead for a particular legislative initiative and the result was a mismatch of complex and interlocking statutes, with intricate registration requirements, that lacked overall coherence and uniformity: 'Half a dozen filing systems covering chattel security devices might be maintained within a state, some on a county basis, others on a state-wide basis, each of which had to be separately checked to determine a debtor's status.'[23]

Article 9 brought rationality and coherence to this 'wilderness of single instances'[24] and one of the ways it did this was by recognising the

---

[20] *Ibid.*

[21] See generally Grant Gilmore *Security Interests in Personal Property* (Little Brown, 1965) vol. I, chaps. 1–8.

[22] Article 9 has been described as 'an anthological collection of the most celebrated security law controversies of the preceding forty years' in Grant Gilmore 'Security Law, Formalism and Article 9' (1968) 47 *Nebraska LR* 659 at 671.

[23] See the official comment attached to the 1972 version of Article 9-101.

[24] As the poet Alfred Lord Tennyson conceived English law in 'Aylmer's Field':

Mastering the lawless science of our law,
That codeless myriad of precedent,
That wilderness of single instances,
Thro' which a few, by wit or fortune lend,
May beat a pathway out to wealth and fame.

functional equivalent of the floating charge.[25] Resort to legal subterfuge was made unnecessary by a provision sanctioning the creation of a 'floating' security interest on shifting collateral. In England Professor Goode has likened the floating charge to a charge over a fund of assets,[26] and the same analogy has been used to capture what has been recognised by an Article 9 security interest:[27] 'The secured creditor's interest is in the stream of accounts flowing through the debtor's business, not in any specific accounts. As with the Heraclitean river, although the accounts in the stream constantly change, we can say it is the same stream.'

The revolution wrought by Article 9 was to recognise the fact that a fixed security interest was not necessarily incompatible with a freedom on the part of the debtor to dispose of the secured property in the ordinary course of business. This conclusion has been mirrored in Canada and in *Royal Bank of Canada* v. *Sparrow Electric Corp.*[28] The Supreme Court of Canada acknowledged that for practical purposes, the distinction between fixed and floating charges and between legal and equitable security interests had been swept away. The court referred to an implicit legislative declaration that, as a matter of public policy, there was nothing objectionable about having a fixed charge on stock-in-trade of a debtor coupled with a licence to deal with the collateral in the ordinary course of business.[29] This declaration is fairly explicit in Article 9-205 which provides that a security interest is not invalid or fraudulent against creditors solely because the debtor has the right or ability to

(a) use, commingle, or dispose of all or part of the collateral, including returned or repossessed goods;
(b) collect, compromise, enforce or otherwise deal with collateral;
(c) accept the return of collateral or make repossessions; or
(d) use, commingle, or dispose of proceeds;

---

[25] Grant Gilmore has said in 'Security Law, Formalism and Article 9' at 672: 'Article 9 draftsmen argued from the premise that, under existing security law, a lender could take an enforceable interest in all of a debtor's present and future personal property to the conclusion that the new statute should provide for the accomplishment of this result in the simplest possible fashion.'

[26] R. Goode *Legal Problems of Credit and Security* (Sweet & Maxwell, 2nd edn. 1988) at p. 49.

[27] See W. Hogan 'Games Lawyers Play with the Bankruptcy Preference Challenge to Accounts and Inventory Financing' (1968) 53 *Cornell L Rev 553* at 560, quoted in Honnold et al. *Security Interests in Personal Property* at p. 459.

[28] (1997) 143 DLR (4th) 385.

[29] See also Article 9 of the Model Inter-American Law on Secured Transactions which provides if the 'security interest is non-possessory, the secured debtor . . . has the . . . right to use and dispose of the collateral and any proceeds derived from the original collateral in the ordinary course of the debtor's business'.

or because the secured party fails to require the debtor to account for proceeds or to replace the collateral.[30]

Perfection of an Article 9 security interest

Effectiveness of a security interest against third parties occurs through perfection. In the preponderance of cases this requires filing, and the date of filing is the reference point for settling the order of priorities between competing security interests in the same collateral. Article 9-308 states that a security interest is perfected (a) when it has attached and (b) when all the steps required for its perfection under any provision of the article have been complied with. A security interest is perfected when it attaches if the applicable requirements are satisfied before the security interest attaches.[31]

Perfection by filing centres around the notion of notice filing. In the concept of notice filing lies one of the fundamental difference between the US and English systems. Under the English system certain particulars of the charge – date of the charge, parties thereto, amount secured and property charged – must be filed with the registrar of companies along with the instrument of charge within twenty-one days of the date of creation of the charge.[32] The registrar compares the filed particulars with the instrument of charge and, if satisfied that the filed particulars are correct, issues a certificate and this certificate is stated to be conclusive evidence that all the requirements of the legislation as to registration have been complied with.[33] The English system may be described as one of transaction filing – details of certain transactions must be recorded – whereas the US system embodied in Article 9-501 is based on notice filing. Under the notice-filing system what is filed is not the security agreement itself but only a simple record – a financing statement – that provides a limited amount of information.[34] The financing statement may be filed either before or after the security interest attaches. The filed notice merely indicates that a person may have a security interest in the collateral concerned but to ascertain the complete state of affairs it would be necessary to make further inquiry from the parties. There is a statutory procedure under

---

[30] See also Article 9-204 which provides that a security agreement may create or provide for a security interest in after-acquired collateral. It is also provided that a security agreement may provide that collateral secures future advances or other value, whether or not the value is given pursuant to commitment. Article 9-204(b) contains an element of consumer protection in that a security interest may not attach under an after-acquired property clause to consumer goods, other than an accession when given as additional security, unless the debtor acquires rights in them within ten days after the secured party gives value.

[31] Article 9-308(a).   [32] The English law is contained in Part 12 Companies Act 1985.
[33] Section 401 (2) Companies Act 1985.   [34] Article 9-502 Official Comment.

Article 9-210 whereby a secured party, at the debtor's request, may be required to make disclosure. Article 9-210 envisages that a debtor may request three types of information by submitting three types of 'requests' to the secured party.[35] In many cases, however, the debtor or another prospective financier may be able to obtain the requisite information without the need to invoke the compulsive aspects of Article 9-210.

Notice filing has proved to be of great use in financing transactions that involve the use of inventory (stock-in-trade) or receivables (book debts) because it removes the necessity of having to make a number of repeated filings where there is a series of transactions between the parties.[36] Another benefit comes where there is a continuing arrangement under which the collateral changes from day to day, and again there is no need to file a different financing statement every time that the collateral changes. Moreover, a financing statement is effective to encompass transactions under a security agreement that was not in existence and not even contemplated by the parties at the time that the financing statement was filed, provided that the indication of collateral in the financing statement is sufficiently broad to cover the collateral concerned. Similarly, a financing statement is effective to cover after-acquired property of the type indicated and to perfect future advances under security agreements, irrespective of whether after-acquired property or future advances are mentioned in the financing statement and even though they may not have been in the contemplation of the parties at the time that the financing statement was drawn up.[37]

In simple terms, a financing statement may cover the entire credit relationship of the parties. Therefore, a seller who is contemplating the supply of goods to a buyer over an extended period of time may take a security interest in all the supplies by filing a simple financing statement instead of having to register each contract of sale separately which would be the case if a retention-of-title clause were held to constitute a registrable clause under present English law.[38] The creditor may state simply that he is taking security in certain collateral to cover advances made to the debtor including future advances irrespective of whether or not there is any commitment on the part of the creditor to make the advance. Save for the special priority position accorded the purchase-money security interest (PMSI), Article 9 adopts generally a simple first-to-file priority rule and priority extends to future advances.

There are simple formal requirements for an effective financing statement: the debtor's name; the name of a secured party or representative of

---

[35] These include a list of collateral and a statement of the aggregate amount of unpaid secured obligations.
[36] See generally Article 9-502 Official Comment.
[37] Article 9-204.   [38] *Clough Mill Ltd v. Martin* [1985] 1 WLR 111.

the secured party; and an indication of the collateral. A financing statement must reasonably identify the collateral, or alternatively it is permissible to state that the financing statement covers all assets or all personal
property.[39] A broad statement of this kind (e.g. all the debtor's personal
property) would not, however, be a sufficient description for the purposes
of a security agreement.[40] Article 9-506 deals with the effect of errors or
omissions in the financing statement. A financing statement substantially
satisfying the formal requirements is stated to be effective, even if it has
minor errors or omissions, unless the errors or omissions make the financing statement seriously misleading, but a financing statement that
fails sufficiently to provide the name of the debtor is deemed to be seriously misleading. If, however, a search of the records of the filing office
under the debtor's correct name, using the filing office's standard search
logic, if any, would disclose a financing statement that fails sufficiently to
provide the name of the debtor, the name provided does not make the
financing statement seriously misleading.[41]

Records filed in the filing office do not require signatures for their effectiveness, though there is a requirement that the debtor authorises the
filing in an authenticated record.[42] A person who files an unauthorised
record is liable for damages.[43] A filed financing statement is effective for
a period of five years after the date of filing.[44] Article 9-516 provides
that communication of a record to a filing office and tender of the filing fee or acceptance of the record by the filing office constitutes filing.
Article 9-517 sets out an exclusive list of grounds set out upon which the
filing office may reject a record and it is also stated that the failure of the
filing office to index a record correctly does not affect the effectiveness of
the filed record.

While filing a financing statement is the standard way of perfecting a
security interest other methods of perfection are permissible in certain circumstances.[45] Moreover, filing does not ordinarily perfect a security
interest in deposit accounts, letter-of-credit rights or money.[46] Certain security interests are perfected automatically upon attachment,
including:[47]

---

[39] Article 9-504.   [40] Article 9-504 Official Comment.
[41] Article 9-506(c).   [42] Article 9-509.   [43] Article 9-625.
[44] Article 9-515.   [45] Article 9-310.   [46] Articles 9-312(b) and 9-314.
[47] Article 9-309. These exceptions are essentially pragmatic, based on industry need or
    lobbying by pressure groups. As one commentator has explained, the principle of auto-
    matic perfection of security interests created by securities intermediaries arises because
    in this situation there is 'a presumption of encumbrance – ostensible non-ownership':
    see J. Schroeder 'Is Article 8 Finally Ready This Time? The Radical Reform of Secured
    Lending on Wall Street' [1994] *Colum Bus L Rev* 291 at 399.

(a) a purchase-money security interest in consumer goods;
(b) an assignment of accounts or payment intangibles which does not by itself or in conjunction with other assignments to the same assignee transfer a significant part of the assignor's outstanding accounts or payment intangibles;
(c) a sale of a payment intangible;
(d) a security interest created by the assignment of a health-care insurance receivable to the provider of the health-care goods or services;
(e) a security interest in investment property created by a broker or securities intermediary.[48]

According to Article 9-313 a secured party may perfect a security interest in negotiable documents, goods, instruments, money or tangible chattel paper by taking possession of the collateral. A security interest in certificated securities may be perfected by taking delivery of the certificated securities. Article 9-314 lays down that a security interest in investment property, deposit accounts, letter-of-credit rights or electronic chattel paper may be perfected by the secured party acquiring control of the collateral.

Priorities under Article 9

Article 9-322 determines priorities among conflicting security interests in the same collateral and, following earlier versions of Article 9, generally recognises the principle that the first secured party to file a financing statement should have priority over competing secured parties with security interests in the same collateral.[49] The revised Article 9 introduces additional variants on the basic priority picture, notably by permitting

---

[48] According to the Official Comment the automatic perfection principle applying to securities intermediaries is designed to facilitate current secured-financing arrangements for securities firms as well as to provide sufficient flexibility to accommodate new arrangements that develop in the future. Under 'agreement to deliver' arrangements, a securities firm retains positions in securities in its own account but records on its books that the positions have been charged and promises that the securities will be transferred to the secured party's account on demand. Under 1994 amendments to Articles 8 and 9 of the UCC a security interest in securities given for new value under a written security agreement was temporarily perfected without filing or possession for twenty-one days. This state of affairs could have been continued indefinitely, however, by rolling over the loans at least every twenty-one days and the principle of automatic perfection makes it unnecessary to engage in the purely formalistic practice of rolling over the loans. Query, however, whether the concept of notice filing is not sufficiently flexible to accommodate these forms of financing arrangement.

[49] The first-to-file priority principle has its critics, however – see e.g. R. Mann 'The First Shall be Last: A Contextual Argument for Abandoning Temporal Rules of Lien Priority' (1996) 75 *Texas L Rev* 11.

perfection by control and investing this method of perfection with a status superior to that of perfection by filing.[50]

Be that as it may, let us return to the basic priority picture. Priority generally dates from the earliest time a filing that covers the collateral is first made or the security interest is first perfected, provided that there is no period thereafter when there is neither filing nor perfection. A perfected security interest has priority over a competing unperfected security interest.[51] The first security interest to attach has priority if competing security interests are unperfected.[52] Article 9, however, does not preclude subordination by the agreement of a person that is otherwise entitled to priority. Subordination agreements are expressly validated by Article 9-339.[53]

The centrality of the 'first-to-file-or-perfect' priority rule must be stressed. The secured party who first registers a financing statement obtains priority even though he is not the first in terms of executing a security agreement with a debtor or indeed acquiring an attached security interest in the collateral. Professors Cuming and Wood have described the policy driving the similar Canadian approach as being quite simple:[54]

Once a financing statement is registered any person who is planning to deal with someone named as debtor in the financing statement has the ability to determine whether or not the interest he intends to acquire will be subject to a security interest having a prior status. If such a person goes ahead and acquires an interest in the personal property described in the financing statement without making some accommodation with a registering party or without obtaining a discharge of the financing statement, there is no reason to give his interest priority over a subsequent security interest acquired by the registered party.

The 'first-to-file' priority rule and subsequent advances

Under Article 9, a security agreement may cover future advances – or indeed any future obligations whatsoever. Additionally, subsequent

---

[50] See generally R. Picker 'Perfection Hierarchies and Nontemporal Priority Rules' (1999) 74 *Chicago-Kent L Rev* 1157 who argues that the revised Article 9 does a better job than previously of matching collateral taken and reliance on it, assuming that control is a good proxy for reliance.

[51] Article 9-322(a)(2).   [52] Article 9-322(a)(3).

[53] The Official Comment makes it clear that a person's rights cannot be adversely affected by an agreement to which the person is not a party. On debt subordination agreements under English law see *Re Maxwell Communications Corp. (No. 2)* [1993] 1 WLR 1402; *Re British & Commonwealth Holdings plc (No. 3)* [1992] 1 WLR 672; *Cheah v. Equiticorp Finance Group Ltd* [1992] BCLC; and see generally E. Ferran 'Subordination of Secured and Unsecured Debt' in *Company Law and Corporate Finance* (Oxford University Press, 1999) chap. 16; R. Nolan 'Less Equal than Others' [1995] *JBL* 485.

[54] See R. Cuming and R. Wood 'Compatibility of Federal and Provincial Personal Property Security Law' (1986) 65 *Canadian Bar Review* 267 at 285.

advances made under a first-in-time perfected security interest have priority over advances made under a security agreement that has been made and perfected in the intervening period.[55] Generally speaking, the date of the advance is not a factor in determining priorities. In other words, a secured party will come after all advances made by a competing secured party having priority under the first-to-file-or-perfect rule, including subsequent advances.[56] Moreover, it does not matter whether or not the subsequent advances have been made pursuant to an obligation. The general tenor of the provision is brought home in the following observations of the United States District Court in *Re Smith*:[57]

Once priority has been achieved by being the first to file, that priority will not be destroyed as to an advance made with the knowledge that a second party has made a prior advance secured by a perfected security interest in the same collateral. This is the case . . . even if it is the first advance made under the prior perfected agreement. Similar treatment should be accorded any interest which attached after filing.

This interpretation is confirmed by Article 9-204(c) which states that a security agreement may provide that collateral secures future advances or other value, whether or not the advances or value are given pursuant to commitment. According to the Official Comment this article rejects the view manifested in some of the earlier case law that asked whether or not the future advance was of a similar class or type as earlier obligations that were secured by the collateral.

In England, by way of contrast to Article 9, the position governing priority of subsequent advances is somewhat more complicated. As far as security over personalty is concerned, the law is contained in section 94 Law of Property Act 1925. This section gives a prior chargee the right in three situations to make further advances which rank in priority to subsequent chargees:

(a) where an arrangement has been made to that effect with the subsequent chargees;
(b) if the prior chargee had no notice of the subsequent charges at the time that the further advance was made;
(c) where the charge imposes an obligation on him to make further advances.

---

[55] Article 9-323.
[56] There is a partial exception to this principle, however, that favours the holders of liens. Under Article 9-323(b) a security interest is subordinate to the rights of a person who becomes a lien creditor to the extent that the security interest secures an advance made more than forty-five days after the person becomes a lien creditor unless the advance is made without knowledge of the lien or pursuant to a commitment entered into without knowledge of the lien.
[57] (1971) 326 F Supp 1311.

The effect of Article 9 filing on subsequent security agreements

The impact of Article 9 goes even further than merely validating 'future advances' clauses in security agreements.[58] The article permits a financing statement to be filed covering more than one security agreement. Take the example where a financing statement has been filed covering particular collateral. The parties then execute a security agreement that commits the creditor to make certain advances. Some time elapses and the obligations arising under the security agreement are spent. Then, within the five-year period from the date of the filing of the original financing statement, the parties execute a subsequent security agreement which covers the same collateral without filing another financing statement. It seems clear from the Article 9 priority rules that advances made under the second security agreement will take priority over any intervening creditor. Initially, there was some judicial hostility against acceptance of this view. In particular, the courts were inclined to the proposition that there should be some linkage between financing statement and security agreement with a secured party having to show that a financing statement was made in connection with a particular security agreement before obtaining priority.

This issue arose in an acute form before the Rhode Island Superior Court in *Coin-O-Matic Service Co.* v. *Rhode Island Hospital Trust Co.*[59] Here the court rejected the proposition that an original financing statement was an umbrella which gave the secured party, X, a priority with respect to its second security transaction notwithstanding the fact that another security interest was established in point of time prior to X's second security transaction. The court did not consider that this result was demanded by the provisions of the UCC and stated:[60]

---

[58] One largely unresolved issue under Article 9, however, concerns whether a first-filed secured party can, as it were, sell his place in line. See generally on this issue S. Walt 'The Case for Laundered Security Interests' (1996) 63 *Tenn L Rev* 369; S. Neth 'The First to File Priority in Article 9: Can you Sell your Place in Line?' (1998) 31 *UCC LJ* 64 and the responses by M. Shanker (1998) 31 *UCC LJ* 82 and S. Walt (1998) 31 *UCC LJ* 217. Shanker, contrary to the views of the other commentators, is strongly of the view that one cannot sell one's place in line and suggests somewhat facetiously at p. 83:

> If Professor Neth's thesis prevails, I suggest that he and I start a business setting up senior financing statements with hosts of companies (perhaps supported by a minimal one dollar loan), and then market them to subsequent creditors of that business. It might turn out to be a lucrative business opportunity. Of course, we may discover that we are engaged in selling an investment security, and thus subject to Article 8, and possibly even state and federal securities laws. But, doesn't Professor Neth's article functionally reach that result: transforming a financing statement from a mere notice of security interest into some kind of marketable investment security?

[59] (1966) 3 UCC Rep 1112.   [60] *Ibid.*

If the Code gives the lender an interest in the collateral for future advances even though no provision is made for such future advances, then the information secured by the debtor and given to a subsequent lender is of little value because the second creditor surely could not rely upon the information. If the defendant's interpretation of the Code is correct, there seems to be hardly any substantive reason why the original lender should be bound to comply with the borrower's request for information concerning a correct statement of the outstanding balance and the collateral covered under the security agreement.

The court concluded that a secured party was not entitled to rely upon the original financing statement in order to make a subsequent loan that ranks ahead of that of the intervening creditor. In its view, a single financing statement made in connection with a security agreement where there was no provision for future advances did not serve as an umbrella for future advances based upon new security agreements, notwithstanding the fact that the same collateral was involved.

The decision can be criticised on the basis that the court confused two issues.[61] One was the question of future advances and the scope of security agreements, and the second was the use of financing statements and notice filing. Clearly, Article 9 does not tie the filing of a financing statement to the execution of a particular security agreement, and indeed it is permissible to file a financing statement long before any security agreement is executed. The provision in Article 9 – now Article 9-204(c) – validating future advance clauses in security agreements was logically and fundamentally distinct from the concept of notice filing and the use of financing statements which formed an essential part of the latter. *Coin-O-Matic* ignored the basic point that Article 9 revolves around the world of notice filing rather than transactional filing where the giving of notice in a publicly accessible register is tied to specific transactions. In a universe determined by transaction filing the priority of the first creditor on the scene is generally confined to the amount of money that is advanced in the initial loan or the amount that the creditor is expressly committed to advance. If there are additional advances then these would require a separate filing. Of course English law, being based on transaction rather than notice filing, is firmly committed to the *Coin-O-Matic* view. If, in England, a lender and corporate borrower make a new or fresh security agreement, and loan obligations are entered into pursuant to this agreement, then the loan will be regarded as unsecured if the borrower goes into liquidation and details of the security agreement (charge) have not been submitted for registration within twenty-one days of the security agreement being executed. This result flows from a number of basic propositions, namely, that the security agreement creates a charge

---

[61] See the Official Comment to the 1972 version of Article 9-204.

and a charge has to be registered within twenty-one days of the date of its creation to escape invalidity in the event of the borrower's liquidation. These consequences are an inherent part of the existing English system.[62]

Article 9, however, was expressly designed to abandon the confined quarters of the old transaction filing system and to embark on a brave and radically new world of notice filing. Undoubtedly transaction filing provides more information to an outside creditor who can ascertain from the register the maximum amount by which the collateral stands as security for the original creditor. On the other hand, there are countervailing advantages which the drafters of Article 9 considered outweighed the disadvantages of notice filing. The notice-filing system offers greater flexibility by removing the necessity of a creditor having to make a fresh filing every time a new advance is made or the debtor subsequently acquires new items of property. As the official comment to the 'old' Article 9-312 put the matter, notice filing safeguarded the integrity of the notice-filing system by 'allowing the secured party who has first filed to make subsequent advances without each time having, as a condition of protection, to check for filings later than his'.

The court in *Coin-O-Matic* referred to policy reasons in support of its decision by implying that the first creditor on the scene should not have a security monopoly as far as the debtor is concerned. On the other hand, there are countervailing considerations and it may be argued that later lenders can buy out the existing secured creditor by loaning the debtor a sufficient amount to repay the earlier indebtedness and terminate the earlier financing statement. In this way, the assets of the debtor are released for subsequent secured borrowings.[63]

Special Article 9 priority rules: the purchase-money security interest

There is an exception to the general first-to-file priority rule in the case of PMSIs.[64] A PMSI will rank ahead of a prior security interest with

---

[62] Even in the proposed reforms the implications of *Coin-O-Matic* and the reversal of the same do not appear to have been taken fully on board by the Law Commission in *Registration of Security Interests* at pp. 106–7. At para. 4.154 the Law Commission provisionally proposes to allow the tacking of further advances only where these are contemplated by the security agreement and are covered by the financing statement. By implication they seem to exclude the possibility that a filed financing statement might cover more than one security agreement.

[63] See generally D. G. Baird and T. H. Jackson *Security Interests in Personal Property* (Foundation Press, 2nd edn. 1987) at p. 363.

[64] Article 9-324 deals with the priority of PMSIs; and see generally on this area P. Shupack 'Defining Purchase Money Collateral' (1992) 29 *Idaho Law Review* 767; K. Meyer 'A Primer on Purchase Money Security Interests under Revised Article 9' (2001) 50 *Kan*

an after-acquired property clause.[65] A PMSI may conveniently be referred to as an interest that favours creditors who extend credit on the understanding that the debtor will use it to acquire the collateral.[66] There is a fairly convoluted definition in Article 9-103 which requires a close nexus between the acquisition of the collateral and the security interest. Basically what is required is the giving of value 'to enable the debtor to acquire rights in or the use of the collateral if the value is in fact so used'. Article 9 distinguishes between PMSIs and general security interests and awards the former a kind of super-priority status that has traditionally been enjoyed by retention-of-title claimants. The possibility of enjoying super-priority status has now been extended to other financiers in certain circumstances.[67] If a debtor has granted an all-assets security interest that extends over future property then, notwithstanding the general first-to-perfect priority rule, a creditor whose advances funded the acquisition of 'new property' in the debtor's hands will outrank the earlier financier in respect of the collateral represented by the new property.[68]

The economic justification for recognising PMSIs focuses on the fact that the release of funds by the creditor increases the debtor's total pool of assets. The debtor is enabled to acquire new assets as distinct from merely rolling over existing debt. The proposition has been neatly put as follows:[69]

LR 143. For an argument against the PMSI super-priority rules see A. Schwartz 'A Theory of Loan Priorities' (1989) 18 *J Legal Stud* 209 at 250–4 who would limit super-priority in inventory and prevent PMSI super-priority in other collateral from trumping secured parties who do not have blanket liens.

[65] See generally on the background to purchase-money super-priority and for an English perspective see Iwan Davies 'The Trade Debtor and the Quest for Security' in Harry Rajak ed. *Insolvency Law: Theory and Practice* (Sweet & Maxwell, 1993) p. 43 at pp. 55–63.

[66] One of the justifications given for recognising purchase-money super-priority is that whereas a general financier takes account of average risk, the PMSI lender may have particular skills and is able to lend on particularly advantageous terms because of its special knowledge of the collateral: see generally A. Schwartz 'The Continuing Puzzle of Secured Debt' (1984) 37 *Vand L Rev* 1051.

[67] Non-seller purchase-money security was possible before the 1998 Article 9 revisions: see generally on this issue G. Nation 'Creation and Perfection of Non-Seller Purchase Money Security Interests: Current Law and Proposed Changes under Revised Article 9' (1998) 31 *UCC LJ* 84.

[68] Under Article 9-324(g) the holder of a PMSI that secures the unpaid purchase price of collateral will prevail over the holder of a conflicting PMSI that enables the collateral to be acquired. Translated into English-law terms, this means that a retention-of-title seller has priority over a lender that makes an enabling loan. For criticism of this rule see Meyer 'A Primer' at 188, which points to some possible inconsistency with Article 9-328, which deals with investment property. Priority in investment property is given to the secured party who has control. Article 9-328(2) provides that if two or more secured parties have control, priority is determined by who obtained control first.

[69] Baird and Jackson *Security Interests in Personal Property* at p. 401. The priority of PMSIs is discussed generally by T. Jackson and A. Kronman 'Secured Financing and Priorities

Purchase money lenders always involve debtors who acquire new assets at the same time they acquire new liabilities. Giving a superpriority to purchase money lenders does not raise the fear that the debtor is simply using the new loan to roll over old debt. It may be that this characteristic of purchase money loans explains why they receive superpriority. Showing that other kinds of loans brought increases in the debtor's net worth equal to the value of the security interests transferred may be much more difficult.

Whereas a security interest granted over property already owned may remove that property from the debtor's estate, a security interest over newly acquired property to secure the price paid for that property is neutral in its effect. The debt in respect of the price is offset by the addition of the property.[70] Moreover, if the new property helped the debtor's business to earn extra profits it would strengthen the position of existing creditors by swelling their security interest. In addition, if an earlier creditor could rely on an after-acquired property clause to the prejudice of a PMSI holder, the earlier creditor would obtain an unjustified windfall at the expense of the later creditor whose money enabled the additional property to be acquired.[71] On the other hand, 'privileging' the PMSI seems to assume that the advance of funds specifically linked to the acquisition of 'new' assets is intrinsically more valuable to the debtor's business than the advance of funds for general funds such as paying the wages of employees.[72] Is the one advance necessarily of greater social utility than the other?

There are, however, special perfection requirements applicable to PMSIs under Article 9 and adherence to these requirements is necessary to obtain super-priority status. The point is illustrated by a Canadian case, *Haibeck v. No. 40 Taurus Ventures Ltd,*[73] where it was held that although the fairness of the situation appeared to support the unpaid seller who would lose the goods as a result, a buyer under an Article 9 regime gained

among Creditors' (1979) 88 *Yale LJ* 1143 at 1171–8. Jackson and Kronman suggest that the purchase-money super-priority is best thought of as a device for alleviating the situational monopoly created by an after-acquired property clause.

[70] See the discussion at para 17.7 of the Diamond report: A. Diamond *A Review of Security Interests in Property* (HMSO, 1989).

[71] For a law and economics perspective on this view see H. Kanda and S. Levmore 'Explaining Creditor Priorities' (1994) 80 *Va L Rev* 2103 at 2138–41.

[72] See the comments in W. J. Gough *Company Charges* (Butterworths, 2nd edn. 1996) at p. 436:

It assumes that financial accommodation for the purpose of, for example, paying wages and salaries through cheques drawn on an overdrawn account is less important than for the purchase of stocks or plant and equipment. This is not a real world distinction. Credit, as a matter of business need, is indivisible in the sense that all business inputs, including wages, overheads, equipment and supplies are all vital to an ongoing business.

[73] (1991) 59 BCLR (2d) 229.

sufficient rights in goods sold subject to a reservation-of-title clause so as to enable a prior security interest given by the buyer in after-acquired property to attach. The consequence of this holding was that the holder of a prior security interest over the buyer's property achieved priority where the unpaid seller did not observe the PMSI super-priority perfection requirements. Article 9-324 distinguishes between inventory and other goods with a claim to PMSI status in inventory being more difficult to establish. 'Inventory' is defined as meaning goods that are held by a person for sale or lease or that have been leased or that are to be furnished or have been furnished under a contract of service, or that are raw materials, work in progress or materials used or consumed in a business or profession. Article 9-324 imposes fairly stringent requirements which must be satisfied before a security-interest clause can qualify as a PMSI. Basically, before the debtor receives possession of the inventory, the purchase-money secured party must give notice in writing to every other secured party who has already registered a financing statement over the same collateral. The notice is required to state that the person giving it has, or expects to acquire, a PMSI in the inventory of the debtor and also the notice is required to describe the inventory.[74]

Where capital equipment rather than inventory is concerned, the qualifications necessary for obtaining PMSI status are somewhat less demanding, with automatic super-priority over prior secured lenders gained if the PMSI is registered within twenty days of the debtor acquiring possession of the collateral.[75] For earlier creditors there are differences in the risk equation in so far as new financing is concerned, and this has been explained as accounting for the difference in legal treatment. 'The rules intimate that the acquisition of new inventory and its associated debt is more threatening to earlier creditors than the debt-financing of new equipment but that debt tied to new inventory is still less threatening than new money unlinked to particular assets.'[76]

While economic reasons have been advanced to justify according a PMSI financier super-priority status, such status has also a respectable

---

[74] Article 9-324 Official Comment explains the purpose of the notification requirement as being to protect a non-purchase-money inventory secured party, which, under an arrangement with the debtor, is typically required to make periodic advances against incoming inventory or periodic releases of old inventory as new inventory is received. If the inventory secured party receives notice it may not make an advance. While the notification requirement is not the same as imposing a consent requirement before a PMSI over inventory can take priority, through the mechanism of an inventory secured party exerting pressure on the debtor, it may function in roughly the same way.

[75] Article 9-324(a).

[76] Kanda and Levmore 'Explaining Creditor Priorities' at 2139; and see generally M. Bridge, R. Macdonald, R. Simmonds and C. Walsh 'Formalism, Functionalism and Understanding the Law of Secured Transactions' (1999) 44 *McGill LJ* at nn. 99–108.

lineage in pre-Article 9 concepts and authority. The conceptual argument is founded on the proposition that the debtor has acquired only the raw shell of ownership with the purchase-money financier keeping the meat. The after-acquired property clause of the first-in-time financier can only attach to the raw shell of ownership in the hands of the debtor or, to put it another way, the 'equities attach to the property simultaneously, and prima facie that of the later lender should prevail, for his money made the acquisition possible'.[77] This view found expression in the decision of the US Supreme Court in *US* v. *New Orleans Railroad*[78] where the court recognised the priority status of a purchase-money financier – namely, a conditional seller – of railway equipment. It was observed:[79]

> The appellants contend . . . that the mortgages being prior in date to the bond given for the purchase-money of these locomotives and cars, and being expressly made to include after-acquired property, attached to the property as soon as it was purchased, and displaced any junior lien. This, we apprehend, is an erroneous view of the doctrine by which after-acquired property is made to serve the uses of a mortgage. That doctrine is intended to subserve the purposes of justice, and not injustice. Such an application of it as is sought by the appellants would often result in gross injustice. A mortgage intended to cover after-acquired property can only attach itself to such property in the condition in which it comes into the mortgagor's hands. If that property is already subject to mortgages or other liens, the general mortgage does not displace them, though they may be junior to it in point of time.

Under Article 9 there are, as we have seen, special perfection requirements that must be satisfied before PMSI status can be attained.[80] In at least one reported case, however, the old 'shell' or 'equities' reasoning was used to circumvent these special perfection requirements. Essentially the Florida Supreme Court held in *International Harvester Credit Corp.* v. *American National Bank*[81] that where a seller retained a security interest

---

[77] Anonymous note 'Defeating the Priority of an After-Acquired Property Clause' (1935) 48 *Harv L Rev* 474 at 476.

[78] (1871) 79 US 362.   [79] *Ibid.* at 365.

[80] Under the Model Inter-American Law on Secured Transactions these perfection requirements are somewhat different. A PMSI is referred to as an 'acquisition security'. Article 40 of the Model Law provides that in order for an acquisition security interest to be publicised and have priority over previously perfected security interests over property of the same type, the secured creditor, must before the debtor takes possession of such property:

  1. Register in the registration form a notation that indicates the special character of the acquisition security interest; and
  2. Notify the holders of previously perfected security interests over property of the same kind that the secured creditor has or expects to acquire an acquisition security interest in the collateral described in the notice.

[81] (1974) 296 So 2d 32, quoted in Baird and Jackson *Security Interests in Personal Property* at p. 394.

in a machine it sold to the debtor the seller's security interest defeated the after-acquired property clause of an earlier creditor with a perfected security interest over all the debtor's property. The court said:[82]

The contention is made that to restrict the prior creditor's priority in the after-acquired property to the debtor's equity therein renders meaningless the requirement for filing a financing statement. We do not think so. There really are no conflicting security interests in this situation. That security interest retained by the subsequent seller in the after-acquired property never passes to the buyer-debtor and thus never became subject to the earlier creditor's claim of security interest in such after-acquired property. On the other hand, the earlier (perfected) creditor does have his security in that interest which is after-acquired by his debtor.

Subsequent to the *International Harvester* decision, a Florida statute was passed rejecting the concept of a 'debtor's equity'. The statute declared that the UCC contained no such concept and, in fact, provided for a complete and logical system of determining priorities.[83]

The purchase-money security interest in England and Comparising with the Article 9 PMSI   There has been some judicial recognition of the concept of a PMSI in England, but this recognition has been limited and in the main confined to cases involving land, though the reasoning employed in the cases is, in principle, applicable in other contexts.[84] The leading authority is now the decision of the House of Lords in *Abbey National* v. *Cann*[85] but this decision is best understood in the light of the earlier authorities such as *Re Connolly Bros. Ltd (No. 2)*[86] and *Wilson* v. *Kelland*.[87]

In *Re Connolly Bros. Ltd (No. 2)*[88] a company issued debentures creating a floating charge upon their undertaking and all their property, including both present and future property. The debentures contained a condition that the company should not be at liberty to create any other mortgage or charge in priority to the debentures. A couple of years later the company wished to purchase premises but did not have the money for that purpose. Consequently, it borrowed a sum from a purchase-money lender to facilitate the acquisition upon terms that the lender should have a charge upon the premises when purchased. The Court of Appeal held

---

[82] (1974) 296 So 2d 32 at 34–5.
[83] See Baird and Jackson *Security Interests in Personal Property* at p. 396.
[84] See generally J. De Lacy 'The Purchase Money Security Interest: A Company Charge Conundrum?' [1991] *LMCLQ* 531; H. Bennett and C. Davis 'Fixtures, Purchase Money Security Interests and Dispositions of Interests in Land' (1994) 110 *LQR* 448.
[85] [1991] 1 AC 56; on which see generally G. Goldberg 'Vicit ac Vivat Scintilla Temporis' (1992) 108 *LQR* 380.
[86] [1912] 2 Ch 25.   [87] [1910] 2 Ch 306.   [88] [1912] 2 Ch 25.

that the debenture holders ranked after the purchase-money lender on the basis that when the company purported to purchase the premises it in fact acquired only an equity of redemption subject to the equitable charge of the purchase-money lender. The full ownership of the premises never constituted part of the company's assets in so far as the charge in favour of the debenture holders was concerned, for the purchase-money lender acquired an interest in the property coincident with its acquisition by the company.[89]

Another case in point is *Wilson* v. *Kelland*[90] where a vendor of land gave up the lien in respect of the unpaid purchase price in return, *inter alia*, for a contractual promise of an equitable charge over the property. The subsequently created charge was held to prevail over a floating charge over all the assets – present and future – of the company, which was prior in point of time. The *raison d'être* of the decision was that the company had only acquired an equity of redemption in the property. Any equity which attached to the purchased property in favour of the debenture holders was subject to the paramount equity of the unpaid vendors.

The problem with many of these old cases is that they turn on quite narrow distinctions rather than on the underlying economic realities.[91] The courts have scrutinised the facts quite minutely to determine whether or not there has been a split second of time (*scintilla temporis*) in which it could be said that a borrower has been the unencumbered owner of property. If there is such a period of time, however minute, then an earlier security interest extending over the borrower's after-acquired assets will have time to bite and consequently outrank a secured lender whose advance enabled the property in question to be acquired. As Professor Goode has stated:[92]

The courts have examined the sequence of operations with meticulous detail to find out whether the debtor's interest in the asset was encumbered at the outset by the purchase-money mortgage (in which case A's after acquired property clause can attach to the asset only in its encumbered form, so that B wins even if taking with notice of his security interest) or whether on the other hand there was a moment of time (*scintilla temporis*) in which B was the unincumbered owner of the asset before granting the purchase-money security interest, in which event A's after acquired property clause flashes in to catch the asset seconds before the purchase-money security interest takes.

In *Abbey National Building Society* v. *Cann*[93] the House of Lords appeared to give wider scope for the recognition of PMSIs by rejecting the

---

[89] *Ibid.* at 31.   [90] [1910] 2 Ch 306.
[91] But for recognition of the PMSI in Malaysia on the basis of the old English authorities see *United Malayan Banking Corp* v. *Aluminex* [1993] 3 MLJ 587.
[92] *Legal Problems* at pp. 98–9.   [93] [1991] 1 AC 56.

doctrine of *scintilla temporis*. The court said that a purchaser of domestic property who relied on a bank or building-society mortgage for completion could not be said to be the unencumbered legal and equitable owner of the property for a split second of time. In the court's view, the acquisition of the legal estate and the charge were not only precisely simultaneous but indissolubly bound up together.[94] In *Cann* it was held that the interest of a mortgagee whose advance of funds financed the acquisition of the property prevailed over the beneficial interest of somebody who was in actual occupation of the property for a mere half an hour before completion took place. The actual result in the case is hardly surprising but it is not entirely clear how far the *Cann* case signifies any wider recognition of the PMSI outside the important, but still relatively narrow, confines of domestic conveyancing. All is plain sailing where a purchaser needs a 100 per cent mortgage or a mortgage approaching that level. Here the reality clearly is that the advance is necessary for completion of the purchase. But what if the loan is in the nature of a top-up? Maybe the purchaser has ample funds to complete out of his own resources but wishes to obtain a loan merely to smooth over potential financial difficulties. Does the purchase-money financier prevail even in this case? The recent decision of the Court of Appeal in *Whale* v. *Viaystems Ltd* [95] does not provide precise answers to these questions but the case does signify a wider recognition of the concept of a PMSI. Speaking for the Court of Appeal, Jonathan Parker LJ said:[96]

It must now be taken as settled law that, in the context of an issue as to priorities between equitable interests, the court will have regard to the substance, rather than the form. Of the transaction or transactions which give rise to the competing interests; and in particular that conveyancing technicalities must give way to considerations of commercial and practical reality . . . this approach is not limited to cases involving the purchase of a property coupled with the grant of a mortgage or charge to secure repayment of the funds which were required

---

[94] *Ibid.* at 92. Lord Oliver pointed out that in many, if not most, cases of building society mortgages there will have been formal offer of acceptance of an advance which will ripen into a specifically enforceable agreement immediately the funds are advanced, which will normally be a day or so before completion. Furthermore, under the Land Registration Rules the registrar was entitled to register the charge even before registration of the transfer to the charger if he was satisfied that both were entitled to be registered. In registered land cases the expression 'the legal estate' is used in the sense of an estate which will become legal when registered. See also the comments of Lord Jauncey at 101.

[95] [2002] EWHC 393; 2002 WC 1876 107.

[96] At para. 72 of the judgment. The court appeared to endorse the sentiments expressed by Professor Goode in *Legal Problems* at pp. 99–100 about 'the inequity that would result in allowing the prior chargee a windfall increase in his security brought about not with the debtor's money or new funds injected by the prior chargee but with financing provided by a later incumbrancer'.

to enable completion of the purchase to take place . . . It falls to be adopted generally, in every case where an issue arises as to priority as between equitable interests.

Be that as it may, legislation may still be useful to fix more precisely the parameters of the principle of the PMSI in English law.

Other special Article 9 priority rules

Article 9-327 also contains special rules for priority of security interests in deposit accounts that serve as original collateral rather than the proceeds of disposition of other collateral.[97] A security interest held by a secured party having control of the deposit account has priority over a competing security interest held by a secured party that does not have control.[98] The same principle applies to letter-of-credit rights.[99] It should be noted that a transferee of money takes the money free of a security interest unless the transferee acts in collusion with the debtor in violating the rights of the secured party. Moreover, according to Article 9-340, a bank with which a deposit account is maintained may exercise any right to recoupment or set-off against a secured party that holds a security interest in the deposit account.[100] It may be added that a bank may hold both a right of set-off against, and an Article 9 security interest in, the same deposit account.

There are also particular provisions in Article 9-335 that govern accessions and commingled goods.[101] A security interest may be created in an accession and continues in collateral that becomes an accession.[102] If a security interest is perfected when the collateral becomes an accession, the security interest remains perfected in the collateral. A security interest in an accession is, however, subordinate to a security interest in the whole

---

[97] See generally on the background to this issue a report by the UCC Permanent Editorial Board study group *Use of Deposit Accounts as Original Collateral* (American Law Institute, 1992); and see also G. McCormack 'Security Interests in Deposit Accounts: An Anglo-American Perspective' [2002] *Insolvency Lawyer* 7.

[98] Moreover, under Article 9-342, a depositary bank may refuse to enter into a control agreement with another prospective secured party even if the customer so requests or directs.

[99] See generally for a discussion of security over letter-of-credit rights J. F. Dolan 'Security Interests in Letter of Credit Rights' (1999) 74 *Chicago-Kent L Rev* 1035; and see also G. Hissert 'Letter of Credit under Revised UCC Article 9' (1999) 31 *UCC LJ* 458.

[100] For the position in England see *Re BCCI (No. 8)* [1998] AC 214.

[101] For a discussion of the intricacies of some of these provisions see E. Reiley 'The Article 9 Revision Process and Interpretation of Original Article 9' (1999) 31 *UCC LJ* 261 at 287–92.

[102] For the law in England see *Hendy Lennox (Industrial Engines) Ltd* v. *Grahame Puttick Ltd* [1984] 1 WLR 485.

which is perfected by compliance with the requirements of a certificate-of-title statute such as a motor-vehicle registration-of-ownership statute. A secured party that removes an accession from other goods is required promptly to reimburse any holder(s) of a competing interest in the goods, other than the debtor, for the cost of repair of any physical injury to the whole of the other goods. 'Accession' is defined in Article 9-102 as meaning goods that are physically united with other goods in such a manner that the identity of the original goods is not lost. Article 9-336 deals with commingled goods, and these are defined as goods that are physically united with other goods in such a manner that their identity is lost in a product or mass. A security interest may attach to a product or mass that results when goods become commingled goods.[103] If a security interest in collateral is perfected before the collateral becomes commingled goods, the security interest that attaches to the product or mass is perfected. If more than one security interest is perfected, the security interests rank equally in proportion to the value of the collateral at the time that it becomes commingled goods.

Comparisons of Article 9 with English law

At the outset of this chapter, the principal differences between Article 9 and the English law of security interests were identified as lying in the more extensive filing or registration obligations contained in Article 9 and, allied to this, a greater Article 9 preference for functionalism over formalism.[104] In England, the requirement to register with Companies House details of certain charges created by a company was first introduced by section 14 Companies Act 1900.[105] This provision laid down a requirement to register in respect of four categories of charges: a charge for the purpose of securing any issue of debentures; a charge on uncalled capital of the company; a charge created or evidenced by an instrument which, if executed by an individual, would require registration as a bill of sale; and a floating charge on the undertaking or property of the company.

---

[103] For the position in England see *Borden* v. *Scottish Timber Products Ltd* [1981] Ch 25.

[104] See generally Iwan Davies 'The Reform of Personal Property Security Law: Can Article 9 of the US Commercial Code be a Precedent?' (1988) 37 *ICLQ* 465.

[105] This follows the recommendations of the 1895 Davey Committee on Company Law Amendment. There were existing obligations, dating from 1862, on a company to keep a register of mortgages and charges at its own registered office, and these provisions still survive in the Companies Act 1985. In a number of cases, however, it was held that failure to comply with the provisions in respect of an internal register did not invalidate the charge, and the provisions had become something of a dead letter. As the Davey report pointed out at para. 47: 'Many companies, even amongst the largest and best-managed, keep no register at all.'

The list of charges requiring registration has been added to over the years. Charges on any land, wherever situated, or any interest therein, and charges on book debts of the company became registrable in 1907.[106] In 1928 there was another extension of the ambit of the registrable charge, with charges on calls made but not paid, on a ship or any share in a ship, and a charge on goodwill, patents, trade marks and copyright becoming subject to the registration obligation.[107] Charges on aircraft were brought within the scope of the obligation by the Mortgaging of Aircraft Order 1972.[108]

Despite these modifications, it is possible to discern essential features of the scheme introduced in 1900 which have remained unchanged.[109] Registration is a requirement imposed in respect of only a limited category of enumerated charges. Certain particulars of the charge as to date of creation, amount secured, property charged and persons entitled thereto, together with the instrument of charge, must be delivered to the registrar of companies within twenty-one days of the date of creation of the charge. The registrar compares the instrument of charge with the filed particulars and once satisfied that everything is in order issues a certificate of due registration which is stated in the legislation to be conclusive evidence that all the requirements as to registration have been complied with. An unregistered but registrable charge becomes void against a certain stated class of persons, namely the liquidator, administrator and secured creditors of the company. There is a facility for registration out of time but this necessitates an application to the court. It should be stressed that while registration is not per se a reference point for determining priorities, the holder of an unregistered but registrable charge is reduced to the ranks of unsecured creditors in the event of the company creating the charge going into liquidation. There is provision for a certificate of due registration issued by the registrar which is stated to be conclusive evidence that all the requirements of the statute as to registration have been complied with. There is a requirement to submit the original instrument of charge along with relevant particulars of the charge to the registrar of companies.[110] The registrar compares the instrument with the particulars submitted, and if there is a correspondence issues a certificate of due registration. While the system has been fine-tuned over the years there are still major

---

[106] Companies Act 1907, s 10.
[107] Companies Act 1928, s 43.   [108] SI No. 1268 of 1972.
[109] For a detailed historical account of the development of the company charge registration provisions see J. De Lacy 'Reflections on the Ambit and Reform of the Part 12 of the Companies Act 1985 and the Doctrine of Constructive Notice' in J. De Lacy ed. *The Reform of United Kingdom Company Law* (Cavendish, 2002) at p. 333.
[110] For more details on the mechanics of registration see chap. 5 below.

shortcomings in that registration is required only of a specific enumerated list of charges, and the time of registration is not a reference point
for determining priorities.

There have been many calls for reform of Part 12 Companies Act 1985
although some of these reform proposals have been at the level of detailed
fine-tuning. A new registration regime was contained in Part 4 of the
Companies Act 1989 but Part 4 has not been implemented. Part 4 draws
on Part 3 of the 1989 Diamond report commissioned by the Department
of Trade and Industry which contained suggestions for immediate interim
changes in the company-charge sphere.[111] The Companies Act 1989 went
for interim reform but what eventually emerged onto the statute book was
introduced only at a very late stage of the parliamentary process. Legislative clauses already widely consulted upon were dropped in favour of
clauses that had not been the subject of any consultation. The end result
was highly technical legislation that may not have been practically workable.[112] A major idea behind Part 4 Companies Act 1989 appears to have
been to alleviate the administrative burden on the registrar of companies.
Henceforth, there was to be no obligation to submit the original instrument of charge and hence no checking of particulars and no conclusive
certificate of due registration. To offset the possibility of a loss of accuracy
in the register a chargee was precluded from asserting rights conferred
by the charging instrument in excess of those referred to in the particulars delivered for registration. There was no enthusiasm, however, in the
commercial world for implementation of Part 4 partly because it was felt
that the provisions might affect the marketability of secured debt. Consequently, Part 4 has not been implemented. The Company Law Review
Steering Group in its final report once again, however, puts the issue of
more fundamental reform of the English law of security interests back
on the agenda.[113] The proposals made by the Company Law Review
Steering Group in relation to registration of company charges are clearly
consistent with Article 9 – notice filing and the time of registration being
used to determine priorities. The Steering Group recognised, though,
that it would not be sensible to consider a notice-filing system for company charges without at the same time considering a similar system for
all charges over personal property and for functionally equivalent legal

---

[111] Diamond report at p. 14.
[112] See generally G. McCormack *Registration of Company Charges* (Sweet & Maxwell, 1994)
at p. 28.
[113] *Modern Company Law*. The initial consultation document from the Company Law Review Steering Group 'Registration of Company Charges', in October 2000 recommended, however, only modest changes to the existing system. For criticism of the
approach adopted by the Steering Group see De Lacy 'Reflections' at p. 333.

devices. The Law Commission developed the recommendations of the Company Law Review Steering Group for the introduction of a notice-filing system as well as its eventual extension to cover quasi-securities.[114] The changes would culminate in a comprehensive restatement of the law of security interests and the enactment of an Article 9 equivalent in England. If England moved over to an Article 9-type system it would probably bring in its wake three distinct advantages: firstly, the end – or the beginning of the end – of compartmentalisation; secondly, less complexity in the law in some respects; and thirdly, more rational rules for determining priorities between competing security interests.[115] These advantages and some possible disadvantages will be considered in the next chapter.

Conclusion

A distinguished civil lawyer, Professor Ulrich Drobnig, has depicted Article 9 as being the 'most modernised, rational and comprehensive system of security interests in the present world'.[116] The wide, majestic sweep of Article 9 is seen in its validation of what the Americans refer to as a shifting lien on changing collateral. Pre-Article 9 US law did not recognise the floating charge as such with the Supreme Court holding in *Benedict v. Ratner* that a security interest over property was incompatible with the debtor's freedom to dispose of that property in the ordinary

---

[114] *Registration of Security Interests.* The Scottish Law Commission, however, has not gone down the route of recommending Article 9-type reform in Scotland: see *Registration of Rights in Security by Companies* (October 2002) available at www.scotlawcom.gov.uk. The Scottish law of security interests, given the Scottish civil-law inheritance, differs significantly from its English counterpart. For example, it was only through statutory intervention in 1961 that the floating charge was recognised in Scotland: see generally G. Gretton 'Registration of Company Charges' (2002) 6 *Edinburgh Law Review* 146. The Scottish Law Commission states at pp. 8–9 of its discussion paper:

> Our own terms of reference do not embrace notice filing. Existing models of notice filing presuppose Anglo-American property law and turn on distinctions between creation, attachment and perfection which are unknown in Scots law or in other systems drawn from the Germanic stream of the civil law tradition. A system of notice filing suited to English property law could not readily be modified or adapted to accommodate the very different structures and concepts of Scots property law.

[115] See generally R. Goode 'The Modernisation of Personal Property Security Law' (1994) 100 *LQR* 234; M. Bridge 'Form, Substance and Innovation in Personal Property Security Law' [1992] *JBL* 1.

[116] Comment quoted by A. Diamond 'The Reform of the Law of Security Interests' (1989) 42 *CLP* 231 at 241. The comment comes from the report *Study on Security Interests* that Professor Drobnig prepared for UNCITRAL: see *UNCITRAL Yearbook* (1977) vol. 8, p. 171 at s 2.6.2.3.

course of business. This decision proved unsatisfactory for business and the credit industry employed a variety of devices to circumvent the effect of the ruling. The enactment of Article 9 put paid to the avoidance industry with its broad proclamation that a security interest over property and freedom on the part of the debtor to dispose of the self-same property in the ordinary course of business were not mutually incompatible. Article 9 brings order and coherence to the law of security. It contains comprehensive or filing obligations and catches 'quasi-security', i.e. functionally equivalent legal devices such as the factoring of receivables and reservation-of-title clauses in sale-of-goods contracts. The difference between security interests strictly so-called and the use of absolute title as security remains, however, in other legal contexts such as tax, securitisation and bankruptcy.[117]

On the other hand, while Article 9 may have a greater conceptual unity than the law applicable to security interests in England it is highly questionable whether it is any less complex. This is particularly so given the recent revision of Article 9, which has significantly added to its length and complexity. The revised Article 9 is certainly not simple and straightforward in its drafting. It is by no means obvious that clarity in communication – an important goal of legislative policy – has necessarily been better achieved in the United States than in England.[118] All that one may safely say on this score is that neither Article 9 nor any legislative restatement of the English position would win any prizes for literary elegance or the quality of the prose. If England moved over to an Article 9-type legal regime, this would have adverse consequences for certain categories of creditors, but above all, the major impediment is likely to be the inertia factor.[119]

---

[117] According to the UCC Permanent Editorial Board Commentary No. 14 inclusion of the sale of accounts within Article 9 does not turn a sale into a non-sale. As Professor Reiley explains in 'The Article 9 Revision Process' at 274:

> There is no residual interest in a sold asset to be included in the seller's bankruptcy estate. If the buyer is a true buyer, liens created by the seller will be cut off, not subordinated to, the buyer's interest. A buyer in an outright sale is not accountable for any surplus generated when the account or chattel paper is paid off.

[118] This is despite the best efforts of the Article 9 drafters to achieve an easily understood text: see generally L. Del Duca, V. DeLiberato, D. Hostetter, K. Kettering and S. Weise 'Simplification in Drafting – the UCC Article 9 Experience' (1999) 74 *Chicago-Kent L Rev* 1309.

[119] See the comment by J. Ziegel 'Canadian Perspectives on How Far is Article 9 Exportable?' (1996) 27 *Can Bus LJ* 226 at 231: 'Non-banking financiers also have a vested interest in maintaining the status quo since there is a general aversion in the United Kingdom to expanding existing registration requirements to hire-purchase and conditional sale agreements and to various forms of consignment and discounting agreements for the financing of inventory and accounts receivable.'

The present system works tolerably well[120] and the inherent conservatism of the English legal profession in the face of major threatened change should not be underestimated. The barriers to reforms and the proposals for Article 9-type reforms made by the Law Commission will be considered in the next chapter.

---

[120] According to P. Ali *The Law of Secured Finance* (Oxford University Press, 2002) at p. 144 the present regime has proved 'surprisingly resilient' in the face of proposals by various law-reform bodies.

4 Implications of Article 9-type reforms for the English law of security interests

There would be both advantages and disadvantages in the transformation to an Article 9-type regime as far as current English law is concerned. This is a somewhat obvious point. In the previous chapter three advantages were identified as being firstly the end of compartmentalisation, or at least the beginning of the end of compartmentalisation; secondly, removal of complexities; and thirdly, simpler and more rationally based priority rules. To this could be added a fourth: the greater convenience and flexibility of notice filing over transaction filing. Two other factors might also be mentioned, i.e. clarification of the position of purchasers of charged property and also abolition of the floating charge, with the latter being seen as a possible source of confusion and obfuscation.

The Law Commission consultation paper on *Registration of Security Interests* highlighted the various deficiencies in English law and particularly emphasised the failings in the current registration of company charges regime. Nevertheless, there would be losers in a straightforward move to an Article 9 system. The Law Commission proposals were framed in such a way as to minimise the impact on groups such as preferential creditors that might otherwise be prejudicially affected by the changeover. The proposals, however, generate their own complications, in particular by the retention of the floating charge that does not feature under Article 9. The merits and demerits of Article 9 for England will be canvassed in this chapter, with special attention being paid to the Law Commission proposals and also the position of the floating charge under a new dispensation.

Advantages of an Article 9-type regime for English law: an end to compartmentalisation

The problem of compartmentalisation or lack of a functional basis in English law has often been highlighted. The point is that transactions that are essentially similar in nature are treated in very different ways by the law, and this has the effect of complicating the legal issues quite unnecessarily.[1] For example, there is often quite a narrow line in practice between the creation of a charge over debts and an undisclosed factoring arrangement involving the self-same debts, but nevertheless the difference in terms of legal consequences is quite profound.[2] The first type of transaction requires registration whereas the second does not. Likewise with retention-of-title clauses where, particularly with the most complex variety of clauses, the courts expend great time and effort in deciding whether the transaction in question constitutes a registrable charge.[3] If the question is answered in the affirmative then the clause will be struck down for non-registration in the event of the buyer's liquidation, whereas if it is answered negatively then the arrangement will be upheld notwithstanding the absence of registration.

On the other hand, not all commentators and creditors would necessarily welcome an end to compartmentalisation. For instance, Article 9 undoubtedly weakens the position of a conditional seller compared with the position prevailing in England. Firstly, the seller has to file notice to protect his interest whereas under the English position 'simple' and 'current account' retention-of-title clauses are not the subject of any requirement of registration. Secondly, the retention-of-title claimant in English law, in so far as the clause is valid, enjoys super-priority status ranking ahead of other creditors with secured claims against the assets that form the subject matter of the retention-of-title clause. Under Article 9, on the other hand, the priority position of the supplier can be preserved only if the latter fulfils the special perfection requirements applicable to PMSIs, and these vary depending on whether the collateral is classed as 'inventory' or 'capital equipment'.

Removal of complexities and simpler priority rules

Another criticism of English law that is often made is of its complexity. For example, influential commentators have suggested that the compartmentalisation of the English law of security interests gives rise to a law that is both complex and uncertain and, in consequence, perfectly legitimate business activities are attended with unnecessary expense and delay.[4]

---

[1] A. Diamond, *A Review of Security Interests in Property* (1989), at pp. 31–3.

[2] *Lloyds & Scottish Finance* v. *Cyril Lord Carpet Sales Ltd* [1992] BCLC 609.

[3] See e.g. *Pfeiffer Weinkellerei-Weineinkauf Gmbh* v. *Arbuthnot Factors Ltd* [1988] 1 WLR 150; *Compaq Computer Ltd* v. *Abercorn Group Ltd* [1991] BCC 484; *Borden* v. *Scottish Timber Products Ltd* [1981] Ch 25; *Re Peachdart Ltd* [1984] Ch 131.

[4] Diamond report at pp. 31–3. Diamond concluded by saying that 'there would be major advantages in Great Britain in adopting a new law that was functional, addressed itself directly to known problems and provided clear solutions, free from historical anomalies and legal fictions'.

If there is one small benefit that the changeover to an Article 9 model might provide it is to do away with the complicated 'tacking' rules. Under Article 9, priorities between different security interests are generally resolved on the basis of a simple first-to-file-prevails principle, and priority extends to subsequent advances made by the secured party having priority. In England, on the other hand, the position governing priority of subsequent advances is somewhat complex. As far as security over personal property is concerned, matters are regulated by section 94 Law of Property Act 1925 which gives a prior chargee the right in three circumstances to make further advances that rank in priority to intervening chargeholders. These are:

(a) where an arrangement has been made to that effect with the subsequent chargees;
(b) if the prior chargee had no notice of the subsequent charges at the time that the further advance was made;
(c) where the charge imposes an obligation on him to make further advances.

The problem of complexity in determining priorities is particularly acute, with practitioners often complaining that confusion and obscurity reign in this area of English law – so much so that negotiated contractual solutions among the different secured parties are often the only answer.[5] A regime modelled on Article 9 would replace the present complexities of English law with a superficially more straightforward 'first-to-file' rule. It is worth noting, however, that there are exceptions to the general Article 9 principle and these exceptions carry their own complexities. Firstly, there is an exception in the case of purchase-money security interests (PMSIs) which will rank ahead of a prior security interest with an after-acquired property clause. Secondly, there are different priority rules for different types of collateral and in certain circumstances 'control' may be more effective than registration.[6]

---

[5] As Richard Calnan of Norton Rose has stated ('Taking Security in England' in M. Bridge and R. Stevens eds. *Cross-Border Security and Insolvency* (Oxford University Press, 2001) p. 17 at p. 33:

> The priority rules are a potential minefield for secured creditors. The rules vary depending on the nature of the assets concerned, floating charges are governed by a different set of rules altogether, and there is yet another set of rules for money lent after the creditor has received notice of a subsequent charge. Even if the creditor knows which set of rules to apply, many of them depend on matters of fact, such as the extent to which the creditor has actual or constructive notice, which makes it very difficult to be confident of the outcome of any dispute. For all these reasons, it is common practice for secured creditors to enter into a priority agreement with any other secured creditor of which they become aware.

[6] Article 9-327–30.

Notwithstanding these points, the advantages of the Article 9 priority rules have often been stressed by law reformers including the Law Commission. In the consultation paper on *Registration of Security Interests* it recommended that all types of charge over property, whether fixed or floating, should be registrable under a system of notice filing and that, irrespective of the nature of the charge, priorities between one or more charges over the same property should generally be determined on the basis that the first to file has priority.[7] This proposal cuts through a lot of current complications. At the moment, and as a matter of broad principle, a duly registered floating charge ranks after a duly registered fixed charge irrespective of the respective dates of creation of the two charges.[8] A floating charge, however, has priority over a subsequent fixed charge, assuming that both charges have been duly registered where the subsequent fixed-charge holder has actual notice of a restrictive clause in the earlier floating charge.[9] A restrictive or negative pledge clause is a provision which prohibits the creation of subsequent fixed charges ranking prior to, or *pari passu* with, the earlier floating charge. It is actual, and not just constructive notice, of a restrictive clause in the floating-charge debenture that is required before the priority of a fixed-charge holder is displaced in favour of a floating-charge holder. In *G & T Earle Ltd* v. *Hemsworth Rural District Council* Wright J said:[10]

The debentures having been duly registered . . . the plaintiffs, like all the world, are deemed to have constructive notice of the fact that there are debentures. But it has never been held that the mere fact that persons in the position of the plaintiffs

---

[7] See Law Commission Consultation Paper No. 164 *Registration of Security Interests* (July 2002) at para. 4.122 and following paragraphs.

[8] A floating charge permits a company to carry on business in the ordinary way in so far as the class of assets charged is concerned. This would include the creation of fixed charges in the ordinary course of business. For statements on the ingredients of a floating charge see the judgment of Romer LJ in *Re Yorkshire Woolcombers Association Ltd* [1903] 2 Ch 284 and the famous 'ambulatory' metaphor employed by Lord Macnaghten in the House of Lords in that case which is reported under the name *Illingsworth* v. *Houldsworth* [1904] AC 355 at 358.

[9] For criticism of knowledge based priority systems see D. Baird and T. Jackson 'Information, Uncertainty and the Transfer of Property' (1984) 13 *J Legal Stud* 299 at 314:

> An inquiry into knowledge is likely to be expensive and time consuming. It is simply much easier to live in a world in which everyone knows that he must comply with a few simple formalities or lose than to live in a world where the validity of someone's property rights turns on whether certain individuals had knowledge at some particular time in the past. Those who are required to make appropriate filings, in the main, either are professionals or engage the services of professionals. We think it likely that everyone is ultimately better off with a clear rule than with a legal regime that is somewhat more finely tuned but much more expensive to operate. Ferreting out those who took with knowledge despite a defective filing generally is not worth the uncertainty and the litigation it generates.

[10] (1928) 44 TLR 605.

have constructive notice of the existence of debentures also affects them with constructive notice of the actual terms of the debentures or that the debentures are subject to the restrictive condition to which these debentures were subject. No doubt it is quite common for debentures to be subject to this limiting condition as to further charges, but that fact is not enough in itself to operate as constructive notice of the actual terms of any particular set of debentures.

More recently, the application of the constructive-notice doctrine in this context was rejected by the Irish Supreme Court in *Welsh* v. *Bowmaker (Ireland) Ltd*[11] after a full review of the authorities. The practice of submitting details of a negative pledge clause among the particulars of a charge delivered for registration does not, it appears, automatically mean that a subsequent fixed-charge holder has notice of the negative pledge clause though registration of the clause is something from which notice may be inferred.[12] Floating-charge holders have endeavoured to rely on the constructive-notice doctrine in this sphere but the prevailing analysis is that registration constitutes constructive notice of matters in relation to which registration is required rather than of what might be termed 'optional extras'.[13] The Companies Act 1989 legislated for details of a negative pledge clause to become compulsorily registrable, and this provision would have impacted on the question of priorities, but the provision was never brought into force.[14] In practice, however, a bank which is thinking about making a secured loan to a corporate borrower will consult the register of charges and through this process details of previous secured borrowings by the company should emerge. If details of a restrictive clause appear on the register then the subsequent secured lender will actually learn of their existence on consulting the register.

If a fixed-charge holder has priority over a floating-charge holder in a particular case because the fixed-charge holder has actual notice of a restrictive clause then this gives rise to a circularity problem that also implicates the preferential creditors who, in terms of priorities, are in between the fixed and floating charges. The issue has provoked judicial disagreement with one view suggesting that, by coming after the floating charge, the fixed charge should therefore come after the preferential

---

[11] [1980] IR 251.

[12] But for a different view see J. Farrar 'The Crystallisation of the Floating Charge'(1976) 40 *Conv* (NS) 397 who argues for the existence of inferred actual knowledge rather than constructive knowledge.

[13] See also *Re Standard Machine Co. Ltd* (1906) 95 LT 829 and *Wilson* v. *Kelland* [1910] 2 Ch 306. See also the decision of the Hong Kong High Court in *ABN AMRO Bank NV* v. *Chiyu Banking Corp. Ltd* [2000] 3 HKC 381 which holds that registration of a floating charge constitutes constructive notice of the charge but not of any restrictive provision therein contained since particulars of such a provision are not required to be registered under the Hong Kong Companies Ordinance.

[14] The recommendations for change which led to the provisions in the Companies Act are set out in the DTI-commissioned 1989 Diamond report at pp. 124–5.

creditors.[15] Another possible solution is to apply the doctrine of subrogation and to hold that, by virtue of the altered priorities between them, the floating-charge holder stands in the shoes of the fixed-charge holder to the extent of the amount secured by the fixed charge and therefore the floating-charge holder will be paid ahead of preferential creditors by the degree to which liabilities are secured by a fixed charge.[16]

One of the major objectives of the Law Commission proposals is to devise a simpler system of priority determined principally by the date of filing. Consequently, the new legislation, in its view, should provide that a floating charge should no longer give a company authority to create subsequent fixed charges that automatically get priority over an earlier floating charge.[17] The first-to-file-has-priority principle is a welcome change from the complexity of the present position. Moreover, the special position accorded purchase-money security interests should help to ensure that a debtor is not restricted to the initial financier and may tap alternative sources of finance. The first creditor on the scene will not have a security monopoly over the assets of the debtor. Later creditors will be able to obtain priority in respect of their advance if the advance is specifically tied to the acquisition of new assets.[18]

The greater convenience of notice filing

The broad thrust of the Law Commission consultation paper is that English law should move over to a system of notice filing, first developed in the US under Article 9 of the UCC[19] and then refined in personal property security legislation in the common-law provinces of Canada and more recently in New Zealand with the Personal Property Securities Act 1999.[20] Under the present Part 12 Companies Act 1985 once a charge

---

[15] *Re Portbase Clothing Ltd* [1993] Ch 388. On the other hand, the court suggested that a different result would follow if the respective secured parties had agreed to exchange their proprietary rights. For criticism of the reasoning in *Portbase* see R. Goode *Principles of Corporate Insolvency Law* (Sweet & Maxwell, 2nd edn. 1997) at pp. 170–1.

[16] See *Re Woodroffes (Musical Instruments) Ltd* [1986] Ch 366.

[17] Law Commission *Registration of Security Interests* at para 4.142.

[18] For criticism of purchase-money super-priority see W. J. Gough *Company Charges* (Butterworths, 2nd edn. 1996) at p. 436.

[19] See generally on notice filing D. Baird 'Notice Filing and the Problem of Ostensible Ownership' (1983) 12 *J Legal Stud* 53; and see also G. McCormack 'Notice Filing versus Transaction Filing – A Comparison of the English and US Law of Security Interests' [2002] *Insolvency Lawyer* 166.

[20] For up-to-date information on the New Zealand legislation see the website www.ppsr.govt.nz/: and see generally M. Gedye, R. Cuming and R. Wood *Personal Property Securities in New Zealand* (Thomson, 2002); L. Widdup and L. Mayne *Personal Property Securities Act: A Conceptual Approach* (Butterworths, rev. edn. 2002); B. Allan *Guidebook to the New Zealand Personal Property Securities Law* (CCH, 2002).

has been created, particulars of the charge along with the instrument of charge must be delivered to the registrar of companies within twenty-one days of creation, and if this is not done the charge is invalid in the event of the corporate borrower going into liquidation. The legislation is premised on the assumption that the registrar compares the filed particulars with the charging instrument and if satisfied that there is a concordance issues a certificate of due registration, which is stated to be conclusive evidence that all the requirements of the Act as to registration have been complied with.[21] Under the notice-filing system, however, only a bare-bones statement needs to be submitted, which states that the lender either has taken or intends to take a security interest in the debtor's property.

There are definite advantages in moving over to a system of notice filing, which stem from deep-rooted problems with the existing process.[22] For a start the process is a burdensome, time-consuming one and the duties imposed on the staff at Companies House may not be ones that are capable of easy fulfilment.[23] Secondly, there is not much flexibility in the procedure as far as the secured lender is concerned. There is no procedure whereby registration may be achieved in advance of negotiations for a loan agreement, and moreover, a single filing cannot cover more than one instrument of charge. Thirdly, the time of registration does not determine priorities if there is more than one charge over the same property. The Law Commission scheme would eliminate these disadvantages and enable notice to be filed in advance of the actual conclusion of a security agreement with priorities set by a simple first-to-file rule subject to an exception for PMSIs.[24]

The effect of an Article 9 regime on purchasers of property that has been used as security

It has sometimes been suggested that the change to an Article 9 regime would make clearer the position of purchasers of secured property.[25] For example, in the Diamond report it is said that under current English

---

[21] It should be noted that this is not an inevitable feature of English-based registration systems. Under section 131 Singapore Companies Act 1993, which is modelled on the English legislation, only the prescribed particulars have to be submitted though the registrar may request that the instrument should be produced for inspection.

[22] See generally Law Commission *Registration of Security Interests* at pp. 48–50.

[23] For a discussion of possible liability on the part of the registrar for mistakes made in the registration process see the comments of Lightman J in *Grove* v. *Advantage Healthcare (T10) Ltd* [2000] 1 BCLC 661 at 665.

[24] Law Commission *Registration of Security Interests* at para. 4.110. The detailed merits of notice filing versus the present English system of transaction filing will be considered in chapter 5.

[25] See Diamond report at pp. 31–3.

law the effect of security interests on purchasers may be difficult to determine and also potentially prejudicial.[26] It is not altogether clear, however, whether the protection afforded purchasers differs significantly between England and the US.

Article 9-317 deals with the position of buyers and unperfected security interests. According to the provision a buyer takes free of a security interest if the buyer gives value and receives delivery of the collateral without knowledge of the security interest and before it is perfected. Article 9-320 deals with the position of buyers and perfected security interests and provides that a buyer in ordinary course of business takes free of a security interest created by the buyer's seller, even if the security interest is perfected and the buyer knows of its existence. The effect of Article 1-201 is, however, to limit the apparent protection afforded by Article 9-320. 'Buyer in ordinary course of business' is defined as meaning a person that buys goods in good faith and without knowledge that the sale violates the rights of another person in the goods, and in the ordinary course from a person, other than pawnbroker, in the business of selling goods of that kind. The end result of these somewhat convoluted definitions is that a buyer takes free of an existing security interest if the buyer merely knows that a security interest covers the goods but takes subject to the same if the buyer knows additionally that the sale violates a term in the agreement with the secured party. There are also special provisions in Article 9-320 to protect buyers of consumer goods.

In England, property that is held by a company subject to a floating charge may be disposed of by the company in the ordinary course of business free from the security interest. The company, by virtue of the floating charge, has an implied authority to dispose of goods in this way. Moreover, it appears that a subsequent assignee of property that is the subject matter of a registered charge takes subject to the rights of the charge holder, where particulars of the charge have been duly registered. The assignee, however, has to be a person who might reasonably have been expected to search the register, whether by reason of prior dealings between the parties or otherwise. If the subsequent assignee is not such a person, and the buyer of goods in the ordinary course of business does not come within the category, then the assignee ranks ahead of the prior security interest. This principle was applied by Neill J in *Feuer Leather Corporation* v. *Frank Johnstone & Sons*[27] who held that a purchaser will not be affected in a commercial transaction by constructive notice. He

---

[26] *Ibid.* at pp. 32–3.
[27] [1981] Com LR 251. For the Court of Appeal decision see [1983] Com LR 12.

emphasised the fact that there was no general duty on a buyer of goods in an ordinary commercial transaction to make inquiries as to the right of the seller to dispose of the goods.[28] The celebrated comments of Lindley LJ in *Manchester Trust* v. *Furness*[29] also come to mind in this context. He said:[30]

The equitable doctrines of constructive notice are common enough in dealing with land and estates, with which the Court are familiar; but there have been repeated protests against the introduction into commercial transactions of anything like an extension of those doctrines, and the protest is founded on perfect good sense. In dealing with estates in land title is everything, and it can be leisurely investigated; in commercial transactions possession is everything and there is not time to investigate title; and if we were to extend the doctrine of constructive notice to commercial transactions we should be doing infinite mischief and paralysing the trade of the country.

It must be said, however, that there is a paucity of authority, still less modern authority, on this particular point but such authority as there is tends to restrict the ambit of the doctrine of constructive notice to subsequent security interest holders and not to extend it to trade purchasers. For instance, in *Channel Airways Ltd* v. *Manchester Corp.*[31] Forbes J said: 'I do not find that the mere registration of a debenture . . . amounts to notice to all the world.' As Dr De Lacy argues, the effects of applying a doctrine of constructive notice to 'all the world' are not edifying, for we cannot really expect purchasers in the ordinary course of business to search the register prior to dealing.[32]

Just to summarise, a buyer in an Article 9 context takes free of a security interest unless it knows that the sale contravenes the terms-of-security agreement. The situation in England is more or less the same. Buyers take free of floating charges and also of fixed charges provided that they do not actually know of the latter's existence. The fixed charge is essentially a security agreement that prohibits the disposition of assets subject to it in the ordinary course of business. So this is an area where there is strong similarity between the existing law in England and the US. It is not clear

---

[28] See also *Greer* v. *Downs Supply Co.* [1927] 2 KB 28; *Goodyear Tyre & Rubber Co.* v. *Lancashire Batteries* [1958] 1 WLR 857; *Wilts United Dairies* v. *Thomas Robinson Sons & Co.* [1957] RPC 220; *Panchaud Freres SA* v. *Etablissements General Grain Co* [1970] 1 Lloyds Rep 53; *Worcester Works Finance* v. *Cooden Engineering Co.* [1972] 1 QB 210.

[29] [1895] 2 QB 539.   [30] *Ibid.* at 551–2.

[31] [1974] 1 Lloyds Rep 456 at 459 and see also the statement of Slade J in *Siebe Gorman & Co* v. *Barclays Bank Ltd* [1979] 2 Lloyds Rep 142 at 160 that registration 'may by itself serve to give subsequent mortgages constructive notice'.

[32] See J. De Lacy 'Ambit and Reform of Part 12 Companies Act 1985' in J. De Lacy ed. *The Reform of United Kingdom Company Law* (Cavendish, 2002) at p. 376.

whether the move to an Article 9 regime would be beneficial to this jurisdiction apart from the clarity of having the law set out in statutory form.[33]

The floating charge and 'reformed' personal property security law

One of the greatest contributions of English lawyers to the creation of a modern system of secured transactions law has been in the development of the floating charge – or universal business charge – which makes it possible to create a security interest in the entirety of a company's business operations.[34] The charge is over a class of assets and the borrower is free to dispose of the assets in the ordinary course of business until some event takes place which brings about the intervention of the charge holder. It is submitted that the benefits of the floating charge in terms of comprehensiveness, lack of formalities and ease of use could be retained if English law moved over to an Article 9-type system.[35] Indeed, the disappearance of the floating charge might be one advantage of the adoption of a radically new system of secured-transactions law. The floating charge is an instrument of great power but perhaps of even greater mystery.[36] Its existence may in fact puzzle foreign observers and cloud understanding of this branch of law by non-specialists. On the other hand, the floating charge was undoubtedly a great invention and its death would be mourned by many. Consequently, the disappearance of the floating charge could not be considered to be an unalloyed blessing. Article 9 has the functional equivalent, but not the English-style floating charge with all its trappings.

---

[33] See generally Law Commission *Registration of Security Interests* at pp. 112–18. The Law Commission in a number of fairly detailed recommendations suggested provisionally that a buyer should not be bound by security interests in goods (other than those that are uniquely identifiable) created by prior owners. The Law Commission also invited comment from consultees on whether a buyer of capital equipment should be expected to search the register.

[34] See generally for a comparative perspective P. Wood *Comparative Law of Security and Guarantees* (Sweet & Maxwell, 1995).

[35] Professor Sir Roy Goode has long propounded this view, arguing that 'a unified concept of security interests in which rules of attachment, perfection and priority are clearly laid out and are designed to produce results that are fair in the typical case is greatly preferable to the uncodified and unsystematised collocation of rules we have painfully developed in this country over the past century': see 'The Exodus of the Floating Charge' in D. Feldman and F. Meisel eds. *Corporate and Commercial Law: Modern Developments* (Lloyds of London Press, 1996) chap. 10 at pp. 202–3.

[36] For accounts of the juridical nature of the floating charge see E. Ferran 'Floating Charges – the Nature of the Security' [1988] *CLJ* 213; S. Worthington 'Floating Charges – an Alternative Theory' [1994] *CLJ* 81; K. Naser 'The Juridical Basis of the Floating Charge' (1994) 15 *Co Law* 11; R. Gregory and P. Walton 'Fixed Charges over Changing Assets – the Possession and Control Heresy' [1998] *CFILR* 68; L. Gullifer 'Will the Law Commission Sink the Floating Charge' [2003] *LMCLQ* 125.

As discussed in the previous chapter, pre-Article 9 US law did not have any equivalent of the floating charge,[37] and essentially there were two grounds for this lack of recognition. Firstly, there was the conceptual point that a debtor could not create a security interest over future property, i.e. property that he did not yet own; and secondly, there was the more instrumental argument that a debtor should have a cushion of free assets to which general creditors were entitled to look for payment. These points come through in various decisions from the courts in New York, including *Zartman* v. *First National Bank of Waterloo*.[38] This is a case where a manufacturer mortgaged all its property, both real and personal, including after-acquired personal property, to secure its negotiable bonds. The manufacturer retained possession of the property, for its own use and benefit, until it defaulted on the mortgage. The question arose whether the mortgage covered 'shifting' assets. The court answered not: firstly, because a man cannot grant what he does not own, actually or potentially; and secondly, because the mortgagor's freedom of disposition permitted by the mortgage rendered the security fraudulent as against other creditors.

The *Zartman* line of authority was confirmed by the United States Supreme Court in *Benedict* v. *Ratner*[39] but over time a sophisticated avoidance industry developed so as to permit large-scale receivables and other financing.[40] Moreover, in the US most types of personal property, whether tangible or intangible, became available as collateral to secure loans as a result of separate legislative initiatives in the individual states.[41] It was often the case, however, that in a single state there might be a number of distinct filing systems, with each of these covering separate security devices. In the case of some filing systems, filing could be accomplished on a state-wide basis whereas with respect to others filing might be done locally or on a county basis. Each of these separate systems would have to be checked to discover the debtor's credit history and the possible existence of prior encumbrances.[42]

---

[37] The progenitor of Article 9, Professor Grant Gilmore, has argued that if floating charges had been accepted in the US, then some of the pressure for change that brought about Article 9 would have been absent: see *Security Interests in Personal Property* (Little Brown, 1965) at pp. 359–61.

[38] (1907) 189 NY 267.

[39] See generally J. O. Honnold, S. L. Harris and C. W. Mooney *Security Interests in Personal Property* (Foundation Press, 3rd edn. 2001) at pp. 452–6.

[40] See generally Gilmore *Security Interests in Personal Property*, chaps. 1–8.

[41] Article 9 has been described as 'an anthological collection of the most celebrated security law controversies of the preceding forty years' in Grant Gilmore 'Security Law, Formalism and Article 9' (1968) 47 *Nebraska LR* 659 at 671.

[42] See the Official Comment attached to the 1972 version of Article 9-101. Grant Gilmore notes in *Security Interests in Personal Property* at p. 463:

Article 9 rationalised and systematised by a straightforward provision that permitted the creation of a 'floating' security interest[43] in a shifting subject matter.[44] The English floating charge has been likened to a charge over a fund of assets and the Article 9 security interest has been analogised in similar terms.[45] Essentially Article 9 recognised that there was no necessary incompatibility between a fixed security interest and the debtor's freedom to dispose of the charged assets in the ordinary course of business. Article 9-205 concretises this proposition, stating that a security interest is not invalid or fraudulent against creditors solely because

(1) the debtor has the right or ability to
    (a) use, commingle, or dispose of all or part of the collateral, including returned or repossessed goods;
    (b) collect, compromise, enforce or otherwise deal with collateral;
    (c) accept the return of collateral or make repossessions; or
    (d) use, commingle, or dispose of proceeds; or
(2) the secured party fails to require the debtor to account for proceeds or replace collateral.

So in the US there is the functional equivalent of the floating charge brought into existence by direct legislative fiat. Essentially an Article 9 security interest is a fixed charge coupled with a licence to deal. In England, if a security giver purported to dispose of assets that were the subject of a fixed charge in the ordinary course of business then this would constitute a breach of a covenant in the loan agreement, whether express or implied.[46] The security taker could appoint a receiver whether under a

---

The typical pre-Code pattern included separate filing systems for chattel mortgages, for conditional sales, for trust receipts, for factor's liens and for assignments of accounts receivable. In such a situation the expense and difficulty of making a thorough credit check are obvious. Since the filing requirements were themselves frequently obscure and tricky, the chances were good that a lender who, through his counsel, was familiar with one device would inadvertently go wrong in attempting to comply with another and fail to perfect his security interest.

[43] Grant Gilmore has said, in 'Security Law, Formalism and Article 9', at 672: 'Article 9 draftsmen argued from the premise that, under existing security law, a lender could take an enforceable interest in all of a debtor's present and future personal property to the conclusion that the new statute should provide for the accomplishment of this result in the simplest possible fashion.'

[44] R. Goode *Legal Problems of Credit and Security* (Sweet & Maxwell, 2nd edn. 1988) at p. 49.

[45] See W. Hogan 'Games Lawyers Play with the Bankruptcy Preference Challenge to Accounts and Inventory Financing' (1968) 53 *Cornell L Rev* 553 at 560, quoted in Honnold et al. *Security Interests in Personal Property* at p. 459.

[46] One commentator has talked about the 'mental block experienced by the courts in the early floating charge cases when they were quite unable to fathom the idea of a fixed mortgage or charge over trading assets coupled with a licence to dispose of those assets in the ordinary course of business': see D. McLauchlan 'Fixed Charges over Book Debts: New *Bullas* in New Zealand'(1999) 115 *LQR* 365 at 367.

provision contained in the debenture or via a court application, since the security is clearly in jeopardy. The English courts have been adamant that a floating charge is not a fixed charge coupled with a licence to deal.[47] As Buckley LJ explained in *Evans v. Rival Granite Quarries Ltd*:[48]

A floating security is not a future security, it is a present security, which presently affects all the assets of the company expressed to be included in it. On the other hand, it is not a specific security: the holder cannot affirm that the assets are specifically mortgaged to him. The assets are mortgaged in such a way that the mortgagor can deal with them without the concurrence of the mortgagee. A floating security is not a specific mortgage of the assets, plus a licence to the mortgagor to dispose of them in the course of his business but is a floating mortgage applying to every item until some event occurs or some act of the mortgagee is done which causes it to crystallise into a fixed security.

Unlike in the US, the floating charge did exist in common-law Canada, where personal property security legislation has been enacted in the footsteps of Article 9.[49] The Canadian Supreme Court in the *Sparrow* case[50] declared that the effect of the new legislation is to sweep away the distinction between fixed and floating charges as well as between legal and equitable security interests notwithstanding the fact that the security agreement used by the parties may have employed the old floating-charge terminology.[51] In the court's opinion the relevant legislation contained an implicit declaration that, as a matter of public policy, there was nothing objectionable about having a fixed charge on stock-in-trade of a debtor coupled with a licence to deal with the collateral in the ordinary course of business.

---

[47] According to P. Ali *The Law of Secured Finance* (Oxford University Press, 2002) at p. 121 the 'licence' theory of floating charges is 'now widely regarded as without any legitimate basis' but cf. R. Calnan 'Priorities between Execution Creditors and Floating Charges' (1982) 10 *NZULR* 111.

[48] [1910]2 KB 979 at 999. See also *Re Gregory Love & Co.* [1916] 1 Ch 203.

[49] See generally G. McCormack 'The Floating Charge in England and Canada' in De Lacy ed. *The Reform of United Kingdom Company Law* at p. 398.

[50] *Royal Bank of Canada v. Sparrow Electric Corp.* (1997) 143 DLR (4th) 385; on which see generally K. Davis 'Priority of Crown Claims in Insolvency' (1997) 29 *Can Bus LJ* 145.

[51] See the comment by Catherine Walsh in 'The Floating Charge is Dead: Long Live the Floating Charge' in Agasha Mugasha ed. *Perspectives on Commercial Law* (Prospect, 1999) p. 129 at p. 146:

Although the Court ultimately divided, the majority and minority opinions were ad idem on the proprietary character of the bank's PPSA security interest in the debtor's inventory: it was fixed and legal in nature . . . In a PPSA statutory regime, all security interests attach on the debtor's acquisition of rights in the collateral, regardless of whether the collateral is specific or circulating, and regardless of the scope of the debtor's licence to deal. In thus establishing a unitary attachment regime independent of the concept of crystallisation, the PPSA legislators had effectively signalled to the courts that all security interests were henceforth to be characterised as fixed and legal in their proprietary effect.

This is also the position in New Zealand where personal property security legislation suggested as a model by the Law Commission has been enacted. Lord Millett presciently remarked in *Agnew* v. *Commissioner of Inland Revenue*:[52] 'A curiosity of the case is that the distinction between fixed and floating charges, which is of great commercial importance in the United Kingdom, seems likely to disappear from the law of New Zealand when the Personal Property Security Act 1999 comes into force.'

This is not the case in England in any brave new world after implementation of the Law Commission proposals. The latter involves retention of the floating charge and preserving the importance of the distinction between fixed and floating charges. It is suggested that this approach gives rise to considerable complexities and it would be conceptually neater were English law to follow the lead set in Canada and New Zealand. In general, while there are undoubtedly certain advantages in moving over to an Article 9-type system there are also certain disadvantages, or at least people who will lose out as the result of a move to a new system. Five disadvantages could be highlighted in this regard. Firstly, there are adverse implications for execution creditors. Secondly, there are potentially adverse implications for preferential creditors. Thirdly, the issue of characterisation continues to be relevant in an Article 9-type environment. Fourthly, there are considerable transition costs in the move to a new system. Finally, there are particular difficulties with the exact scheme of reform envisaged by the Law Commission.

Implications for execution creditors

Firstly, the changeover to an Article 9 system would impact adversely on execution creditors. The full implications of Article 9 in this respect may not have been fully appreciated by the drafters of the original Article 9, though the Official Comment said that the approach in *Benedict* v. *Ratner* was rejected not because it was wrong but because it was ineffective. The principal drafter, Grant Gilmore, has commented after the event as follows:[53]

If we had listened to what the courts were trying to tell us, we might have come closer to the mark. Surely the substance of the rule in *Benedict* should have been preserved . . . Furthermore, there was something worth thinking about in the limitations that the nineteenth century courts had placed on a mortgagee's claim to after-acquired property: does it make any sense to award everything to a secured party who stands idly by while a doomed enterprise goes down the slippery slope into bankruptcy?

[52] [2001] 2 AC 710 at 716.   [53] 'Security Law, Formalism and Article 9' at 671–2.

In England, at the moment, assets subject to an uncrystallised floating charge may be used to discharge the debtor's general debts and are also amenable to judgment creditors endeavouring to levy execution on the debtor's property.[54] While these possibilities arguably provide only a small window of opportunity for an extremely nimble and fleet-footed unsecured creditor,[55] clearly half a loaf is better than no bread at all. Moreover, it could be contended that a creditor should not be able to blow hot and cold – to permit a debtor to carry on business in the normal way until a crystallising event occurs while at the same time denying execution creditors an entitlement to enforce a judgment against the debtor's assets.

This small window of opportunity is not available to creditors under Article 9 at all. This conclusion becomes evident when one considers the basic structure of Article 9 which centres around the concepts of attachment and perfection of a security interest.[56] The objective of Article 9 is to permit lenders and sellers to register their interest in the personal property of a debtor so as to secure payment of the debt and to mark out their priority position in the collateral (secured property). A security interest attaches when it becomes enforceable vis-à-vis creditor and debtor. The expression 'attachment' therefore identifies the process whereby the security interest is regarded as creating an obligation. Since floating charges were unknown to pre-Article 9 US law, they are not specifically referred to in Article 9. It seems, however, that if a security agreement covers after-acquired property, the security agreement will attach once the debtor acquires the property, since at that time the debtor 'has rights in the collateral'. Moreover, the parties may agree to postpone the time for attachment, in which case the security interest attaches at the agreed time.[57]

---

[54] See generally on this Calnan 'Execution Creditors and Floating Charges'.

[55] See J. Ziegel 'Canadian Perspectives on How Far Article 9 is Exportable' (1996) 27 *Can Bus LJ* 226 at 237:

> The equitable floating charge promises more than it can deliver. It only assists the unsecured creditor so long as the charge has not been crystallised. Given the ease with which a floating charge may be crystallised, the unsecured creditor is left empty-handed just when she needs equity's help most. The result comes about because a floating charge does not create an estoppel in favour of unsecured creditors after as well as before the debtor's insolvency.

[56] The reference is to the 1989 Ontario Personal Property Security Act. The first Personal Property Security Act was enacted in Ontario in 1967 but this did not come into force until 1976. Revisions of the statute were recommended by the Catzman Committee: see *Report of the Minister's Advisory Committee on the Personal Property Security Act* (Toronto, June 1984), on which see J. Ziegel 'Recent and Prospective Developments in the Personal Property Security Law Area' (1985) 10 *Can Bus LJ* 131.

[57] Article 9-203(a).

The legislative structure is basically the same under the Personal Property Security Acts in Canada and there has been a lot of litigation concerning the effect of attachment of security interests on execution creditors. It has been held by the courts that assets subject to an attached security interest are no longer available for seizure by an execution creditor.[58] However, despite the language used in the personal property security legislation, which makes floating charges subject to the general rules on attachment, judges initially expressed some hesitation in coming to this conclusion.[59] The reluctance has been explained on the basis that:[60]

> The threat of execution creditor super-priority operated to significantly encourage closer monitoring as well as crystallization and enforcement on the first sign of cessation of the debtor's economic viability. Absent that threat, unsecured creditors can no longer rely on the debtor's general secured lender to terminate the debtor's business dealings sufficiently early to minimize their losses.

The reluctance could also be rationalised on legal grounds by using the argument that because the parties had employed the old terminology of the floating charge in their security agreement they had implicitly agreed to postpone the time for attachment until crystallisation had taken place in the traditional conception of things. The courts now reject this view,[61] and the theory of implied contracting out has effectively been abandoned.[62] In other words, an unsecured creditor who seeks payment from the collateral takes subject to all prior perfected security interests, including those held in floating assets.

A case in point is *Canadian Imperial Bank of Commerce* v. *Otto Timm Enterprises Ltd*,[63] where a bank provided finance to a farm-equipment

---

[58] See the analysis in Walsh 'The Floating Charge is Dead' at 143–4:

> Under the pre-reform floating charge theory, an unsecured creditor could sue the debtor and enforce its judgment against any assets subject to a floating charge so long as the charge remained uncrystallised, that is so long as the chargee had not yet terminated the debtor's licence to deal freely with the relevant assets in the ordinary course of business. But under the fixed charge concept of attachment adopted by the PPSAs, the enforcement rights of a judgment creditor are subject to all prior perfected security interests from the point of perfection forward, even against assets of a circulating character over which the debtor is still empowered to deal freely.

[59] See *Royal Bank of Canada* v. *Mohawk* (1985) 49 OR (2d) 734; and *Re Standard Modern Technologies Corp.* (1992) 6 OR (3d) 161, 87 DLR (4th) 44; and see generally Ziegel 'Canadian Perspectives' at 238.

[60] See M. Bridge, R. Macdonald, R. Simmonds and C. Walsh 'Formalism, Functionalism, and Understanding the Law of Secured Transactions' (1999) 44 *McGill LJ* 567 – text accompanying n. 206.

[61] The leading case is *Canadian Imperial Bank of Commerce* v. *Otto Timm Enterprises Ltd* (1995) 130 DLR (4th) 91 on which see generally R. Harason and D. Denomme 'The PPSA and Floating Charges Again' (1997) 115 *Banking and Finance Law Review* 115.

[62] See also *Credit Suisse Canada* v. *Yonge Street Holdings Ltd* (1996) 62 ACWS (3d) 497.

[63] (1995) 130 DLR (4th) 91. See generally on the case Harason and Denomme 'The PPSA and Floating Charges Again'.

dealer; it took a general security agreement covering existing and future property and registered financing statements in respect of the agreement. Under the terms of the security agreement the dealer was expressly authorised to sell inventory in the ordinary course of business but the agreement also provided that the security interest attached when it was signed and delivered to the bank. Subsequently the dealer entered into conditional sale agreements with a supplier in respect of a number of deliveries of tractors. Financing statements were filed in relation to some of these deliveries. The question arose who had best claim to the proceeds of sale of the tractors – the bank or the conditional seller. At first instance, the conditional seller prevailed,[64] with the judge holding that the parties did not intend attachment upon delivery of future inventory to the dealer; because the agreement permitted sales in the ordinary course of business. Perfection was impossible without attachment and therefore the bank could not invoke the priority protection normally given to the first-registered security interest.

A completely different analysis was adopted in the Ontario Court of Appeal.[65] The court held that the bank's security interest attached when the tractors were delivered to the dealer; since the parties intended it to attach, the bank had given value and the dealer had rights in the collateral. The bank's security interest became perfected at that stage since previously it had registered a financing statement and maintained it in force. By way of contrast, the distributor's security interest was only perfected subsequently whether by filing an appropriate financing statement or by taking possession of the inventory. It was held that the first-instance judge had erred in applying common-law concepts referable to the crystallisation of floating charges.[66]

Implications of Article 9 for preferential creditors

While the enactment of Article 9-type reforms in England would have adverse implications for execution creditors the consequences for preferential creditors are potentially even more serious. This point becomes clear when the overlap between the law of credit and security and insolvency law in the two countries is considered. In England, by virtue of sections 40 and 175 of the Insolvency Act 1986, preferential creditors enjoy priority over a floating-charge holder. The categories of preferential claim are set out in Schedule 6 to the Insolvency Act and, prior to the Enterprise Act 2002, basically cover certain tax and employee claims.

---

[64] (1991) 79 DLR (4th) 67.   [65] (1995) 130 DLR (4th) 91.
[66] See also *Euroclean Canada Inc.* v. *Forest Glade Investments Ltd* (1985) 49 OR (2d) 769 and see generally Ziegel 'Recent and Prospective Developments' at 148–54.

There have been various arguments put forward for acceding to claims by particular categories of creditors to preferential status.[67] Governmental entities, for example, are said to be involuntary creditors and not consciously to have assumed the risk of the debtor's insolvency. It is also arguable, though highly debatable, that such creditors are not in an effective position to monitor the debtor's behaviour and to assess the risk of default or insolvency. As far as claims by employees to preferential status are concerned, an inequality-of-bargaining-power argument can be deployed in support of the proposition that such claimants are too weak economically to bargain for security rights. Unpaid employees also are protected under the National Insurance Fund which serves partly as a wage-guarantee scheme in the event of employer insolvency.[68] Part 12, Employment Rights Act 1996 requires the Secretary of State for Employment to pay employees their unpaid remuneration and other entitlements and the Secretary of State is then subrogated to the employees' rights as preferential creditor. This provision endeavours to ensure that employees are paid promptly and that the receiver or liquidator has a certain freedom in realising the assets of the company.

The Insolvency Act 1986 essentially restricted the Crown's claim to priority in respect of unpaid taxes to withholding taxes (e.g. PAYE) and social insurance contributions. Here the business entity acts as an agent for the transmission of funds to the government and has no right to hold on to the funds in the first place. On the other hand, the government is in a better position to shoulder the losses arising from insolvency of a business than anybody else, with debts owing to the state from a single corporate insolvency being completely insignificant compared with total government expenditure. The Enterprise Act abolished Crown preference, but only as part of an integrated package of measures under which the general right of floating-charge holders to appoint an administrative receiver is curtailed.[69] Moreover, a certain proportion of

---

[67] See generally A. Keay and P. Walton 'The Preferential Debts Regime in Liquidation Law: In the Public Interest? [1999] *CFILR* 84; and see also for a Canadian perspective S. Cantlie 'Preferred Priority in Bankruptcy' in J. Ziegel ed. *Current Developments in International and Comparative Corporate Insolvency Law* (Oxford University Press, 1994).

[68] Employment Rights Act 1996, Part 12. See generally V. Finch *Corporate Insolvency Law: Perspectives and Principles* (Cambridge University Press, 2002) at pp. 425–37, who points out that the Employment Rights Act (ERA) offers employees of an insolvent company more extensive protection than the Insolvency Act 1986 and that less than a quarter of the money paid out under the ERA scheme can be claimed by the Crown as preferential.

[69] The abolition applies only with respect to new floating charges: see Enterprise Act 2002, s 250. Also, holders of qualifying floating charges are given a new power to appoint administrators out of court, though the administrator has an overarching duty of trying

floating-charge – but not fixed-charge – realisations is set aside for the benefit of unsecured creditors so that the fruits flowing from the abolition of Crown preference do not go exclusively to floating-charge holders.[70] Perhaps recognising the vulnerability of employees, the Enterprise Act leaves unchanged their preferential rights and also, to avoid any shifting of burdens from secured creditors onto the central exchequer, it also leaves unchanged the subrogation rights of those who satisfy employee preferential claims.

In the US, according to Article 541 of the Bankruptcy Code, the bankrupt's estate generally includes 'all legal and equitable interests of the debtor in property as of the commencement of the case'. Statute fixes up the slicing of the corporate pie amongst the various creditors. The law generally respects the non-bankruptcy entitlements of creditors with security-interest holders ordinarily entitled to the value of their collateral. Those with unsecured claims may only share in the value collateral to the extent that it exceeds the secured debt. Article 544(a) is the so-called strong-arm clause of the Bankruptcy Code because it confers extensive powers on the bankruptcy trustee. Basically, the bankruptcy trustee is afforded the status of a hypothetical judicial lien creditor and can avoid security interests that are unperfected at the commencement of bankruptcy.[71] Perfected secured creditors are paid off first to the extent of their security, and then it is the task of the trustee in bankruptcy to distribute the remaining funds among the 'general' creditors.[72] General creditors are classed into three groups: priority creditors; general unsecured creditors; and subordinated creditors. The kind of claims accorded priority status by Article 507 – basically certain tax and employee claims – are roughly equivalent to those accorded preferential status in the Insolvency Act. The major difference between the two countries lies in the relative priority position of secured claims which in the US outrank all other claims but which in England are subdivided into fixed and floating security interests with only the former having priority over preferential creditors.

to rescue the company whenever reasonably practical – and even in cases where this is not reasonably practical, the administrator must not unnecessarily harm the interests of company creditors as a whole. For details see Enterprise Act 2002, Sch. 16 and for the abolition of Crown preference see section 251.

[70] Enterprise Act 2002, s 252 and the Insolvency Act 1986 (Prescribed Part) Order 2003.

[71] Article 725 US Bankruptcy Code. The point has been expressed pithily by Karen Gross *Failure and Forgiveness: Rebalancing the Bankruptcy System* (Yale University Press, 1997) at p. 155: 'In essence, then, secured creditors have a priority over all other creditors to the extent of the value of their collateral.'

[72] See generally on the theoretical underpinnings of the US bankruptcy system T. H. Jackson *The Logic and Limits of Bankruptcy Law* (Harvard University Press, 1986).

On the other hand, US corporate reorganisation law in the shape of Chapter 11 of the US Bankruptcy Law[73] is much less respectful of secured creditor rights than the corresponding English corporate reorganisation provisions in the Insolvency Act 1986. A stay on enforcement proceedings may be obtained simply by filing under Chapter 11, and the existing corporate management remain in place – at least initially – during the course of the reorganisation process. In England there is no concept of 'debtor-in-possession' and the procedure for getting an out-of-court stay on enforcement proceedings has only recently been introduced.[74] In the US, the balance between security-interest holders and preferential creditors is struck not by giving the preferential creditors any prior claim over assets in the bankruptcy distribution process but rather by restricting the rights of secured creditors in the corporate reorganisation process in such a way as to maximise the prospects of an ailing business being restored to financial good health. The hope is that by creating a climate conducive to corporate rescue, ultimately preferential debts will be paid. As the DTI review of company rescue and business reconstruction mechanisms points out, on the standard tests, the US should be classed as pro-debtor rather than pro-creditor: it allows an automatic stay on assets; allows unimpeded petition for reorganisation; and allows the company's board to remain in control during reorganisation.[75] One distinguished American commentator has observed:[76]

If an American banker is very, very good, when he dies he will go to the United Kingdom. British banks have far more control than an American secured lender could ever hope to have. Receiverships on the British model are unknown and almost unthinkable in the US. A US banker could barely imagine a banker's Valhalla in which a bank could veto a reorganisation as a UK bank may effectively veto an administration by appointing an administrative receiver.

The Enterprise Act shifts English law in the direction of the US position but still there is no concept of debtor-in-possession.[77]

---

[73] US Bankruptcy Code 1978.   [74] Insolvency Act 2000.

[75] *A Review of Company Rescue and Business Reconstruction Mechanisms* (London, 2000) at pp. 38–41. At p. 33, however, the review group observes that 'it would be wholly inappropriate to attempt to replicate Chapter 11 in the UK, where the business culture and economic environment are quite different'.

[76] See J. Westbrook 'A Comparison of Bankruptcy Reorganisation in the US with the Administration Procedure in the UK' (1990) 6 *Insolvency Law and Practice* 86 at 87; and see also J. Franks and W. Torous 'Lessons from a Comparison of US and UK Insolvency Codes' (1993) 8 *Oxford Review of Economic Policy* 70.

[77] For an argument that English law is moving gradually in the direction of 'debtor-in-possession' see D. Milman 'Reforming Corporate Rescue Mechanisms' in De Lacy ed. *The Reform of United Kingdom Company Law* at p. 415. The Insolvency Act 2000 allows small companies to obtain out-of-court moratoria on creditor enforcement proceedings when they are proposing a voluntary arrangement with the company creditors.

The New Zealand approach would perhaps be more familiar to English observers. There is no corporate rehabilitation statute as such but preferential creditors take priority over holders of security interests in respect of claims to particular categories of assets – namely, inventory and receivables.[78] This is a possible approach for consideration in England but it involves giving preferential creditors slightly greater rights than they enjoy under existing law. It is theoretically possible at least, at the moment, to have a fixed charge over receivables, and if such a charge exists, the holder of the security interest will outrank preferential creditors.

Under the new dispensation proposed in England by the Law Commission floating-charge language employed in a loan agreement is more than a matter of mere terminology and would have major substantive impact. The Law Commission strove to minimise the substantive implications of its proposals and so aimed to preserve the priority that preferential creditors currently enjoy over the floating charge. It said:[79]

Since a charge that permits the debtor to dispose of the assets in the ordinary course of business free of the charge may still be described accurately as a floating charge, it would still be subject to the provisions of the Insolvency Act 1986 requiring that preferential creditors be paid before the floating charge-holder, but if preferential debts are to be retained it would be sensible to provide this expressly in order to avoid any doubt. The same applies to the provisions for the avoidance of certain floating charges contained in the Insolvency Act 1986, section 245.

It is easy, however, to see why the Law Commission recommendations are cast as they are. Firstly, as various commentators have remarked, the floating charge is very much the workhorse of the secured-credit industry and has been the mainstay of bank lending for over a century.[80] One of the precursors to the Law Commission consultation paper, the Crowther report, observed that the floating charge was so fundamental a part of commercial lending practice that its abolition could not seriously be contemplated.[81] The centrality of the floating charge in English lending practice was also acknowledged recently by the Privy Council in *Agnew* v. *Commissioner of Inland Revenue*.[82] Lord Millett said:

The floating charge is capable of affording the creditor, by a single instrument, an effective and comprehensive security upon the entire undertaking of the debtor

---

[78] Companies Act 1993 Sch 7 para. 9; and for a general discussion of this matter see Gedye et al. *Personal Property Securities* at p. 21.

[79] *Registration of Security Interests* para 4.133.

[80] See J. Ziegel 'The New Provincial Chattel Security Regimes' (1991) 70 *Canadian Bar Review* 681 at 712.

[81] Committee on Consumer Credit *Consumer Credit* (1971) Cmnd 4596 at para. 5.7.77.

[82] [2001] 2 AC 710.

company and its assets from time to time, while at the same time leaving the company free to deal with its assets and pay its trade creditors in the ordinary course of business without reference to the holder. Such a form of security is particularly attractive to banks, and it rapidly acquired an importance in English commercial life which . . . should not be underestimated.

Secondly, and relatedly, banks and bank lending documentation are very rooted in the language and concepts of the floating charge and might be most reluctant to see its disappearance.[83] Thirdly, abolishing the floating charge as such, or in other words assimilating fixed and floating charges, would disadvantage preferential creditors – that is, unless some alternative provisions were put in place to safeguard the interests of this category of creditors. In other words, if fixed and floating charges were brought together in a new unitary concept of a single security interest the Law Commission would have to craft a whole new set of compromises, and that is outside its terms of reference.

The continued importance of characterisation issues under Article 9

Article 9 does not completely remove the need to consider characterisation issues. Article 9 is stated to apply to any transaction which is intended to create a security interest, irrespective of differences of form and irrespective of title to the secured property, but problems of characterisation and recharacterisation are endemic in all systems and Article 9 is no exception.[84] There are many different categories of collateral in Article 9. The classification exercise is difficult, but important, for there are different perfection rules for different types of collateral as well as different priority rules for different types of collateral. Moreover, the fact that absolute transfers and security transfers are assimilated for certain Article 9 purposes does not mean that the same rules apply to them in other legal contexts. For example, Article 9 is specifically stated to apply to 'any sale

---

[83] See, for example, the comments by Professor M. Bridge in 'How Far is Article 9 Exportable?: The English Experience' (1996) 27 *Can Bus LJ* 196 at 221:

> The English bank has obtained all the freedom it needs to make its position ironclad. It is therefore hardly surprising that the banks are not pressing for reform along the lines of Article 9. The position in English law is a world away from the strict line on accounts receivable financing by the United States Supreme Court in *Benedict v. Ratner*. If England were to adopt an Article 9 statute, these hard-won gains would be surrendered for something new whose implications would take some time to be felt.

[84] For a penetrating account see Bridge et al. 'Formalism, Functionalism and Understanding'.

of accounts or chattel paper'. In England this would be known broadly as the assignment of receivables or factoring. The fact, however, that Article 9 registration requirements apply to a factoring transaction does not mean that the transaction is also subject to other Article 9 rules.[85] As one commentator observes:[86]

> The basic distinction between the sale and securing of accounts is seen in the fact that any surplus from collections goes to the buyer in the case of a sale and to the seller in the case of a security assignment. The limited purpose for which Article 9 applies to the sale of accounts is to avoid litigation on characterization and to notify third parties of the assignee's interest. But this limited purpose does not prevent characterization of absolute assignments as sales for other purposes albeit that Art. 9 does have a bankruptcy impact insofar as the failure of the buyer to file allows the trustee to grab the accounts.

Moreover, apart from bankruptcy, the absolute-sale/security-interest distinction retains its importance in other spheres such as accounting, tax and securitisation. The courts are still required correctly to characterise a transaction and the major continuing significance of this characterisation exercise in a post-Article 9 era is illustrated by the decision of the Supreme Court of Canada in *R* v. *Alberta (Treasury Branches)*,[87] where the distinction between absolute assignments of debts and security assignments was crucial. The issue in the case arose because of a provision in the Canadian Income Tax Code which stated that a secured creditor who had a right to receive a payment that, but for a security interest in favour of the secured creditor would be payable to a tax debtor, could be required to make direct payment to the Revenue. It was further provided that the money so required to be paid should, 'notwithstanding any

---

[85] See the comments by Professor Ronald Cuming in 'The Internationalisation of Secured Financing Law' in Ross Cranston ed. *Making Commercial Law: Essays in Honour of Roy Goode* (Oxford University Press, 1997), at pp. 522–3:

> There are two features of the UCC, Article 9 approach that appear to be troublesome even to those who are attracted to it. The first is the total reconceptualisation that it requires in the context of types of transactions that traditionally are not viewed as secured financing devices . . . The second feature . . . is the extent to which it requires a bifurcated approach to the characterisation of certain types of transactions. Since a title retention sales contract or a lease falls within a secured financing regime because it functions as a security device, it follows that the seller or lessor is not the owner of the goods sold or leased . . . What is troublesome is that outside this regime, the recharacterisation might not be acceptable with the result that the same transaction is viewed differently depending on the legal issues being addressed.

[86] B. Clark *The Law of Secured Transactions under the Uniform Commercial Code* (Warren, Gorham & Lamont, 1996; Cumulative Supplement) at S1.11–S1.12, cited by Bridge et al. 'Formalism, Functionalism and Understanding' at n. 64.

[87] (1996) 133 DLR (4th) 609.

security interest in those moneys, become the property of Her Majesty and should be paid to the Receiver General, in priority to any such security interest'. 'Secured creditor' was defined as 'a person who has a security interest in the property of another person' and 'security interest' as 'any interest in property that secures payment or performance of an obligation'.

In a number of instances tax debtors had executed assignments of debts in favour of lenders, and in each of these instances the Revenue claimed priority over the lender. The assignments were specifically stated to be by way of 'continuing collateral security'. The key issue was whether the lender was a secured party within the meaning of the statutory provision. This question was answered in the affirmative by a majority of the Supreme Court of Canada. The court, however, distinguished between 'absolute' and security assignments of debts. An absolute assignment meant that no property remained in the hands of the assignor. In commercial parlance it was the business of factoring – the sale of book debts of the company. In this particular case, though, the borrower retained the right to redeem the book debts once the debt had been paid off, and this right of redemption demonstrated that the assignment was something less than absolute. An assignment could not be both absolute and leave an equity of redemption with the assignor.[88] Nevertheless, the court stressed that those engaged in the factoring business were protected from the provision in the Income Tax Code since the factoring of debts was based upon an absolute assignment of them. Factoring was, in effect, a sale by a company of its debts at a discounted value to the factoring company for immediate consideration.

Transitional matters

If England adopted Article 9 or some variant thereof then lawyers would have to learn a whole different vocabulary. Words and concepts such as 'attachment' and 'perfection' would replace 'crystallisation' and 'registration'. Lawyers working in this field have acquired a specialised body of knowledge and experience that they might be reluctant to see consigned to the realms of legal history. Moreover, looking at the matter from the perspective of the banking industry, there is a risk that moving over to a new system would reignite old controversies pertaining to the extent of secured creditors' rights. Banks may feel that they are adequately

---

[88] Clearly, the court is here using the word 'absolute' in a different sense from that used in section 136 English Law of Property Act 1925. Under that section an assignment could still be both 'absolute' and 'by way of security'.

protected at the moment and that any change would be detrimental change from their point of view.[89] We are very much at a time where the prevailing economic orthodoxy suggests that secured credit is a 'good' thing. Given this climate of opinion the views of banks are likely to command great weight.

Complications with the Law Commission recommendations

Apart from the intrinsic disadvantages of the move over to an Article 9 regime it is submitted that there are particular difficulties in the scheme envisaged by the Law Commission. In particular, the principle behind the Law Commission consultation paper that the floating charge is to be preserved generates a number of complications. Firstly, what is a 'floating charge' under the new dispensation? The Law Commission does not offer much in the way of real guidance, though it did proffer the following comment:[90] 'Since a charge that permits the debtor to dispose of the assets in the ordinary course of business free of the charge may still be described accurately as a floating charge.' Over the years there has been an enormous amount of effort expended in trying to define a floating charge, as distinct from a fixed charge, not least because of the profound practical consequences of the distinction. The latest significant salvo in the definition stakes was the judgment of the Privy Council in the *Agnew*[91] case. It seems clear that implementation of the Law Commission proposals will not decrease the definitional battle but may even heighten it.[92]

The seminal account of a floating charge is contained in the judgment of Romer LJ in *Re Yorkshire Woolcombers Association Ltd*,[93] which refers to the nature of the assets over which the security is taken. While the nature of the property charged provides a reasonably safe guide for characterising the type of security it is not completely reliable. The Law Commission comment and the general trend of the case law focus more on the management autonomy which a floating charge confers on the security giver. With a floating charge, the security giver has management autonomy with respect to the assets within the security umbrella until that autonomy is

---

[89] See the comment by Professor Michael Bridge quoted in n. 83 above.

[90] *Registration of Security Interests* at para 4.133.

[91] *Agnew* v. *Commissioner of Inland Revenue* [2001] 2 AC 710. The case is often referred to as the *Brumark* case.

[92] A floating charge was first mapped out by the Court of Appeal in Chancery in *Re Panama, New Zealand and Australian Royal Mail Co.* (1870) 5 Ch App 318. See generally on the history of the floating charge R. Pennington 'The Genesis of the Floating Charge' (1960) 23 *MLR* 630.

[93] [1903] 2 Ch 284.

brought to an end by the process known as crystallisation, whereupon the floating charge becomes fixed.[94] On the other hand, a floating charge is clearly compatible with some restrictions on the debtor's management autonomy.[95] For example, the existence of a negative pledge provision in the security documentation does not turn what would otherwise be a floating charge into a fixed charge. The real issue is about how extensive these restrictions must be before the charge becomes a fixed charge. In *Agnew v. Commissioner of Inland Revenue*[96] the Privy Council suggested that where a charge is created over receivables and where the proceeds of the receivables are required to be paid into a blocked bank account under the control of the lender, the charge in question may be a fixed charge.

The second complication stemming from the Law Commission recommendations is the seeming ambiguity in the report on the effect of labelling. Under existing law, it is clear that characterisation of the nature of a security interest by the parties is not conclusive. To use an analogy, and to borrow language used in a different context, a four-pronged instrument for manual digging cannot be changed into a spade merely by the parties calling it a spade.[97] If a security agreement has the usual attributes of a floating charge in terms of debtor autonomy the parties cannot transform the agreement into a fixed charge merely by labelling it as such. There is a whole line of cases, particularly in the context of receivables financing, where the courts have disregarded the characterisation applied to a security interest by the parties and instead construed the parties' agreement in the round and in the light of the surrounding circumstances.[98] Nevertheless, in this respect, while the consultation paper is ambiguous, it may involve a change in existing law. At one point it is said that if the charge is stated in the financing statement to be a floating charge the purchaser can be confident that, provided the sale is in the ordinary course of business, she will take free of it.[99] At another

---

[94] [1904] AC 355 at 358.

[95] See the comments of Hoffmann J in *Re Brightlife Ltd* [1987] Ch 200 at 209: 'But a floating charge is consistent with some restriction upon the company's freedom to deal with its assets. Floating charges commonly contain a prohibition upon the creation of other charges ranking prior to or pari passu with the floating charge.' Professor John Farrar has suggested in 'Floating Charges and Priorities' (1974) 38 *Conv* (NS) 315 that restrictive clauses may be inconsistent with the nature of a floating charge but reaches the conclusion that 'it would now seem too late for the point to be raised' (at 318).

[96] [2001] 2 AC 710; and see also the decision of the House of Lords in *Smith v. Bridgend County BC* [2002] 1 AC 336.

[97] See the judgment of Lord Templeman in *Street v. Mountford* [1985] AC 809.

[98] Cases indeed such as *Agnew v. CIR* [2001] 2 AC 710.

[99] Law Commission *Registration of Security Interests* at para 4.141.

juncture, however, the report provides that a financing statement should not be required to state the nature of the charge.[100]

The third difficulty arising from the Law Commission recommendation is that in a new, supposedly simpler and conceptually more coherent system, it proposes retaining the concept of crystallisation of a floating charge. The consultation paper suggests that it should not be necessary to register the existence of an automatic crystallisation clause, but that it should be necessary to register the fact in the event that such a charge has crystallised if the charge holder wishes to rely on it. The floating charge has been described as an instrument of power and mystery,[101] and part of the mysterious aura derives from the concepts of crystallisation and automatic crystallisation. The expression 'crystallisation' refers to the process whereby a floating charge becomes fixed and, as traditionally understood, the process occurred when the company went into liquidation or when the charge holder appointed a receiver over the company's assets or went into possession of the assets. In *Re Woodroffes (Musical Instruments) Ltd*[102] it was held that crystallisation also took place when the debtor ceased to carry on business in the ordinary way and in *Re Brightlife Ltd*[103] Hoffmann J took the view that lender and borrower could agree upon the events on which crystallisation was deemed to have occurred – so-called 'automatic crystallisation'.[104] The effect of crystallisation is to terminate the company's management authority, i.e. its freedom to dispose of assets in the ordinary course of business free from the security interest. It seems, however, on the basis of normal agency principles that a third party who is unaware that crystallisation has occurred pursuant to an automatic crystallisation clause is entitled to assume the continuance of a company's managerial authority implied by the floating charge until cessation of that authority has been brought explicitly to its attention.[105]

---

[100] *Ibid.* at para 4.144.

[101] See generally Goode 'Exodus of the Floating Charge' at p. 203.

[102] [1986] Ch 366.   [103] [1987] 1 Ch 200.

[104] Pre-PPSA Canadian courts, however, took the view that floating-charge holders were required to intervene in an overt fashion so as to give public notice to other creditors that the debtor's freedom of dealing with its assets in the ordinary course of business had been terminated. See generally *R* v. *Consolidated Churchill Copper Corp.* (1978) 90 DLR (3d) 357; *Esket Wood Products Ltd* v. *Starline Lumber Inc.* (1991) 61 BCLR (2d) 359. See also Gough *Company Charges* at pp. 408–31; and see also A. J. Boyle 'The Validity of Automatic Crystallisation Clauses' [1979] *JBL* 231.

[105] See Goode *Legal Problems* at pp 70–1. See also the comments of McGarvie J in the Australian case *Horsburgh* v. *Deputy Commissioner of Taxation* (1984) 54 ALR 397 at 413, who doubted whether 'modern equity would be forced to run in such established grooves that if employees received pay and customers bought goods from a company, while reasonably unaware that the property of the company had become subject to a fixed equitable charge, they would be losers'.

Logically, in a reformed law of security interests, there is no place for concepts such as crystallisation and automatic crystallisation.[106] An Article 9 security interest is totally consistent with a debtor's freedom to dispose of assets subject to the security interest in the ordinary way.[107] In so far as the debtor's authority to dispose of assets is restricted by provisions in the security agreement, such provisions cannot be relied upon against third parties who are unaware of the existence of such provisions. Farewell, therefore, to crystallisation; but this is not how the Law Commission viewed things.

Another complication that would arise if the Law Commission recommendations were enacted in their present form relates to charges that are currently subject to dual registration, i.e. registration in the company charges register and registration in some other specialist register such as the patents register. One of the reasons why Part 4 Companies Act 1989 was not implemented was because of such dual-registration problems and in that case the problem of the interrelationship between the land register and the company charges register following the loss of the conclusive evidence status attributed to the Companies House registration certificate.[108] The difficulty was never satisfactorily resolved, and it may be that the issue of dual registration will return to haunt the Law Commission. The Law Commission provisionally proposed to exclude all charges registrable in a specialist register from the notice-filing system. Its suggestion was that the validity and priority of charges created by companies over land or other assets that are registrable in specialist registers should not depend on the filing of a financing statement in the company charges register.[109] One could question the merits of the exclusion on the basis that the company charges register thereby becomes much less valuable as a source of information. Be that as it may, the proposal may not be workable because it relates only to fixed charges. Floating charges that extend to property that is subject to registration in another specialist

---

[106] For a discussion of more convoluted concepts such as selective crystallisation, decrystallisation and reflotation of crystallised floating charges see C. Rickett 'Automatic Reflotation of a Crystallised Floating Charge' (1992) 22 *UWALR* 430; Tan Cheng Han 'Automatic Crystallisation, De-Crystallisation and Convertibility of Charges' [1998] *CFILR* 41; and see generally Ali *Law of Secured Finance* at pp. 127–9.

[107] See the comment by Walsh 'The Floating Charge is Dead' at p. 143:

> The PPSAs themselves provide a statutory licence to deal of sorts: the debtor is empowered to sell or lease goods in the ordinary course of business free of the security interest, and the newer PPSAs explicitly affirm the freedom of the debtor to utilise collateral in the form of its liquid assets in the voluntary payment of ordinary course of business debts.

[108] See generally Law Commission *Registration of Security Interests* at pp. 9 and 71–2.

[109] *Ibid.* para 4.208.

register, e.g. intellectual property rights, would still be subject to dual registration.[110] Therefore it would be necessary to distinguish between fixed and floating charges over intellectual property rights, and this may not be an easy task.

Conclusion

If Article 9-type reforms were enacted in England, it would bring greater order and coherence to the law of security interests. We would have the end of a situation where economically similar transactions are regarded by the law in a substantially different light. Moreover, the complexity of some aspects of the law such as 'tacking' would be removed and we would have more rational rules for determining priorities between competing security interests in the same property. The Law Commission consultation paper on security interests in endorsing the Article 9 approach has much to commend it. Apart from simplifying the registration process, it also provides for the introduction of a simpler, more straightforward and conceptually more coherent method for determining priorities between competing security interests in the same property.[111]

The paper, however, tries to marry the old and the new by proposing the retention of the floating charge instead of its assimilation into a new, unified concept of security interest. It is submitted that in the last respect the consultation paper creates unnecessary complications. In other PPSA jurisdictions the advent of reform has spelt the demise of the traditional floating charge. Not so in England where the legacy of the past lives on and which means that business, lawyers and financiers will have to cope with two systems running in tandem – the old and the new. Be that as it may, it seems that the Law Commission recommendations are couched as they are with at least one eye to the political realities. The obliteration of the floating charge would have meant upsetting the traditional bedrock of the secured-finance industry in England and overturning over a century of learning. It would also impact adversely on existing categories of creditors unless alternative provisions were put in place to protect their interests. Execution creditors would be potential losers under a new system, but the major disadvantage is likely to be suffered by preferential creditors. At the moment, preferential creditors are paid after claims secured by fixed charges, but outrank floating-charge holders. If no measures were put in

---

[110] See the discussion of this point in *ibid.* at pp. 37–8. All charges, including floating charges, over patents, trade marks or registered designs are registrable at the Patent Office; see Patents Act 1977, s 33(3)(b); Trade Marks Act 1994, s 25(2)(c); Registered Designs Act 1949, s 19.

[111] See Law Commission *Registration of Security Interests* at para 4.124.

place to protect the position of preferential creditors they would be a lot worse off under the new dispensation. At one stage it seemed unlikely that this state of affairs would be socially or politically acceptable. Crown preference has, however, been recently abolished. Consequently, the major losers from Article 9-type reforms in England would be employees, or rather those subrogated to employee preferential claims, namely, the government in another guise. Having sacrificed its 'privileges' through the abolition of Crown preferences, the question arises whether the central exchequer would be prepared to shoulder any more of the losses arising from business insolvency. That question remains to be determined.[112] Ultimately, however, the acceptability and enactability of the proposals may turn not on overcoming outright opposition but rather in overcoming apathy. The 1989 Diamond report floundered on a sea of indifference and it remains to be seen whether the Law Commission consultation paper will suffer a similar fate.

[112] See generally Bridge 'How Far is Article 9 Exportable?'.

5   Notice filing versus transaction filing

The Company Law Review Steering Group in its final report, *Modern Company Law for a Competitive Economy*, suggested that the law relating to registration of company charges is of real importance to the capital markets as it guards against fraud and facilitates commercial borrowing.[1] The Law Commission endorsed this conclusion and suggested that the system performs a useful commercial function. In its view, it was a means of providing information on the financial position of companies that the business community and its professional advisers find important and helpful. Both bodies, however, provisionally concluded that the present system was open to substantial criticism and should be replaced with a system based on the 'notice-filing' model employed in the US under Article 9 of the UCC and in Canada and New Zealand under PPSA statutes.[2] Most types of security interest created by corporate borrowers in England require registration in order to ensure validity of the security interest in

---

[1] (July 2001) at para. 12.1. A slightly more sceptical view on the company charge registration procedure was expressed by Lord Hoffmann in the *Cosslett Contractors* case – *Smith* v. *Bridgend County Borough Council* [2002] 1 AC 336 at para. 19:

> It was intended to give persons dealing with a company the opportunity to discover, by consulting the register, whether its assets were burdened by floating and certain fixed charges which would reduce the amount available for unsecured creditors in a liquidation. Whether this was a realistic form of protection and whether the choice of registrable charges was entirely logical is not presently relevant.

[2] For a polemical attack on the PPSA model and its appropriateness to New Zealand see B. Dugan 'PPSA – The Price of Certainty' [2000] *NZLJ* 241 at 243, who argues that the expensive PPSA registration system embraces information which is, for the large part, already available in financial statements, in company records and at credit-reporting agencies. He concludes by stating that

> there is little reason to believe that the PPSA will lower the cost of credit. Registration will increase out of pocket costs of lenders and borrowers by millions of dollars annually. As the PPSA does not significantly increase the amount of relevant credit information, it seems highly unlikely that the statute will make lending relationships more transparent. If North American experience is any guide, the PPSA will create a new quagmire for the next generation of lawyers. Instead of looking for solutions suited to current reporting practices and emerging forms of personal property, we have opted again for an overseas relic.

the event of the borrower going into liquidation or administration. The list of registrable charges is set out in Part 12 Companies Act 1985. The position is broadly similar in the US though there the registration or filing obligation applies to a broader range of security interests. This chapter will examine the mechanics of the registration system in England and compare it with notice filing under Article 9.[3] The English system is essentially one of transaction filing, with the instrument creating the security interest being delivered to the registration office along with the filed particulars. The basic difference between the two systems carries in its wake certain other differences of detail, and these differences will be highlighted with attention being paid to the respective roles of the various parties to the process: the holder of the security interest, the debtor, other creditors and the judicial authorities. On the other hand, there are noted similarities: firstly, the fact that there is a filing or registration system in the first place; and secondly, the fact that failure to file is attended with certain civil consequences.[4] The purposes served by the filing system will be considered after a brief overview of the two systems. The appropriateness of the sanctions for failure to file will also be addressed.

An overview of the Article 9 system of perfection by notice filing

Article 9 revolves around the concepts of attachment and perfection of a security interest. A security interest is said to attach when it becomes enforceable between creditor and debtor, i.e. an obligation has been created, and for this to occur the secured party must have given value and the debtor must have rights in the collateral.[5] Perfection refers to the procedure whereby the security interest becomes effective against third parties, i.e. a property right is created. Filing (registration) is the principal method of perfecting a security interest. Under Article 9 what is required to be filed is not the security agreement itself, but only a simple record – a financing statement – that provides a limited amount of information. The financing statement may be filed either before or after attachment of the security interest. The effect of a filed financing statement is merely to

---

[3] For access to the text of Article 9 see http://www.nccusl.org. See also Corinne Cooper ed. *The New Article 9* (American Bar Association, 2nd edn., 2000) and also J. Honnold, S. L. Harris and C. W. Mooney *Security Interests in Personal Property: Cases, Problems and Materials* (Foundation Press, 3rd edn. 2001).

[4] In England failure to register a registrable charge is also subject to criminal penalties. For an up-to-date explanation of the registration system under English law see H. Bennett 'Registration of Company Charges' in J. Armour and H. Bennett eds. *Vulnerable Transactions in Corporate Insolvency* (Hart Publishing, 2002) at p. 217.

[5] Article 9-203.

note that a person may have a security interest in the collateral concerned and further inquiries from the parties will be necessary if one wants to find out the exact state of affairs.[6]

Under the old pre-Article 9 chattel-mortgage and conditional-sale statutes what was required to be filed was the security agreement itself.[7] Article 9 does away with this requirement and, in this respect, borrows from the Uniform Trust Receipts Act 1933 which merely required a finance company to make a single filing for each dealer it did business with.[8] This Act, drafted by the distinguished jurist Karl Llewellyn, has been described as one of breathtaking complexity, but nevertheless it established the important principle that a filing system did not need to contain elaborate and detailed information about each single transaction. Article 9 develops and extends this principle. According to Article 9-502(a) a financing statement is sufficient only if it '(1) provides the name of the debtor; (2) provides the name of the secured party or a representative of the secured party; and (3) indicates the collateral covered by the financing statement'. As Professor Grant Gilmore, the principal author of Article 9, notes:[9]

The typical pre-Code pattern included separate filing systems for chattel mortgages, for conditional sales, for trust receipts, for factor's liens and for assignments of accounts receivable. In such a situation the expense and difficulty of making a thorough credit check are obvious. Since the filing requirements were themselves frequently obscure and tricky, the chances were good that a lender who, through his counsel, was familiar with one device would inadvertently go wrong in attempting to comply with another and fail to perfect his security interest.

According to the Article 9-502 Official Comment, notice filing is of great convenience and flexibility particularly where the collateral includes inventory, accounts and chattel paper. A notice-filing system removes the necessity of having to file a series of financing statements where there is an ongoing arrangement between debtor and creditor and the collateral changes on a frequent basis. Moreover, a financing statement can be used to cover situations where the security agreement is not in existence, and perhaps not even in the contemplation of the parties at the time that the notice is filed; provided of course that the description of collateral in the financing statement is sufficiently broad to encompass the collateral

---

[6] Article 9-210 sets out a process under which the secured party, at the debtor's request, may be required to make disclosure. In many cases, however, information may be forthcoming without the need to invoke this procedure.

[7] See revised Article 9-502 Official Comment.

[8] See generally Honnold et al. *Security Interests in Personal Property* at p. 169.

[9] *Security Interests in Personal Property* (Little Brown, 1965) at p. 463.

concerned. In the same way, a financing statement is effective with respect to after-acquired property and future advances.[10]

It should be stressed that, under Article 9, the financing statement is a short, simple document that describes the collateral in quite general terms. It simply acts as a bulletin board or pointer as to where to look for more information.[11] It will not, for instance, indicate the amount of the secured debt or indeed whether there is any secured indebtedness, nor will it say whether particular property is actually subject to a security agreement as distinct from being possibly the subject of a security agreement. Neither is there any information provided on the amount of interest payable or other terms of the loan agreement.[12]

An overview of registration under Part 12 Companies Act 1985

Part 12 Companies Act 1985 imposes an obligation on corporate borrowers to register certain types of security interest created by the borrower. Section 399 Companies Act 1985 provides that it is the duty of a company to send to the registrar of companies for registration particulars of every charge created by the company that falls within the list of registrable charges set out in section 396.[13] The instrument (if any) by which the charge is created or evidenced must be delivered along with the prescribed particulars of the charge. This task may be effected, however, by any person interested in the charge.[14] In such an eventuality the person is entitled to recover from the company the amount of any fees paid to the registrar in connection with the registration. If particulars are not submitted for registration within the twenty-one-day period then the

---

[10] Article 9-204.

[11] See generally D. Baird 'Notice Filing and the Problem of Ostensible Ownership' (1983) 12 *J Legal Stud* 53.

[12] See also the Scottish Law Commission discussion paper *Registration of Rights in Security by Companies* (October 2002) at p. 8:

> The most characteristic difference between notice filing and traditional systems of registration is that notice filing is parties-specific rather than transaction-specific. What is filed are not the details of a particular security but notice that certain parties have entered into, or may in future enter into, a secured transaction in relation to specified property. This approach has certain implications. A notice may be filed in advance of the transaction and the proposed transaction may never take place. The same notice may serve a series of connected transactions. And the information given on the register is necessarily rather general in character, being an invitation to further inquiry rather than a full account of the right in security.

[13] The obligation applies to charges created by companies that are registered in England and Wales.

[14] Section 399(2).

company and every officer of it who is in default is liable to a fine and, for continued contravention, to a daily default fine.[15] In practice, registration is done on the application of the beneficiary of the charge, as the economic incentive to register is stronger from the point of view of the beneficiary. Non-registration or, as more correctly stated, non-delivery of particulars for registration will result in a loss of priority. Where a charge has been created by a company and particulars are not delivered within the twenty-one-day period, the charge is, so far as it confers any security over the company's property or undertaking, void against the liquidator or administrator and any creditor of the company.

Section 395(1) Companies Act 1985 talks about delivery to the registrar of 'prescribed particulars' and these prescribed particulars are set out in Form 395. Form 395 refers to the name of the company creating the charge, date of creation of the charge, description of the instrument (if any) creating or evidencing the charge, the amount secured by the mortgage or charge, names and addresses of the mortgagees or persons entitled to the charge and short particulars of the property mortgaged or charged.[16] The prescribed particulars do not as a matter of law have to be on Form 395 though the Court of Appeal, in *R v. Registrar of Companies, ex parte Central Bank of India*,[17] interpreting earlier legislation in similar terms, made it clear that it would be unwise for a chargee not to put the particulars on that form. In *Sun Tai Cheung Credits Ltd v. AG*[18] the Privy Council emphasised the importance of achieving accuracy with respect to the prescribed particulars. Lord Templeman said that it was for the applicant to provide the prescribed particulars in the form and, if he failed to do so, the registrar was entitled to reject the application unless the registrar was able and willing to complete his register and to issue a certificate on the basis of the information available to him. The registrar was clearly not bound to analyse and understand a bundle of documents submitted by the applicant for registration and then to draft the necessary particulars.[19]

The original instrument of charge together with the requisite particulars has to be submitted to the company registrar. The registrar compares the charge document with the filed particulars and is required to issue a certificate of due registration. The checking and comparison function is not an easy one and many commentators have expressed the view that the burden is unreasonable, with the process of registration being unduly

---

[15] Section 399(3).
[16] The relevant particulars do not include the company number of the security provider: see *Re Grove Advantage (T10) Ltd* [2000] 1 BCLC 661.
[17] [1986] 1 QB 1114.   [18] (1987) 3 BCC 357.   [19] *Ibid.*, at 361.

slowed as a result.[20] For instance, the Jenkins Committee on Company Law Reform stated:[21]

We understand that the Registrar has been advised that the effect of these provisions is to impose upon him an absolute duty to enter on the register the effect of every instrument of charge delivered to him. Thus, he may receive an instrument of charge which is extremely complicated or is obscurely drafted, but in fact creates both a specific charge on land and a floating charge over the remaining assets of the company, although the prescribed particulars furnished to him may mention only the fixed charge: if he fails to detect the existence of the floating charge and therefore omits any reference to it from his register, he may be liable to anyone who suffers loss in consequence of the omission.

The certificate of due registration issued by the registrar is stated to be conclusive evidence that the requirements of the Act as to registration have been complied with.[22] The courts have held the certificate effective even where a false date had been inserted on the charge;[23] where the amount secured was misstated;[24] and where the particulars did not accurately represent the full coverage of the charge.[25] Indeed, in judicial review proceedings, the Court of Appeal held that the 'conclusive evidence' formula precluded the receipt of information to rebut the facts stated on the certificate.[26]

Purposes served by the filing system

It has been argued that, as a result of the development of modern techniques for the collection and dissemination of credit information, traditional filing systems have been rendered unnecessary and obsolete and these developments call into question the usefulness of the Article 9 model.[27] On the other hand, Article 9, as well as providing public notice

[20] There is also the possibility of liability on the part of the registrar for mistakes made in the registration process: see the comments of Lightman J in *Grove* v. *Advantage Healthcare (T10) Ltd* [2000] 1 BCLC 661 at 665.

[21] Cmnd 1749, para. 302. See also Professor Aubrey Diamond's report for the Department of Trade and Industry (the Diamond report), *A Review of Security Interests in Property* (HMSO, 1989) at pp. 98–101.

[22] CA 1985, s 401(2)(b). The certificate is required to be either signed by the registrar or authenticated by his official seal.

[23] *Re Eric Holmes Ltd* [1965] 1 Ch 1052; *Re C. L. Nye Ltd* [1971] 1 Ch 442.

[24] *Re Mechanisations Eaglescliffe Ltd* [1966] 1 Ch 20.

[25] *National Provincial and Union Bank of England* v. *Charnley* [1924] 1 KB 431.

[26] *R* v. *Registrar of Companies, ex parte Central Bank of India* [1986] QB 1114.

[27] This point is discussed generally by Grant Gilmore in *Security Interests in Personal Property* at pp. 462–5. Professor Gilmore made the point as long ago as 1965, and it has obviously been reinforced by the passage of years. For a strong New Zealand flavour see Dugan 'The Price of Certainty' at 242: 'On the one hand, the expensive PPSA registration system embraces information which is, or the large part, already available in financial

of the existence of security interests, performs a whole host of other functions.[28] For example, it streamlines the methods for the creation of security interests, removes conceptual barriers to the creation of security in certain types of property and provides a method for determining priorities between competing security interests in the same property. It is a complete restatement of the law of security interests. Moreover, although the information contained in the Article 9 filing system is somewhat sparse, secured creditors in particular have been opposed to any abandonment of the notion of a central filing system. A filed financing statement puts subsequent creditors on notice that the debtor's property is possibly encumbered. The description of the collateral does not operate to identify the collateral and define property that a creditor may definitely claim, but rather to warn other subsequent creditors of the prior interest. Secured creditors can ascertain from the system whether or not any asset of the debtor is possibly subject to a prior-ranking encumbrance, and this may influence both the decision to lend and the conditions of any loan. In addition, it may prevent misrepresentations about the state of the debtor's financial position and this is of benefit to general creditors as well:[29]

The trade creditor may decide whether to send the goods on open account or to insist upon retaining a purchase money security interest only after checking the filing system. A compulsory public filing system is more accurate than any private system because security interests not properly noted in a public filing system are not enforceable against such competing property claimants as a lien creditor or a trustee in bankruptcy.

Nevertheless, there have been critics, vociferous and otherwise, of the place that the filing system occupies in the secured-credit world. One of the more moderate of the critics has been Professor James J. White.[30] On Professor White's analysis one of the ten commandments of mercantile

---

statements, in company records and at credit reporting agencies. On the other hand, secured financing is flourishing in jurisdictions which have rejected the art 9 model in favour of registrationless regimes for personal property security.'

[28] For an argument that the promulgation of Article 9 in a sense facilitated a movement from status to contract, i.e. credit became available to persons not previously on first-name terms with bankers, see A. Dunham 'Inventory and Accounts Receivable Financing' (1949) 62 *Harv L Rev* 588 at 611: 'One banker thought the questions [about sources of debtor information] "silly" because his bank did not make a loan unless the borrower "was properly introduced", and therefore a fraudulent borrower was an impossibility.'

[29] See D. Baird and T. Jackson *Security Interests in Personal Property* (Foundation Press, 2nd edn. 1987) at p. 80.

[30] See J. White 'Reforming Article 9 Priorities in Light of Old Ignorance and New Filing Rules' (1995) 79 *Minn LR* 529. Professor White adds the following, perhaps slightly tongue-in-cheek, comment (at 530):

The filing system is an integral part of the most sophisticated secured lending known to mankind. Only by an effective filing system can a secured lender know of other lenders and only by it can later secured lenders and unsecured lenders be encouraged to

law is that an effective filing system is the centre pole that holds up the entire personal-property-security tent. In his view, this 'commandment' or proposition rests on the assumption that a significant percentage of lenders, secured and unsecured, rely on the state of the filing records to find out about prior perfected secured creditors and also that the behaviour of these creditors would be different if there were no such system.[31] His intuition is that the filing system hardly looks like a significant variable in the formula for a successful mercantile economy.[32]

More trenchant critics see the filing system as a 'tax' on secured transactions. A proponent of this view is Professor Bowers,[33] who suggests that the filing system is little more than a 'rip-off'. He points to the proposition that secured lending ought not to be made more difficult or expensive (an assumption reflected in the Article 9 revision) and argues that proper application of such a policy mandates that the filing requirement be lifted from the backs of those who contract to grant or take security. In his view, the filing system has the prospective future lender paying search fees to a bureaucracy rather than buying the necessary information from the borrower and agreeing to pay for it in setting the terms of the loan agreement. On his analysis, potential contractors are turned by the system into potential free riders.[34]

Professor Bowers' arguments come from a free-market perspective but perhaps are not entirely convincing. Not only does the filing system serve a notice function, it also serves a validation function. In other words, when a secured party invests fees and effort in making an appropriate filing it is essentially buying an insurance policy. The filing system could be regarded as a form of insurance against fraud in that it provides creditors with insurance against the risk that a debtor has imposed or will impose secret liens on its assets to frustrate the claims of creditors.[35] Clearly the

---

lend. Without such a system, lenders would grow wary, commerce would be hobbled, and the manifold commercial ends that are met by commercial lenders would be stunted, rendered more costly, or stymied altogether . . . I can see generations of law students writing this down and repeating this incantation in negotiations, in court, and elsewhere. This view even extends to Americans abroad who approach the English, Dutch and Germans with an air of superiority, asserting the superiority of our filing system and belittling the European efforts to put together a filing system worthy of the name.

[31] *Ibid.* at 531.   [32] *Ibid.* at 534.

[33] See J. Bowers 'Of Bureaucrats Brothers-in-Law and Bankrutpcy Taxes: Article 9 Filing Systems and the Market for Information' (1995) 79 *Minn LR* 721 at 722–3.

[34] For a rebuttal of this view see J. Ayer 'Some Comments on Bowers' (1995) 79 *Minn LR* 745; and for a cautious embrace of the idea of partial privatisation of the system see C. Bjerre 'Bankruptcy Taxes and Other Filing Facts' (1995) 79 *Minn LR* 757.

[35] See generally P. Alces 'Abolish the Article 9 Filing System' (1995) 79 *Minn LR* 679; E. Smith 'Commentary' (1995) 79 *Minn LR* 715.

filing system is not an adequate substitute for a thorough credit investi-gation, and no careful lawyer would suggest otherwise. Nevertheless, the filing system, even when it works imperfectly, does provide information about prior claims to the debtor's assets. The system does not need to provide perfect and complete information to be a valuable source of in-formation. Moreover, the filing system does provide other benefits by creating a means of public notice for transactions that the parties might not want to publicise. Furthermore, the system could be used by debtors to provide some reassurance to the commercial community about their financial well-being. The financing statements that are recorded in favour of secured lenders provides reassurance to a debtor's suppliers that the debtor has lines of credit to pay for the goods supplied. It may be that unsecured creditors do not use the filing system on a large scale as a means of gleaning information about a debtor's borrowings because later events could render the information moot, i.e. a security interest could be filed the day after a search of the register was conducted. Neverthe-less, the system, however imperfect, is there as an information source if unsecured creditors choose to use it.

Perhaps the clinching argument in favour of the continued existence of the Article 9 notice-filing system is its role in determining priorities. The first secured party to file generally has priority. An alternative priority system would be first in time equals first in right, but such a system gives rise to evidentiary difficulties in establishing exactly who is first in time. Also, the effect of notice of a prior security interest on subsequent security-interest holders would have to be worked out.[36] It is far better to have a clear baseline, i.e. the public act of registration, as a priority reference point.[37]

Both the Company Law Review Steering Group and the Law Com-mission, in addressing the purpose of the filing system, highlighted the failure of the present English system in sorting out priorities. The Steering Group suggested that the express intention of the existing system is to penalise the concealment of secured credit and thus to prevent markets being misled by the apparent ownership by companies of assets which were in fact already encumbered in favour of prior creditors. The system provides public notice of any charges over a company's specified assets and only determines priorities as an incidental effect of failure to register

---

[36] See generally D. Baird and T. Jackson 'Information, Uncertainty and the Transfer of Property' (1984) *13 J Legal Stud* 299.

[37] See also C. Felsenfeld 'Knowledge as a Factor in Determining Priorities under the Uniform Commercial Code' (1967) 42 *NYULR* 246; S. Nickles 'Rethinking Some UCC Article 9 Problems' (1980) 34 *Ark LR* 1 at 72–103; D. Carlson 'Rationality, Accident and Priority under Article 9 of the Uniform Commercial Code' (1986) 71 *Minn LR* 207.

in timely fashion. This, in their view, was a major failing.[38] The Law
Commission spoke in similar terms, stating:[39]

We believe that a registration scheme should perform two basic functions: (1) to
provide information to persons who are thinking of extending secured lending
(and occasionally unsecured lending, where the amount is large), credit rating
agencies and potential investors about the extent to which assets that may appear
to be owned by the company are in fact subject to securities in favour of other
parties, in particular creditors; and (2) to determine the priority of securities . . .

In relation to priority the system should, in general, enable potential secured
parties to be confident (1) that they can take a security without any risk that it
will be subject to other existing interests of which they had no reasonable means of
knowing; (2) that, having checked the register, they will be able by taking simple
steps to ensure the priority of any security they subsequently take over one that is
taken in the meantime by another party; and (3) that registration will ensure the
priority of their security against any subsequent security interest (unless there are
good reasons of policy for the later interest to have priority).

Comparisons between perfection by filing under Article 9 and registration under Part 12 Companies Act 1985

While there seems little doubt that notice filing is more convenient and
flexible than transaction filing, it is also easy to overestimate these advantages. For example, after-acquired property clauses, future advances
clauses and 'floating' security interests are fully recognised by English
substantive law and, while registration must relate to a particular instrument of charge rather than the entire credit relationship of the parties,
the registered particulars can capture the full flexibility of the legal provisions. The major difference between the two systems lies in the fact
that in England the registrar checks off the registered particulars against
the instrument of charge whereas under Article 9, of necessity, no such
checking function is performed. The security agreement may not yet
be in existence and therefore it is impossible to match it up against the
financing statement.

The ability to register a financing statement in advance of the conclusion of a security agreement carries significant practical advantages.
A similar facility exists under the Canadian PPSA legislation and the
advantages accruing there have been described as follows:[40]

---

[38] *Modern Company Law* at pp. 248–9.
[39] Consultation Paper No. 164 *Registration of Security Interests* (July 2002) at pp. 46–7.
[40] J. Ziegel and D. Denomme *The Ontario Personal Property Security Act: Commentary and Analysis* (Canada Law Book, 1994) at p. 337. The same point was made by the Company Law Review Steering Group in its final report, *Modern Company Law*, at para. 12.22:

Where multiple parties are involved in a security agreement, pre-registration avoids delays arising from difficulties in arranging execution of the agreement by all parties. As well, there is no necessity to allow a period of time to elapse between the attachment of the security interest and its perfection because of the physical delay required to attend at the registry or branch registry or instruct someone else to do so after the conclusion of the security agreement. Advance registration also allows a secured party to confirm that the registration has occurred, and occurred correctly, before taking steps in reliance on the security interests perfected by registration (e.g. advancing funds under a secured loan). Pre-registration also facilitates line of credit financing when the parties anticipate that several security agreements will be reached, or changes made to existing security agreements, in the course of their relationships.

The advantage of being able to register a financing statement in advance of the conclusion of a security agreement was also noted by the Company Law Review Steering Group, which made the following point:[41] 'Notice-filing allows an intending chargee to preserve his priority during negotiations for the loan by filing the particulars in advance of the creation of the charge. The registered particulars then give notice of intention to take a charge with its priority being determined by the date of filing, even though this preceded its creation.' The fact that there is no facility for advance registration under the present English system was also highlighted by the Law Commission. As the Law Commission pointed out:[42]

A potential lender seeking to take a security may check the register, discover the state of the company's charges at the date of search and decide that the company can offer adequate security for an advance. However, during the period it takes to negotiate and set up the security there is no way in which he can ensure that the company will not create further charges that will rank ahead of his.

This practical problem could be solved by the adoption of a notice-filing system which the Law Commission advocated.

On the other hand, there are critics who suggest that the so-called practical problem is not a major one and that the notice-filing system leads to the underproduction of valuable information.[43] A searcher of the register does not know whether a particular registration relates to an actual transaction or to an intended transaction that never in fact materialised.

'Notice-filing allows an intending chargee to preserve his priority during negotiations for the loan by filing the particulars in advance of the creation of the charge. The registered particulars then give notice of intention to take a charge with its priority being determined by the date of filing, even though this preceded its creation.'

[41] *Modern Company Law* at para. 12.22.

[42] *Registration of Security Interests* at para. 3.29.

[43] See the unpublished paper prepared by Richard Calnan, a partner in Norton Rose, for the Queen Mary, University of London, conference on Registration of Security Interests (September 2002).

Moreover, far fewer details of the transaction are available than under a transaction-filing system. One might ask the rhetorical question whether, in the modern electronic information age, there is any justification for providing less detailed information on a publicly accessible register as to the state of a debtor's borrowings. Similar considerations appealed to the Scottish Law Commission in their discussion paper *Registration of Rights in Security by Companies*.[44] The Scottish Law Commission canvassed the possibility of requiring registration of the deed of charge rather than summarised particulars. In their view, the proposal would reduce the chances of error in that a system which registers only particulars, and not the deed itself, runs the risk of the particulars being inaccurate. According to the Scottish Law Commission:[45]

By making the security document publicly accessible, the proposed system would provide those searching the register with precisely the information they would wish to have, namely the nature and extent of the security. From the point of view of a third party, a copy of the deed itself is almost always better than an abbreviated summary . . . In any event it may be assumed that existing creditors would prefer to consult a public, and online, register than to have the inconvenience, and possible embarrassment, of making an approach to the company itself.

It may be that the only answer to these critics is to say that the register merely alerts searchers to the possible existence of conflicting third-party rights and no matter how perfect the information on the register it would be unrealistic to expect any register to render obsolete inquiries being made of the debtor or of the third party.

Identity of the person making the filing

In England the primary filing obligation is cast on the debtor, although in practice the creditor will attend to registration because the consequences of non-registration are much more serious from the point of view of the creditor, i.e. loss of priority. Under Article 9, on the other hand, the perfection duty resides with the would-be secured party though a debtor must provide authorisation before filing can occur.[46] The revised Article 9

---

[44] (October 2002).
[45] *Ibid.* at p. 47. The Commission recognised that there were counter-arguments such as the fact that registration of the deed might reveal more information than the parties to it would wish. Moreover, internet registration of a deed was likely to be awkward and internet registration was the way of the future. See also R. Calnan 'Registration of Company Charges: Proposals for Reform' [2001] *Butterworths Journal of International Banking and Financial Law* 53 at 56.
[46] Article 9-509(a)(1).

removes the requirement that the financing statement should be signed by the debtor. All that is required now is that the filing be authorised by the debtor in an authenticated record. Article 9-509(b) even stipulates that the debtor's authentication of a security agreement *ipso facto* constitutes the debtor's authorising the filing of a financing statement which covers the collateral described in the security agreement. Nevertheless, while the authorisation requirement minimises the risk, there is still the potential problem of malicious filings under Article 9. There is a remedy for unauthorised filings under Article 9-625, which entitles the debtor to recover $500 from a person who files a record that the person is not entitled to file. There is also a more general provision in Article 9-625 stipulating that a person is liable for damages in the amount of any loss caused by a failure to comply with Article 9, including the making of an unauthorised filing. Article 9-518 also allows the debtor to file a corrective statement where, in its view, there has been a bogus filing. The provision enables a person to file in the filing office a correction statement with respect to a record indexed there under the person's name, if the person believes that the record is inaccurate or has been wrongfully filed.[47] While the correction statement becomes part of the record, it does not destroy the effectiveness of the filed financing statement.

Continuation and termination of perfection

Under Article 9 a filed financing statement remains in force for five years after which it lapses unless it has been renewed within six months prior to the end of the five-year period. Again to avoid cluttering up the record, a secured creditor is obliged to file, or provide the debtor with a termination statement where there are no secured obligations and no commitment to advance credit. Article 9-509(d)(2) authorises the debtor to file a termination statement where the secured party was required to file or provide a termination statement but failed to do so.

The provisions on this score in the Companies Act are less detailed but arguably accomplish the desired objective just as effectively. Section 403 of the Act is concerned with entries of satisfaction and release. There is provision whereby if the registrar of companies receives a statutory declaration, in the prescribed form, that the debt for which the charge was given has been paid or satisfied in whole or in part, or that

---

[47] According to the Article 9-518 Official Comment this provision does not displace any available judicial remedies.

part of the property or undertaking charge has been released from the charge or has ceased to form part of the company's property or undertaking, he may make appropriate entries to the relevant effect on the register. If the registrar has issued a memorandum of satisfaction in whole, he must, if so required, furnish the company debtor with a copy of it.

Sufficiency of description in the filed particulars or security instrument
This is not a major issue as far as English law is concerned; it has no problem with general or indeed supergeneric descriptions either in the instrument of charge or in the filed particulars. It has long been the case that a floating charge over a company's undertaking is sufficient to create a security interest over the entirety of its business operations. On the other hand, the question of sufficiency of description has generated extensive litigation in the United States under Article 9.[48]

It is provided that a financing statement is effective to cover collateral if either it reasonably describes the collateral or else indicates that the financing statement refers to all assets or all personal property.[49] A broad, sweeping statement of this kind, which would be perfectly adequate in the context of a financing statement, would not be good enough in the case of a security agreement. Article 9-108 specifically provides that supergeneric descriptions such as 'all the debtor's assets' or 'all the debtor's personal property' do not reasonably identify the collateral in a security agreement. What is required is a description by specific listing, category, type, quantity, computational or allocational formula or procedure, or any other method that provides objectively determinable identification. In fact, the bulk of the case law under the 'old' Article 9 rejected supergeneric descriptions in the financing statement as well.[50] The logic of this reasoning is difficult to fathom, for as one judge has pointed out:[51] 'One of the basic words in English is "all". It is actually easier to understand "all" than a compilation of all of the UCC generics. Why must a security document state 1+1+1 when 3 is easily understood.' The judge added: 'There is a T-shirt available in resort areas with the legend: "What part of NO don't you understand?"'

---

[48] For an interesting but now somewhat dated account of the case law see I. Davies 'The Reform of Personal Property Security Law: Can Article 9 of the US Uniform Commercial Code be a Precedent?' (1988) 37 *ICLQ* 465 at 497–503.

[49] Article 9-504.

[50] See generally Honnold et al. *Security Interests in Personal Property* at pp. 161–7.

[51] *Re Legal Data Systems Inc.* (1991) 135 B.R. 199 at 201. This is a case from the Massachusetts bankruptcy courts that is referred to by Honnold et al. *Security Interests in Personal Property* at p. 167.

*Effect of errors or omissions in the financing statement
or filed particulars*

According to Article 9-506 a financing statement substantially satisfying the requirements of part 5 of Article 9 is effective, even if it has minor errors or omissions, unless the errors or omissions make the financing statement seriously misleading. A financing statement, however, is deemed to be seriously misleading if it fails sufficiently to provide the name of the debtor. If, nevertheless, a search of the records of the filing office under the debtor's correct name, using the filing office's standard search logic, if any, would disclose a financing statement that fails sufficiently to provide the name of the debtor, the name provided does not make the financing statement seriously misleading. Financing statements are indexed according to the name of the debtor and so it is logical that there should be a lot of attention paid to the use of the debtor's correct name. Whether a search turns up a particular financing statement depends on how the debtor has been named in the financing statement and the name against which the search is made. Article 9-503 provides a list of circumstances where a financing statement is regarded as having sufficiently stated the name of the debtor. Basically, Article 9-506 tells the courts to ignore minor errors in a financing statement. The predecessor provision has been characterised as an injunction to 'discourage the fanatical and impossibly refined reading of statutory requirements in which courts occasionally have indulged themselves'.[52] Nowadays, the courts can dismiss as irrelevant common slip-ups such as a reference to what is in reality a blue car as being red.

In England issues concerning the debtor's name have not been the subject of much judicial consideration[53] but the effect of other errors in the filed particulars has been extensively litigated. In large part, however, these decisions simply affirm the conclusiveness of the registrar's certificate of due registration. Indeed, there was a large outcry when the Companies Act 1989 proposed to do away with the checking function on the part of the registrar and, consequently, the conclusive evidence certificate. To reduce the possibility of any consequent increase in the number of inaccuracies on the register, a charge holder was not allowed to assert rights conferred by the instrument of charge that were greater than those mentioned in the particulars delivered for registration. These changes

---

[52] Article 9-506, Official Comment.
[53] See, however, *Re Grove Advantage (T10) Ltd* [2000] 1 BCLC 661. Registered companies have a unique registration number and Part 12 Companies Act applies principally to companies registered in England, though there is the so-called 'Slavenburg' register for foreign registered companies.

were not brought into force because of fears that they might compromise the marketability of debentures, and also on account of practical difficulties arising out of the interrelationship between the company charge registration process and the land registry.[54] More recently, the Company Law Review Steering Group made a number of recommendations to address the problem of the delivery of defective particulars.[55] Firstly, it proposed to make it an offence knowingly or recklessly to deliver false information to the registrar; secondly, that while filing of defective particulars should not invalidate the charge as a whole, a charge should only be valid as to the property or classes of property properly included in the particulars; thirdly, the charge holder should be under civil liability with respect to the accuracy of the particulars irrespective of who actually filed the particulars; fourthly, the registrar should not be liable for any inaccuracy in the information filed. The Law Commission was more tentative on some of these points but its general approach was somewhat similar.[56] In its view, the person filing would take responsibility for the contents of the financing statement. If an error occurred – as, for instance, in relation to the scope of the property covered by the charge – the party filing could not claim more than was stated although the filing would be effective for what was correctly filed. It was only in cases of a seriously misleading error that the filing would be invalidated. Consultees' views were invited on whether a person must actually have been misled in order for an error to be seriously misleading and whether that person should actually have been prejudiced by such an error.[57]

The full spirit of the present regime is captured in certain judicial decisions, including *National Provincial and Union Bank of England* v.

[54] See generally Law Commission *Registration of Security Interests* at p. 9.
[55] See *Modern Company Law* at pp. 255–6.
[56] See *Registration of Security Interests* at pp. 72–6.
[57] The Law Commission *ibid.* at p. 73 n. 67 made reference to the following statement of principle from the Supreme Court of British Columbia in *Coates* v. *General Motors Acceptance Corporation of Canada Ltd*:

> 1. The test of whether a registration is seriously misleading is an objective one, independent of whether anyone was or was not misled by the search, or whether a search was in fact conducted. 2. Total accuracy in registration by name or registration by serial number is not necessary. 3. A seriously misleading description of either the name or the serial number in the registration will defeat the registration. 4. A seriously misleading registration is one that, (a) would prevent a reasonable search from disclosing the registration or, (b) would cause a reasonable person to conclude that the search was not revealing the same chattel (in the case of a serial number search) or the same debtor (in the case of a name search). The obligation is on the searcher to review the similar registrations to make this determination. 5. Whether a registry filing and search program is reasonable in the sense that its design will reveal simple discrepancies without arbitrary distinction, will not be assessed in determining if a reasonable search would disclose a registration. The only question to be answered is whether a registry search will reveal the incorrect registration.

Charnley.[58] Here a company granted a mortgage to the bank of a certain leasehold factory together with all the movable 'plant used in or about the premises'. The bank sent the indenture to the registrar of companies for registration. The instrument was described as a mortgage of the leasehold premises, no mention being made of the chattels. The registrar entered the description of the instrument in the register in similar terms, identifying it by date, and omitting all mention of any charge on the chattels. He also issued a certificate stating 'that a mortgage or charge dated' – specifying the date and the parties to the instrument – 'was registered pursuant to s. 93 of the Companies Act'. A priority dispute subsequently arose between the bank and a judgment creditor of the company who had seized certain chattels on the mortgaged premises. The bank emerged victorious. The Court of Appeal held that as the certificate identified the instrument of charge, and stated that the mortgage or charge thereby created had been duly registered, it must be understood as certifying the due registration of all the charges created by the instrument, including that of the chattels. The fact that the register was misleading to a potential creditor of the company did not sway the court which said that it was incumbent upon a person to look at the charging instrument itself to discover the precise nature of the security granted by the company. The fact of registration only puts a person on notice that there is a charge.[59]

A slightly different situation arose in *Re Mechanisations (Eaglescliffe) Ltd.*[60] Here the particulars supplied for registration gave the amount secured as the principal sum only, with no mention being made of the payment of interest. The registrar's certificate again referred only to the principal sum. It was held, nevertheless, that the charges constituted valid security for the full amount due under them. The court said that the certificate was not conclusive evidence that the amount thereby stated to be secured by the charge was in fact the amount secured by the charge. It was, in fact, only conclusive evidence that the requirements as to registration had been complied with. Although no doubt the legislature contemplated that when particulars were submitted they would be accurate and that when the registrar made entries in the register he would have checked the accuracy of such particulars against the instrument which he had for that purpose, the legislature had not made accuracy in that respect a condition of the validity of the charge. In *Re C. L. Nye Ltd*[61] there is a detailed discussion as to the reasons why evidentiary conclusiveness is attributed to the registrar's certificate. According to the court,

[58] [1924] 1 KB 431.   [59] *Ibid.* at 447–8.
[60] [1966] 1 Ch 20.   [61] [1971] 1 Ch 442 at 470.

the registration provisions should provide for a marketable security. This could not be achieved unless the certificate of the registrar was, in every respect, conclusive and unassailable.[62]

An attempt was made to sidestep the effect of *Re C. L. Nye Ltd* in *R v. Registrar of Companies, ex parte Central Bank of India*.[63] Here the prescribed particulars of the charge sent to the registrar of companies for registration were defective. The registrar returned the form for amendment and later accepted a corrected form of the particulars after the twenty-one-day period had elapsed. A judicial review order was sought quashing the certificate of registration. It was contended that, in accordance with standard administrative law principles, an exercise of a statutory authority to make decisions affecting the rights and obligations of other persons was normally subject to review by way of *certiorari*. The Court of Appeal held, however, that while the jurisdiction of the court to grant judicial review had not been ousted, it was not permissible to adduce evidence to challenge the registrar's certificate. If an unsecured creditor sought judicial review solely on the ground that the chargee did not deliver the prescribed particulars, then the necessary evidence could not be put before the court. Therefore, the judicial review application was doomed to failure.[64]

There were a number of cases, however, where a certificate of due registration issued by the registrar of companies might be set aside. Firstly, the certificate did not operate to confer validity on a charge that was invalid for reasons other than lack of registration.[65] Secondly, the Companies Act was not expressed to bind the Crown. Therefore, it was possible that the Attorney General was not constrained by the conclusive evidence provision if he were to seek judicial review so as to quash a certificate.[66] Thirdly, an applicant could conceivably increase his chances of success by demonstrating an error of law on the face of the certificate or by proving that it had been procured by fraud or duress.[67] Moreover, the Court of Appeal approved the revised practice of the registrar whereby he will not accept for registration particulars of charge, whether in original or revised form, submitted after the twenty-one-day period had elapsed subject to

---

[62] *Ibid.* at 474.   [63] [1986] QB 1114.   [64] *Ibid.* at 1169–70.
[65] *Grove* v. *Advantage Healthcare (T10) Ltd* [2000] 1 BCLC 661.
[66] Lawton LJ referred at 1169 to the Divisional Court decision in *R* v. *Registrar of Companies, ex parte Attorney General* [1991] BCLC 476. Here the Attorney General applied successfully for the registration of a company to be quashed despite the provisions of what is now section 13 Companies Act 1985 that a certificate of incorporation shall be conclusive evidence that all the requirements of the Act as to registration have been complied with.
[67] [1986] 1 QB 1114 at 1169, 1177.

the qualification that obvious clerical or typing errors could be corrected without recourse to the courts.[68]

In the US, the complete divorce between security agreement and financing statement means that there is no scope for a conclusive evidence certificate issued by the filing office. A financing statement may be filed long before a security agreement is executed; and moreover, the financing statement may be intended to cover more than one security agreement. What is clear is that, in the US, the filing office performs a purely ministerial function. Article 9-516 provides an exhaustive list of grounds upon which the filing office may reject a record. Some of these are grounds that have the effect of rendering the financing statement itself ineffective, but some grounds are not ones that would have this effect. The latter include failure to provide a name and mailing address for the secured party of record. It should be noted that it is not the function of the filing office to check the accuracy of the information provided:[69] 'A filing office may not reject . . . an initial financing statement indicating that the debtor is a State A corporation and providing a three-digit organizational identification number, even if all State A organizational identification numbers contain at least five digits and two letters.' If the filing office improperly rejects a financing statement that complies with all the requirements of Article 9 then the financing statement is still regarded as effective[70] 'except as against a purchaser of the collateral which gives value in reasonable reliance upon the absence of the record from the files'. In England, wrongly rejected particulars of charge do not detract from the validity of the security interest. What is crucial is the actual delivery of the particulars of charge within twenty-one days of the charge's creation and not the actual acceptance by the registrar of those particulars. If delivery of the correct particulars takes place within the twenty-one-day period, then the charge is valid. There is, however, no proviso to protect a purchaser of collateral who is misled by the absence of any record appearing on the register to denote the creation of a security interest in the collateral.

Unperfected security interests

Article 9-201(a) lays down that 'a security agreement is effective according to its terms between the parties, against purchasers of the collateral, and against creditors'. A security agreement means an agreement that

---

[68] *Ibid.* at 1171, 1178. Lawton and Slade LJJ issued a warning that copies of instruments will not be accepted.
[69] See Article 9-516 Official Comment.   [70] Article 9-516(d).

creates or provides for a security interest. An unperfected security interest remains valid as between debtor and creditor. Moreover, Article 9-201(a) states the general principle of effectiveness of security agreement vis-à-vis third parties though there are some notable exceptions to this principle. Indeed, one may question which in practice is the general rule and which is the exception. Article 9-317 subordinates an unperfected security interest to a lien creditor but, more importantly, the Bankruptcy Code deprives such a security interest of force and effect when it is most needed – namely, in the debtor's bankruptcy. The bankruptcy trustee is afforded the status of a hypothetical judicial lien creditor. Article 544(a)(1) Bankruptcy Code 1978 gives the trustee, as of the commencement of the case, the rights and powers of a creditor that extends credit to the debtor at the time of the commencement of the case, and that obtains, at that time and with respect to that credit, a judicial lien on all property on which a creditor on a simple contract could have obtained a judicial lien, whether or not such a creditor exists. This provision, known as the strong-arm power,[71] reflects a long-established bankruptcy policy directed against unperfected security interests and similar secret liens.[72] The 'provision deprives the secured party of its victory because it has come at the expense of unsecured creditors, who may have been prejudiced by the secret lien'.[73]

Article 9-317 also protects buyers and lessees of collateral who take free of unperfected security interests if they give value and receive delivery of the collateral without knowledge of the security interest and before it is perfected. Where the collateral consists of intangibles such as investment property, similar protection is extended to a licensee as well as a buyer or lessee. As regards competing security interests there is generally speaking a 'first-to-file' rule for determining priorities.[74] A fortiori, a perfected security interest will take priority over an unperfected security interest. So in the US all that is left of the supposed validity of an unperfected security interest in relation to third parties is priority over unsecured creditors outside bankruptcy. Survival in the wake of bankruptcy may be

---

[71] For some history on why it is known as the strong-arm power see J. McCoid 'Bankruptcy, the Avoiding Powers, and Unperfected Security Interests' (1985) 59 *American Bankruptcy Law Journal* 175 at 181 n. 52.

[72] See e.g. *Sampsell v. Straub* (1951) 194 F 2d 228 at 231; and see generally C. Scott Pryor 'Revised Uniform Commercial Code Article 9: Impact in Bankruptcy' (1999) 7 *American Bankruptcy Institute Law Review* 465.

[73] Honnold et al. *Security Interests in Personal Property* at p. 441; and see also McCoid 'Bankruptcy, the Avoiding Powers and Unperfected Security Interests'.

[74] Article 9-322.

regarded as the acid test of a security interest, and an unperfected security interest fails badly on this score.

In England, it is clear from Section 395(1) Companies Act 1985 that a registrable but unregistered charge is invalid as against the liquidator, administrator or creditors of a company.[75] It should be stressed that an unregistered charge remains valid with respect to the company creating it outside liquidation or administration. This state of affairs is well established. A case in point is *Mercantile Bank of India Ltd* v. *Central Bank of India, Australia and China*[76] where it was held that letters of security over goods amounted to floating charges which should have been registered. Nevertheless, the charges remained valid against the company and consequently the chargee was able to convert the floating charges into fixed charges and take possession of the goods subject to the security interest prior to liquidation of the security giver. This seizure was then good as against the liquidator of the company creating the security interest. The same result would obtain in the US, for Article 9-201 makes a security agreement effective between the debtor and secured party, irrespective of perfection. Moreover, outside bankruptcy, ordinary creditors cannot challenge the supremacy of an unperfected security interest. It is only in formal bankruptcy proceedings where the bankruptcy trustee, representing unsecured creditors, can claim the mantle of a hypothetical judicial lien creditor.

Invalidity of unperfected or unregistered security interests in liquidation

In both England and the US the broad policy principle is that unperfected or unregistered security interests are invalid in the event of the corporate debtor going into liquidation. This result has been subjected

---

[75] For a discussion of the scope of the provision (section 395) invalidating unregistered charges see generally *Smith* v. *Bridgend County Borough Council* [2002] 1 AC 336. 'Creditors' has been construed as meaning only secured creditors: *Re Cardiff Workmen's Cottage Co. Ltd* [1906] 2 Ch 627; *Re Telomatic Ltd* [1994] 1 BCLC 90; and see generally E. Ferran *Company Law and Corporate Finance* (Oxford University Press, 1999) at p. 543. The issue would assume some practical importance if an unsecured creditor obtained judgment and tried to execute against property that was subject to an unregistered fixed charge. If the charge, though unregistered, was still valid vis-à-vis unsecured creditors, then the execution would be ineffective. Similar legislation has generated difficulties of interpretation in Singapore: see *Ng Wei Teck Michael* v. *Oversea-Chinese Banking Corporation Ltd* [1998] 2 SLR 1; on which see Tan Cheng Han 'Unregistered Charges and Unsecured Creditors' (1998) 114 *LQR* 565.

[76] [1937] 1 All ER 231.

to forceful criticism, particularly in the US.[77] It is argued that bankruptcy trustees are thereby given an incentive to litigate the issue of perfection and to plead errors in a financing statement that would not in fact have misled any reasonable searcher. Unsecured creditors gain an undeserved windfall, so the argument goes, if a filing is held to be defective.[78] By deciding not to require collateral, unsecured creditors are agreeing to be subordinated to later-in-time perfected secured parties. Even if an unsecured creditor does search and rely upon the existing state of the register, subsequent events could render the information of little value. In other words, the filing system cannot possibly protect an unsecured creditor from having its claim primed by a secured party, because the day after the unsecured creditor's search is made, the debtor could grant a security interest and a filing be made.

Addressing the current law in England, Professor Sir Roy Goode accepts that the effect of avoidance is to give unsecured creditors who did not act in reliance on the want of registration an apparently unjustified windfall in addition to the assets available for distribution. Nevertheless, in his view, there are sound policy reasons for the avoidance of unregistered securities:[79]

In the first place, the avoidance rule reflects the law's dislike of the secret security interest, which leaves the debtor's property apparently unencumbered and at common law was considered a fraud on the general creditors. Secondly, the registration provisions help to curb the fabrication or antedating of security agreements on the eve of the winding-up. Thirdly, though unsecured creditors have no existing interest in the company's assets outside winding up, [upon winding up] . . . their rights become converted from purely personal rights into rights more closely analogous to that of beneficiaries under an active trust. Fourthly, there may well be unsecured creditors who were misled by the want of registration into extending credit which they would not otherwise have granted. But it would be expensive and impracticable to expect the liquidator (or administrator) to investigate each unsecured creditor's claim to see whether he did or did not act

---

[77] See the statement by McCoid 'Bankruptcy, the Avoiding Powers, and Unperfected Security Interests' at 190 that

> invalidation of unperfected security interests by the bankruptcy trustee takes from innocent secured parties to give to unsecured creditors who are not prejudiced by the failure to perfect. Even if avoidance did not take time and effort, one might seriously question this structure which requires those who meant no harm to compensate those who have not been injured, particularly when both bargained for the extension of credit on a different assumption.

[78] See Smith 'Commentary' at 718; and see also more generally Scott Pryor 'Revised Uniform Commercial Code Article 9'.

[79] *Principles of Corporate Insolvency Law* (Sweet & Maxwell, 2nd edn. 1997) at pp. 420–1.

on the assumption that the unregistered charge did not exist. So a broad brush approach which in effect assumes detriment to unsecured creditors at large is justified. Finally, the registration provisions serve a general public notice function as well as being a registration requirement.

These arguments were not accepted in New Zealand where, in a conscious departure from the Article 9 and Canadian PPSA models, a notice-filing system was introduced without any invalidation of unperfected security interests in liquidation.[80] One of the New Zealand Law Commissioners responsible for the preparation of the legislation specifically took issue with the propositions advanced by Professor Goode and suggested that they rested on an outdated conception of how business was actually conducted.[81] The policy against secret security interests was misplaced because nowadays there was little danger of a creditor being induced to give credit on the assumption that goods in the debtor's possession are his own property. In his view, the reliance on apparent ownership to extend credit argument was seriously out of date in the light of modern business conditions.[82]

The matter was not considered by the Law Commission in England, which simply recommended that the effect of a failure to file should be invalidity against an administrator and liquidator, and a loss of priority against a subsequent secured creditor who files first.[83] There was no discussion of the New Zealand legislation but it is submitted that, on balance, the latter approach is not one that should be followed in this

---

[80] See the New Zealand Law Commission Report No. 8 *A Personal Property Securities Act for New Zealand* (1989) at p. 115:

> In practice, only two parties are possibly misled by the absence of a registration statement. The first is the prospective creditor who would normally advance credit only against a first ranking security in a debtor's goods. Under the proposed statute, if such a creditor files a registration statement, it is protected against any unperfected security interests . . . Creditors, who supply goods or funds on an unsecured basis are generally either not concerned about the presence of outstanding interests or assume that such interests exist. Prospective buyers and lessees, like prospective secured creditors, also rely heavily on the ostensible ownership of their transferor. Accordingly, they are protected from unperfected security interests . . . unless they have knowledge of the security interest.

[81] See D. F. Dugdale 'The Proposed PPSA' [2000] *NZLJ* 383 at 384.

[82] See generally on the New Zealand legislation L. Widdup and L. Mayne *Personal Property Securities Act: A Conceptual Approach* (Butterworths, 2000); and see also D. Webb 'The PPSA – a New Regime for Secured Transactions' [2000] *New Zealand Law Review* 175; D. McLauchlan 'Fundamentals of the PPSA: An Introduction' (2000) 6 *NZBLQ* 166; R. Scragg 'Personal Property Securities Law Reform in New Zealand' (1999) 7 *Insolvency Law Journal* 163.

[83] See Law Commission *Registration of Security Interests* para. 4.58.

jurisdiction.[84] Although, as one commentator has pointed out, an unsecured creditor may not actively seek a proprietary right against the company, the register provides important information about the existence of creditors who possess such rights.[85] A wider reliance interest is promoted in that the general credit assessment of the company would involve the receipt of such information. Regular inspections of the register enable an unsecured creditor to police any negative pledge covenants that might exist in the loan agreement and also to police the borrower more generally.[86] The presence of a security interest on the register could cause an unsecured creditor to alter the conditions of the loan or the other terms of the business relationship with the debtor. The fact that a particular individual unsecured creditor may not have relied on the register in this way is irrelevant. As Dr De Lacy comments:[87] 'The hypothetical nature of the unsecured creditor in this context is designed to remove complex factual inquiries that would otherwise occur at considerable expense to the liquidation process thereby prejudicing creditors as a whole. Indeed the concept of reliance in this context would be exceedingly difficult to establish or refute were it to be made fact specific.'

As far as secured parties are concerned registration does not seem too high a price to pay to assume priority over unsecured creditors. Allowing unperfected security interests to prevail over unsecured creditors would contribute to the further marginalisation of the latter in the insolvency process, and this state of affairs is hardly socially or politically acceptable.

Unperfected security interests and the European Convention on Human Rights

The European Convention on Human Rights (now incorporated in domestic English law through the Human Rights Act) provides a possible,

---

[84] The Dugdale view is not one that appeals to all New Zealand commentators. See, for instance, D. McLauchlan 'Unperfected Securities under the PPSA' [1999] *NZLJ* 55 who argues that if the policy objective of adherence to the perfection requirement is to be achieved then failure to perfect should have the meaningful penalty of defeating the security interest on the insolvency of the debtor. In McLauchlan's view this is a bare minimum step that the law should take in redressing the balance somewhat in favour of unsecured creditors.

[85] See J. De Lacy 'Ambit and Reform of Part 12 of the Companies Act 1985 and the Doctrine of Constructive Notice' in J. De Lacy ed. *The Reform of United Kingdom Company Law* (Cavendish, 2002) p. 333 at pp. 362–3; but cf. Baird 'Notice Filing' at 60.

[86] On the possible prejudice that may be suffered by unsecured creditors through 'springing' security interests and so-called affirmative negative pledge clauses see Tan Cheng Han 'Charges, Contingencies and Registration' (2002) 2 *Journal of Corporate Law Studies* 191.

[87] 'Ambit and Reform' at pp. 356–7. De Lacy refers in this connection to the observations of Lord Wilberforce in *Midland Bank Trust Co. Ltd* v. *Green* [1981] AC 513 at 530.

though superficially unlikely, vehicle for challenging the legislative in-validation of unperfected security interests. Article 1, Protocol 1 to the Convention provides:[88] 'Every natural or legal person is entitled to the peaceful enjoyment of his possessions. No one shall be deprived of his possessions except in the public interest and subject to the conditions provided for by law and by the general principles of international law.' Article 1 adds, however, that the preceding prescriptions do not in any way impair the right of a state to enforce such laws as it deems necessary to control the use of property in accordance with the general interest or to secure the payment of taxes or other contributions of penalties.[89]

By analogy with the decision of the Court of Appeal in *Wilson v. First County Trust Ltd (No. 2)*[90] it has been argued that the sanction of invalidity for failure to register a security interest constitutes a disproportionate deprivation of property rights. In the *Wilson* case certain provisions of the Consumer Credit Act were declared incompatible with the Human Rights Convention. It is submitted that there is a clear difference between the Consumer Credit Act provisions and the existing company charge registration provisions and any future notice-filing regime. Under the Consumer Credit Act an improperly executed regulated agreement is unenforceable as between the parties thereto and not just vis-à-vis certain named third parties; and, moreover, there is no mechanism of application to the court whereby the defects can be cured.

Nevertheless, somewhat surprisingly, the Company Law Review Steer-ing Group accepted the *Wilson* analogy at face value and suggested that the present avoidance power needed to be amended to reflect that decision.[91] Consequently, it suggested that the beneficiary of an unregis-tered security interest should be given the right to apply to a court for re-lief from the invalidity.[92] Implementation of this recommendation might create uncertainty and produce practical difficulties, and it is submitted that the avoidance power does not fall foul of the Convention being le-gitimate, proportionate and justifiable in the public interest. Fortunately, the Law Commission took a more robust line than the Company Law

---

[88] See generally for an assessment of the implications of these provisions in the commercial law sphere A. Dignam and J. Allen *Company Law and Human Rights* (Butterworths, 2000) at pp. 263–85.

[89] For a discussion of the position in the US under the Fifth Amendment ('no taking without due process') see J. Rogers 'The Impairment of Secured Creditors' Rights in Corporate Reorganisation: A Study of the Relationship Between the 5th Amendment and the Bankruptcy Clause' (1983) 96 *Harvard L Rev* 973; D. Baird and T. Jackson 'Corporate Reorganization and the Treatment of Diverse Ownership Interests: A Com-ment on Adequate Protection of Secured Creditors in Bankruptcy' (1984) 51 *U Ch L Rev* 97.

[90] [2002] QB 74.   [91] *Modern Company Law* at para. 12.16.

[92] See generally De Lacy ed. *The Reform of United Kingdom Company Law* at pp. 382–4.

Review Steering Group. In its view, the avoidance power was not incompatible with the European Convention because[93] 'the provision merely invalidates the unregistered charge as against third parties in certain circumstances, not as between the parties themselves in all cases; because the sanction is imposed for the important purpose of securing publicity of charges that may have a serious effect on third parties; and because the sanction is easy to avoid by registration'.

The decision of the Court of Appeal in the *Wilson* case has now been overturned by the House of Lords, who held that the Consumer Credit Act was a proportionate regulation of property rights and served a legitimate social end.[94] Lord Nicholls said:[95] 'The fairness of a system of law governing the contractual or property rights of private persons is a matter of public concern. Legislative provisions intended to bring about such fairness are capable of being in the public interest, even if they involve the compulsory transfer of property from one person to another.' He added:[96]

It is open to Parliament, when Parliament considers the public interest so requires, to decide that failure to comply with certain formalities is an essential prerequisite to enforcement of certain types of agreements. This course is open to Parliament even though this will sometimes yield a seemingly unreasonable result in a particular case. Considered overall, this course may well be a proportionate response in practice to a perceived social problem. Parliament may consider the response should be a uniform solution across the board. A tailor-made response, fitting the facts of each case as decided in an application to the court, may not be appropriate. This may be considered an insufficient incentive and insufficient deterrent.

Knowledge of unperfected security interests and effect on priorities

What if a subsequent security-interest holder has knowledge of a prior unperfected or unregistered security interest? How does this affect the issue of priorities? The matter has been considered at length, both in England and the US, with broadly similar results being reached in the two countries.

In England, the issue in its starkest form arises where an interest in charged assets is acquired outside the twenty-one-day period from the date of creation of the initial charge with the acquirer of the interest having actual notice of the prior unregistered charge. The Act does not

---

[93] Law Commission *Registration of Security Interests* at p. 58.
[94] *Wilson v. Secretary of State for Trade and Industry* [2003] 40 UKHL (10 July 2003).
[95] *Ibid.*, at para. 68 of the judgment.   [96] *Ibid.*, at para. 74 of the judgment.

specifically address the question and the case law is 'old', with the leading authority being *Re Monolithic Building Co.*[97] In this case, the Court of Appeal had no hesitation in deciding in favour of the subsequent charge holder with the court stating unequivocally that notice was immaterial. It was acknowledged that, in cases of fraud, the court proceeds upon a different footing, and that any security may be postponed if one could find fraud in its inception. On the other hand, the Court of Appeal stressed that it was not fraud to take advantage of legal rights, the existence of which may be taken to be known to both parties.[98]

One could vary the facts slightly, however, and ask what the position would be if a subsequent charge holder acquires an interest in or right over property and the acquisition is expressly subject to the unregistered charge. In that event, the first charge, although it has not been registered, may take priority. There is direct authority to this effect in the Republic of Ireland,[99] where it was held that in such circumstances the second charge holder's rights were at all times limited and qualified ones, with the right to a second charge ranking after the first. Moreover, while the case is not directly in point, the proposition favouring postponement of the second charge holder also derives some support from the decision of Vinelott J in *Re Fablehill Ltd.*[100]

In the US, knowledge of a prior unperfected security interest will not deprive a perfected security-interest holder of priority. Article 9 made a change to pre-existing law where actual notice of an earlier unperfected interest in the property would prevent the second interest from obtaining

---

[97] [1915] 1 Ch 643. Cf. *Ram Narain* v. *Radha Kishen Moti Lal Chamaria Firm* (1929) LR 57 Ind App 76. See also the Land Charges Act and Land Registration Act cases: *Midland Bank Trust Co Ltd* v. *Green* [1981] AC 513; *Peffer* v. *Rigg* [1977] 1 WLR 285; *De Lusignan* v. *Johnson* (1973) 230 EG 499; and *Lyus* v. *Prowsa Developments Ltd* [1982] 1 WLR 1044. In *Midland Bank Trust Co. Ltd* v. *Green* [1981] AC 513 Lord Wilberforce at 530 specifically approved the words of Lord Cozens-Hardy MR in *Re Monolithic Building Co.* [1915] 1 Ch 643. Lord Wilberforce's speech has been subjected to some criticism by Kevin Gray and Susan Frances Gray in *Elements of Land Law* (Butterworths, 3rd edn. 2001) at p. 1098. They say that the decision of the House of Lords in *Midland Bank Trust Co. Ltd* v. *Green* epitomises the traditional view of the busy property lawyer that there is much to be said in favour of trading off a little justice in return for enhanced security and certainty in commercial transactions. In their view, however, this pragmatic approach will never satisfy all of the people all of the time. They suggest that while it may well be that, in the eyes of the law, it is not fraud to take advantage of the folly of another, it remains an uncomfortable fact of life that most fraud consists in doing precisely that.

[98] See [1915] I Ch 643 at 663. It was suggested that to engraft a notice exception onto the section might be to render the whole provision unworkable and absurd.

[99] *Re Clarets Ltd* (1978) which is discussed by G. McCormack *Registration of Company Charges* (Sweet & Maxwell, 1984) at pp. 106–7.

[100] [1991] BCLC 830. See also *Barclays Bank plc* v. *Stuart Landon Ltd* [2001] 2 BCLC 316.

priority.[101] The change in legislative policy reflects an assumption that making the issue of priorities turn on factual inquiries based on the state of knowledge generates uncertainty and breeds litigation. For example, it may be difficult to determine what exactly happened before the event in question, and this makes life more difficult for subsequent parties who may not know whether to negotiate subordination agreements or to adjust interest rates accordingly. Moreover, it could be argued that a system which makes priorities turn on knowledge tends to reward careless creditors who do not make inquiries about their debtors rather than the diligent creditor who examines a debtor's credit history and prior lending agreements before entering into the commitment to lend.

The merits of the Article 9 approach have been commended by its principal progenitor, Grant Gilmore, who points out that a good-faith or knowledge requirement creates evidentiary problems:[102] 'The presence or absence of "knowledge" is a subjective question of fact, difficult to prove. Unless there is an overwhelming policy argument in favor of using such a criterion, it is always wise to discard it and to make decision turn on some easily determinable objective event – as, for example, the date of filing.'

The statement from Gilmore was approved by the United States District Court in *Re Smith*.[103] This is a case where a second lender advanced credit and perfected a security interest at the time that it had knowledge of a prior unperfected security interest. The court held that Article 9 did not make good faith a requirement for obtaining priority. The provision legislated for a race to the filing office with actual knowledge of a prior unperfected security interest being irrelevant if one perfected first by filing. Knowledge of an earlier unperfected interest had no bearing on priority. The court suggested that there were good reasons for disregarding knowledge and creating a race-to-file situation. The integrity of the filing system was protected only if perfection of interests took place promptly. It was appropriate therefore that a secured party who failed to file promptly should run the risk of subordination to a later, more diligent, party. Stepping back from the case for a minute, one might say that the law rewards diligence and punishes indolence in many different contexts and this situation is fundamentally no different.

---

[101] This was also the case under early versions of Article 9: see Baird and Jackson *Security Interests in Personal Property* at p. 369 'Until 1956, Article 9 followed the traditional rule of granting unperfected secured parties priority over all subsequent property claimants who took with knowledge of their interests.'
[102] *Security Interests in Personal Property* at p. 902.   [103] (1971) 326 F Supp 1311.

Leading scholars, writing more recently, have also endorsed the Grant Gilmore view as to the inappropriateness of a 'knowledge' criterion in this context. Professors Baird and Jackson suggest:[104]

> First, even if there are advantages from insisting that subsequent [security-interest holders] meet the traditional requirement of being without knowledge, these advantages seem to pale beside the costs they impose. Any inquiry into knowledge is likely to be expensive and time consuming. It is simply much easier to live in a world in which everyone knows that he must comply with a few simple formalities or lose than to live in a world where the validity of someone's property rights turns on whether certain individuals had knowledge at some particular time in the past. Those who are required to make appropriate filings, in the main, either are professionals or engage the services of professionals. We think it likely that everyone is ultimately better off with a clear rule than with a legal regime that is somewhat more finely tuned but much more expensive to operate. Ferreting out those who took with knowledge despite a defective filing generally is not worth the uncertainty and the litigation it generates.

Under Article 9, however, there is nothing to prevent a secured party from giving up priority, whether voluntarily or in a contractual arrangement. Indeed, Article 9-339 expressly validates subordination agreements, stating that this article does not preclude subordination by a person entitled to priority. As the Official Comment points out, only the person entitled to priority may make such a subordination agreement. Certainly, a security-interest holder's rights cannot be adversely affected by an agreement to which the person is not a party.[105]

One final point in this area concerns the distinction between the presence of notice or knowledge, which is irrelevant, and an affirmative showing of bad faith, which may or may not be relevant. In fact, there is a suggestion in some of the case law that the priorities established under Article 9 might be disturbed by a positive demonstration of bad faith.[106] There is indeed an overarching good-faith requirement embodied in Article 1-203 of the UCC. It seems clear, however, that knowledge alone does not amount to bad faith. This would require something akin to positive misleading actions. This might encompass the situation, as in England, where a security interest is expressly taken subject to a prior unperfected security interest and the subsequent security-interest holder

---

[104] 'Information, Uncertainty and the Transfer of Property' at 314; and see also Carlson 'Rationality, Accident and Priority'.

[105] For the validity of subordination agreements see *Re Maxwell Communications Corp plc (No 2)* [1993] 1 WLR 1402; *Cheah v. Equiticorp Finance Group Ltd* [1992] BCLC 371; Ferran *Company Law and Corporate Finance* chap. 1; R. Nolan 'Less Equal than Others' [1995] *JBL* 485.

[106] See Honnold et al. *Security Interests in Personal Property* at pp. 235–6.

then tries to rely on the non-perfected status of the earlier security interest to achieve priority.[107]

Late registration

If a charge has not been registered as required under section 395 within the period of twenty-one days from the date of creation, then the court has jurisdiction to make an order sanctioning late registration.[108] The discretion in the court arises if the omission to register on time was accidental, or due to inadvertence or to some other sufficient cause, or is not of a nature to prejudice the position of creditors or shareholders of the company, or that on other grounds it is just and equitable to grant relief. The discretion to permit late registration is normally exercised in favour of the charge holder save where there is evidence that the company granting the charge is actually or imminently insolvent.[109] It is customary to make an order permitting late registration subject to a proviso protecting the rights of parties who acquired such rights in the period between the date of creation of the charge and the date of its actual registration.[110] The proviso, as typically worded, will protect only proprietary-rights holders, and hence secured – but not unsecured – creditors.[111] It has often been suggested that the requirement of having to apply to the court for late registration should be abolished with the consequent saving of court time and avoidance of administrative inconvenience. For instance, the Company Law Review Steering Group suggested that late registration should be possible without application to the court provided that at the time of registration no winding-up petition has been presented and no meeting has been convened to pass a resolution for a creditors' voluntary winding-up petition.[112] Moreover, in the event of late registration the charge should be treated from then on as if it were registered within time, save that it should rank behind any prior registered charges. In fact, under the status quo, the court accedes to late registration applications almost as a matter of course save where a

---

[107] See *General Insurance Co.* v. *Lowry* (1976) 412 F Supp 12, affirmed (1978) 570 F 2d 120; and see generally the discussion in Honnold et al. *Security Interests in Personal Property* at pp. 228–36.

[108] Section 404 Companies Act 1985.   [109] *Re Ashpurton Estates Ltd* [1983] 1 Ch 110.

[110] See generally *Watson* v. *Duff Morgan & Vermont Holdings Ltd* [1974] 1 WLR 450.

[111] *Re Joplin Brewery Co. Ltd* [1902] 1 Ch 79; *Re Cardiff Workmen's Cottage Co. Ltd* [1906] 2 Ch 627.

[112] *Modern Company Law* at para. 12.44. The Company Law Review Steering Group suggested that the court should not be able to change the relative priority of charges and that under the new notice-filing system priority between competing charges would be determined by their dates of registration.

company is in liquidation or, more controversially, where liquidation is imminent.[113]

In the US there is no criminal sanction for failure to file a financing statement and, as we have seen, filing may take place either before or after execution of a security agreement. Of course, a security agreement that has not been perfected, whether by filing or otherwise, is vulnerable to a lien creditor – and doubly so if the debtor goes into bankruptcy, for the trustee in bankruptcy is accorded the status of a hypothetical judicial lien creditor.[114]

Security interests existing on property acquired

It is important to note the distinction between charges created by a company and charges existing on property which has been acquired by the company. Both categories of charge are registrable in England but the consequences of non-registration are fundamentally different in each case. Non-registration of a charge created by a company leads to avoidance of the charge against certain categories of persons.[115] Non-registration, on the other hand, of a charge which is already subsisting on property that is acquired by the company does not lead to invalidation of the charge. Rather, the consequence is simply the imposition of a fine and, for continued contravention, a daily default fine.[116] The distinction is a time-honoured one with the relevant provisions of the Companies Act 1985 mirroring ones found in earlier companies legislation. Generally, however, when a company acquires property that is subject to a charge, the charge will usually be discharged by the seller of the property out of the proceeds of sale of the property. Also, the buyer of an asset in the ordinary course of business will generally take free of existing security interests in that asset. Therefore the issue of registration of security interests on property acquired is not likely to arise very often.

In the US a lot of attention has been paid to the 'double-debtor' problem.[117] The problem arises whenever a person acquires collateral that is subject to a security interest created by another, and secondly, the acquirer then proceeds to create a different security interest in the same property in favour of another secured party. The issue of priority of security interests in transferred collateral is dealt with in Article 9-325, which provides that a security interest created by a debtor is subordinate to a

---

[113] See G. McCormack 'Extension of Time for Registration of Company Charges' [1986] *JBL* 282 at 283–9.
[114] Article 544(a)(1) US Bankruptcy Code 1978.
[115] Section 395(1).   [116] Section 400(4).
[117] See generally on the 'double-debtor' problem Honnold et al. *Security Interests in Personal Property* at pp. 480–6.

security interest in the same collateral created by another person that was perfected when the debtor acquired the collateral.

Perhaps the matter is best looked at through the prism of specific cases. Take the situation where a secured party files a financing statement against all a debtor's assets, both existing and future, and the debtor also executes a security agreement in favour of the secured party, covering specific items of property. Then the debtor disposes of a specific item of property, subject to the security agreement, to a buyer. The first question to ask is whether the buyer takes free of the security interest created by the debtor (seller). Article 9-315 provides that a security interest continues in collateral notwithstanding sale. But there is a very substantial exception to this provision in Article 9-320, which states that a buyer in ordinary course of business takes free of a security interest created by the buyer's seller, even if the security interest is perfected and the buyer knows of its existence. 'Buyer in ordinary course of business' is defined in Article 1-201 as buyers 'from a person, other than a pawnbroker, in the business of selling goods of the kind'. So essentially the double-debtor problem only arises with sales not in the ordinary course of business, for otherwise the security interest will not survive the sale. For sales not in the ordinary course of business the original security interest remains perfected for the normal five-year period from the date of the filing of the initial financing statement, which period may of course be renewed. What if the buyer creates a new security interest in the same collateral in favour of a new secured party – who has priority? Pervasive principles of property law support the priority of the first secured party, namely the 'first-in-time, first-in-right' notion and the idea that a man cannot convey a better title than he has himself. The proposition is that once a debtor encumbers his interest in the goods with a security interest, any person whose interest derives from the debtor will take subject to the existing encumbrance. The same result will obtain even if the second secured party has filed a financing statement vis-à-vis the buyer before the competing secured party filed against the debtor. This seems to mark a departure from the normal 'first-to-file-has-priority' rule, but the seller's creditor's security interest was the first to attach to the specific item of collateral. The buyer's creditor could have investigated the source of the property before making advances against it. The seller's creditor, on the other hand, had no good reason for making searches against the buyer before making advances because the buyer's existence and identity at that stage is purely hypothetical. As one commentator observes:[118]

---

[118] S. Harris 'The Interaction of Articles 6 and 9 of the Uniform Commercial Code: A Study in Conveyancing, Priorities and Code Interpretation' (1986) 39 *Vand L Rev* 179 at 223–4.

In the case under consideration – [the buyer] acquires goods subject to SP1's perfected security interest, SP2's security interest attaches automatically to the after-acquired [property], and SP2 has filed before SP1 – the reason for [the first-to-file-or-perfect rule] is inapplicable. Prior to the contract of sale between the buyer and the seller, the buyer had no rights in the [property]. Accordingly, SP2 had no interest in the goods and could not not have been disadvantaged by a secret security interest in favor of SP1. SP1 publicized its interest by filing before SP2's interest attached, and SP2 could have discovered the encumbrance by checking the files. Having failed to discover SP1's security interest, SP2 should take subject to it.

Conclusion

Both the Law Commission and the Company Law Review Steering Group highlighted the differences between transaction filing or, as it is sometimes called, ex post registration, and notice filing. The system of ex post registration represents current English law as contained in Part 12 Companies Act 1985 whereas Article 9 is based on notice filing. There is a difference between the two systems in terms of primary purpose. Part 12 Companies Act 1985 provides public notice of any charges over a company's specified assets and only determines priorities as an incidental effect of failure to register in timely fashion. A notice-filing system, on the other hand, determines the relative priority of registered security interests, with registration of the security interest ensuring that it is on the public record. Under transaction filing, registration does not confer priority over a pre-existing charge that is duly registered later in time, whereas the opposite is true under a notice-filing system. Moreover, under a notice-filing system, what is filed is not the security instrument itself but a financing statement that contains abridged details of whatever security interests have been created or may be created between the parties.

In the long run, notice filing seems more convenient and flexible than transaction filing. To give but one example, notice filing allows an intending charge holder to preserve its priority during negotiations for a loan by filing the particulars in advance of the creation of the charge. On the other hand, there are significant administrative and other burdens arising from a changeover to a new system. Such a fundamental change would inevitably result in costs for the users of the system, not least in the learning costs as users adapt to change. Practitioners and more generally 'repeat' users of the existing system have also acquired a body of knowledge and experience that would, in effect, be jettisoned with a move to a new regime. The question for practitioners is whether the advantages of the new system are sufficiently practical rather than merely theoretical to warrant the abandonment of the old regime. Article 9 is clearly not a panacea for every problem thrown up by the existing provisions. It may be cold comfort for legal and banking professionals to know that many of the same issues and difficulties such as the effect or otherwise of errors in the submitted particulars arise in relation to Article 9 as they do in relation to the existing registration of company charge provisions.

6 Retention-of-title clauses under English law and Article 9

One of the fundamental differences between Article 9 and English law lies in the treatment of conditional sale agreements, or reservation-of-title clauses, as they are referred to in England. Under Article 9 basically all conditional sale agreements come within the functional definition of security and perfection by filing is required. In England, on the other hand, some kinds of reservation-of-title clause constitute a registrable charge whereas others do not. This chapter will compare and contrast the English and US positions pertaining to reservation of title with particular reference to registration/filing requirements.[1] In its consultation paper on *Registration of Security Interests* the Law Commission recommended that all retention-of-title clauses should be registrable; but as a partly counterbalancing measure, the Commission canvassed the possibility that at least simple retention-of-title clauses should enjoy super-priority status, i.e. such clauses would rank ahead of pre-existing security interests granted by the debtor which contain an after-acquired property clause.

Background

A reservation-of-title clause is a provision in a contract for the sale of goods under which the seller keeps to itself title to the goods until some condition specified in the contract has been fulfilled. Such provisions are also referred to as retention-of-title clauses, or *Romalpa* clauses, and in this chapter the various expressions are used interchangeably. The seller

---

[1] For a comprehensive discussion of reservation-of-title clauses see G. McCormack *Reservation of Title* (Sweet & Maxwell, 2nd edn. 1995); J. Parris *Effective Retention of Title Clauses* (Blackwell, 1986); I. Davies *Effective Retention of Title* (Fourmat Publishing, 1991); and for an empirical study of the operation of such clauses in practice see S. Wheeler *Reservation of Title Clauses: Impact and Implications* (Oxford University Press, 1991). See also, for a useful synthesis of the cases, G. McMeel 'Retention of Title: The Interface of Contract, Unjust Enrichment and Insolvency' in Francis Rose ed. *Restitution and Insolvency* (Mansfield Press, 2000) at p. 134.

is 'retaining' or 'reserving' title. The phrase 'reservation' comes from section 19 of the Sale of Goods Act 1979 which is headed 'reservation of a right of disposal'. The section provides that where there is a contract for the sale of specific goods or where goods are subsequently appropriated to the contract, the seller may, by the terms of the contract of appropriation, reserve the right to disposal of the goods until certain conditions are fulfilled. Hence the expression 'reservation of title'. The popular shorthand expression – *Romalpa* clauses – comes from the seminal case of *Aluminium Industrie Vaassen B. V.* v. *Romalpa Aluminium Ltd.*[2] While the concept of reservation of title is older than the Sale of Goods Act 1893[3] it was not until the mid-1970s that the legal consequences of the concept began to be explored fully by the courts. The breakthrough came in the *Romalpa* case. Perhaps by way of completeness one should point out that the expression 'conditional sale' is not in common vogue in England, though it is sometimes used in contradistinction to 'hire-purchase' agreement, which is basically an agreement for the hiring of goods coupled with an option to purchase.[4] 'Conditional sale' is the standard way of referring to retention of title in the US.

In the US it appears that reservation of title was quite a widespread phenomenon before the promulgation of the UCC in the 1950s, with many state jurisdictions having Conditional Sale Acts. The major breakthrough effected by the UCC was to assimilate the treatment of conditional sales with other financing techniques that serve a security-type function.[5] 'Security interest' is defined in what is now Article 1-201(37) as meaning an interest in personal property or fixtures which secures payment or performance of an obligation. It is specifically provided that the retention or reservation of title by a seller of goods notwithstanding shipment or delivery to the buyer is limited in effect to a reservation of a 'security interest'.

Types of reservation-of-title clause

There are five different types of reservation-of-title clause, four of them purporting to go one step further than the original 'simple' clause. The objectives of each of these clauses can be summarised as follows:

---

[2] [1976] 1 WLR 676.
[3] Such a clause was used in the Irish case of *Bateman* v. *Green and King* (1868) IR 2 Ch 607. The case is discussed by J. Phillips and A. Schuster, 'Reservation of Title in the Commercial Laws of England and Ireland' [1978–80] *DULJ* 1.
[4] *Helby* v. *Matthews* [1895] AC 471; *McEntire* v. *Crossley Bros Ltd* [1895] AC 457.
[5] See generally J. O. Honnold, S. L. Harris and C. W. Mooney *Security Interests in Personal Property: Cases, Problems and Materials* (Foundation Press, 3rd edn. 2001) chap. 1.

1. Simple clause: the seller retains ownership in the goods delivered as against the buyer until the full purchase price for goods has been paid.
2. Current-account clause: the seller retains ownership in the goods delivered as against the buyer until all debts or other obligations owed by the buyer to the seller have been paid.
3. Extended (or 'continuing') clause: the seller retains ownership in the goods delivered as against the buyer, and any sub-buyer, either until the full purchase price for goods has been paid or until all debts owed by the buyer to the seller have been paid.[6]
4. Tracing (or 'prolonged') clause: the seller retains ownership in the goods delivered as against the buyer either until the full purchase price for those goods has been paid or until all debts owed by the buyer to the seller have been paid, but if the goods are resold to a sub-buyer, then the seller acquires ownership either of the proceeds of sale or of the right to sue the sub-buyer for the proceeds of sale.
5. Aggregation (or 'enlarged') clause: the seller retains ownership in the goods delivered as against the buyer until the full purchase price for those goods has been paid, but, if the goods are manufactured into some other property, with or without the addition of other goods, then the seller acquires ownership of the resulting property or of a proportionate part of it equal to the contribution made to the manufacturing process by the original goods.

As the wording of the summaries indicates, a current-account clause (2) may be combined with an extended clause (3), a tracing clause (4) or an aggregation clause (5). In addition, an extended clause (3) or a tracing clause (4) may be added to an aggregation clause (5). However, 3 and 4 cannot be combined in the same clause. In the end, therefore, one might have a clause that represents 2 and (3 or 4) and 5.

Reasons for the use of reservation-of-title clauses

Undoubtedly, the principal reason behind the use of retention-of-title provisions is to provide security for payment of unpaid purchase price. In *Clough Mill Ltd* v. *Martin*,[7] however, Oliver LJ suggested that the purpose of the clause goes well beyond a mere security for payment of the

---

[6] Extended reservation-of-title clauses are not much used in practice, for they are unlikely to be effective against sub-buyers. Section 25 Sale of Goods Act 1979 enables a buyer in possession to pass a good title to a sub-buyer even though the buyer may not itself have a good title; on which see generally *Forsythe International (UK) Ltd* v. *Silver Shipping Co. Ltd* [1993] 2 Lloyd's Rep 268 and *Re Highway Foods* [1995] 1 BCLC 209.
[7] [1985] 1 WLR 111 at 122.

price. In more general terms its purpose is to protect the seller from the insolvency of the buyer in circumstances where the price remains unpaid.

Goods sold subject to a retention-of-title clause may be repossessed by the seller if the buyer defaults in payment. Alternatively, if the goods have been resold by the buyer prior to discharge of the original contract debt, the original seller's claim lies against the proceeds of sale. Where the goods have been incorporated into other products, or formed part of the raw material for a process of manufacture, the seller may have an entitlement to the finished product, either alone or in common with others. The important point to note is that the seller is not left with an unsecured claim in respect of the purchase price in the event of the buyer's insolvency.

Registration or filing requirements

Section 395 Companies Act 1985 requires that certain charges created by corporate buyers should be registered. Otherwise, the charge will be invalid in the event of the buyer's insolvency. Section 396 Companies Act 1985 contains the list of registrable charges. Retention-of-title clauses are not specifically identified as such, but there are certain categories of registrable charge that may catch at least particular types of retention of title clause: subsection (1)(e), a charge on book debts; and subsection (1)(f), a floating charge on the whole or part of the company's property. If, for example, a proceeds-of-sale clause is held to constitute a charge, then it would be registrable as a charge over book debts. With other types of retention-of-title clause the application of the company charge registration regime is somewhat less certain. If simple retention-of-title, current-account or aggregation clauses are held to constitute charges, then they are most logically characterised as charges over goods. While a charge on goods is among the categories of registrable charge, the actual legislative reference is somewhat oblique. Section 396(1)(c) Companies Act 1985 makes registrable 'a charge, created or evidenced by an instrument which, if executed by an individual, would require registration as a bill of sale'. The law on bills of sale is contained in the Bills of Sale Acts 1878–82, as amended, and the Companies Act provision effectively incorporates all the old learning as to what constitutes a 'bill of sale'.[8] The Bills of Sale Acts are verbose and unclear, and their application in the

---

[8] See generally on the bills of sale legislation McCormack *Reservation of Title* chap. 8; and see also the Law Commission Consultation Paper No. 164 *Registration of Security Interests* (2002) at pp. 207–16.

reservation-of-title context is not easy to discern.[9] Certainly they were not drafted with reservation-of-title clauses specifically in mind.

Bills of sale that fall within the Bills of Sale Acts are of two kinds: those that constitute absolute assurances of chattels; and bills of sale given by way of security. The former are regulated by the 1878 Act whereas the latter are affected both by the 1878 and 1882 Acts. The 1878 Act has the long title 'An Act to consolidate and amend the law for preventing frauds upon creditors by secret Bills of Sale of Personal Chattels'. The *raison d'être* of the Act was explained by Lord Herschell in *Manchester, Sheffield and Lincolnshire Railway Co.* v. *North Wagon Railway Co.*[10] as being designed for the protection of creditors, and to prevent their rights being affected by secret assurances of chattels which remained in the possession of the grantor of the bill of sale.[11] The Act requires that a bill of sale should be attested and also registered in a public register within seven days of its execution. Failure to comply with the registration requirement renders the bill void, but only as against creditors or their representatives.[12] The rationale of the Bills of Sale Act 1882 is somewhat different. As Lord Herschell said:[13]

It was to prevent needy persons being entrapped into signing complicated documents which they might often be unable to comprehend and so being subjected by their creditors to the enforcement of harsh and unreasonable provisions. A form was accordingly provided to which bills of sale were to conform, and the result of non-compliance with the statute was to render the bill of sale void even as between the parties to it. But this being the object, the enactment is, as we have seen, limited to bills of sale given 'by way of security for the payment of money by the grantor thereof'.

Section 3 Bills of Sale Act 1878 lays down that the Act shall apply to 'every bill of sale . . . whereby the holder or grantee has power . . . to seize or take possession of any personal chattels'. Section 4 of the same Act sets out three categories of bill of sale:

(i) assignments, transfers, declarations of trust without transfer, inventories of goods with receipt thereto attached, or receipts for purchase monies of goods, and other assurances of personal chattels;

(ii) powers of attorney, authorities or licences to take possession of personal chattels as security for any debt;

(iii) agreements by which a right in equity to any personal chattels or to any charge or security thereon shall be conferred.[14]

---

[9] A. Diamond *A Review of Security Interests in Property* (HMSO, 1989) at para. 23.9.14.
[10] (1880) 13 App Cas 554.   [11] *Ibid.* at 560.   [12] Section 8.
[13] (1880) 13 App Cas 554 at 560–1.
[14] The expression 'bill of sale' is accorded the same meaning in the 1882 Act – see section 3.

Aggregation clauses pose particular problems in so far as the application of the bills of sale legislation is concerned. The position is complicated by the fact that the first two categories of bills of sale – transfer of ownership and right to possession as security – apply only to property which the grantor owns at the time that the document is executed.[15] A document concerning after-acquired property, such as an aggregation clause, is only a bill of sale if it comes within the third limb of the definition, i.e. an agreement conferring a right in equity to chattels or to any charge or security thereon. The precise scope of this third category of bill of sale was considered in *Reeves* v. *Barlow*.[16] In this case a clause in a building contract whereby all building and other materials brought by the builder upon the land should become the property of the landowner was held not to constitute a bill of sale. The court held that the builder's agreement was not an equitable assignment of anything but a mere legal contract that, upon the happening of a particular event, the legal property should pass in certain chattels. In its judgment, an agreement that created a legal right over future goods, without any preceding equitable right, was not a bill of sale.

Generally, however, assignments of future property, including manufactured goods not yet in existence at the time that a contract of sale is drawn up, only take effect in equity rather than at law. The leading case is *Holroyd* v. *Marshall*[17] where it was held that an assignment of future property operates in equity by way of assignment, binding the conscience of the assignor, and so binding the property from the moment when the contract becomes capable of being performed on the principle that equity regards as done that which ought to be done. A legal interest may pass, however, if the grantor is required to perform some new act manifesting an intention to pass the property. According to *Lunn* v. *Thornton*[18] the act must be done for 'the avowed object and with the view of carrying the former grant or disposition into effect'. In *Reeves* v. *Barlow* the taking of possession of goods by the transferee was held to be a new act within this doctrine. In practice, however, this option is not likely to be available to a seller where new products have been manufactured out of raw materials supplied subject to a reservation-of-title provision.[19]

Certain transactions that prima facie fall within the definition of a bill of sale are excluded from the ambit of the legislation, with section 4 Bills

[15] See B. Allcock 'Romalpa Clauses and Bills of Sale' (1981) 131 *NLJ* 842.
[16] (1884) 12 QBD 436.   [17] (1862) 10 HL Cas 191.   [18] (1845) 1 CB 379.
[19] See Allcock 'Romalpa Clauses' at 843. Presumably one should insist that the new products be separated from the buyer's own goods. The courts, however, may not take the view that such separation is effected, in the words of Tindal CJ, 'for the avowed object and with the view of carrying the former grant or disposition into effect'.

of Sale Act 1878 setting out a list of documents that are specifically ex-
empted. The exceptions include transfer of goods in the ordinary course
of any trade or calling. If what purports to be a reservation-of-title clause
is held, in reality, to amount to a charge, and the charge is neither a charge
over book debts nor a floating charge over the undertaking or property of
the company, then the charge will only be avoided if it comes within the
statutory definition of a bill of sale. A fall-back position is for the seller of
goods to argue that the charge, while prima facie a bill of sale, falls within
one of the excepted categories such as the transfer of goods in the ordinary
course of any trade or calling. At first, though, it appears a little incon-
gruous to imagine how this provision might apply in a reservation-of-title
context. The exception presupposes, initially, the transfer of title to the
goods to the buyer, contrary to the express purpose of the reservation-of-
title clause and secondly, the retransfer of rights back to the seller in the
ordinary course of a trade or calling.[20] It has been suggested, however,
that, in theory at least, there seems no reason not to apply the exception
to retention-of-title clauses.[21] Most of the decided cases have covered letters of hypothecation and lien over trading stock executed by traders in
need of short-term finance, but the object is the same in this situation and
the reservation of title sphere – namely, the regular use of trading-stock
as security for recurring obligations.

The leading case on the exception is *Re Young, Hamilton and Co., ex
parte Carter*.[22] The case concerned a textile partnership which required
a bank loan and, to facilitate the borrowing, the partnership provided,
in accordance with its business practice, letters of equitable charge over
goods in its possession or in possession of its bailees. The partnership
went bankrupt and the trustee in bankruptcy claimed that the letters
constituted bills of sale and, being unregistered, were void. The court rejected this contention on the ground, *inter alia*, that the letters amounted
to a transfer of goods in the ordinary course of business.

The *Young* case was invoked unsuccessfully by a reservation-of-title
claimant anxious to avoid registration requirements in *Ian Chisholm
Textiles Ltd* v. *Griffiths*.[23] The court said that the onus of proof was on
the plaintiff to show that what was in effect a charge was created in the
ordinary course of the buyer's trade. The plaintiff contended unsuccessfully that the absolute volume of cases on retention-of-title agreements

---

[20] See J. Farrar and N. Furey 'Reservation of Ownership and Tracing in a Commercial
Context' (1977) 36 *CLJ* 27.
[21] A. Tettenborn 'Reservation of Title: Insolvency and Priority Problems' [1981] *JBL* 173
at 175.
[22] [1905] 2 KB 772. See also *Re Slee, ex parte North Western Bank* (1872) LR 15 Eq 69.
[23] [1994] BCC 96.

was enough to discharge the onus of proof, with the court holding that it would require a very exceptional case before it was prepared to conclude, merely on the volume of reported cases on a particular topic, that something was 'in the ordinary course of business of any trade'. Moreover, the plaintiff did not normally deal with its customers, who were mostly in the same sort of business as the buyer, on the basis of reservation-of-title arrangements. Furthermore, it only entered into a reservation-of-title agreement with this particular buyer when the financial condition of the latter became parlous.

Comparisons between the English position and that in the United States under Article 9

In England, it is fair to say that the registration of company charge provisions are not drafted adequately to deal with the reservation-of-title phenomenon. The particulars requiring registration cover the date of creation of a charge, the amount secured by the charge, short particulars of the property charged and the persons entitled to the charge. Difficulties arise in relation to the phrase 'date of creation' and these difficulties are highlighted if, for example, a contract for the sale of goods includes an aggregation clause as well as a 'simple' reservation-of-title provision – is the 'date of creation' the date of the making of the original supply contract or the date of manufacture? If the latter is the date of creation then it would be almost impossible for the seller to fulfil the registration requirements, for it may not know the precise date when the goods supplied have become part of the process of manufacture. Another potential difficulty arises where goods have been delivered on reservation-of-title terms over a prolonged period and the question arises whether the 'date of creation' is every single invoice recording the delivery of goods subject to these conditions.[24] It is simply not feasible to expect a seller to register each contract of sale individually.[25]

Compare all this with the position in the US. There a supplier can take a security interest in the goods themselves as well as proceeds and

---

[24] See Parris, *Effective Retention of Title Clauses* at pp. 129–30. See also the comment by the Law Commission at para. 3.30 of their consultation paper *Registration of Security Interests*: 'Each individual charge must be registered even when it is just one of a long series between the same parties. For example, the difficulty and expense this causes is the explanation usually given for suppliers not registering extended retention of title clauses even though these frequently create registrable charges.'

[25] Professor Aubrey Diamond, in his report on *Security Interests in Property* for the Department of Trade and Industry, when suggesting that a supplier need file only one financing statement for each customer, was conscious of the burden even this requirement might impose. The work involved for a seller with thousands of customers would be enormous. See Diamond report paras. 17.16 and 17.17.

products by filing a simple financing statement. The financing statement will expire at the end of five years unless renewed, but clearly can cover multiple deliveries of goods during that period. Therefore, there is no need to register each contract of sale individually. Transaction costs are kept to a minimum but of course there is the initial filing expense. It should be noted, however, that a purchase-money security interest in consumer goods is automatically perfected upon attachment. In other words, it does not have to be filed. A PMSI arises where value is given to enable the debtor to acquire rights in or the use of collateral, if the value is in fact so used. This definition clearly covers the case of a simple reservation-of-title clause.

Under English law, in so far as a simple reservation-of-title clause is recognised as being effective without registration, it will enjoy super-priority status.[26] In other words, it will outrank security interests strictly so-called that are subject to a requirement of registration. If a reservation-of-title clause is held to constitute a registrable charge, however, the position is much less favourable from the point of view of a seller. Where there is more than one charge over the same property, and assuming that all charges have been duly registered, the priority position, somewhat simplified, is as follows: fixed charges rank among themselves according to the order of creation, whereas a floating charge is postponed, priority-wise, to a fixed charge irrespective of the order in which the two charges were created.[27] In practice, however, a registrable retention-of-title clause is unlikely to be registered, and the claimant relying on such a clause will be reduced to the ranks of the unsecured creditors.

Superficially, the picture under Article 9 is more straightforward, with a 'first-to-file' rule for determining priorities. There is, however, an exception in the case of PMSIs. A PMSI will rank ahead of a prior security interest with an after-acquired property clause, though Article 9 undoubtedly weakens the position of a conditional seller as compared with the position prevailing in England. Firstly, the seller has to file to protect his interest whereas, under the English position, simple and current-account retention-of-title clauses are not the subject of any requirement of registration. Secondly, there are special perfection requirements that must be complied with so as to acquire PMSI status, and observance of these statutory formalities is necessary before super-priority status can be achieved. In other words, a person who has bought goods that have been sold subject to a reservation-of-title clause will have acquired sufficient rights in these goods to enable an earlier security interest given

---

[26] Put shortly, the property never comes into the beneficial ownership of the insolvent.
[27] See G. McCormack 'Priority of Charges and Registration' [1994] *JBL* 587.

by the buyer in after-acquired property to attach. In consequence, a prior security-interest holder will assume priority in the event that an unpaid seller fails to comply with the super-priority perfection requirements for PMSIs.[28]

The point is illustrated by *Hongkong and Shanghai Banking Corp. v. HFH USA Corp.*[29] where a German Company sold and shipped machinery to a US customer pursuant to a reservation-of-title clause. The supplier did not file a financing statement until becoming aware of the buyer's financial problems. At that time the grace period for filing had expired and so it was held that the supplier's PMSI could not defeat the general security interest held by the buyer's principal financier. The sales contract contained a choice of law clause which subjected the contract, including the reservation-of-title element, to German law, but the New York court refused to enforce the provision. It said that if German law were applied under the present circumstances, it would violate a fundamental purpose of Article 9 'to create commercial certainty and predictability by allowing third party creditors to rely on the specific perfection and priority rules that govern collateral within the scope of Article 9'.[30]

The rationale for awarding the PMSI super-priority status has been canvassed extensively in a previous chapter, and will be rehearsed only briefly here.[31] Basically, a distinction should be drawn between a security interest granted over property already owned by the debtor and a security interest granted over newly acquired property so as to secure the price paid for that property. The former operates to remove existing property from the debtor's estate whereas the latter is neutral in its effect as the debt incurred in respect of the price is offset by the addition of the

---

[28] See generally K. Meyer 'A Primer on Purchase Money Security Interests under Revised Article 9 of the Uniform Commercial Code' (2001) 50 *Kan LR* 143; P. Shupack 'Defining Purchase Money Collateral' (1992) 29 *Idaho LR* 767.

[29] (1992) 805 F Supp 133. The case is discussed by J. Hausmann in 'The Value of Public-Notice Filing under Uniform Commercial Code Article 9: A Comparison with the German Legal System of Securities in Personal Property' (1996) 25 *Georgia Journal of International and Comparative Law* 427 at 477–8.

[30] (1992) 805 F Supp 133 at 141.

[31] See also the justification offered at Law Commission *Registration of Security Interests* para. 4.159:

Someone who simply advances further funds to a company, whilst providing new value in exchange for any security she takes, is not contributing to the property available to secured creditors: she is not making their position any better. In contrast, where the fresh finance was to enable the debtor to acquire further property, if the property subject to the purchase-money interest in favour of the second (or later) creditor was available to the earlier creditors, they would be better off as a result of that later creditor, who would probably lose out.

property.[32] Moreover, if the new property helped the debtor's business to earn extra profits it would strengthen the position of existing creditors by swelling their security interest.[33] There is an additional argument that if an earlier creditor could rely on an after-acquired-property clause to the prejudice of a PMSI holder, the earlier creditor would obtain an unjustified windfall at the expense of the later creditor whose advance of funds enabled the additional property to be acquired. Finally, it is contended that the first creditor on the scene should not be permitted to obtain a security monopoly over the assets of the debtor.[34] The effect of this might be to preclude the debtor from procuring further credit elsewhere or to force later creditors to contract on a riskier basis, having to settle for lower-ranking security or no security at all.[35]

Basically a PMSI can only be created in goods or software but Article 9 distinguishes between inventory and other goods for the purpose of conditioning entitlement to PMSI status. Article 9-324 states that a PMSI in inventory has priority over any other security interest in the same collateral. Purchase-money super-priority over the proceeds of inventory may also be established in certain circumstances. 'Inventory' is defined as meaning goods that are held by a person for sale or lease or that have been leased or that are to be furnished or have been furnished under a contract of service, or that are raw materials, work in progress or materials used or consumed in a business, with 'proceeds' defined as meaning whatever property, in any form, is derived, directly or indirectly, from any dealing with collateral and including any payment representing indemnity or compensation for loss of, or damage to, the collateral.

Thus, interpreting Article 9, a reservation-of-title clause is valid as a PMSI in so far as the clause is a simple one and possibly as regards proceeds generated by a resale of the goods in their original unprocessed state. Article 9-324, however, enunciates some stringent conditions which must be satisfied before a retention-of-title clause can qualify as a PMSI.

---

[32] See the discussion in the Diamond report *A Review of Security Interests in Property* at para. 17.7 and there is also a discussion of the issue in Law Commission *Registration of Security Interests* at para. 7.5.

[33] For a law and economics perspective on the issue see H. Kanda and S. Levmore 'Explaining Creditor Priorities' (1994) 80 *Va L Rev* 2103 at 2138–41.

[34] See generally T. Jackson and A. Kronman 'Secured Financing and Priorities among Creditors' (1979) 88 *Yale LJ* 1143 at 1167: 'The purchase-money priority is best thought of as a device for alleviating the situational monopoly created by an after-acquired property clause.'

[35] The Law Commission makes the point in *Registration of Security Interests* at para. 7.69 that not having a concept of purchase-money super-priority under a functional system would make it more difficult for a company to obtain vendor credit.

Basically, during the five-year period before the debtor receives possession of the inventory, the purchase-money secured party must send an
authenticated notification to the holder of a conflicting security interest
in the same collateral. The notification is required to state that the person giving it has or expects to acquire a PMSI in inventory of the debtor
and describing such inventory.[36] The Official Comment to Article 9-324
explains the purpose of the notification requirement as being to protect
a non-purchase-money inventory-secured party. The financing arrangement between an inventory-secured party and its debtor may typically
require the secured party to make periodic advances against incoming
inventory. If the inventory-secured party receives notification it may decide not to make the advance whereas if it does not receive notification it will ordinarily have priority under the first-to-file priority rule of
Article 9-322.

Where the retention-of-title clause relates to goods other than inventory, such as capital equipment, the qualifications necessary for gaining PMSI status are somewhat less demanding.[37] Essentially, automatic
super-priority over prior secured lenders is gained if the PMSI is perfected
within twenty days of the debtor obtaining possession of the collateral as a
debtor. The differences in legal treatment between capital equipment and
inventory have been explained on the basis that the risks to earlier creditors are greater in the case of inventory financing: 'The rules intimate that
the acquisition of new inventory and its associated debt is more threatening to earlier creditors than the debt-financing of new equipment but
that debt tied to new inventory is still less threatening than new money
unlinked to particular assets.'[38]

---

[36] Article 9-324(b).

[37] See generally Meyer 'A Primer' at 170 who argues that the relevant requirements are
relatively easily satisfied. He states:

> It is probably easy for sellers to control when the debtor obtains possession and file
> before transferring the goods. Lenders, on the other hand, face some dangers. First,
> they must prove that the advance was in fact used to purchase the goods and that the
> loan enabled the debtor to buy the goods, which normally requires that the goods be
> purchased after the advance or substantially contemporaneously with it. Next, lenders
> must be certain when the debtor obtains possession of the goods and file within twenty
> days. The lender can avoid this issue by filing a financing statement before it releases
> any funds. Finally, another potential problem is the possibility that the previous secured
> creditor will declare the debtor in default when it learns of the lender's PMSI.

[38] See Kanda and Levmore 'Explaining Creditor Priorities' at 2139; and see generally
M. Bridge, R. Macdonald, R. Simmonds and C. Walsh 'Formalism, Functionalism
and Understanding the Law of Secured Transactions' (1999) 44 *McGill LJ* 567 at
nn. 99–108.

By way of exception to the general rule, Article 9-309 provides for the automatic perfection of a PMSI in consumer goods, i.e. the security interest is perfected automatically when it attaches. There is no need for filing or the creditor acquiring possession of the same. The principle of automatic perfection does not apply, however, in the case of consumer goods governed by certificate-of-title statutes, such as motor cars. The pre-Article 9 history of American personal property security law has been likened to a crazy quilt evolution of various security devices designed to solve particular problems. Article 9 brought in its wake the single, unitary security device, but there are traces of the inheritance scattered throughout the article – in particular there is not a single mode of perfection of security interests, and different legal rules sometimes apply depending on the nature of the collateral.[39] The principle of automatic perfection of PMSIs in consumer goods might be viewed as a descendant of the pre-Article 9 conditional sale – in English terms, a simple retention-of-title clause which is valid without registration, as will now be considered.

Simple retention-of-title clauses

The English case law has affirmed the effectiveness of 'simple' reservation-of-title clauses. The principal authority is the decision of the Court of Appeal in *Clough Mill* v. *Martin*.[40] In that case the court rejected the notion, propounded by the judge at first instance, that if the purpose of a reservation-of-title clause is to provide security for the payment of the purchase price, then the clause should be construed as creating a charge.[41] In *Re Bond Worth Ltd*,[42] however, it was held that where a clause purported to reserve 'equitable and beneficial ownership' legal and equitable title to the goods passed to the buyers and an equitable interest was granted back to the sellers by way of charge after a split second

---

[39] See generally D. Baird and T. Jackson *Security Interests in Personal Property* (Foundation Press, 2nd edn. 1987) at pp. 30–5.

[40] [1985] 1 WLR 111. It makes no difference that the buyer has been given a power of resale over the goods or a right to consume the goods in a process of manufacture. Robert Goff LJ was adamant on this point. He said (*ibid.* at 116): 'I see nothing objectionable in an agreement under which A, the owner of goods, gives possession of those goods to B, at the same time conferring on B a power of sale and a promise to consume the goods in manufacture though A will remain the owner of the goods until they are either sold or consumed.' Furthermore, the fact that certain provisions of the contract of sale could only operate by way of charge did not warrant the conclusion that all efforts by the seller to obtain security for payment of goods must necessarily be by way of charge.

[41] The first-instance decision is reported [1984] 1 WLR 1067.

[42] [1980] Ch 228. See also *Coburn* v. *Collins* (1887) 35 CPD 373.

(*scintilla temporis*) had elapsed.[43] *Re Bond Worth Ltd* may require reconsideration, though, in the light of the decision of the House of Lords in *Abbey National Building Society* v. *Cann*.[44] Briefly stated, it was held in *Cann* that where a purchaser relies on a loan for completion of the transaction, to be secured by a charge on the property, he could not be said to have acquired, even for a split second, the unencumbered interest in the property. The court refused to countenance application of the doctrine of *scintilla temporis* in this connection. Despite the *Cann* decision, *Re Bond Worth Ltd* was nevertheless followed in *Stroud Architectural Services Ltd* v. *John Laing Contruction Ltd*.[45] This is a case where goods were supplied subject to a reservation-of-title clause which purported to retain in the seller the 'equitable and beneficial ownership in all or any goods supplied'. The court held that the clause necessarily involved the creation of a charge and, in its view, the status and authority of *Bond Worth* remained unaffected by *Cann*.[46]

Current-account clauses

Clauses which attempt to reserve ownership of the goods supplied in the seller until all obligations owed to the seller by the buyer have been discharged, and not just those flowing from the contract of sale, give rise

---

[43] The sellers argued that all they had passed to the purchasers was the shell of legal ownership from which the crabmeat of equitable ownership had been skilfully extracted. Slade J said ([1980] Ch 228 at 253):

> However, no authority has been cited which satisfies me that on the transfer of the legal property in land or chattels, it is competent to a vendor expressly to except from the grant in favour of himself an equitable mortgage or charge thereon to secure the unpaid purchase price (in addition to or in substitution for any lien which may arise by operation of law), in such manner that the exception will take effect without any express or implied grant back of a mortgage or charge in the vendor's favour by the purchaser.

[44] [1991] 1 AC 56. See generally J. De Lacy 'The Purchase Money Security Interest: A Company Charge Conundrum' [1991] *LMCLQ* 531. On the other hand, *Cann* derives some support from the comments of Lord Browne-Wilkinson in *Westdeutsche Landesbank Girozentrale* v. *Islington London Borough Council* [1996] AC 669 at 706:

> A person solely entitled to the full beneficial ownership of money or property, both at law and in equity, does not enjoy an equitable interest in that property. The legal title carries with it all rights. Unless and until there is a separation of the legal and equitable estates, there is no separate equitable title. Therefore to talk about the bank 'retaining' its equitable interest is meaningless.

[45] (1993) 35 Con LR 135.
[46] Judge Newey said (at 145): 'Slade J did speak of the sale being 'followed' by the giving back of security, but he described both events as occurring eo instanti. I think that the House of Lords and Slade J each envisaged transfers of title and grants of security occurring completely simultaneously.'

to potentially more legal problems. In particular, it is argued that with-holding ownership until a long overdue debt has been paid is creating something over and above what was in existence when the clause was first incorporated, unless it simply replaces another security right already provided for. Thus it is more difficult to disguise as something other than the creation of a security interest. The reason for the use of 'all-liabilities' clauses is to circumvent problems of identification that arise if a buyer company has gone into liquidation or receivership. In that circumstance, one may have the situation where goods originally supplied by the seller are now in the buyer's warehouse, and while some consignments have been paid for, others have not. The seller has a difficult task in iden-tifying the goods actually unpaid for. Its task is easier when there are 'all-liabilities' reservation-of-title clauses in respect of all consignments, and it can therefore say to the buyer: 'You do not have title to any of the consignments in the warehouse because all of them have not been paid for.'[47]

The House of Lords upheld the effectiveness of 'all-liabilities' retention-of-title clauses in the Scottish case *Armour* v. *Thyssen Edelstahl-werke AG*.[48] Reference was made to section 17(1) Sale of Goods Act 1979 which provides that, in a contract for the sale of specific or ascertained goods, the property in them is transferred to the buyer at such time as the parties to the contract intend it to be transferred. Moreover, section 19(1) stipulates that where is a contract for the sale of specific goods the seller may reserve the right of disposal of the goods until certain conditions are fulfilled. In this particular case the sellers, by the terms of the contract of sale, had in effect reserved the right of disposal of the goods until all debts due to them by the buyer had been paid. The relevant clause reads: 'All goods delivered by us remain our property (goods remaining in our ownership) until all debts owed to us including any balances existing at relevant times – due to us on any legal grounds – are settled.' The court acknowledged that such a provision did, in a sense, give the seller secu-rity for the unpaid debts of the buyer but it did so by way of a legitimate retention of title and not by virtue of any right over his own property conferred by the buyer.

The *Armour* case did not involve a situation where the supplier re-covered possession of goods because of the non-discharge of some

---

[47] In *Clough Mill Ltd* v. *Martin* the Court of Appeal was faced with a contract to be performed in stages rather than an 'all-monies' clause *stricto sensu*. Nevertheless there are some helpful *dicta* concerning 'all-monies' clauses by Robert Goff LJ at 117, Oliver LJ at 123 and Sir John Donaldson MR at 126.

[48] [1991] 2 AC 339; this is discussed by counsel for the suppliers Jonathan Mance in 'The Operation of an "All Debts" Reservation of Title Clause' [1992] *LMCLQ* 35.

indebtedness extraneous to the sales contract containing the reservation-of-title clause. It has been argued that if a seller retains legal and beneficial ownership in goods supplied, it must follow that if, after payment of the full purchase price of those goods, the seller recovers possession of them because of non-discharge of some other liability, the seller must refund the purchase price to the customer on the ground of total failure of consideration.[49] This would, of course, defeat the object of the clause. In almost all instances, it would be the intention of the seller that he should be entitled to recover the goods and resell them elsewhere without having to refund the purchase price. The leading authority is *Rowland* v. *Divall*,[50] where it was held that under a sales contract, the essential consideration for which the buyer pays the price is the transfer of ownership by the seller.[51] On this basis, where no title is transferred because of a defect in the seller's title, the buyer can recover the price on the grounds of total failure of consideration regardless of any use of the goods in the interim period. It is possible to argue, however, by relying upon the doctrine of set-off, that an all-liabilities reservation-of-title clause is of benefit to a supplier of goods. According to Rule 4.90 of the Insolvency Rules 1987, set-off is compulsory in a liquidation where before the commencement of the winding up there have been mutual credits, mutual debts or other mutual dealings between the parties.[52] If a repossessing supplier has to refund the purchase price on grounds of total failure of consideration, at the same time, however, the supplier has a claim against the buyer for non-payment of the outside indebtedness. The two claims should be set off against one another.[53]

An 'all-liabilities' clause, in essence, purports to reserve title to the seller until all indebtedness arising between buyer and seller has been met, but are there theoretical difficulties if 'indebtedness' is construed as referring to future indebtedness? If there is a running account between buyer and seller that oscillates from debit to credit, the question arises whether property moves to and fro according to the momentary state of

---

[49] See W. Goodhart '*Clough Mill Ltd* v. *Martin* – a Comeback for Romalpa?' (1986) 49 *MLR* 96. See also the article by William Goodhart QC and Professor Gareth Jones, 'The Infiltration of Equitable Doctrine into English Commercial Law' (1980) 43 *MLR* 489 at 508; but cf. G. McCormack ' "All Liabilities" Reservation of Title Clause and Company charges' [1989] *Conv* 92.

[50] [1923] 2 KB 500. See also *Butterworth* v. *Kingsway Motors* [1957] 1 WLR 1286; *Warman* v. *Southern Counties Car Finance Corp* [1949] 2 KB 576; *Karflex Ltd* v. *Poole* [1933] 2 KB 251; and *Linz* v. *Electric Wire Co. of Palestine* [1948] AC 371.

[51] See R. Bradgate 'Retention of Title in the House of Lords: Unanswered Questions' (1991) 54 *MLR* 726.

[52] See also section 323 Insolvency Act 1986 which applies in the case of bankruptcy.

[53] See Bradgate 'Retention of Title' at 735.

the account.[54] The better view seems to be that title passes when the account comes into credit and does not revert to the seller when the account once again falls into debit. Consider also the situation where there is a continuous trading relationship between buyer and seller and the parties make it clear that title to a particular consignment of goods should only pass when all possible future debts between them have been met irrespective of the momentary state of the account. If the trading relationship between the parties may extend indefinitely into the future, clearly then it is impossible to say, at any particular point in time, that there will be no future debts arising from buyer to seller. This means that title will never pass to the buyer, and seems to place the agreement between the parties outside the statutory definition of a contract for the sale of goods. A contract for the sale of goods is defined in section 2(1) Sale of Goods Act 1979 as a contract by which the seller transfers or agrees to transfer the property in goods to the buyer for a money consideration called the price. One approach by the courts to resolve this difficulty would be to say that the parties clearly intended a contract for the sale of goods, and the surest way of ensuring this result and making sense of their agreement is to hold that title passes from seller to buyer on delivery of the goods. Such a construction of the agreement is not in the seller's interests, and therefore it may be best to make it clear that the 'indebtedness' referred to in the sales contract is purely past indebtedness. On the other hand, it may be that the courts will brush aside as of no practical consequence theoretical problems stemming from potential future indebtedness. After all, disputes over reservation-of-title clauses only arise if the buyer has gone into liquidation/receivership. The seller will be endeavouring to repossess goods not because some possible future indebtedness has not been cleared but rather on account of an existing indebtedness.

In the US, the main 'problem' with current-account reservation of title concerns entitlement to PMSI status and the issue of 'cross-collateralisation'.[55] In other words, if a current-account clause conditions the passing of property on the payment of debts that are extraneous to the particular contract of sale will it still qualify as a PMSI? Take the situation where there are two separate contracts of sale of goods with each containing a current-account clause. The buyer pays for consignment 2 but not for consignment 1, which has been 'consumed' by the buyer in such a manner as to leave no traceable exchange product. There is a prior

---

[54] Norman Palmer, reviewing Professor T. B. Smith's book *Property Problems in Sales* (Sweet & Maxwell, 1978) at (1981) 1 *Legal Studies* 326 at 328.

[55] For a discussion of these general issues see Honnold et al. *Security Interests in Personal Property* at pp. 247–52.

secured party with a conflicting security interest in consignment 2. It is submitted that the seller's claim in consignment 2 for the unpaid purchase price of consignment 1 will have super-priority PMSI status under Article 9-103 which provides that a

> security interest in goods is a purchase-money security interest to the extent that the goods are purchase-money collateral with respect to that security interest; if the security interest is in inventory that is or was purchase-money collateral, also to the extent that the security interest secures a purchase-money obligation incurred with respect to other inventory in which the secured party holds or held a purchase-money security interest.[56]

Article 9-103(f) also provides that a PMSI does not lose its status as such, even if the purchase-money collateral also secures an obligation that is not a purchase-money obligation. In other words, the fact that an item of inventory secures not only the price paid for it but also other obligations does not negate the purchase-money character of the security interest.[57]

Other jurisdictions with 'reformed' personal property security law do not necessarily recognise cross-collateralisation in this context.[58] The New Zealand Personal Property Securities Act is a case in point where a security interest will be a PMSI only to the extent that it secures the outstanding purchase price in respect of the particular goods secured.[59] The example has been given of a retailer with ten stereos in its inventory that have been supplied by a particular supplier, and five of these stereos have been paid for.[60] The seller's security interest will not have PMSI status in so far as it relates to the stereos already paid for. The seller can have a non-PMSI in these stereos, but such a security interest may lose out in a priority battle with a bank that holds a general security interest

---

[56] See the example given at the Official Comment to Article 9-103:

> Seller (S) sells an item of inventory (Item-1) to Debtor (D), retaining a security interest in Item-1 to secure Item-1's price and all other obligations, existing and future, of D to S. S then sells another item of inventory to D (Item-2), again retaining a security interest in Item-2 to secure Item-2's price as well as all other obligations of D to S. D then pays to S Item-1's price. D then sells Item-2 to a buyer in ordinary course of business, who takes Item-2 free of S's security interest . . . S's security interest in Item-1 securing Item-2's unpaid price would be a purchase-money security interest.

[57] See the Article 9-103 Official Comment which states that for non-consumer-goods transactions, this article rejects the 'transformation' rule adopted by some cases, under which any cross-collateralisation, refinancing or the like destroys the purchase-money status entirely. See also a leading case on the former Article 9, *Southtrust Bank of Alabama* v. *Borg-Warner Acceptance Corp* (1985) 760 F 2d 1240, which holds that a PMSI requires a one-to-one relationship between the debt and the collateral.

[58] There is an interesting discussion of this issue in a paper by Professors Cuming and Walsh on the reform of the Canadian personal property security legislation on the Canadian Uniform Law Commissioners' website: www.ulc.ca/.

[59] See sections 74 and 75 New Zealand Personal Property Securities Act.

[60] See B. Brown and J. Sampson 'Retention of Title under New Zealand's Personal Property Securities Act 1999' (2002) 17 *JIBL* 102 at 105.

over the retailer's property. To get around these limitations on the recognition of PMSIs it has been suggested that a supplier should make use of a price-allocation clause if there is a running account between supplier and buyer. This approach has been advocated by certain New Zealand commentators who argue:[61]

One alternative, which would maximise the extent of the supplier's PMSI priority, is to provide that payments are deemed to relate first to the purchase price of goods the debtor has already sold. If upheld by a court, this would have the effect of allocating remaining debt to goods which remain in the debtor's possession, hence maximising the extent of the supplier's PMSI priority.

Proceeds-of-sale clauses

In many retention-of-title clauses a provision has been inserted conferring on the original supplier an entitlement to resale proceeds. This is referred to as a 'proceeds-of-sale' clause, or 'tracing' clause, and it seems clear that a tracing right arising by operation of law is not registrable. In this situation, the seller's 'security' rights have not been conferred or created by the buyer company. Similarly, where traceable funds have been mingled with other funds in a bank account the courts may declare a charge on the mixed fund[62] but again, since this charge has not been created by the buyer company, it is not registrable under Part 12 Companies Act 1985. The courts, however, are loath to uphold a tracing clause in the reservation-of-title context.

It seems reasonably clear now from a series of decisions throughout the common-law world that the mere fact that there is a reservation-of-title clause in a sale-of-goods contract does not give the seller an automatic claim against resale proceeds. The contrary view might be described as the automatic fiduciary relationship proposition, and derived some support from the seminal *Romalpa* case. Moreover, there was also some support for this proposition in Ireland in cases such as *Re Stokes & McKiernan Ltd*[63] and *Sugar Distributors Ltd v. Monaghan Cash and Carry Ltd.*[64] That view, however, is no longer in the ascendancy in Ireland and the prevailing judicial opinion is illustrated by the decision of Murphy J. in *Carroll Group Distributors Ltd v. Bourke.*[65] That decision followed the more recent English case law and rejected a claim to resale proceeds.[66]

---

[61] *Ibid.*
[62] See *Re Diplock* [1948] Ch 465; *Re Hallett's Estate* (1879) 13 Ch D 696; *Re Oatway* [1903] 2 Ch 356; *James Roscoe (Bolton) Ltd* v. *Windsor* [1915] 1 Ch 62; *Re Tilley's Will Trusts* [1967] Ch 1179; *Boscawen* v. *Bajwa* [1996] 1 WLR 328; *Foskett* v. *McKeown* [2001] 1 AC 102.
[63] [1978] ILRM 240.   [64] [1982] ILRM 399.   [65] [1990] ILRM 285.
[66] See J. De Lacy 'The Anglicisation of Irish Retention of Title?' (1990) 8 *Irish Law Times* (NS) 279.

The *Romalpa* case is the first of the modern cases on proceeds-of-sale retention of title – indeed, on any aspect of retention of title – and for this reason alone merits extended treatment even though it has been almost distinguished to death in subsequent cases. In *Romalpa* the plaintiffs, a Dutch company, supplied aluminium foil to the defendants, an English company, and some of this foil had been resold in its original unprocessed state before a receiver was appointed to the defendant company. The conditions of sale gave the buyers a seventy-five-day period of credit and also contained a current-account retention-of-title clause. The buyers were required to store the goods separately from their own property and it was conceded that this provision rendered the buyers bailees of any foil in their possession while money was still owing to the suppliers. The courts upheld the suppliers' claim to resale proceeds even though there was no clause in the conditions of sale dealing expressly with the claim to resale proceeds where the goods had been resold in their original state. Roskill LJ said:[67]

I see no difficulty in the contractual concept that, as between the defendants and their sub-purchasers, the defendants sold as principals, but that, as between themselves and the plaintiffs, those goods which they were selling as principals within their implied authority from the plaintiffs were the plaintiffs' goods which they were selling as agents for the plaintiffs to whom they remained fully accountable. If an agent lawfully sells his principal's goods, he stands in a fiduciary relationship to his principal and remains accountable to his principal for those goods and their proceeds.

In subsequent English cases, however, the *Romalpa* decision has been heavily distinguished, with the courts disallowing successive claims to resale proceeds on the grounds that, in the particular cases, charges have been thereby created which are void for want of registration.[68] The decisions may be viewed in a very pragmatic light. It is almost as if the courts are drawing a line in the sand and saying to a supplier, 'You can have your simple and current-account reservation-of-title clauses, but thus far and no further.' There are various strands of reasoning apparent in the different cases, though some of these seem mutually contradictory. It is possible to isolate perhaps six different strands of reasoning which have led courts to reject claims to resale proceeds.

---

[67] [1976] 1 WLR 676 at 690. For a full critical discussion of this area see J. De Lacy 'Romalpa Theory and Practice under Retention of Title in the Sale of Goods' (1995) 27 *Anglo-American Law Review* 327.

[68] According to Phillips J in *Pfeiffer Gmbh & Co. v. Arbuthnot Factors Ltd* [1988] 1 WLR 150 at 159 the normal implication is that when a buyer resells the goods he does so on his own account and will not hold any proceeds thereby received in a fiduciary capacity on behalf of the seller.

Firstly, in some of the cases emphasis has been placed on the fact that the buyer has not been under any obligation to store the seller's goods separately from his own. For example, in *Hendy Lennox (Industrial Engines) Ltd v. Grahame Puttick Ltd*,[69] in rejecting a claim to resale proceeds, the judge pointed to the absence of an express obligation on the buyers to store the goods in such a way that they were clearly the property of the seller. Similarly, in *Re Andrabell Ltd* [70] Peter Gibson J relied on the fact that the buyers were not bound to store the goods in such a way as to manifest the continued ownership of the sellers.

Secondly, again in some of the cases the courts have drawn adverse inferences from the fact that the buyer has not been expressly designated as a 'fiduciary' for the seller and, in particular, the courts have not been willing to infer fiduciary obligations to segregate buyer's assets and seller's assets in the absence of express contractual provision to that effect. This factor was a consideration in *Hendy Lennox (Industrial Engines) Ltd v. Grahame Puttick Ltd*.

Thirdly, the presence of express credit terms in conditions of sale has also been taken as militating against the validity and effectiveness of proceeds-of-sale retention of title. In other words, courts have rejected claims to resale proceeds on the basis that the buyer has been afforded a period of credit. This clause has been taken as impliedly acknowledging that the buyer may use the proceeds in the ordinary course of business during the period of credit. Such freedom of action would be incompatible with the existence of a fiduciary relationship between buyer and seller in respect of resale proceeds. In *Re Andrabell Ltd*,[71] for example, the court reasoned that the forty-five day credit period afforded the buyers in the particular case meant that the buyers were free to use resale proceeds in their business and this was irreconcilable with the equitable duty to account.[72] One leading commentator has however argued to the contrary, suggesting that:[73]

---

[69] [1984] 1 WLR 485.   [70] [1984] 3 All ER 407.

[71] *Ibid.* at 416. See also the *Hendy Lennox* case [1984] 1 WLR 485 at 499.

[72] For a different interpretation see the views expressed by the High Court of Australia in *Associated Alloys Pty Ltd v. ACN 001 452 106 Pty Ltd* (2000) 202 CLR 588 at 610:

> The express term in the agreement . . . which provides for a period of credit within which the debt need not be paid by the Buyer is, in turn, incorporated as an express term of the trust. This term thereby prescribes the period within which the Seller, as beneficiary, cannot call upon the trust property (if the trust is constituted during the credit period). The implied term thus provides one means of discharging the debt by performance. No relevant inconsistency arises between this implied term and the express term in the agreement providing for a period of credit for the Buyer.

> See also *Len Vidgen v. Timaru Marine Supplies* [1986] 1 NZLR 349 at 364.

[73] R. Goode, *Proprietary Rights and Insolvency in Sales Transactions* (Sweet & Maxwell, 2nd edn. 1989) at p. 100.

The sale agreement may, for example, be construed as providing that the buyer is to have 45 days' credit but subject to a duty to account for proceeds of sale on receipt, the transfer of such proceeds pro tanto reducing the buyer's price indebtedness. The duty to account thus cuts down the scope of the provision for credit but does not deprive it of effect, for the buyer remains entitled to avail himself of the full period of the credit except insofar as he receives proceeds of sale during that period.

A fourth factor has been overelaboration in the conditions of sale. This is regarded as a possible vice because the source of the seller's rights is taken to be the agreement between the parties and not equitable principles that might have applied had the parties not made such an agreement. If seller and buyer by express contractual statement have brought into existence security-type rights then they run the risk that the parties will categorise their agreement as creating a charge. Therefore, a person drafting a retention-of-title clause has to steer between the twin perils of underprovision, which has proved fatal in some notable cases such as *Re Andrabell Ltd*, and that of overelaboration, which was the supplier's undoing in other cases such as *Tatung (UK) Ltd v. Galex Telesure Ltd*.[74] In *Tatung*, for example, the plaintiffs supplied goods to the defendants under two separate sets of conditions. The first set of conditions declared that the proceeds of resales of the goods belonged to the supplier absolutely. The second, and more elaborate, set of conditions obliged the defendants to keep the proceeds of resales in a separate account for the benefit of the plaintiffs. It was held that a charge had been created over the proceeds of sale. The court noted that the contracts made express provision for the interest that the plaintiffs were to have in the proceeds of dealing with the goods. In these circumstances, the court considered that the source of the plaintiffs' rights was the contract between the parties and not equitable principles that might have otherwise obtained had the parties not made such a contract. Basically, in *Tatung* the plaintiffs were penalised for precision in their supply contracts, and some commentators might see this result as being somewhat strange.

A fifth consideration has been the question of entitlement to any profits generated by resales. The rationale of a contract for the sale of goods is that the buyer should have the use of the goods along with any profits from resales. This issue of entitlement to profits on resales is often used to distinguish between sales, strictly so-called, and security interests. In some celebrated comments Romer LJ in *Re George Inglefield Ltd* said:[75]

If the mortgagee realizes the subject-matter of the mortgage for a sum more than sufficient to repay him, with interest and the costs, the money that has passed

---

[74] (1989) 5 BCC 325.   [75] [1933] Ch 1 at 26–7.

between him and the mortgagor he has to account to the mortgagor for the surplus. If the purchaser sells the subject-matter of the purchase, and realizes a profit, of course he has not got to account to the vendor for the profit.

If the buyer is simply reselling the goods supplied under a contract of sale as an agent or other fiduciary for the original seller, then logically the original seller should be entitled to the entire resale price, but instinctively this seems contrary to the intention of the parties.[76] Implying a contractual or restitutionary duty on the part of the original seller to account to the buyer for the profit element on resales may be a way out of the conceptual conundrum, but the courts appear reluctant to make the implication.

A sixth, and overarching, reason why proceeds-of-sale retention-of-title clauses are not recognised flows from the fact that the original seller's interest or claim in resale proceeds comes to an end once the original purchase price, plus any outstanding expenses, have been discharged. For this reason, one might cynically observe that there is very little chance of a reservation-of-title clause receiving judicial approval. This view tends to be confirmed by *Compaq Computer Ltd* v. *Abercorn Group Ltd*.[77] In this case the plaintiff sold computer equipment to the first defendant, Abercorn. The latter resold the equipment and also entered into a factoring arrangement with another company, Kellock. The factoring arrangement included debts arising from the resales of the computer equipment. The equipment had been sold subject to a reservation-of-title clause in favour of the seller. Resales, though, were permitted subject to the following qualification:

Insofar as the dealer may sell or otherwise dispose of the Compaq products or receive any monies from any third party in respect of the Compaq products, he shall strictly account to Compaq for the full proceeds thereof (such monies as the dealer shall receive) as the seller's bailee or agent and shall keep a separate account of all such proceeds or monies for such purpose.

---

[76] See the comments of the High Court of Australia in *Associated Alloys Pty Ltd* v. *ACN 001 452 106 Pty Ltd* (2000) 202 CLR 588 at 607:

The present case is not an example of an arrangement whereby, upon its proper construction, proceeds subject to the trust in favour of the seller were defined otherwise than by reference to the state of indebtedness between the Buyer and the Seller, and the beneficial interest of the Buyer in a greater sum might have been appropriated by the Seller to give it a windfall. Equity favours the identification and protection of an equity of redemption and, in that regard, prefers substance to form . . . [This] might have provided a footing for the treatment of the interest of the seller as no more than a charge upon the proceeds to secure the indebtedness of the Buyer. It is unnecessary to express any concluded view upon the matter.

[77] [1991] BCC 484.

The court held that the sub-sales claims and proceeds were effectively charged to the seller as security for the price of the goods. As the charge had not been registered it became void when the buyer went into liquidation. The court came to the conclusion that the buyer was not a trustee for the seller because the seller's interest in sub-sales and proceeds was not absolute but was defeasible on payment of the purchase price. In its view, analysing the contract in this way led inevitably to a charge construction. Once it was conceded that the beneficial interest in the proceeds of sale was determinable on payment of the debts, the seller had to confront the difficulty that the rights and obligations of the parties were in reality, and in substance, characteristic of those of the parties to a charge, and not of those in a fiduciary relationship. Reference was made to the following observations in *Re Bond Worth Ltd*:[78] 'Any contract which, by way of security for the payment of a debt, confers an interest in property defeasible or destructible upon payment of such debt, or appropriates such property for the discharge of the debt, must necessarily be regarded as creating a mortgage or charge, as the case may be.' Reasoning by analogy, the buyer was empowered to redeem the charge in favour of the seller if the outstanding debts were paid but the seller was not entitled to retain out of resale proceeds a sum that was more than sufficient to pay those debts. If the resale proceeds were deficient in this respect, the seller had a right of action against the buyer for the balance of the purchase price as a simple contract debt. It is submitted that this reasoning is open to criticism if one contrasts it with the judicial approach towards 'simple' reservation-of-title clauses where the courts have brushed aside a charge construction notwithstanding the fact that the seller's interest in the goods comes to an end when the buyer pays the outstanding sums due. If the seller repossesses and realises the goods for less than the original purchase price, then the seller may sue the buyer for the balance. The analysis adopted in *Compaq Computer* is very much in line with the purposive approach towards 'simple' reservation that found favour at first instance,[79] but was decisively rejected by the Court of Appeal, in *Clough Mill Ltd v. Martin*.[80]

Claims to trace resale proceeds have been upheld in pre-PPSA New Zealand[81] and Australia[82] with the courts not recognising or enforcing the limits placed on the *Romalpa* decision in England. The leading authority

---

[78] [1980] Ch 228 at 248.
[79] The first-instance decision is reported [1984] 1 WLR 1067.
[80] [1985] 1 WLR 111.
[81] See, e.g., *Len Vidgen v. Timaru Marine Supplies Ltd* [1986] 1 NZLR 349; *Bisley Ltd v. Gore Engineering & Retail Sales Ltd* [1989] 2 NZBLC 103, 593; *Peerless Carpets Ltd v. Moorhouse Carpet Market Ltd* [1992] 4 NZBLC 102, 747.
[82] See *Puma Australia Pty Ltd v. Sportman's Australia Ltd* [1994] 2 QD R 149; but cf. *Chattis Nominees Pty Ltd v. Norman Ross Homeworks Pty Ltd* (1992) 28 NSWLR 338.

in Australia is the decision of the High Court of Australia in *Associated Alloys Pty Ltd* v. *ACN 001 452 106*.[83] This is a case where steel was supplied by the plaintiffs to the defendants and allegedly used in a complex manufacturing process so as to produce industrial equipment which was then sold to a third party. The defendants went into liquidation with substantial amounts owing to the plaintiffs remaining unpaid, and the latter claimed the proceeds of sale of the industrial equipment on the basis of a reservation-of-title clause in their invoices which provided, *inter alia*:

> In the event that the [buyer] uses the goods/product in some manufacturing or construction process of its own or some third party, then the [buyer] shall hold such part of the proceeds of such manufacturing or construction process as relates to the goods/product in trust for the [seller]. Such part shall be deemed to equal in dollar terms the amount owing by the [buyer] to the [seller] at the time of the receipt of such proceeds.

One of the questions the High Court of Australia had to decide was whether the clause in question constituted a charge requiring registration under the Australian Corporations Law. The majority took the view that the proceeds sub-clause was an agreement to constitute a trust of future-acquired property. It was not a charge within the meaning of the Corporations Law and the detailed provisions of the law pertaining to charges did not apply to it. The majority recognised that this holding had commercial significance and for third parties, such as financial institutions seeking to assess the creditworthiness of the buyer, the non-registration of the proceeds sub-clause on a public register could create practical difficulties. On the other hand, it was not for the courts to destroy or impair property rights, such as those arising under trusts, by supplementing the list of registrable interests. Moreover, reference was made to considerations that might militate against any extension of registration requirements:[84]

> The lack of any statutory obligation to register the proceeds subclause . . . creates commercial incentives for entities, in the position of both the Buyer and the Seller, to incorporate clauses such as the proceeds subclause into their purchase agreements. These clauses reduce the risk of non-payment by the buyer. To the extent that this financial, or credit, risk is reduced, the commercial viability of the transaction for both parties may be increased. For example, the availability of this means of reducing credit risk for the seller may result in the seller accepting a lower cost price per unit of steel. Competitive pressures may thus operate upon the parties to incorporate clauses such as the proceeds subclause in their transactions.

It should be noted that the original seller was only claiming a proportionate part of resale proceeds and not the entirety thereof. Whether

---

[83] (2000) 202 CLR 588. The case is dicussed, *inter alia*, by J. De Lacy 'Corporate Insolvency and Retention of Title Clauses: Developments in Australia' [2001] *Insolvency Lawyer* 64.
[84] (2000) 202 CLR 588 at 611.

such claim was sustainable, in the eyes of the court, is not entirely clear. Reference was made to the observations of Robert Goff LJ in *Clough Mill Ltd* v. *Martin*[85] that it was a manifestly peculiar outcome to find that the parties intended that the seller should obtain the windfall of the full value of the newly manufactured products. Counterbalancing this, however, were the comments of Windeyer J in *Garfunkel* v. *Bentley Pty Ltd* that the law ordinarily will take the parties at their word and the court will be slow to find that a bargain is not as the parties expressed it. The court appeared to lean in favour of this interpretation. There are some unsatisfactory features about the *Associated Alloys* decision, however, which, it is submitted, will reduce the possibility of it gaining judicial acceptance in England. Firstly, as far the seller's claim is concerned, there was a break in the proprietary chain. The seller's steel was used in the manufacturing process and, at that point, according to the English authorities, title vested in the buyers. The latter, in selling the finished article, were selling their own goods and consequently, the proceeds of sale of these goods belonged to them too. The original seller's claim against such proceeds amounted to a claim over the property of another and fell within the classic definition of a charge.[86] Secondly, in *Associated Alloys* the seller's claim fell on the facts as the sellers failed to establish a necessary and direct link between particular unpaid invoices and payments received from the third party. Consequently, the views expressed on the permissible limits of proceeds-of-sale reservation-of-title clauses might be regarded as strictly *obiter*. It is submitted that, all in all, an English court is likely to be more persuaded by the strong dissent of Kirby J in the case:[87]

The most that [the clause] can amount to for [the seller] is an unregistered charge on a 'book debt'. Any other construction . . . would permit the easy defeat of the clear purpose of the Law, namely that creditors of companies which become insolvent must, unless they are secured creditors that are afforded priority, participate pari passu in the available assets of the company. It would be contrary to principle to adopt a restrictive or confined construction of the provisions of the Law, which is designed to ensure that a company's charges on book debts are registered and that those which are not registered are unenforceable against the administrator or liquidator of that company. In effect, [the seller] seeks . . . to have a priority by virtue of its own undisclosed contractual stipulation.

[85] [1985] 1 WLR 111 at 120.
[86] See the comments by De Lacy 'Corporate Insolvency' at 65:

Should a seller seek to claim the proceeds of sub-sale resulting from the buyer's sale of manufactured/processed goods (including the seller's goods) then as the manufacturing process will cause the seller's title to be lost no claim can exist against the process. Any such claim will be dependent upon a contractual provision granting such an interest and will be construed as a registrable security interest.

[87] (2000) 202 CLR 588 at 626.

Claims to proceeds of collateral in the United States

In the US there are no conceptual or other difficulties about a supplier asserting a claim to resale proceeds. In the case of a contract of sale containing a reservation-of-title clause, the contract itself constitutes the security agreement within Article 9 parlance and, if the reservation-of-title clause contains a resale-proceeds element, then obviously the security agreement covers proceeds. Proceeds could be referred to specifically as such in the filed financing statement. This step, however, is not necessary. Article 9 regards a filing against the original collateral as filing against the proceeds with the policy being one of automatic perfection of security interests in proceeds. The assumption underlying Article 9 is that the absence of a specific reference to proceeds in Article 9 would not mislead third parties. It has been argued that in addition to rescuing some secured parties from careless omissions, the automatic-perfection-of-security-interests-in-proceeds approach also saves the costs of extended negotiations. It is also arguable that it inhibits abuse and overreaching by some secured parties who, if it were necessary to protect one's claim to proceeds by explicit provision, might use unnecessarily detailed and all-encompassing language.[88] Article 9-315(d) states that a perfected security interest in proceeds becomes unperfected on the twenty-first day after the security interest attaches to the proceeds, subject to three exceptions. These exceptions are, however, so broad that they seem to cover most proceeds cases in practice. Even the first exception would seem to cover most cases. It refers to the situation where a filed financing statement covers the original collateral and the proceeds are collateral in which a security interest may be perfected by filing in the same office in which the financing statement has been filed. The second exception permits continued perfection of 'identifiable cash proceeds' and the third exception refers to a situation where an actual financing statement has been filed before the expiry of the twenty-one-day period.

When do cash proceeds cease to be 'identifiable'? Article 9-315(b)(2) refers to identification of the proceeds by 'a method of tracing, including application of equitable principles, that is permitted under law'. Courts in the US, like those in England, generally apply the 'lowest intermediate balance' principle when tracing commingled funds.[89] In *Universal CIT*

---

[88] See generally on this point Honnold et al. *Security Interests in Personal Property* at p. 202; and see also *Buhr* v. *Bardays Bank P/C* [2002] BPIR 25.

[89] See generally *Foskett* v. *McKeown* [2001] 1 AC 102; *Roscoe* v. *Winder* [1915] I Ch 62; *Re Goldcorp Exchange Ltd* [1995] 1 AC 74; *Bishopsgate Investment Management Ltd* v. *Homan* [1995] Ch 211. For a broader, more pragmatic approach to the question of tracing in the PPSA context see the Saskatchewan decision *Agricultural Credit Corp of Saskatchewan* v. *Pettyjohn* (1991) 79 DLR (4th) 22.

Credit Corp. v. *Farmers Bank*[90] the US District Court stated the general rule that in tracing commingled funds it is presumed that any payments made were from other than the funds in which another had a legally recognised interest. The court invoked the following passage from the *Restatement of Trusts*:[91]

Where the trustee deposits in a single account in a bank, trust funds and his individual funds, and makes withdrawals from the deposit and dissipates the money so withdrawn, and subsequently makes additional deposits of his individual funds in the account, the beneficiary cannot ordinarily enforce an equitable lien upon the deposit for a sum greater than the lowest intermediate balance of the deposit.

If a security interest in goods has PMSI status then the PMSI character of the security interest will not necessarily carry into the proceeds of the goods. A distinction in this context is again drawn between inventory and other goods, with PMSI status in the proceeds of inventory being more difficult to establish. According to Article 9-324 a perfected security interest in the identifiable proceeds of goods other than inventory has priority over a conflicting security interest if the PMSI is perfected when the debtor receives possession of the collateral or within twenty days thereafter. On the other hand, the PMSI status of a perfected security interest in inventory will only extend to identifiable cash proceeds of the inventory and will not, for example, apply if the proceeds of the inventory are, say, accounts. The Official Comment to the Revised Article 9-324 states that matter as follows:

Debtor creates a security interest in its existing and after-acquired inventory in favour of SP-1, who files a financing statement covering inventory. SP-2 susbsequently takes a purchase-money security interest in certain inventory and, under subsection (b), achieves priority in the inventory over SP-1. This inventory is then sold, producing accounts. Accounts are not cash proceeds, and so the special purchase-money priority in the inventory does not control the priority in the accounts. Rather, the first-to-file-or-perfect rule of Section 9–322(a)(1) applies.[92]

Moreover, purchase-money super-priority only extends to the proceeds of inventory if 'identifiable cash proceeds are received on or before the

---

[90] (1973) 358 F Supp 317.
[91] Second edition, para 202, comment j. For further details see the American Law Institute website: www.ali.org.
[92] The point is also discussed by Catherine Walsh 'The Floating Charge is Dead; Long Live the Floating Charge' in Agasha Mugasha ed. *Perspectives on Commercial Law* (Prospect, 1999) p. 129 at pp. 139–40. The PMSI status or otherwise of a claim to the proceeds of purchase-money collateral differs in the various Canadian PPSA jurisdictions. For details see the Canadian Conference on Personal Property Security Law section on the Uniform Law Commissioners of Canada website: www.chlc.ca/.

delivery of the inventory to a buyer'. This is an extremely restrictive condition but, as the Official Comment explains, cash supplied by the receivables financier will often be used to pay off the inventory financing. Indeed, the party financing the inventory on a purchase-money basis may insert provisions in the contract to the effect that receivables financing obtained from another financier should be devoted to paying off the inventory security interest.[93]

PMSI status in inventory may, however, under certain conditions carry through into the proceeds of inventory that consist of 'chattel paper'. In this respect there is an interesting analogy between the Article 9 provisions and the English case *Re Highway Foods Ltd*.[94] 'Chattel paper' is defined in Article 9-102 as a record or records that evidence both a monetary obligation and a security interest in specific goods. Where goods are sold on retention-of-title terms, the written conditions of sale constitute 'chattel paper' in the Article 9 parlance. In *Re Highway Foods Ltd* goods were sold subject to a reservation-of-title clause and the buyer then sold the goods on to a sub-buyer with that sale also being subject to a reservation-of-title clause. The goods were also delivered to the sub-buyer. The court concluded on a review of the relevant statutory provisions, principally section 9 Factors Act 1889 and section 25 Sale of Goods Act 1979, that unless and until the sub-buyer paid the buyer the price of the goods, the original seller could lay claim to the goods in the hands of the sub-buyer. If the buyer had actually sold the meat to the sub-buyer, it could not be disputed that title had passed to the sub-buyer but, translated into the relevant statutory language, the contract between the buyer and sub-buyer was not a sale but an agreement for sale. In Article 9 language inventory subject to a purchase-money security had been sold, producing proceeds in the form of chattel paper. The PMSI in the inventory carried through into the proceeds of the inventory.

Mixture of goods: accessions

If goods supplied subject to a retention-of-title clause have been altered, mixed or refined in some way the question arises whether the claim by the supplier is still effective. In England the common law appears to distinguish between three basic situations.[95] The first situation, that of accession, occurs where one chattel is added to a more dominant chattel.

---

[93] Official Comment to revised Article 9-324 para. 8.   [94] [1995] 1 BCLC 209.
[95] See, however, the comments of Oliver LJ in *Clough Mill* v. *Martin* [1985] 1 WLR 111 at 124: 'English law has developed no very sophisticated system for determining title in cases where undistinguishable goods are mixed or become combined in a newly manufactured article.'

The second situation involves the mixing of goods, and the third involves the manufacture of a 'new product' or *nova species*.[96]

Cases of accession are sometimes encountered in the retention-of-title context, with a retention-of-title clause often being accompanied by a provision to the effect that the goods supplied should not be attached to other chattels without the consent of the seller. The purpose clearly is to prevent the supplier from losing title to the goods by virtue of the doctrine of accession. Under this doctrine where a subsidiary chattel is attached to a dominant chattel, ownership therein inheres in the owner of the dominant chattel.[97] If the goods are attached without the supplier's knowledge or consent, he might have a personal claim against the buyer for breach of contract but this personal claim does not involve any right to priority in the event of the buyer's insolvency.

The principles of accession were applied in *Hendy Lennox (Industrial Engines) Ltd* v. *Grahame Puttick Ltd.*[98] The case concerned diesel engines, supplied subject to reservation-of-title clauses, which had been incorporated into generating sets. It was held that the proprietary rights of the sellers in the engines were not affected when the engines were wholly or partially incorporated into the generator sets. The title of the original seller remained because the diesel engines could be removed without serious injury to or destruction of the whole so formed. The judge explained that the engines were not like the acrilan which became yarn and then carpet (*Bond Worth*)[99] or the resin which became chipboard (*Borden*)[100] or the leather which became handbags (*Peachdart*).[101]

Another approach might be for the seller to state that any additions to the goods supplied become the seller's property. The danger in this attempt at drafting lies in the fact that if the additions are identifiably separate from the goods supplied, then the buyer can only be regarded as transferring his own property to the seller. If this is done for the purpose of ensuring payment of the purchase price under the sale-of-goods

---

[96] For a comparison between English and Roman law in this area see P. Birks 'Mixtures' in N. Palmer and E. McKendrick eds. *Interests in Goods* (Lloyds of London Press, 2nd edn. 1998) at p. 227; but see the comments by Lord Hope in *Foskett* v. *McKeown* [2001] 1 AC 102 at 121–2, who points to uncertainties in the Roman-law position (not easily resolved in the present day!):

> It is worth noting that even in the well known case of the picture painted by Apelles on someone else's board or panel differing views were expressed: see *Stair's Institutions* (1832, vol. 1, 11.1.39). Paulus thought that the picture followed the ownership of the board as accessory to the picture (*Digest*, 41.1.9.2). Justinian's view, following Gaius, was that the board was accessory to the picture, as the picture was more precious (*Institutes of Justinian*, 11.1.34).

[97] See generally G. McCormack 'Mixture of Goods' (1990) 10 *Legal Studies* 293; A. Guest 'Accession and Confusion in the Law of Hire-Purchase' (1964) 27 *MLR* 505.
[98] [1984] 1 WLR 485.   [99] [1980] Ch 228.   [100] [1981] Ch 25.
[101] [1984] Ch 131.

contract, then the arrangement will probably be struck down by the courts as creating a registrable charge over goods.[102]

In Article 9 there are special rules governing accessions. The term is defined as meaning goods that are physically united with other goods in such a manner that the identity of the original goods is not lost. Article 9-335 provides that a security interest may be created in an accession and continues in collateral that becomes an accession. Moreover, if a security interest is perfected when the collateral becomes an accession, it remains perfected in the collateral. A security interest in an accession is stated, however, to be subordinate to a security interest in the whole which is perfected by compliance with the requirements of a certificate-of-title statute. After default, a secured party may remove an accession from other goods if the security interest in the accession has priority over the claims of every person having an interest in the whole. A secured party that removes an accession is required promptly to reimburse any holder of a security interest or other lien on, or owner of, the other goods, other than the debtor, for the cost of physical injury to the whole or the other goods. Moreover, a person entitled to reimbursement may refuse permission to remove until the secured party gives adequate assurance for the performance of the obligation to reimburse. The provision adds, however, that a secured party need not reimburse the holder or owner for any diminution in value of the whole or the other goods caused by the absence of the accession removed or by any necessity for replacing it.

Article 9-335 on accessions leaves a lot of questions to be governed by other aspects of Article 9, including matters of attachment and perfection and some matters of priorities. One issue that arises is whether a perfected security interest in the dominant chattel will attach to the inferior chattel once the latter has been affixed to the dominant chattel. This question will turn on whether the description of the collateral in the security agreement is sufficiently extensive. Similarly, the question arises whether a perfected security interest in the inferior chattel will attach to the whole. Again, this depends on the breadth of the description of the collateral in the financing statement. Apart from the reference to a certificate-of-title statute, Article 9-335 has nothing to say about priority questions. These are left to be regulated by other aspects of Article 9, namely the first-to-file-or-perfect priority rule and the super-priority status applicable to PMSIs. The Official Comment provides an example of how such priority questions would be resolved in the context of accessions:[103]

---

[102] *Specialist Plant Services Ltd* v. *Braithwaite Ltd* [1987] BCLC 1.
[103] Article 9-335 Official Comment Example 3.

Debtor owns an office computer subject to a security interest in favor of SP-1. Debtor acquires memory and grants a perfected security interest in the memory to SP-2. Debtor installs the memory in the computer, at which time (one assumes) SP-1's security interest attaches to the memory. The first-to-file-or-perfect rule of Section 9–322 governs priority in the memory. If, however, SP-2's security interest is a purchase-money security interest, Section 9–324(a) would afford priority in the memory to SP-2, regardless of which security interest was perfected first.

Mixture of goods without loss of physical identity

Where goods belonging to different parties are mixed together but not so as to affect the physical characteristics of the commingled goods, different rules may apply depending on whether one of the parties has been guilty of intentional wrongdoing in bringing about the mixing. In particular there was some authority supporting the existence of a penal rule whereby a party who was guilty of intentional wrongdoing in bringing about the mixing forfeited his share in the resultant mixture.[104] More recently, however, in *Indian Oil Corporation* v. *Greenstone Shipping SA (Panama)*,[105] the existence of a penal rule was denied. The court held that where a party wrongfully mixed the goods of another with his own goods which were substantially of the same nature and quality, and they could not be separated for practical purposes, the mixture was held in common. The innocent party, however, could claim from the wrong-doer any loss sustained by reason of the admixture, whether in respect of quality or otherwise.[106]

Where commingling has been effected in good faith or with the consent of the respective owners then the authorities suggest that the owners of the constituent items become tenants in common of the mass in proportion to

---

[104] See *Lupton* v. *White* (1808) 15 Ves 432; and *Sandeman & Sons* v. *Tyzack and Branfoot Steamship Co. Ltd* [1913] AC 680 at 695 where Lord Moulton said: 'If the mixing has arisen from the fault of "B", "A" can claim the goods.' See also the comments of Lord Millett in *Foskett* v. *McKeown* [2001] 1 AC 102 at 132–3.

[105] [1988] 1 QB 345.

[106] See the statement of principle by Moore-Bick J in *Glencore* v. *Metro Trading International* [2001] 1 Lloyds Law Reports 284 who concluded (at 330) that

> when one person wrongfully blends his own oil with oil of a different grade or specification belonging to another person with the result that a new product is produced, that new product is owned by them in common. In my view justice also requires in a case of this kind that the proportions in which the contributors own the new blend should reflect both the quantity and the value of the oil which each has contributed. As in other cases of mixing, any doubts about the quantity or value of the oil contributed by the innocent party should be resolved against the wrongdoer. The innocent party is also entitled to recover damages from the wrongdoer in respect of any loss which he has suffered as a result of the wrongful use of his oil.

their respective contributions.[107] Cases usually cited in this connection are *Buckley* v. *Gross*[108] and *Spence* v. *Union Marine Insurance Co.*[109] In *Buckley* v. *Gross*, tallow in a warehouse belonging to a number of persons flowed out as a result of a fire into a common sewer. Blackburn J said:[110]

> The tallow of the different owners was indeed mixed up into a molten mass, so that it might be difficult to apportion it among them . . . Probably the legal effect of such a mixture would be to make the owners tenants in common in equal portions of the mass, but at all events they do not lose their property in it.

In this case there was no proof of the respective contributions of the owners of the separate goods. Therefore, a tenancy-in-common-in-equal-shares solution was adopted.

In *Spence* v. *Union Marine Insurance Co.* it was possible to quantify the contributions of each party to the mixture and, accordingly, a tenancy in common was declared in line with the contribution of each party to the whole. This was a case where a ship carrying a cargo of cotton from the American South to Liverpool became shipwrecked. Consequently, distinguishing marks on the bales of cotton were obliterated. The court took the view that[111] 'by the mixture of the bales, and their becoming undistinguishable by reason of the action of the sea, and without the fault of the respective owners, these parties became tenants in common of the cotton, in proportion to their respective interests'. More generally, the court said:[112] 'If . . . separation is not practicable, then the former proprietors of the things now connected will be joint owners of the whole, whenever the mixture has been made with the consent of both parties, or by accident.' The English authorities in this area are of respectable antiquity, to say the least, but were applied in a modern setting by the New Zealand Court of Appeal in *Coleman* v. *Harvey*.[113] The New Zealand Court of Appeal accepted the view that where the goods of two persons are intermixed by consent or agreement, so that the several portions can no longer be

---

[107] See the comments of Lord Millett in *Foskett* v. *McKeown* [2001] 1 AC 102 at 141:

> A mixed fund, like a physical mixture, is divisible between the parties who contributed to it rateably in proportion to the value of their respective contributions, and this must be ascertained at the time they are added to the mixture . . . If 20 gallons of A's oil are mixed with 40 gallons of B's oil to produce a uniform mixture of 60 gallons, A and B are entitled to share in the mixture in proportions of 1 to 2. It makes no difference if A's oil, being purchased later, cost £2 a gallon and B's oil cost only £1 a gallon, so that they each paid out £40. This because the mixture is divisible between the parties rateably in proportion to the value of their respective contributions and not in proportion to their respective cost.

For a somewhat more complicated analysis see Birks 'Mixtures'.
[108] (1863) 3 B & S 566; 122 ER 213.   [109] (1868) LR 3 CP 427.
[110] (1863) 3 B & S 566 at 574–5; 122 ER 213 at 216.
[111] (1868) LR 3 CP 427 at 438–9.   [112] *Ibid.* at 438.   [113] [1989] 1 NZLR 723.

distinguished, the proprietors have an interest in common in proportion to their respective shares. In principle, this body of doctrine should apply in the reservation-of-title context. Consequently, where goods supplied under a reservation-of-title clause have been mingled with other goods without resulting in a loss of physical identity, the supplier should be able to claim co-ownership of the mixture. Under English law, no security interest in the mixture has been created in favour of the supplier and, as a result, there are no registration requirements to fulfil before the supplier's co-ownership is recognised.

Article 9 appears to assimilate the treatment of mixtures of heterogeneous goods and mixtures of homogeneous goods. If physical separation of the product or mass is not possible then the same rules apply irrespective of whether the constituent items are homogeneous or heterogeneous.

Mixture of heterogeneous goods or the manufacture of a new article

It seems to be the rule under English law that where heterogeneous goods are mixed together in a manufacturing process so as to result in the manufacture of what might be called a 'new product', the manufacturer becomes the owner of the new product and the title of owners of the constituent items disappears.[114] This rule would apply unless the manufacturing work was done on a contract or agency basis for the owners of the raw materials. The question obviously arises as to what kind of 'process' goods must be subjected to before the title of the original owner or owners disappears. The issue has been considered on a pragmatic basis by the courts, and while the general principle is clear the detailed aspects of the issue are not. One may state a general rule of somewhat uncertain ambit that where substantial work is done on raw materials then the title of the supplier of the raw materials is lost. Certainly the courts in England have made it clear that where goods supplied under

---

[114] Subject to what was said in *Clough Mill Ltd* v. *Martin* [1985] 1 WLR 111; and see also the judgment of Moore-Bick J in *Glencore* v. *Metro Trading International* [2001] 1 Lloyds Law Reports 284 at 322 who was prepared to hold that

> in a case where title to newly manufactured goods would otherwise vest solely in the manufacturer, there is no reason in principle why the manufacturer and a supplier should not by agreement cause title to vest originally in the supplier rather than the manufacturer. Other considerations would clearly arise if more than one supplier had entered into an agreement of that kind with the same manufacturer.

> Moore-Bick J rejected the submission of counsel that in all cases title must necessarily vest for an instant in the manufacturer before passing to the supplier as 'contrary to both principle and authority'.

a reservation-of-title clause form part of a process of manufacture, then the supplier must make express contractual provision if it wishes to acquire rights in the finished product. It cannot simply rely on its ownership of the raw material. This proposition was firmly stated in *Borden (UK) Ltd v. Scottish Timber Products Ltd.*[115] In this case the plaintiffs supplied resin to the defendants and the resin was mixed with certain hardeners, wax emulsion and wood chippings so as to manufacture chipboard. The resin was supplied subject to the following reservation-of-title clause:

(2) Risk and Property. Goods supplied by the company shall be at the purchaser's risk immediately on delivery to the purchaser or into custody on the purchaser's behalf (whichever is the sooner) and the purchaser should therefore be insured accordingly.

Property in goods supplied hereunder will pass to the customer when:

(a) the goods the subject of this contract, and (b) all other goods the subject of any other contract between the company and the customer which, at the time of payment of the full price of the goods sold under this contract, have been delivered to the customer but not paid for in full, have been paid for in full.

The plaintiffs made a claim to the chipboard manufactured with the resin or to any money or property representing the proceeds of sale of such chipboard. The Court of Appeal held, however, that the plaintiffs' title to the resin disappeared once it was used in the manufacturing process.[116] In the court's view, the tracing remedy recognised in *Romalpa* did not apply where there was a mixture of heterogeneous goods in a manufacturing process wherein the original goods lost their character and what emerged was a wholly new product.[117] The court said that what had happened was fairly analogous to instances where cattle cake was sold to a farmer, or fuel to a steel manufacturer, in each case with a reservation-of-title clause, but on terms which permitted the farmer to feed the cattle cake to his herd and the steelmaker to fuel his furnaces, before paying the purchase price. It was universally agreed that the seller could not trace into the cattle or the steel. If the seller wished to acquire rights over the finished product, this could only be done by express contractual stipulation.[118]

---

[115] [1981] Ch 25.   [116] *Ibid.* at 41 *per* Bridge LJ and at 44 *per* Templeman LJ.
[117] See Bridge LJ *ibid.* at 41.
[118] *Ibid.* at 42. Templeman LJ was of the same opinion. He said at 44: 'When the resin was incorporated in the chipboard, the resin ceased to exist, the plaintiff's title to the resin became meaningless and their security vanished. There was no provision in the contract for the defendants to provide substituted or additional security. The chipboard belonged to the defendants.'

If title to the new products belongs to the buyer and is transferred to the seller as a means of security for the discharge of an indebtedness, then the arrangement will probably be viewed as creating a charge over goods. This charge will then be void for non-registration in the event of the buyer's insolvency.

The question arises when exactly title to goods is lost by incorporation in a new product or use in a manufacturing process. At what moment of time does the title of the supplier disappear? This question is by no means easily answered. Various tests have been applied in the decided cases, though often without clearly distinguishing between these tests. One test asks whether the goods have been 'appropriated' to the manufacturing process; another whether they have lost any significant value as raw material; and a third whether they have been subjected to more than minor physical manipulation or alteration. The overwhelming tendency, however, is to hold that the title of the supplier is 'lost' in processed goods. A case in point is Re Peachdart Ltd,[119] where leather was sold to a company which used it to manufacture handbags. The relevant provision in the supply contract read:

If any of the products are incorporated in or used as material for other goods before such payment the property in the whole of such other goods shall be and remain with the seller until such payment has been made or the other goods have been sold as aforesaid and all the seller's rights hereunder in the products shall extend to those other goods. (c) Until the seller is paid in full for all the products the relationship of the buyer to the seller shall be fiduciary in respect of the products or other goods in which they are incorporated.

The court used the Borden case in support of the proposition that title to the leather vanished once the handbag-making operation was embarked upon. In the court's view, the parties must have intended that, at least after a piece of leather had been appropriated to the manufacturing process and work had started on it (when the leather would cease to have any significant value as raw material), the leather would cease to be the exclusive property of the sellers. Thereafter, the sellers would have a charge on handbags in the course of manufacture and on the distinctive products which would come into existence at the end of the process of manufacture. The value of these products would be derived for the most part from the buyer's reputation and skill in design and the skill of its workforce.[120] In this respect at least, the Peachdart decision seems in line with the traditional proposition that where a party applies his own labour to another's

---

[119] [1984] Ch 131.   [120] Ibid. at 142–3.

raw materials in bringing out the formation of a new product, the worker, as it were, becomes owner of the new product.[121]

Peachdart was applied in *Modelboard* v. *Outer Box Ltd.*[122] The latter is a case where cardboard sheets, supplied under retention-of-title terms, were subjected to a 'process' by the buyer. There was no evidence before the court as to the exact nature of this process but, at the end of it, the cardboard sheets had lost any significant value as raw material. The court concluded that the suppliers' interest in the goods was lost and their interest in the processed goods was in the nature of a charge.

Peachdart was also applied in *Ian Chisholm Textiles Ltd* v. *Griffiths*[123] – a case which concerned cloth that was sold for use in the manufacture of clothes. The court took the view that once the cloth was combined to any significant extent by the buyer with goods owned by the buyer or by a third party, the beneficial ownership of the seller in the cloth changed into that of a security-interest holder over the clothes in the course of manufacture or the finished articles.

Aggregation clauses and claims against manufactured goods

A seller of goods that are likely to be used in a manufacturing process may, by virtue of an 'aggregation' retention-of-title clause in the conditions of sale, try to claim ownership of all or part of the finished articles. If such a provision is employed in the conditions of sale the question arises whether it constitutes a security interest over the finished article in favour of the seller. If the provision is so characterised then, prima facie, it will be invalid in the event of the corporate buyer's liquidation unless details of the security interest have been submitted for registration. The matter was addressed by the Court of Appeal in *Clough Mill Ltd* v. *Martin*, a case in which yarn was supplied for manufacture into fabrics. Robert Goff LJ said:[124]

---

[121] See the Scottish case *International Banking Corp* v. *Ferguson, Shaw & Sons* [1910] SC 182. In that case Lord Low said at 192 that 'the mixer, whether he be one of the proprietors or a third party, must, as the maker of the new species, become the sole proprietor of the subjects mixed'.

[122] [1992] BCC 945.   [123] [1994] BCC 96.

[124] [1985] 1 WLR 111 at 119. Oliver LJ was of the same opinion. He failed to see any reason in principle why the original legal title in a newly manufactured article composed of materials belonging to A and B should not lie where A and B had agreed that it should lie. Sir John Donaldson, on the other hand, was more tentative on the issue.

Now it is no doubt true that, where A's material is lawfully used by B to create new goods, whether or not B incorporated other material of his own, property in the new goods will generally rest in B, at least where the goods are not reducible to the original materials (see Blackstone's Commentaries (17th ed., 1830), Vol. 2, pp. 404–405). But it is difficult to see why, if the parties agree that the property in the goods shall vest in A, that agreement should not be given effect to. On this analysis the buyer does not confer on the seller an interest in property defeasible upon the payment of the debt; on the contrary, when the new goods come into existence the property in them ipso facto vests in the seller, and he thereafter retains his ownership in them, in the same way and on the same terms as he retains his ownership in the unused material.

In *Clough Mill* the relevant clause provided that if any of the material supplied was incorporated in or used as material for other goods before payment the property in the whole of such goods shall be and remain with the seller until such payment had been made. It was not strictly unnecessary to decide whether this condition created a registrable charge, but nevertheless both of the judges stated that it did, largely for two reasons.[125] The first reason stemmed from the so-called third-party problem, and the second from the windfall-profit problem. The first scenario arose where there were two lots of raw material, each supplied by different sellers, which were both used by the buyer to make or manufacture a new article. Assume also that each sale was made subject to an aggregation clause which vested in the seller the sole legal title to 'products'. Clearly, it is impossible to give effect to both aggregation clauses as drafted, and the most logical way out of the conundrum seems to be to hold that each supplier has a limited claim by way of charge against the new product in respect of the original contract debts.

The 'windfall-profit' problem raises an even more extensive barrier against the recognition of aggregation clauses. An aggregation clause confers a windfall on the seller in that he gains the benefit of the buyer's labour plus any raw materials that might have belonged originally to the buyer; but is such a windfall, profit really intended? It might be argued that seller and buyer never really intended to grant the seller such a windfall, particularly where the value of the raw materials was only a small part of the value of the finished article. Consequently, there is a risk, even a likelihood, that the courts will recharacterise the transaction as creating a charge in favour of the seller that secures the amount of the original sale price. If the transaction is not recharacterised, however, the windfall-profit problem could be surmounted by holding that the seller is under a duty to account to the buyer for the surplus value based on

---

[125] [1985] 1 WLR 111 at 120, 124.

the principles of unjust enrichment. The law of unjust enrichment has now been accepted at the highest judicial levels as an inherent feature of English law.[126]

Moreover, if supplier and buyer are free to agree where ownership of a new product shall lie then they should be free to agree, at least in theory, that ownership should be shared between them in whatever proportions they like. Such a provision avoids any question of a large windfall profit that would otherwise arise if ownership of the entirety of the new goods was given to the supplier. In the Irish case *Kruppstahl AG* v. *Quitmann Products Ltd*[127] the drafter of the reservation-of-title clause dealt with this problem by providing that the seller and buyer were to hold the new product jointly in the ratio of the invoice value of the seller's goods to those of the buyer's goods. Gannon J held that the provision constituted a registrable charge. He interpreted the contract as meaning that the accountability of the buyers was limited to the extent of their indebtedness. In consequence, the agreement was construed as conferring on the suppliers a means of security for the discharge of an indebtedness. It may be that if accountability was not restricted to the amount of indebtedness on the original sales contract, the agreement would have been upheld. Certainly, in the New Zealand case *Coleman* v. *Harvey*[128] there is strong support for the view that where the goods of two parties are mixed together even in such a way as to result in a loss of physical identity the parties should be free about ownership of the new product.

Mixing of goods and Article 9

Article 9 of the UCC contains special rules dealing with commingled goods. The expression is defined as meaning goods that are physically united with other goods in such a manner that their identity is lost in a product or mass. If there is a perfected security interest in collateral before the collateral becomes commingled goods, the security interest attaches to, and becomes perfected in, the product or mass. In other words, the security interest is transferred from the original collateral to the product or mass. A perfected security interest in collateral that becomes a product or mass will prevail over a security interest that is unperfected at the time that the collateral becomes commingled goods. If, however, there are

---

[126] See, e.g., *Lipkin Gorman* v. *Karpnale Ltd* [1999] 2 AC 548; *Westdeutsche Landesbank* v. *Islington LBC* [1996] AC 669. See also the comment of Moore-Bick, J. in *Glencare* [2001] 1 Lloyda Law Reports 284 at 322.

[127] [1982] ILRM 551. See also Goode *Proprietary Rights and Insolvency* at pp. 98–9.

[128] [1989] 1 NZLR 723.

competing perfected security interests in the different constituent items of commingled goods, the security interests rank equally in proportion to the value of the collateral at the time it became commingled goods. The following example from the Article 9 Official Comment illustrates the point:[129]

SP-1 has a perfected security interest in Debtor's eggs, which have a value of $300 and secure a debt of $400, and SP-2 has a perfected security interest in Debtor's flour, which has a value of $500 and secures a debt of $600. Debtor uses the flour and eggs to make cakes, which have a value of $1000. The two security interests rank equally and share in the ratio of 3:5. Applying this ratio to the entire value of the product, SP-1 would be entitled to $375 (i.e. 3/8 × $1000), and SP-2 would be entitled to $625 (i.e., 5/8 × $1000).

There is a threshold question about what sort of situations the commingling provision of Article 9-336 covers. In one case – *First National Bank* v. *Bostron*[130] – a supplier that had a security interest in cattle feed sold to a rancher contended that its interest continued in the cattle that consumed the feed. The argument proceeded on the basis that the feed had become part of the cattle, but the court rejected this proposition, stating that the cattle were neither a 'product' nor a 'mass' as these terms were used in Article 9. According to the court:

The feed which the cattle ate did not undergo any of these transformations, that is, it was not manufactured, processed, assembled or commingled with the cattle. Cattle consume food as motor vehicles do gasoline. Once eaten the feed not only loses its identity but in essence it ceases to exist and thus does not become part of the mass in the sense that the code uses the phrase.

There does not appear to be any reported case raising precisely the same issues in the UK but there is a Scottish case – *Kinloch Damph Ltd* v. *Nordvik Salmon Farms Ltd*[131] – which does raise some interesting parallels. In this case salmon smolts were supplied by the plaintiffs to the defendants subject to a reservation-of-title clause. The clause provided that until the price for the goods is paid for in full, the goods shall, notwithstanding delivery, remain the property of the seller. The contract went on to provide that the buyer should, so far as practicable, keep the goods in such a way that they were identifiable as the property of the supplier and, until property passed, the buyer would 'rear the goods in accordance with good husbandry as applicable to the farming of salmon in Scotland'. It

[129] Official Comment to Article 9-336 – Example 1.
[130] (1977) 564 P2d 964. The case is discussed in Baird and Jackson *Security Interests in Personal Property* at p. 440.
[131] (1999) – available through www.scotcourts.gov.uk/.

was also stated that the buyer 'accepts that no amount of growth in the size of the fish or weight or change of growth class of any fish delivered under this contract shall prevent the operation of this condition nor shall it permit the buyer to make any claim that title to the fish has passed to him by such fact alone'.

Despite this clause, however, it was argued on the basis of the doctrine of *specificatio* that a fish farmer who feeds and husbands large numbers of *Salmo salar* while they develop from smolts into mature salmon creates a *nova species* ownership which vests in him. The court dismissed this contention, holding that the mere fact that the salmon are larger and more valuable than the smolts from which they have grown had no adverse effect on the validity of the retention-of-title clause. In its view the doctrine of *specificatio* was inapplicable to the process of growth of living creatures.

While the English case *Chaigley Farms Ltd* v. *Crawford, Kaye & Grayshire Ltd*[132] raises broadly similar issues it was not referred to by the Scottish Court of Session in *Kinloch Damph Ltd* v. *Nordvik Salmon Farms Ltd* but perhaps the two cases are distinguishable on their facts. In *Chaigley Farms* a farmer supplied cattle to an abattoir on credit terms, retaining title to 'the goods' until paid for. The cattle were slaughtered and the question arose whether the retention-of-title clause was effective vis-à-vis the dead animals – in particular, whether the carcasses could be classed as goods supplied under the contract of sale. The court said not, holding that there was 'an inescapable difference between a live animal and a dead one, particularly a dead one minus hide or skin, offal, etc. not sold on as butcher's meat'.[133]

Generally speaking, the normal priority rules of Article 9 – first-to-file-or-perfect has priority and the PMSI principle – govern priorities in commingled goods. Take the case where flour is combined with other materials and baked into cakes. SP-1 has a perfected security interest in debtor's existing and after-acquired baked goods while SP-2 has a subsequently perfected security interest in debtor's flour. When the flour is turned into cakes SP-2 will acquire a perfected security interest in the cakes but this will rank after SP-1's security interest. The latter prevails in the priority conflict under the first-to-file principle unless SP-2 has acquired PMSI status in the flour which will continue into the baked goods.

---

[132] [1996] BCC 457.

[133] As Moore-Bick J explained in *Glencore* v. *Metro Trading International* [2001] 1 Lloyds Law Reports 284 at 325 the case turned essentially on whether the word 'goods' in the retention-of-title clause should (as the judge in fact held) be construed as referring only to livestock.

English and European reform initiatives

In Part II of the 1989 Diamond report commissioned by the Department of Trade and Industry the point was made that, at least in economic terms, the retention of title by the seller under a contract for the sale of goods was, in truth, a security interest taken by the supplier.[134] As Diamond acknowledged, there was nothing new in this observation. It formed the basis of the recommendation of the Crowther Committee in 1971 that a new scheme for security interests should apply to every agreement having as its true purpose the creation or retention of rights in property other than land for the purpose of securing payment of money or performance of an obligation, whatever the form of the agreement used by the contracting parties.[135] The Crowther Committee suggested that the retention of title for the purpose of security was in reality a chattel mortgage securing a loan.[136] In the Diamond scheme of things reservation-of-title clauses in non-consumer contracts would be registrable in the new register of security interests. Pending implementation of this fundamental recasting of personal property security law – which of course has not come to pass – Diamond did not argue for any major changes in the way reservation-of-title clauses are treated by the Companies Act registration provisions. The issue of company-charge registration and reservation-of-title clauses was also considered by the Company Law Review Steering Group. In its final report[137] the Steering Group pointed out that 'the broad thrust of case law is that complex retention of title clauses, where the title protecting the indebtedness shifts from one good to another on transformation, are charges over the goods and thus registrable but that simple retention of title clauses, where the seller merely retains title on transfer, are not'. The Steering Group suggested that 'such questions, which give rise to difficult issues in a developing area of commercial practice, are best left to the courts'. A different tack was taken by the Law Commission which, as has been noted earlier, recommended that all retention-of-title clauses should be subjected to filing obligations.[138] In its view even 'simple' retention-of-title clauses served a clear security purpose, and it was pointed out that in the case of an 'all-monies' clause, security was effectively being taken over goods already delivered and paid for.[139] The Law Commission

---

[134] Diamond report at pp. 11 and 87.
[135] Cmnd 4596, para. 5.2.8.   [136] *Ibid.* para 5.2.8.ii.
[137] *Modern Company Law for a Competitive Economy: Final Report* (July 2001) at p. 265.
[138] Law Commission *Registration of Security Interests* para. 7.24.
[139] In *ibid.* at para 7.10 the Commission wondered 'whether there might be a risk that in time overseas investors may be hesitant before investing in United Kingdom companies if we persist in having a system that does not take a functional approach, instead retaining the application of any system only to charges'.

proposals have been criticised on the basis that they do not contain the corresponding compensating benefits for trade creditors that are generally found in Article 9 and PPSA systems[140] though it asked consultees whether secured parties who have given value should, to the extent of that value, be given priority over existing perfected security interests.[141] Moreover, the Law Commission's proposals may lead to complications in practice when it comes to the entitlement to the 'surplus' when goods supplied subject to a retention-of-title clause are recovered by the original seller.

In principle, where a seller reclaims property that has been sold subject to a retention-of-title clause the seller is not obliged to account to the original buyer for any profits made on a resale of the goods. The seller is simply selling his or her own property and is entitled to keep the totality of what is obtained. In practice, this entitlement was watered down by the Court of Appeal in *Clough Mill Ltd* v. *Martin*[142] which read certain implied clauses into the first contract of sale, but nevertheless the point of principle remains.[143] The Law Commission proposes that the notice-filing system proposed for security interests including quasi-securities should be introduced without any provision that quasi-securities are to be subjected to the rules governing traditional security instruments.[144] In other words, retention-of-title clauses are to be recharacterised for certain purposes but not necessarily for others, and it is unclear how the courts will tackle the matter in the absence of more specific legislative guidance. Perhaps harshly, the Law Commission, along with Article 9 regimes more generally, could be accused of conceptual incoherence on this point as has been noted by a distinguished Canadian proponent of such legislation, Professor R. C. Cuming:[145]

---

[140] In *ibid.* at para. 8.77 the Commission asks whether a restatement of the law of security (which would be largely concerned with personal property) should set out rules on fixtures, accessions and processed or commingled goods.

[141] *Ibid.* para. 7.74.   [142] [1985] 1 WLR 111.

[143] See the comments of Robert Goff LJ *ibid.* at 117–18 who suggested that if the seller of goods chose to exercise its power under a retention-of-title clause to repossess goods that were worth considerably more than the outstanding debt, an implied term would prevent it repossessing and reselling more than was necessary to pay the outstanding debt. The matter is discussed in Law Commission *Registration of Security Interests* at para. 6.21; but cf. *R. V. Ward Ltd* v. *Bignall* [1967] 1 QB 534.

[144] *Registration of Security Interests* para 11.47.

[145] In 'The Internationalisation of Secured Financing Law' in Ross Cranston ed. *Making Commercial Law: Essays in Honour of Roy Goode* (Oxford University Press, 1997) p. 499 at pp. 522–3. *Clough Mill Ltd* v. *Martin* [1985] 1 WLR 111 and the theoretical entitlement of a retention-of-title seller to a 'surplus' is not good law under Article 9. Generally speaking, Article 9 stipulates that the debtor and not the secured party is entitled to a surplus on the disposition of collateral. There is an exception to this principle in the case of sales of accounts and chattel paper, but not as regards the sale of goods under retention-of-title terms: Article 9-615(d) and (e).

There are two features of the UCC, Article 9 approach that appear to be troublesome even to those who are attracted to it. The first is the total reconceptualization that it requires in the context of types of transactions that traditionally are not viewed as secured financing devices . . . The second feature . . . is the extent to which it requires a bifurcated approach to the characterisation of certain types of transactions. Since a title retention sales contract or a lease falls within a secured financing regime because it functions as a security device, it follows that the seller or lessor is not the owner of the goods sold or leased . . . What is troublesome is that outside this regime, the recharacterisation might not be acceptable with the result that the same transaction is viewed differently depending on the legal issues being addressed.

Another criticism of the Law Commission proposals concerns the failure to consider the provisions of the EU Directive on Late Payment in Commercial Transactions.[146] The Directive is designed to alleviate suppliers from the consequences of delayed receipt of payment for goods or services provided and introduces an entitlement to interest on overdue debts. But as part of the overall package of 'pro-supplier' measures it appears that member states are obliged to recognise simple retention-of-title clauses throughout the EU. Article 4(1) of the Directive reads: 'Member States shall provide in conformity with the applicable national provisions designated by private international law that the seller retains title to goods until they are fully paid for if a retention of title clause has been expressly agreed between the buyer and the seller before the delivery of the goods.' 'Retention of title' is defined in Article 2 as meaning the contractual agreement according to which the seller retains title to the goods in question until the price has been paid in full. The most straightforward interpretation of the relevant provisions would be to say that if passing-of-property questions under a contract for the sale of goods are governed by the law of an EU member state, then the member state must recognise a simple retention-of-title clause contained in the contract of sale. It is possible, however, to interpret the reference to private international law in Article 4 in such a way as to deprive the provision of substantive meaning. On such a construction, if the legal system invoked by the choice of law rules in a forum member state does not recognise simple retention-of-title clauses or requires observance of formalities for

---

[146] Directive 2000/35/EC of the European Parliament and of the Council of 29 June 2000 on combating late payment in commercial transactions (OJ 2000 L2000/35); and see generally G. McCormack 'Retention of Title and the Late EC Payment Directive' (2001) 1 *Journal of Corporate Law Studies* 501. For general background see G. Monti, G. Nejman and W. Reuter 'The Future of Reservation of Title Clauses in the European Community' (1997) 47 *ICLQ* 866; J.-H. Dalhuisen 'The Conditional Sale is Alive and Well' in J. Norton and M. Andenas eds. *Emerging Financial Markets and Secured Transactions* (Kluwer, 1998) at p. 83; and also E. Kieninger 'Securities in Movable Property within the Common Market' (1996) 4 *European Review of Private Law* 41.

their enforcement, such as compliance with registration requirements, then the forum member state is not compelled to recognise the clause. The so-called European rule would not be in accordance with the relevant national law whose application is dictated by the choice of law rules. In the case of an ordinary domestic sales contract governed by English law, then English law prevails over the European norm because English law is the governing law under the choice of law rules whose effect has not been altered by the Directive.[147] If this interpretation is correct then the Late-Payment Directive is devoid of much content because a retention-of-title clause could always be enforced according to the applicable law. If the governing law in a forum member state recognises retention of title, then, by that fact alone and without reference to the provisions of any EU directive, retention of title should be recognised in that forum.[148]

While the proper interpretation of the Directive is shrouded in some uncertainty, on one view it may act as a barrier to the full implementation of an Article 9 regime that extends to title retention. Article 9 is intended to regulate what, in economic terms, are designed to serve as security interests. Of course, what is important under Article 9 is the substantive purpose and effect of the agreement and not the label which has been applied to it by the parties. If the essence of the agreement is to secure payment or performance of an obligation, then Article 9 characterises it as a security interest and it will be governed by the Article 9 principles. Article 9 applies irrespective of the location of title to the secured property, and the retention of title by a seller of goods is limited in effect to a reservation of a 'security interest'.

Conclusion

One can see that there is a fundamental difference in the English and US approaches in the treatment of reservation-of-title clauses. Attempts by the seller to postpone the passage of title until some condition has been fulfilled is not regarded in English law as the creation by the buyer

---

[147] See McCormack 'Retention of Title' at 505–6.

[148] In many EU member states retention-of-title clauses are valid without registration; for a general discussion see the chapters on taking security in France and Germany in M. Bridge and R. Stevens eds. *Cross-Border Security and Insolvency* (Oxford University Press, 2001), and note the following comment on German law (at p. 94): 'Apart from charges on land which have to be registered in the land register, none of the security based on the BGB (namely the pledge over goods and rights, the transfer of title for security purposes, the security assignment, and the reservation of title) require registration against the asset.' See also Dalhuisen 'Conditional Sale'; and J.-H. Dalhuisen *Dalhuisen on International Commercial, Financial and Trade Law* (Hart Publishing, 2002) at pp. 432–52 and 567–716.

of a security interest in favour of the seller. Rationalising this conclusion on conceptual grounds, the buyer has no ownership right which he can confer on the seller by way of security. The buyer only acquires ownership once the condition has been fulfilled. Before that time there is nothing in the nature of an interest in the goods which he can give to the seller. The US approach towards characterisation is radically different. The reservation of ownership by a seller is specifically stated to amount to the creation of a security interest. Article 9-202 lays down that, in determining the application of Article 9, the locus of title is immaterial. Due to Article 9 perfection requirements, filing (registration) is necessary in the case of reservation-of-title clauses. This is in contrast with the position in England where 'simple' and 'current-account' reservation-of-title clauses enjoy validity without registration. The countries are at one in requiring registration of more complex aspects of the reservation-of-title phenomenon, i.e. proceeds of sale and aggregation clauses. The task of registration is made somewhat easier and more practicable in the US by the possibility of filing a financing statement covering multiple deliveries of goods over an extended period.

Reservation-of-title clauses in so far as they are recognised as valid in England enjoy super-priority status outranking pre-existing security interests containing after-acquired property clauses. Super-priority status is, in effect, confined to simple and current-account reservation-of-title since these are the only types of clauses whose validity is not conditioned on registration. In the US, while perfection by registration is of course a condition of validity, a reservation-of-title clause covering the original purchase price plus proceeds thereof is invested with super-priority status as a PMSI. Moreover, in the US there are special provisions dealing with the recognition of claims to proceeds and commingled goods. All in all, leaving aside the special case of perfection requirements, there are more similarities between the English and US approaches to reservation of title than appear at first sight.

7   Receivables financing

A large part of the wealth of the economy is locked up in debts or, to use the American expression, 'receivables'.[1] Unlocking that wealth so that it can be used as a basis for the development of commercial activity is a key task facing business people and policy makers. In both England and the US debts may be used as security and 'quasi-security'. In this respect the law in the two countries is versatile and flexible and facilitates lending. There are, however, differences of approach between the two countries. This chapter will compare and contrast the treatment of receivables as security and 'quasi-security' in England and the US. In England receivables financing may take one of two main forms: either the creation of charges, whether fixed or floating, on receivables; or else the outright assignment of receivables. The latter practice is referred to as factoring, and many of the major financial institutions have factoring subsidiaries. Traditionally, receivables were used as security through the medium of the floating charge but the courts have recognised that it is also possible, at least in theory, to create a fixed charge over receivables including future receivables. Before this can be done, however, the grantee of the security interest must, in some way, be restricted in the manner that he can deal with the debts themselves or debt proceeds.[2] More recently, the Court of Appeal in *Re New Bullas Trading Ltd*[3] held that it is possible to create a crossover form of security, i.e. a floating charge on book debts while uncollected, coupled with a floating charge on debt collections.[4] This decision, however, was disapproved of by the Privy Council in *Agnew* v. *Commissioner of Inland* Revenue.[5]

In the US, one of the hallmarks of Article 9 has been to sweep away the formalistic distinctions between different ways of securing a claim. Similar

---

[1] See generally on legal aspects Fidelis Oditah *Legal Aspects of Receivables Financing* (Sweet & Maxwell, 1991); and Freddy Salinger *Factoring Law and Practice* (Sweet & Maxwell, 3rd edn. 1999).

[2] *Siebe Gorman & Co. Ltd* v. *Barclays Bank Ltd* [1979] 2 Lloyd's Rep 142; *Re Brightlife Ltd* [1987] Ch 200.

[3] [1994] 1 BCLC 485.

[4] *Ibid.*; but cf. *Royal Trust Bank* v. *NatWest Bank* [1996] BCC 613.   [5] [2001] 2 AC 710.

rules are intended to apply to transactions that serve the same economic ends irrespective of differences of form. According to Article 9-109, Article 9 is specifically stated to apply to a transaction, regardless of its form, that creates a security interest in personal property or fixtures by contract and also to 'a sale of accounts, chattel paper, payment intangibles, or promissory notes'. The distinction in the US, however, between the absolute transfer of receivables and the security transfer of receivables remains and retains profound significance in many contexts. Article 9 does not provide a test or tests for distinguishing between sale transactions and the transfer of receivables by way of security. Essentially what Article 9 does, in bringing sale transactions within its scope, is to subject the sale of receivables to the perfection and priority rules of Article 9. Even though the outright sale and transfer of receivables is within Article 9 it is important to note that the debtor/seller retains no residual ownership in the receivables once the transfer has been effected. The revised Article 9 makes this clear. If, however, the buyer of receivables fails to comply with the Article 9 perfection rules, then for the purpose of determining the rights of creditors and purchasers for value from the seller of the receivables, the seller is taken as having retained the rights that it sold. This conclusion is the result of specific provisions in Article 9.[6]

Mortgages and charges over receivables in England

In England it is possible both to mortgage and charge receivables to serve as security. A mortgage of a debt is effected by assignment of the debt to the mortgagee, coupled with a provision for reassignment of the debt once the obligation to which the mortgage relates has been discharged. The creation of a charge over a debt is conceptually distinct, however. A charge of a debt gives the chargee not ownership of the debt but rather preferential rights thereto.[7] Denman J stated in *Tancred* v. *Delagoa Bay and East Africa Rly Co.*[8] that 'a document given "by way of charge" is not one which absolutely transfers the property with a condition for reconveyance, but is a document which only gives a right to payment out of a particular fund or particular property, without transferring that fund

---

[6] Article 9-318. See also Article 9-207, which provides that a secured party shall use reasonable care in the custody and preservation of collateral in the secured party's possession. This obligation, however, does not apply where the secured party is a buyer of accounts unless the secured party is entitled under an agreement either to charge back uncollected collateral or otherwise to full or limited recourse against the debtor or secondary obligor based on the non-payment or other default of an account debtor or other obligor on the collateral.

[7] See generally Oditah *Receivables Financing* at pp. 95–6.

[8] (1889) 23 QBD 239 at 242.

or property'. One leading commentator has suggested that to facilitate a transfer of the legal title to the debt in case the chargee wishes to dispose of it, the default provisions in the charge should (1) confer a power of attorney on the chargee to collect or dispose of the debt and (2) convert the charge into a mortgage by executing an assignment in the name of the chargor.[9] Such provisions, if inserted in a loan agreement, would eviscerate in practice the distinction between a mortgage and a charge[10] but, nevertheless, the conceptual differences remain intact.

Fixed and floating charges over receivables

It is possible in theory to create both fixed and floating charges over receivables.[11] Until relatively recently the boundary between the fixed and floating charge was fairly settled in England, judging by the nature and volume of reported cases. Fixed charges were taken over specific assets of the company whereas floating charges were taken over circulating assets. While the well-known judgment of Lord Macnaghten in *Illingworth* v. *Houldsworth*[12] is more an attempt at definition, it also tends to signify the kind of assets over which the respective charges are taken. He said:[13]

A specific charge, I think, is one that without more fastens on ascertained and definite property or property capable of being ascertained and defined: a floating charge, on the other hand, is ambulatory and shifting in its nature, hovering over and so to speak floating with the property which it is intended to affect until some event occurs or some act is done which causes it to settle and fasten on the subject of the charge within its reach and grasp.

While the kind of assets over which the security is taken provides a reasonably safe guide for characterising the nature of the security, it is not fail-safe. The real distinction turns on the management autonomy which a floating charge confers on the chargor. With a floating charge the chargor has management autonomy in so far as the category of assets charged is concerned until that autonomy is brought to an end by a process known as crystallisation, whereupon the floating charge becomes fixed. The floating charge has been likened to a charge over a fund of assets. When crystallisation occurs the charge settles on the assets then

---

[9] See R. Goode 'The Effect of a Fixed Charge on a Debt' [1994] *JBL* 172 at 174.
[10] Oditah *Receivables Financing* at p. 96.
[11] See generally P. Ali *The Law of Secured Finance* (Oxford University Press, 2002) at pp. 284–92.
[12] [1904] AC 355.
[13] *Ibid.* at 358. The characteristics of a floating charge were also recently considered by the House of Lords in *Smith* v. *Bridgend County* BC [2002] 1 AC 336.

within the fund. As Lord Millett observed in *Agnew* v. *Commissioner of Inland Revenue*:[14]

The floating charge is capable of affording the creditor, by a single instrument, an effective and comprehensive security upon the entire undertaking of the debtor company and its assets from time to time, while at the same time leaving the company free to deal with its assets and pay its trade creditors in the ordinary course of business without reference to the holder of the charge. Such a form of security is particularly attractive to banks, and it rapidly acquired an importance in English commercial life.

A fixed or specific charge, on the other hand, precludes the chargor from disposing of an unencumbered title to the assets that form the subject matter of the charge. The chargor would be in breach of the provisions of the loan agreement if he purported to do so and this would entitle the charge holder to exercise the default remedies including the appointment of a receiver over the chargor's assets. Moreover, the buyer of the asset would acquire the property subject to the charge if, in accordance with general principles, he was aware of its existence.[15] As well as impacting on the position of buyers, the fixed/floating charge distinction also has important consequences for preferential creditors. The effect of sections 40 and 175 of the Insolvency Act is that, in a receivership or liquidation, holders of floating charges are paid after preferential creditors as set out in Schedule 6 to the Insolvency Act 1986 – basically unpaid taxes and certain employee claims. It is often the case that a company in financial difficulties has accumulated large revenue debts – taxes are not remitted to the Revenue as expeditiously as is required by statute.[16] Fixed-charge

---

[14] [2001] 2 AC 710 at para. 8 of his judgment. See generally on this case G. McCormack 'The Nature of Security over Receivables' (2002) 23 *Co Law* 84; P. Watts 'The Rending of Charges' (2002) 118 *LQR* 1; A. Berg 'Brumark Investments Ltd and the Innominate Charge' [2001] *JBL* 532; P. Wood 'Fixed and Floating Charges' [2001] *CLJ* 472. For a recent application of the fixed/floating-charge distinction in the context of a charge over shares see *Arthur D. Little* v. *Ableco Finance* [2002] 3 WLR; and see also a leading Singaporean authority in this area *Dresdner Bank AG* v. *Ho Mun-Tuke Don* [1993] 1 SLR 114.

[15] *Feuer Leather Corp* v. *Frank Johnstone & Sons* [1981] Com LR 251.

[16] In *Agnew* v. *Commissioner of Inland Revenue* [2001] 2 AC 710 at 721 Lord Millett observed: 'By the 1970's, however, the banks had become disillusioned with the floating charge. The growth in the extent and amount of the preferential debts, due in part to increases in taxation and in part to higher wages and greater financial obligations to employees, led banks to explore ways of extending the scope of their fixed charges.' Section 251 Enterprise Act 2002 abolishes Crown preference but not employee preference. Nevertheless, the fixed/floating distinction retains its importance not least because under section 252 Enterprise Act 2002 (which inserts a new section 176A into the Insolvency Act 1986) a certain percentage of floating charge, but not fixed charge, realisations are set aside for the benefit of unsecured creditors. The percentage has now been on a sliding-scale basis by the Insolvency Act 1986 (Prescribed Part) Order 2003.

lenders are, on the other hand, paid ahead of preferential creditors. In other words, the hierarchy of payment runs as follows: fixed-charge creditors; preferential creditors; floating-charge holders; and then unsecured creditors at the bottom of the pile. Any extension of the scope of the fixed charge has adverse consequences for third parties, particularly preferential creditors. Drafters of debentures, however, have tried to push forward the frontiers of security by trying to get the fixed charge to take up territory that had traditionally been occupied exclusively by the floating charge.[17] In particular, receivables have traditionally been the subject of a floating charge in that they are a class of circulating assets and normally the company creating the security expects to be able to continue to collect the receivables and use the proceeds thereof in the ordinary course of its business. Nevertheless, in a seminal case, *Siebe Gorman & Co. Ltd* v. *Barclays Bank*,[18] a company gave a debenture to a bank which purported to include a first fixed charge on existing and future book debts. The court upheld the characterisation and said that the security in question was a fixed rather than a floating charge.

In *Siebe Gorman* there were three particular aspects of the debenture that were relevant to the characterisation exercise. Firstly, the charge was described as a first fixed charge on existing and future book debts. This point alone, however, was not conclusive, for the test is one of substance rather than form. Secondly, the debenture contained what might be referred to as a negative pledge clause – the company was prohibited from charging or assigning the debts in favour of anybody other than the bank. But again this aspect itself was not conclusive. The judge was more persuaded by a third feature of the debenture, which obliged the debtor, even before the bank had taken any steps to enforce its security, to pay into the debtor's account with the bank all monies which it might receive in respect of the debts. While there were no express prohibitions on withdrawals from this account, Slade J held that the debenture, on its true construction, gave the bank rights to prevent the company from spending, in the ordinary course of business, all or any of the proceeds of book debts paid into the account. Were this not so, he would have been inclined to regard the charge, for all the wording of the debenture, as doing no more than 'hovering over' and, so to speak, floating with the book debts.

It may be argued that *Siebe Gorman* is a lenient decision from the point of view of the security-interest holder. The judge was prepared to infer the existence of provisions, nowhere expressly stated in the debenture, which

---

[17] See generally R. Goode 'Charges over Book Debts: A Missed Opportunity' (1994) 110 *LQR* 592; and also S. Griffin 'The Effect of a Charge over Book Debts: The Indivisible or Divisible Nature of the Charge' (1995) 46 *NILQ* 163.

[18] [1979] 2 Lloyd's Rep 142. Overruled in *Re Spectra*.

ultimately proved decisive in the resolution of the fixed/floating charge debate. Hoffmann J was not prepared to make similar inferences in *Re Brightlife Ltd*.[19] This is a case where the debenture described the charge as a first specific charge and the chargor was not allowed to sell, factor or discount the debts without the written consent of the chargee. There was, however, no provision referring to collection of debts or disposal of the proceeds thereof other than a general clause that the chargor should not deal with the debts 'otherwise than in the ordinary course of getting in and realising the same'. Hoffmann J pointed out that a floating charge was consistent with some restriction on the company's freedom to deal with its assets. Such charges commonly contained a prohibition on the creation of other charges ranking prior to or *pari passu* with the floating charge. According to the judge the significant feature of this case is that the chargor was free to collect its debts and pay the proceeds into its bank account and once in the account, they would be outside the charge over debts and at the free disposal of the company. The judge went on to say that a 'right to deal in this way with the charged assets for its own account is a badge of a floating charge and is inconsistent with a fixed charge'.[20]

Siebe Gorman was distinguished on the basis that, in that case, there were restrictions, albeit implied, on withdrawals from the account. Reference was also made to the decision of the Irish Supreme Court in *Re Keenan Bros Ltd*.[21] The facts of this case were much stronger than those in *Siebe Gorman*. In the *Keenan* case a debenture was created in favour of a bank with the chargor being obliged to pay the proceeds of all debts into a designated account with the bank and 'not without the prior written consent of the bank in writing make any withdrawals or direct any payment from the said account'. The Irish Supreme Court took the view that the charge was a floating charge. According to the court the degree of sequestration of the debts when collected made those monies incapable of being used in the ordinary course of business and meant that they were put, specifically and expressly, at the disposal of the bank. Assets thus withdrawn from ordinary trade use, put in the keeping of the debenture holder, and sterilised and made indisposable save at the absolute discretion of the debenture holder, had the distinguishing features of a fixed charge.

There have, however, been decisions where a fixed charge over receivables has been recognised even though the assets in question have not been sterilised and made unavailable to the chargor. In *Re Atlantic*

[19] [1987] Ch 200. See also *Hart v. Barnes* (1982) 7 ACLR 310; *Supercool Refrigeration and Air Conditioning v. Hoverd Industries Ltd* [1994] 3 NZLR 300; *Re Cosslett (Contractors) Ltd* [1998] Ch 495.
[20] [1987] Ch 200 at 209.   [21] [1986] BCLC 242.

Computer Systems plc[22] and *Re Atlantic Medical Ltd*[23] the courts held that it was possible to create a fixed charge over receivables even though the chargor was allowed to continue to collect the receivables and to use the proceeds in the ordinary course of its business. These decisions have been criticised on the basis that the characterisation of a charge over receivables as fixed or floating cannot be divorced from contractual provisions relating to the application of proceeds of the receivables.[24] It is also arguable that the decisions are doctrinally unsound, for they ignore the necessary conditions formulated in *Siebe Gorman* before a fixed charge over book debts could be upheld. Moreover, they have the effect of jeopardising the statutory protection afforded preferential creditors vis-à-vis floating-charge holders. If more charges are regarded as fixed rather than floating, then this, inescapably, reduces the amount of assets available for distribution to preferential creditors.

At the heart of the fixed/floating charge characterisation exercise lies an unresolved tension. The chargee wants to have a fixed charge. The chargor wants to be able to use the proceeds of charged debts in the ordinary course of its business. Doctrine, however, in the shape of *Siebe Gorman* seems to insist that some restrictions on this freedom are necessary before a fixed-charge label can be attached to the security interest. To use a somewhat muddled metaphor, there are obvious tensions pulling in opposite directions. Of course an attempt can be made to resolve these tensions by imposing formal restrictions on the withdrawal of proceeds of debts from a bank account but, at the same time, establishing a 'consent to withdrawals' procedure whereby the chargor is, in practice, enabled to benefit from the collections. This was, in effect, done in the *Keenan* case. According to McCarthy J if the chargor was driven to such financial straits that it was prepared to effect an immediate charge upon its book debts, the existence of which was published to the commercial world through the registration-of-company-charges procedure, the fact that an elaborate system was set up to enable the company to benefit by the collection of such debts did not detract from it qualifying as a fixed charge. Another decision of the Irish Supreme Court – in *Re Wogan's (Drogheda) Ltd*[25] – goes even further. There, to cite the Chief Justice, the court held that:

If a lender, having availed of a debenture in these terms, as a concession delays the designation of a bank account or suspends for some period the operation of direct control over the bank account into which the proceeds of book debts are paid,

---

[22] [1992] Ch 505.   [23] [1992] BCLC 653.

[24] See Goode 'Charges over Book Debts' at 601; and also S. Worthington 'Fixed Charges over Book Debts and other Receivables' (1997) 113 *LQR* 562 at 566.

[25] [1993] IR 157.

thus permitting the company to carry on trading in a more normal fashion than strict compliance with the terms of a fixed charge would permit, there does not appear to be any principle of law or justice which would deprive such a lender of the rights agreed by the debtor company of a fixed charge over the assets, whereas, a lender with a more draconian approach to the rights which were granted to it by a debenture would be in a more advantageous position.[26]

A different approach, however, would be to say that the lender is estopped by its conduct from denying that the charge is a floating charge. Alternatively, but reaching the same result, one could say that the lender has consented to an implied variation of the terms of the debenture contract. This whole issue raises the logically anterior question of the relevance of post-contractual behaviour in interpreting the terms of a contract and determining rights and obligations of the parties under the contract. There is a general principle that a contract should not be construed by reference to the subsequent conduct of the parties. Lord Reid, in the leading case, *Whitworth Street Estates Ltd* v. *Miller*,[27] said that a contrary proposition might have the result that a contract meant one thing the day it was signed but, by reason of subsequent events, it meant something different a month or a year later. On the other hand, there is another general principle that a commercial contract such as a debenture should be interpreted in its general commercial context.[28] If the evidence is that the parties never seriously intended that restrictions in a debenture should operate, then this is part of the general business backdrop and points to a floating-charge construction.

The leading authority in this area of law is now the decision of the Privy Council in *Agnew* v. *Commissioner of Inland Revenue*. The importance of this case in the general context of charges over book debts is its reiteration of the point that 'labelling' and 'non-assignment' clauses in the debenture are insufficient to constitute a charge over book debts as a

---

[26] *Ibid.* at 170–1. The *Wogan* decision is, however, of questionable authority in Ireland following the subsequent decision of the Irish Supreme Court in *Re Holidair Ltd* [1994] IR 416. For a discussion of *Holidair* see G. McCormack 'Company Law – Secured Creditors Succumb' (1994) 16 *DULJ* (NS) 160.

[27] [1970] AC 583 at 603.

[28] See the statement of principle by Lord Hoffmann in *Investors Compensation Scheme Ltd* v. *West Bromwich Building Society* [1998] 1 WLR 896 at 912–13:

> Interpretation is the ascertainment of the meaning which the document would convey to a reasonable person having all the background knowledge which would reasonably have been available to the parties in the situation in which they were at the time of the contract . . . Subject to the requirement that it should have been reasonably available to the parties and . . . [the background] includes absolutely anything which would have affected the way in which the language of the document would have been understood by a reasonable man . . . The law excludes from the admissible background the previous negotiations of the parties and their declarations of subjective intent.

fixed charge. Lord Millett said categorically:[29] 'A restriction on disposition which nevertheless allows collection and free use of the proceeds is inconsistent with the fixed nature of the charge; it allows the debt and its proceeds to be withdrawn from the security by the act of the company in collecting it.'

The court appeared to approve *Siebe Gorman*, subject to the caveat that the implied restrictions on withdrawals of the proceeds of debts, once collected, were real and substantial in practice. In other words, a charge on book debts could be a fixed charge if the proceeds of the debts collected by the chargor were required to be paid into a blocked account with the charge holder. It was said:[30]

Such an arrangement is inconsistent with the charge being a floating charge, since the debts are not available to the company as a source of its cash flow. But their Lordships would wish to make it clear that it is not enough to provide in the debenture that the account is a blocked account if it is not operated as one in fact.

Hybrid fixed/floating charges over debts

As far as the lender is concerned, the ideal state of affairs is that the borrower should have freedom to conduct normal business operations while solvent yet be in a state of servitude while insolvent. The debenture used, and accorded the judicial imprimatur, in *Re New Bullas Trading Ltd* appeared successfully to combine these ideals. Rationalising the conclusion of the court Nourse LJ stated:[31]

There being usually no need to deal with it before collection, [a company's book debt] is at that stage a natural subject of the fixed charge. But once collected, the proceeds being needed for the conduct of the business, it becomes a natural subject of the floating charge. While the company is a going concern, it is no less an advantage to the lender that the debt should be collected and the proceeds used in the business. But on insolvency, a crystallised floating charge on proceeds which, in the event supposed, are all the more likely to have been dissipated, may be worthless; whereas a fixed charge enabling the lender to intercept payment to the company may be of real value.

Re New Bullas Trading Ltd has been criticised on conceptual grounds. In particular, it has been argued that the distinction drawn in the case

---

[29] [2001] 2 AC 710 at 726.
[30] *Ibid.* at 730. The decision of the Court of Appeal in *O'Donnell & Sons* v. *Midland Bank* 2001 WL 1676963 confirms that there is nothing objectionable or impossible in law to creating a fixed charge over debts. For a discussion of how 'blocked-account mechanisms' can be made to work in practice see C. Hanson and G. Yeowart 'Book Debt Charges after Brumark: where are we Now.' [2001] *Butterworths Journal of International Banking and Financial Law* 456.
[31] [1994] I BCLC 485 at 487.

between the book debts before collection and after realisation is unrealistic and artificial because a debt is worth nothing unless and until it is turned into money. Professor Sir Roy Goode has been a forceful proponent of this view, asserting that the characterisation of a security over book debts cannot be divorced from contractual provisions relating to the application of the proceeds.[32] His reasoning proceeds as follows:[33]

> The distinctive feature of debts as an object of security is that they are realised by payment, upon which they cease to exist. If the chargor is authorised to collect them, then so long as his authority to do so continues, the only way in which the chargee can assert his security interest as a fixed interest is through the proceeds. It is by a contractual provision controlling the proceeds that the chargee establishes that the debts themselves are collected for his account, not for that of the chargor. Without such a contractual control, the chargee's supposed fixed security over the debts has no meaning, for the chargor is then collecting the debts for his own account.

It is submitted that these criticisms of *New Bullas* may be less than convincing for a number of reasons. Firstly, a book debt is clearly worth something in money terms if it is sold as distinct from being collected. A creditor may obtain something of value from his debts either by selling them or collecting them. Charges over debts are not simply realised by payment; they may also be realised by sale. Secondly, in a number of different contexts debts and debt proceeds have been treated as separate items of property. This matter was adverted to by Walsh J in the influential Irish Supreme Court case *Re Keenan Bros Ltd*.[34] He said that as the relationship between banker and customer is one of debtor and creditor, all sums from time to time standing to credit in a special book debts receivable account were owed by the bank to the company and were not book debts due to the company or debts in the contemplation of the deed of charge or the debenture. This was so even though the account was opened to receive the collected book debts due to the company. Debts ceased to be debts once they were collected. There was at least a tacit recognition of the same principle in *Re Brightlife Ltd*,[35] with Hoffmann J holding that a bank account in credit did not come within the phrase 'book debts' as used in a commercial debenture. In his view, while it was not legally inaccurate to describe a credit balance with a banker as a debt, since the banker–customer relationship was a debtor–creditor one, this was not normal linguistic usage for an accountant or business person. In their minds the accepted usage was 'cash at bank' rather than 'debt'.[36]

---

[32] Goode 'Charges over Book Debts'.   [33] *Ibid.* at 602.
[34] [1986] BCLC 242 at 244.   [35] [1987] Ch 200 at 208–9.
[36] Some support was offered for the overall philosophy articulated in *Re Brightlife Ltd* by the House of Lords in *Re BCCI (No 8)* [1998] AC 214.

Thirdly, the courts have held that a contractual prohibition on the assignment of debts does not prevent the assignee from having to account for the proceeds of the debts, once received, to the assignor.[37] This conclusion strongly suggests that debts and debt proceeds are being viewed through separate lenses.

In *Agnew v. Commissioner of Inland Revenue* the Privy Council rejected *New Bullas* as wrongly decided. In *Agnew* the question was whether a charge over the uncollected book debts of a company which left the company free to collect them and use the proceeds in the ordinary course of its business was a fixed charge or a floating charge. The chargor was in receivership and the only assets available for distribution to creditors were the proceeds of book debts which were outstanding when the receivers were appointed and which they had since collected. If the charge was a fixed charge, then the proceeds were payable to the charge holder but if the charge was a floating charge, then under the relevant New Zealand legislation which, at the material time, was equivalent to that in England, the preferential creditors took precedence.[38]

The bank debenture was essentially modelled on that employed in *Re New Bullas Trading Ltd*[39] and endeavoured to create a fixed charge on uncollected book debts. According to Lord Millett, who delivered the judgment of the Privy Council, the debenture purported[40]

to create a fixed charge on the book debts which were outstanding when the receivers were appointed and the proceeds of the debts which they collected. Prior to their appointment, however, the company was free to collect the book debts and deal with the proceeds in the ordinary course of its business, though it was unable to assign or factor them. The question is whether the company's right to collect the debts and deal with their proceeds free from the security means that the charge on the uncollected debts, though described in the debenture as fixed, was nevertheless a floating charge until it crystallised by the appointment of the receivers.

Lord Millett adopted a more subtle and sophisticated critique of *Re New Bullas Trading*, recognising that property and its proceeds were

---

[37] *Linden Gardens Trust Ltd v. Lenesta Sludge Disposals Ltd* [1994] 1 AC 85; *Re Turcan* (1888) 40 Ch D 5.

[38] Schedule 7 Companies Act 1993 and section 30 Receivership Act 1993. The first-instance judge, Fisher J, held that it was a fixed charge ((1999) 15 NZTC 15, 159) but his decision was reversed by the Court of Appeal which decision is reported at [2000] 1 BCLC 353. For a comment on the first instance decision see D. McLauchlan 'Fixed Charges over Book Debts: *New Bullas* in New Zealand' (1999) 115 *LQR* 365; and for a discussion of the New Zealand Court of Appeal judgment see also D. McLauchlan '*New Bullas* in New Zealand: Round Two' (2000) 116 *LQR* 211. Before the case reached the Privy Council it is reported as *Re Brumark Investments*.

[39] [1994] 1 BCLC 485.   [40] [2001] 2 AC 710 at 716.

clearly different assets.[41] He drew an analogy with the sale of goods and said that where goods were sold the seller exchanged one asset for another. Both assets continued to exist with the goods in the hands of the buyer and the proceeds of sale in the hands of the seller. In the same way if a book debt was assigned, the debt was transferred to the assignee in exchange for money paid to the assignor. The seller's former property right in the subject matter of the sale gave him an equivalent property right in the exchange product. Lord Millett, however, added:[42]

While a debt and its proceeds are two separate assets . . . the latter are merely the traceable proceeds of the former and represent its entire value. A debt is a receivable; it is merely a right to receive payment from the debtor. Such a right cannot be enjoyed in specie; its value can be exploited only by exercising the right or by assigning it for value to a third party. An assignment or charge of a receivable which does not carry with it the right to the receipt has no value. It is worthless as a security. Any attempt in the present context to separate the ownership of the debts from the ownership of their proceeds (even if conceptually possible) makes no commercial sense.

It was argued on behalf of the chargor that the company had no power to withdraw either the book debts or their proceeds from the embrace of the fixed charge. In other words, the debts were automatically extinguished by collection and their proceeds never became subject to a fixed charge. Lord Millett was not convinced by this line of reasoning, suggesting that it was merely playing with words. He observed:[43]

Whether conceptually there was one charge or two, the debenture was so drafted that the company was at liberty to turn the uncollected book debts to account by its own act. Taking the relevant assets to be the uncollected book debts, the company was left in control of the process by which the charged assets were extinguished and replaced by different assets which were not the subject of a fixed charge and were at the free disposal of the company. This is inconsistent with the nature of a fixed charge.

The essence of the decision in *Agnew* v. *Commissioner of Inland Revenue* is quite straightforward, namely, it is not possible as a practical proposition to create a fixed charge over uncollected book debts and couple this in the same debenture with a floating charge on the proceeds of realisation of the self-same debts.[44] Given the composition of the Privy Council

---

[41] *Ibid.* at 728.   [42] *Ibid.* at 729.   [43] *Ibid.* at 730.
[44] The judgment smacks of commercial common sense. The court said that it was not bound by subjective indications of intention and reference was made in this connection to the comments of Lord Templeman in *Street* v. *Mountford* [1985] AC 809 at 826. Rather, the task of the court was to discover what mutual rights and obligations the parties, objectively speaking, intended to create. Once this task had been completed, then the court would engage in the characterisation exercise. This was a legal exercise that was

in *Agnew* it is perhaps not surprising that the court reached the conclusion it did. As well as Lord Millett the court included Lord Hoffmann, and these judges have previously demonstrated a strong preference for an objective approach towards the representation of security interests.[45] In *Royal Trust Bank* v. *NatWest Bank plc*[46] Millett LJ (as he then was) suggested that the proper characterisation of a security as 'fixed' or 'floating' depends on the freedom of the chargor to deal with the proceeds of the charged assets in the ordinary course of business, free from the security. Indeed, he invoked the observations of Hoffmann J in *Re Brightlife Ltd* that a contractual right on the part of the chargor to collect the proceeds of debts and pay them into its own bank account for use in the ordinary course of its business was a badge of a floating charge and was inconsistent with the existence of a fixed charge.

Application of registration (perfection) requirements to charges over debts

Section 396 Companies Act 1985 makes registrable all types of floating charge including floating charges over book debts and other receivables. The application of the company-charge-registration provisions to fixed charges over book debts has provoked some controversy. Essentially the debate has been over precise definitions, but the appropriateness of the registration obligation per se has gone largely unquestioned. Many of the reasons underlying the registration obligation were articulated in the Diamond report, which made the point that it is common for trade debtors to be given a period of credit. Thus many companies had substantial sums due to them for services rendered or, goods supplied, by

---

unconstrained by the label which the parties had chosen to apply to their agreement. Although not referred to expressly in *Agnew* Lord Templeman also said notably in *Street* v. *Mountford* [1985] AC 809 at 819 that the manufacture of a five-pronged instrument for manual digging results in a fork even if the manufacturer, unfamiliar with the English language, insists that he intended to make and has made a spade. See also the comments of Lord Scott in *Smith* v. *Bridgend County Borough Council* [2002] 1 AC 336 at 355 that 'once contractual rights have, by the process of construction, been ascertained, the question whether they constitute security rights is a question of law that is not dependent on their intentions'.

[45] On the other hand, the court in *Agnew* also included Lord Nicholls who, as Nicholls LJ, handed down the decision of the Court of Appeal in *Re Atlantic Computer Systems plc* [1992] Ch 505. In the *Atlantic Computers* case it was held that a charge over lease-rental payments was a fixed charge notwithstanding the fact that the chargor could collect the rents and spend the proceeds as it wished. In the light of *Agnew* this degree of freedom on the part of the chargor seems incompatible with the nature of a fixed charge and *Atlantic Computers* may be taken as having been impliedly disapproved in *Agnew* although it is not expressly referred to in the case.

[46] [1996] 2 BCLC 682 at 704.

the company. In Diamond's view, a charge over book debts was a major weapon in the hands of the charge holder and a considerable disadvantage to other creditors.[47]

Section 396 uses the phrase 'book debts' rather than the more modern and somewhat wider expression 'receivables', with the old authority *Shipley* v. *Marshall*[48] defining book debts as debts that could or would, in the ordinary course of a business, be entered in well-kept books relating to that business. Buckley J amplified this definition somewhat in *Independent Automatic Sales Ltd* v. *Knowles and Foster*[49] saying that a debt arising in the course of business and due or growing due to the proprietor of that business could properly be called a book debt. This was so whether, in fact, the debt was entered in the books of the business or not.[50] It is clear that actual entry in books of account of a company is not required in England.[51]

It is submitted that the registration requirements embrace both existing and future debts but not contingency contracts. On this analysis, the law can be summed up in three propositions:[52]

(i) Registrability is tested at the date of creation of the charge.
(ii) If, at the date of creation of the charge, what is charged is a contract which does not of itself constitute a book debt, the charge will not be registrable even if a book debt may arise out of the contract at some future date.
(iii) If, however, on its true construction the charge is over book debts arising in the future, the fact that the debts are not in existence when the charge is created does not preclude the charge from registration.

The leading case is *Independent Automatic Sales Ltd* v. *Knowles and Foster*. Here a company that manufactured and dealt in automatic washing

---

[47] See A. Diamond *A Review of Security Interests in Property* (HMSO, 1989) at pp. 109–10. The Diamond report suggested that the relevant legislation should substitute 'receivables' for 'book debts'. In Diamond's view the concept of 'book debts' should be expounded as 'debts due or to become due to the company in respect of goods supplied or to be supplied or services rendered or to be rendered by the company in the course of the company's business, whether entered in a book or not'. See also the somewhat blunt statement at para 7.35 of the Law Commission Consultation Paper No. 164 *Registration of Security Interests* (2002): 'A security over receivables should be registrable under a notice-filing system as a charge.'

[48] (1863) 14 CB NS 566.   [49] [1962] 1 WLR 974.

[50] In *Robertson* v. *Grigg* (1932) 47 CLR 257 at 262, Gavan Duffy CJ and Starke J in the High Court of Australia construed the expression 'book debts' as pointing to debts owing to a business of a kind usually entered in books of account of the business and in fact so entered.

[51] In *M. O'Donnell & Sons (Huddersfield) Ltd* v. *Midland Bank plc* 2001 WL 1676963 it was decided by the Court of Appeal that a sum arising from the sale of the entirety of a company's business operations was not a 'book debt' but came within the expression 'other debts' in a bank debenture.

[52] See M. Lawson 'Registration of Retention of Title Clauses under S. 395 of the Companies Act 1985' [1988] *LMCLQ* 141 at 145.

machines from time to time entered into hire-purchase agreements for the disposal of its machines. Subsequently, the company obtained borrowing facilities from a lender and, as part of the 'lending package', created a security interest in favour of the lender over the benefits flowing to the company from the hire-purchase agreements.[53] The court held that the lending agreement constituted a charge on book debts and, consequently, was void against the liquidator of the company for non-registration. There was an argument that the registration of charge provisions did not, on their true construction, require a charge on future book debts to be registered; in other words, 'book debts' in the statute meant only existing book debts. Buckley J had two answers. His first point was that the hirer became liable immediately upon the agreement coming into operation to the extent of his minimum liability under it notwithstanding that some part of that liability was to be discharged by future payments and that the debts so constituted were existing book debts at the date of the deposit. Secondly, he held that a charge exclusively on future book debts of a company was registrable, stating:[54]

That it is competent for anyone to whom book-debts may accrue in the future to create an equitable charge upon those book-debts which will attach to them as soon as they come into existence is not disputed (see *Tailby* v. *Official Receiver*).[55] That such a charge can accurately be described as a charge on book-debts does not appear to me to be open to question . . . A charge of book-debts, present and future, is not an unusual form of security in the commercial world, and it would seem to me strange if such a charge were registrable (as it undoubtedly is) and a charge confined to future book-debts were not.

There is a school of thought,[56] relying on *Paul & Frank Ltd* v. *Discount Bank (Overseas) Ltd*,[57] which argues that a charge on future book debts is non-registrable but the *Paul & Frank* case appears distinguishable from *Independent Automatic Sales Ltd* v. *Knowles and Foster*. In *Paul & Frank* it was held that a letter of authority authorising the payment of the proceeds of an insurance policy to the defendant did not create a registrable charge. The court held that where the item of property charged was the benefit of a contract and, at the date of the charge, the benefit of the contract did not comprehend any book debt, the contract was not registrable merely by reason of the fact that it might ultimately result in a book debt.[58]

---

[53] In American Article 9 parlance the lender is a chattel-paper financier.
[54] [1962] 1 WLR 974 at 985.   [55] (1888) 13 App Cas 523.
[56] See J. Parris *Effective Retention of Title Clauses* (Basil Blackwell, 1986) at p. 114. See generally on this area G. McCormack 'Reservation of Title – the Controversy Continues' [1989] *LMCLQ* 198 at 206–9.
[57] [1967] Ch 348.
[58] The court distinguished *Independent Automatic Sales Ltd* v. *Knowles and Foster* on the basis that if a charge upon its proper construction covers future debts, in the sense of debts

Factoring or the outright assignment of debts

It is vitally important to distinguish between the outright assignment ('factoring') of book debts and the creation of a charge over such debts. Section 136 Law of Property Act 1925 specifies the following conditions which must be met before an assignment of debts or other choses in action can operate as a legal assignment: (1) the assignment must be absolute and not by way of charge; (2) the assignment must relate to the whole of the debt; (3) the assignment must be in writing under the hand of the assignor; (4) notice in writing of the assignment must be given to the debtor. Even if these conditions are not met, an assignment may still be effective in equity provided that consideration has been provided and the intention to assign is clear. As Lord Macnaghten remarked in *Tailby* v. *Official Receiver*,[59] it has long been settled that future property, possibilities and expectancies are assignable in equity for value. In his view, the mode or form of assignment was absolutely immaterial provided that the intention of the parties was clear. The judge added that to effectuate the intention 'an assignment for value, in terms present and immediate, has always been regarded in equity as a contract binding on the conscience of the assignor and so binding the subject-matter of the contract when it comes into existence, if it is of such a nature and so described as to be capable of being ascertained and identified'.

Notice to the debtor is not required to perfect the title of an equitable assignee, contrary to what was said by Lord Watson in *Tailby* v. *Official Receiver*.[60] Lord Macnaghten emphasised this point in *Ward* v. *Duncombe*.[61] It should be noted too that assignments of part of a debt are possible only in equity. In commercial practice, factoring of debts is often done on a non-notification basis and necessarily involves equitable assignment. The distinction between notification factoring and non-notification factoring is quite crucial in practical terms. With the former, notice of the assignment is given to the debtor and the factor invariably collects the debts. In the second situation, the assignor maintains direct relations

---

under a future contract which, when that contract comes to be made, will constitute book debts, e.g. an ordinary contract for the sale of goods on credit, there was no reason why the registration requirement should not be fairly applicable to the charge.

[59] (1888) 12 App Cas 523.

[60] (1888) 13 App Cas 523 at 543. There are many other judicial pronouncements to the same effect: see, e.g., *Mutual Life Assurance Society* v. *Langley* (1886) 32 Ch D 460 at 471 per Bowen LJ. The matter is discussed generally by J. De Lacy 'Reflections on the Ambit of the Rule in Dearle v Hall and the Priority of Personal Property Assignments' (1999) 28 *Anglo-American Law Review* 87 at 109–11.

[61] [1893] AC 369 at 392; and see also the comments of Lord Reid in *B. S. Lyle Ltd* v. *Rosher* [1959] 1 WLR 8 at 19–20.

with its customers by continuing to collect the debts. The factor remains in the background with the proceeds of the debts being remitted to it. The distinction between legal and equitable assignment has some practical consequences in terms of actions against the debtor. Basically a legal assignee can sue a debtor in his name without involving the assignor in the proceedings whereas in the case of an equitable assignment the assignor should be joined as a co-plaintiff if he is willing and as a co-defendant if he is not.[62] In certain circumstances, however, this rule may be waived.[63]

While the legal/equitable distinction may have some practical import, the difference between outright assignments, on the one hand, whether legal or equitable, and charges, on the other, is of far more profound consequence. Factoring, or the outright sale of book debts, is a business that is outside the ambit of the company-charge registration system.[64] As the Privy Council noted in *Chow Yoong Hong* v. *Choong Fah Rubber Manufactory*:[65] 'There are many ways of raising cash besides borrowing. One is by selling book debts.'

In *Welsh Development Agency* v. *Export Finance Co. Ltd*[66] Browne-Wilkinson VC explained that it has been firmly established for many years that debt-factoring agreements and agreements for the block sale of hire-purchase agreements at a discount are not secured loans but sales. The respective rights of a finance house and other creditors of the 'seller' depended entirely on the legal garb in which the finance house clothed the transaction. The judge went on to say:[67]

The transaction is essentially the same in commercial terms whatever legal structure is adopted: the finance house has advanced money to a company in need of money on terms that the finance house is to recoup itself (either from a third party or from the borrower/seller) the sum advanced plus its 'turn' on the deal. If the advance is by way of secured loan, it will be registrable: others dealing with the company will know of the secured position of the finance house and can adjust their dealings accordingly. If, on the other hand, the advance is by way of sale, the finance house is, in commercial terms, fully secured but others dealing with the company are ignorant of the fact.

Leaving aside the key question of registration, there may be other reasons why it makes sense to distinguish between the assignment of debts

---

[62] *Weddell* v. *J. A. Pearce & Major* [1988] Ch 26 at 40 1.

[63] See *Brandt's Sons & Co.* v. *Dunlop Rubber Co. Ltd* [1905] AC 454; *Hendry* v. *Chartsearch Ltd* [1998] CLC 1382; and see also *Raffeisen Zentralbank* v. *Five Star* [2001] 3 All ER 258.

[64] See generally on factoring Salinger *Factoring Law and Practice*.

[65] [1962] AC 209 at 216.   [66] [1990] BCC 393.

[67] *Ibid.* at 405; and see also the view expressed by Staughton LJ when the case went on appeal: [1992] BCLC 148 at 185–6.

and the creation of charges over the same.[68] Firstly, in an assignment, the debtor is obliged to pay the assignee upon receiving notice of the assignment but it seems that the debtor, once it receives notice of a charge, is not obliged to pay the chargee. Indeed, unless the charge is combined with an authority from the chargor to pay the chargee, the debtor is not even entitled to make payment to the chargee, but remains committed to paying the chargor.[69] Secondly, in an assignment, the assignee takes subject to all rights of set-off and other defences which are available against the assignor, provided that such rights of set-off etc. existed when the debtor received notice of the assignment. A chargee, however, is not the owner of a debt and there is some theoretical support for the proposition that a debtor can exercise rights of set-off and defences against the chargor irrespective of whether or not the debtor has received notice of the charge.[70] Nevertheless, decided cases such as *Business Computers Ltd* v. *Anglo-African Leasing Ltd*[71] tend to ignore the point.[72]

Exploring the outright-assignment/security-interest distinction

While the distinction is of profound practical significance, often the difference between, for example, an equitable assignment of debts and a security interest in debts may seem like an exercise in splitting hairs. Nevertheless, the distinction was confirmed by the House of Lords in *Lloyds & Scottish Finance* v. *Cyril Lord Carpet Sales*[73] (the 'Cyril Lord' case). This is a case where Lloyd & Scottish (the factor) agreed to buy credit-sale agreements from Cyril Lord (the assignor). The parties entered into a master trading agreement which was stated to govern all subsequent transactions. The trading agreement provided that every assignment of debts should be an absolute assignment and sale, and that it should be in the form specified in a schedule to the master agreement. The purchase price was calculated as 80 per cent of the balances due under the credit-sale agreements purchased less a discount to be agreed from time to time.

---

[68] See, however, the comments of Millett LJ in *Bovis International Inc.* v. *Circle Ltd Partnership* (1995) 49 Con LR that an assignment does not cease to be absolute merely because it is given by way of security and is subject to an express or implied obligation to reassign on redemption. See also in this connection *Burlinson* v. *Hall* (1884) 12 QBD 347.

[69] See Goode 'The Effect of a Fixed Charge' at 172–4 and R. M. Goode *Legal Problems of Credit and Security* (Sweet & Maxwell, 2nd edn. 1988) at p. 117.

[70] See Goode 'The Effect of a Fixed Charge' at 172–4.   [71] [1977] 2 All ER 741.

[72] For possible different priority rules in the cases of assignment of debts and charges over debts see L. Smith *The Law of Tracing* (Oxford University Press, 1997) at p. 359.

[73] [1992] BCLC 609. The case was originally decided in 1979 and is reported at (1979) 129 *NLJ* 366. On the case see A. Giddins 'Block Discounting – Sale or Charge' (1980) 130 *NLJ* 207.

This discount was the factor's 'turn' or profit on the deal. The factor was entitled to give notice of assignment to the debtors but, at its discretion, however, it could choose not to do so, and, in that situation, the assignor would continue to collect the debts as agent for the factor. The assignor gave bills of exchange or banker's orders to the assignor in respect of an agreed percentage of the debts. This percentage was in practice always 80 per cent, payable by twenty-four or thirty monthly instalments.

Of course, 100 per cent of the debts remained due to the factor, and the assignor guaranteed payment of this. A provision in the master trading agreement stated that upon fulfilment of the assignor's obligations in respect of all assignments, the factor would pay a further purchase price of what was, in effect, the further 20 per cent of the value of the debts assigned. After entry into the trading agreement, 200 assignments of batches of credit-sale agreements were carried out by the parties in the agreed form.

The House of Lords held that the transaction constituted a genuine sale and purchase of debts. In its view, the trading agreement formed the basis of the contract and all subsequent assignments took place subject to it. The circumstances indicated that when the original negotiations took place a lot of importance was placed on the trading agreement being executed before any assignment had been effected. The trading agreement was a central feature in the parties' contractual intentions and there was no evidence that they intended to execute an agreement for a loan secured by a charge. Lord Wilberforce stated quite clearly that the court should not scrutinise documents minutely so as to produce a contractual intention that was manifestly negated by the trading agreement and by other evidence.[74]

The factor did not seek to recover the surplus of debts due above the 80 per cent figure. Their sole objective was to collect the amount that they had paid to the assignor and, in addition, the service fee. The account in respect of an individual assignment was closed as soon as this amount was received, with the assignor collecting and keeping the balance. The House of Lords, however, likened this situation to one of set-off and said that the fact did not demonstrate the existence of a loan. The assignor was liable to account to the factor in respect of the 20 per cent balance; yet under another clause in the trading agreement the factor was under an eventual obligation to pay to the assignor a further purchase price equivalent to that balance. It was common sense, and simplified matters, if the assignor was allowed to retain the 20 per cent balance.

---

[74] The precedent value of three old cases was stressed by the House of Lords: *Re George Inglefield Ltd* [1933] 1 Ch 1; *Olds Discount Co. Ltd* v. *John Playfair Ltd* [1938] 3 All ER 275; and *Olds Discount Co. Ltd* v. *Cohen* [1938] 3 All ER 281n.

The *Lloyds & Scottish* case involved an example of non-notification factoring. Often this form of factoring seems suspiciously like the creation of a charge, and the same is true where factoring of debts is done on a recourse basis. This circumstance alone, however, will not lead to recharacterisation of the transaction by the courts.[75] In other words, the fact that the 'purchaser' of book debts has a right of recourse against the 'seller' of the debts in the event of the debtor's non-payment is not necessarily incompatible with the transaction being one of sale. An option to repurchase is viewed as being essentially different from an equity of redemption.[76]

Legal issues arising from the factoring transaction

While factoring as a discrete and independent legal and commercial institution is well established, there are some potential problems from the point of view of the factor or assignee of the debts. Article 9 deals with many of these matters in a clearer, more detailed and comprehensive way than current English law. The main Article 9 innovations are the introduction of an extensive registration obligation and a first-to-file principle for determining priorities between competing assignments. These issues will be considered later, but Article 9 makes provision for a whole host of other matters such as (a) non-assignment clauses;[77] (b) negative-pledge clauses; (c) effect of notice to the debtor on cross-claims; and (d) potential positive liability of a factor to the debtor.

Non-assignment clauses

Non-assignment clauses are inserted in contracts for a number of reasons.[78] Firstly, and most importantly, such clauses are designed to prevent a debtor having to deal with someone he would have refused to contract with directly.[79] In a leading case, *Don King Productions Inc.* v.

---

[75] For further exploration of the distinction between charges and factoring of debts see the judgment of Browne-Wilkinson VC in *Welsh Development Agency* v. *Export Finance Co. Ltd* [1990] BCC 393.

[76] See *Orion Finance Ltd* v. *Crown Financial Management Ltd* [1996] BCC 621, and in particular the comments of Millett LJ at 626–7.

[77] See generally B. Allcock 'Restrictions on the Assignment of Contractual Rights' [1983] *CLJ* 328 at 344–5; R. Goode 'Inalienable Rights' (1979) 42 *MLR* 553.

[78] See generally on this area G. McCormack 'Debts and Non-Assignment Clauses' [2000] *JBL* 422; and see also L. Sealy and R. Hooley *Commercial Law: Text, Cases and Materials* (Butterworths, 2nd edn. 1999) at pp. 860–73.

[79] Certain contracts are, by their nature, non-assignable, such as contracts of personal service: see *Nokes* v. *Doncaster Amalgamated Colleries Ltd* [1940] AC 1014. In *Tolhurst* v. *Associated Portland Cement Manufacturers* [1902] 2 KB 660 at 668 Collins MR remarked

Warren,[80] which involved management and production agreements in the world of boxing, Lightman J said that the purpose of a non-assignment clause is the genuine commercial interest of a party in ensuring that contractual relations are only with the person he has selected as the other party to the contract and no one else. Building contracts are another important case in point. In *Linden Gardens* v. *Lenesta Sludge* Lord Browne-Wilkinson analysed the factors that led to the use of a non-assignment clause as follows:[81] 'The reason for including the contractual prohibition viewed from the contractor's point of view must be that the contractor wishes to ensure that he deals, and deals only, with the particular employer with whom he has chosen to deal. Building contracts are pregnant with disputes: some employers are more reasonable than others in dealing with such disputes.'

The second factor behind the use of non-assignment clauses is that a debtor cannot rely upon 'new equities' against the assignor after he receives notice of the assignment to the assignee. The assignee may be somebody with whom the debtor has no existing or potential future business relationship, and therefore there is no possibility of setting off equities against the assignee. Thirdly, it might be argued that an assignee would be less interested in the performance of his side of the contractual bargain if he has assigned his right to benefits under the contract to a third party.[82] Moreover, since debtor and assignee are possibly in a once-off relationship, the assignee has no incentive to preserve the debtor's goodwill.

There are, nevertheless, competing considerations which support the principle of the free assignability of debts. These are based on the ideas of free negotiability and protection of the good-faith purchase, i.e. lenders and assignees are potentially at risk from non-assignment clauses and should be protected.[83] The arguments favouring free assignability of debts have met with substantial acceptance in the US. Article 9-406(d) of the UCC provides that[84]

---

that the benefit of the performance of a contract is only assignable in 'cases where it can make no difference to the person on whom the obligation lies to which of two persons he is to discharge it'. See also *Don King Productions Inc.* v. *Warren* [1999] 2 All ER 218.

[80] [1998] 2 All ER 608; [1999] 2 All ER 218.   [81] [1994] 1 AC 85 at 429.

[82] These matters are discussed in Salinger *Factoring Law and Practice* chaps. 7 and 8.

[83] The distinguished theorist Grant Gilmore has argued that despite the absence of anything resembling an 'instrument', good-faith purchase is once more running its normal course under the stimulus of the same commercial pressures that have so many times in the past led to the creation of negotiable instruments, quasi-negotiable instruments and just-a-little-bit-negotiable instruments: 'The Commercial Doctrine of Good Faith Purpose' (1954) 63 *Yale LJ* 1057 at 1121.

[84] More or less the same principle is enshrined in the UNIDROIT (Ottawa) Convention on International Factoring (1988). Article 6 of the Convention provides that an assignment

a term in an agreement between an account debtor and an assignor . . . is ineffective to the extent that it: (1) prohibits, restricts or requires the consent of the account debtor . . . to the assignment or transfer of, or the creation, attachment, perfection or enforcement of a security interest in, the account . . .; or (2) provides that the assignment or transfer or the creation, attachment, perfection or enforcement of the security interest may give rise to a default, breach, right of recoupment, claim, defense, termination, right of termination or remedy under the account.

In England, while the law started from a position of non-assignability, courts of equity have permitted the assignment of debts and other choses of action since the seventeenth century.[85] In *Linden Gardens Ltd* v. *Lenesta Sludge*[86] the House of Lords rejected the proposition that the law had moved so far that contractual prohibitions on assignment of rights were contrary to public policy. The court held that an attempted assignment in breach of such a prohibition was ineffective to vest the contractual rights in the assignee. According to Lord Browne-Wilkinson, if the law were otherwise it would defeat the legitimate commercial reason for inserting the contractual prohibition, namely, to ensure that the original parties to the contract are not brought into direct contractual relations with third parties. In his view, the most normal construction of a non-assignment clause is that it would prevent the assignee enjoying direct relations with the debtor but would not prevent the assignor from accounting to the assignee for whatever he receives from the debtor.[87] In other words, the assignor would be obliged to hand over receipts to the assignee. Another possibility holds that a clause forbidding the assignment of a contract does not exclude declarations of trust of the benefit of the contract. This construction runs the risk, however, of circumventing altogether the effect of non-assignment clauses.[88]

should be effective notwithstanding an agreement between the client and the debtor prohibiting such assignment. The article goes on to state, however, that an assignment in contravention of such an agreement is not effective as regards the debtor if at the time of the contract of sale his place of business is in a contracting state that has made a declaration that this provision is not to apply to debtors within its borders. See also for a similar statement Article 9 of the more comprehensive United Nations Convention on the Assignment of Receivables in International Trade (2001).

[85] See generally O. Marshall *The Assignment of Choses in Action* (Pitman, 1950); W. Holdsworth 'The History of the Treatment of Choses in Action by the Common Law' (1920) 33 *Harv L Rev* at 997; S. Bailey 'Assignment of Debts in England from the Twelfth to the Twentieth Century' (1931) 47 *LQR* 516 and (1932) 48 *LQR* 248, 547; and for a contemporary restrictive interpretation of non-assignment clauses see the Court of Appeal decision *Foamcrete (UK) Ltd* v. *Thrust Engineering Ltd* [2002] BCC 221.

[86] [1994] AC 85.

[87] This construction was in fact adopted in *Re Turcan* (1888) 40 Ch D 5.

[88] It was, nevertheless, the interpretation adopted in *Don King Productions Inc.* v. *Warren* [1999] 2 All ER 218, on which see A. Tettenborn 'Trusts and Unassignable Agreements – again' [1999] *LMCLQ* 353.

Negative-pledge clauses

Since assignments and charges are conceptually different, in principle a non-assignment clause in a contract should not catch the creation of a charge. There is nothing, however, to stop a contracting party from stipulating that the other contracting party should not create a charge or security interest over the debt. There are various reasons why an anti-charging clause might be inserted in the contract. In a building contract, for example, the employer may wish the contractor to receive the benefit of stage payments rather than to see these payments being funnelled to a bank with a security interest over debt proceeds. The employer wishes to see the building works completed and this is less likely to happen if the contractor is deprived of cash flow, which would occur if contractual payments were directly earmarked for security-interest holders. An anti-charging clause could be referred to as a negative-pledge clause though the context is slightly different from the circumstances in which negative-pledge clauses normally operate, i.e. a company purports to create a fixed charge over its existing and future book debts in favour of a lender and a clause in the instrument of charge provides that the company will not factor or assign the debts in favour of anybody else. The borrower has entered into contracts that give rise to debts but the party extracting the negative-pledge clause is not the other contracting party, but rather a third-party lender who does not want the debts assigned or charged to a fourth party.

A breach of a negative-pledge clause would render the person giving the covenant (the covenantor) exposed to a contractual claim from the covenantee. The latter could institute enforcement proceedings under the terms of the loan agreement with the covenantor. Moreover, it has been argued that if the factor, with knowledge of the covenant, enters into a factoring agreement with the person who has given the covenant, then the factor, as assignee, would be liable to the beneficiary of the covenant for assisting in or inducing its breach.[89] The proprietary rights of the factor would not be impeached[90] but the factor runs the risk of being

---

[89] See Salinger *Factoring Law and Practice* at p. 185. See also R. Goode *Commercial Law* (Penguin, 2nd edn. 1996) at pp. 816–18.

[90] There seems little doubt that a pure negative-pledge clause – that is, a clause not to factor or encumber without any obligation to furnish security – does not of itself amount to a security interest. The clause does not purport to give the covenantee any rights, even contingently, over the debtor's present or future assets. Since *Re BCCI (No. 8)* [1998] AC 214 it is apparent that a debtor can have the benefit of a charge over his own indebtedness to a creditor and so, in the situation of two contracting parties, there is no conceptual barrier in one contracting party having a charge over the obligations he owes the other. A negative-pledge clause in the contract does not, however, create

declared personally liable to the covenantee under the tort of inducing a breach of contract. It appears, however, that actual knowledge of the anti-charging clause is a precondition of tortious liability[91] and that inferred knowledge is not enough. In support of this proposition one can refer to an extensive body of case law concerned with the non-application of the doctrine of constructive notice – 'what a person ought to have known' – in commercial transactions. As Lord Browne-Wilkinson remarked in *Westdeutsche Landesbank Girozentrale* v. *Islington LBC*,[92] wise judges have often warned against the wholesale importation into commercial law of equitable principles inconsistent with the certainty and speed that are essential requirements for the orderly conduct of business affairs.

In the US negative-pledge clauses are governed by Article 9-401(b), which provides that an agreement between the debtor and secured party which prohibits a transfer of the debtor's rights in collateral or makes the transfer a default does not prevent the transfer from taking effect. An agreement restricting or prohibiting assignment is not, however, declared to be ineffective. Consequently, the debtor's actions in purporting to effect an assignment may constitute a default under the terms of the debtor's agreement with the secured party and entitle the latter to institute enforcement proceedings under the security agreement. Nevertheless, the security interest created in breach of the negative-pledge clause is still a valid security interest though the security taker might, in certain circumstances, be liable for the tort of inducing a breach of contract. A case in point is *First Wyoming Bank* v. *Mudge*[93] where a family business

---

such a charge. So the factor is not faced with a situation of competing proprietary rights. See generally on this area J. Maxton 'Negative Pledges and Equitable Principles' [1997] *JBL* 458; P. Gabriel *Legal Aspects of Syndicated Loans* (Butterworths, 1986) at pp. 84–90.

[91] See the decision of Browne-Wilkinson J in *Swiss Bank* v. *Lloyds Bank* [1979] Ch 548, who held that it was a requisite element in establishing that the defendant had committed the tort, that the defendant should have been possessed of actual knowledge, at the time the defendant acquired its interest, of the contractual rights which it was claimed had been breached. It may be, however, that this viewpoint is inconsistent with the more general approach of the courts in cases of alleged wrongful interference with contractual rights, particularly in the context of industrial disputes; on which see generally *Merkur Island Shipping Corp.* v. *Laughton* [1983] 2 AC 570. See also on the test for knowledge in the specific area of lending agreements *Mac-Jordan Construction Ltd* v. *Brookmount Erostin Ltd* [1992] BCLC 350. The conflict in the authorities is reviewed by A. McKnight 'Restrictions on Dealing with Assets in Financing Documents: Their Role, Meaning and Effect' [2002] *JIBL* 193; and see also Tan Cheng Han 'The Negative-Pledge as a "security device"' [1996] *Singapore Journal of Legal Studies* at 415; J. Arkins '"OK – So you've Promised, Right?" The Negative-Pledge Clause and the Security it Provides' [2000] *JIBL* 198.

[92] [1996] AC 669.   [93] (1988) 748 P 2d 713.

was sold with the purchaser being able to make staged payments of the purchase price. To provide protection for the unpaid price, the sellers extracted from the purchaser a negative-pledge covenant that covered the business's assets but, in breach of the covenant, the purchaser granted the bank a security interest over part of the assets. It was held by a jury that the bank had actual knowledge of the negative-pledge covenant and had damaged the covenantee by intentionally and unjustifiably interfering with the covenantor's obligations to them. This conclusion was confirmed by an appellate court.

Commentators differ on whether the possibility of tortious liability is a real deterrent to later lenders. One observer surmises that few tortious interference actions are brought by negative pledgees because the later lender must induce the breach rather than lend to a debtor that had already decided to breach, and most debtors that approach later lenders have already made the breach decision.[94] On the other hand, a doctrine such as tortious interference that depends on an actor's actual knowledge or purpose tends to exacerbate uncertainty, and there is a question mark over where strong suspicion ends and actual knowledge begins. These sentiments led another US commentator to conclude:[95]

Whether a court will find tortuous interference on any given set of facts remains nebulous enough to encourage negative-pledgees' attorneys to feel relatively free to press their luck, and the opportunity for a large jury verdict, complete with punitive damages, provides them with an incentive to continue their efforts . . . Prospective lenders are both overdeterred by the threat of a large judgment and underdeterred by the tort device's cumbersome dependence on litigation.

Notice to the debtor and cross-claims

Article 9-406 UCC provides that an account debtor may discharge its obligation by paying the assignor until, but not after, the account debtor receives a notification, authenticated by the assignor or the assignee, that the amount due or to become due has been assigned and that payment is to be made to the assignee. After receipt of the notification, the account debtor may discharge its obligation by paying the assignee and may not discharge the obligation by paying the assignor. The principle is basically the same under English law where, if no notice of assignment is received,

---

[94] See A. Schwartz 'A Theory of Loan Priorities' (1989) 18 *J Legal Stud* 209 at 210.
[95] See C. Bjerre 'Secured Transactions Inside Out: negative-pledge Covenants, Property and Perfection' (1999) 84 *Cornell L Rev* 305 at 330–1. Bjerre's article contains an invaluable study of all the potential liabilities of later lenders where negative-pledge covenants are used in lending agreements.

the debtor will obviously get a good discharge for the debt on paying the original creditor irrespective of whether the latter accounts for the debt proceeds to the factor.[96] It is also the case in England that if a debtor ignores a notice of assignment and still pays the assignor, the debt is not discharged and the debtor remains liable to pay the assignee.[97] The two systems differ somewhat when it comes to assignment of part of a debt. Under English law it seems that if part of a debt has been assigned but a debtor disregards the notice of assignment and pays the part assigned to the assignor, the debtor remains liable to pay that part to the assignee.[98] The rule is different under Article 9-406(b)(3), which entitles a debtor to disregard a notice of assignment if it requires the account debtor to make less than the full amount of any instalment or other periodic payment to the assignee. Article 9-407 also contains a valuable protection for the debtor, which is entitled to require that an assignee should furnish reasonable proof that the assignment has been made and, unless the assignee complies, the debtor may discharge its obligation by paying the assignor.

In England the giving of notice of the assignment to the debtor is important because it will preclude the debtor from setting up, as against the assignee, cross-claims and other equities which arise against the assignor subsequent to the receipt of the notice of assignment. Basically, a debtor is entitled to set up cross-claims against the creditor up until the time that notice of assignment is received. These cross-claims will operate to reduce the value of the assigned debt and, if sufficiently large, may even operate to extinguish it altogether. The authorities were reviewed by Mance J in *Marathon Electrical Manufacturing Corp.* v. *Mashreqbank PSC.*[99] The case was concerned with the assignment of the proceeds of a letter of credit and the right of a collecting bank to set off against payment a liquidated sum due from the assignor which had accrued before notice of assignment had been received. Set-off was allowed and, in doing so, the court invoked the observations of Templeman J in *Business Computers Ltd* v. *Anglo-African Leasing Ltd:*[100]

The result of the relevant authorities is that a debt which accrues due before notice of an assignment is received, whether or not it is payable before that date, or a debt which arises out of the same contract as that which gives rise to the assigned debt, or is closely connected with that contract, may be set off against the assignee.

---

[96] *Bence* v. *Shearman* [1898] 2 Ch 582.   [97] *Brice* v. *Bannister* (1878) 3 QBD 569.
[98] See, however, the comments of Simon Brown LJ in *Deposit Protection Board* v. *Dalia* [1994] 2 AC 367 at 382.
[99] [1997] 2 BCLC 460.   [100] [1977] 2 All ER 741 at 748.

One of the relevant authorities is the old case *Watson* v. *Mid Wales Rly Co.*,[101] where Boyill CJ said:

> No case has been cited to us where equity has allowed against the assignee of an equitable chose in action a set off of a debt arising between the original parties subsequently to the notice of assignment, out of matters not connected with the debt claimed, nor in any way referring to it . . . In all the cases cited . . . some qualification occurred in the original contract, or the two transactions were in some way connected together, so as to lead the court to the conclusion that they were made with reference to one another.

If the cross-claim is closely connected to the transaction under which the debt assigned arose, then wider set-off rights may be available. Article 9-404 UCC achieves the same result in the US. It provides that unless an account debtor has made an enforceable agreement not to assert defences or claims, the rights of an assignee are subject to (1) all terms of the agreement between the account debtor and assignor and any defence or claim in recoupment arising from the transaction that gave rise to the contract; and (2) any other defence or claim of the account debtor against the assignor which accrues before the account debtor receives a notification of the assignment authenticated by the assignor or the assignee.[102]

Potential positive liability of factor to debtor

It seems that, by virtue of the assignment alone, an assignee is under no positive liability to the debtor. This is true in both England and the US. Article 9-402 provides that the existence of a security interest or authority given to a debtor to dispose of or use collateral, without more, does not subject a secured party to liability in contract or tort for the debtor's acts or omissions. According to the Official Comment, this provision rejects theories on which a secured party might be held liable on a debtor's contracts or in tort merely because a security interest exists. Perhaps more directly relevant in the present context is Article 9-404(b), which provides that the claim of an account debtor against an assignor may be asserted against an assignee only to reduce the amount that the account debtor owes. As the Official Comment points out, the account debtor is not afforded the right to an affirmative recovery from an assignee. The revised Article 9 makes explicit what was held to be implicit in a number of cases in the old version. A leading authority is *Michelin Tyres (Canada)*

---

[101] (1867) LR 2 CP 593 at 598.

[102] For roughly similar principles see Article 9 of the Ottawa Convention on International Factoring and Article 18 of the UN Convention on Assignment of Receivables in International Trade. Note too, however, Article 9-405 UCC, which provides that good-faith modifications of an assigned contract are effective against an assignee.

Ltd v. *First National Bank of Boston*,[103] where the First Circuit Court of Appeals took the view, on an analysis of the statutory language, that no affirmative right of recovery was contemplated. Moreover, this was a sound policy choice in that allowing affirmative suits would make every banker who had taken an assignment of accounts for security purposes a deep-pocket surety for every bankrupt contractor in the state to whom it had loaned money.[104]

In England the leading authority is *Pan Ocean Shipping Ltd* v. *Creditcorp Ltd*,[105] which concerned the assignment of the right to receive rental payments (freight) in respect of the hire of a vessel (a charterparty). Some of the rental payments were payable in advance and upon receiving notice of the assignment the account debtor paid these amounts to the assignee. The vessel, however, was unavailable to the account debtors (the hirers) during the rental period and the hirers sought to recover the advance payment from the assignees. The claim was brought against the assignees, as the owners of the vessel were insolvent and the contractual right of action against them for failing to make the vessel available was consequently not worth pursuing. The House of Lords decided that the hirers only had this claim against the assignors with whom they were in a contractual relationship and the purely fortuitous, from their point of view, fact of assignment should not give them an additional claim against the assignees. In Lord Woolf's view there was no justification for subjecting an assignee, because he had received a payment in advance, to an obligation to make a repayment because of the non-performance of an event for which he has no responsibility.[106]

---

[103] (1981) 666 F 2d 673.

[104] On affirmative recovery under the Ottawa Convention see Article 10, which provides that 'non-performance or defective or late performance of the contract of sale of goods shall not by itself entitle the debtor to recover a sum paid by the debtor to the factor if the debtor has a right to recover that sum from the supplier'. Article 10, however, is subject to exceptions: a debtor will be entitled to recover from the factor (to the extent of the debtor's right to recover from the client) a sum paid to the factor when the latter has not discharged his obligation to pay the client for the debt in question or when the factor has made payment for it in the knowledge of the client's default. Article 10 is to be contrasted with Article 21 of the UN Convention on Assignment of Receivables in International Trade, which simply states that failure 'of the assignor to perform the original contract does not entitle the debtor to recover from the assignee a sum paid by the debtor to the assignor or the assignee'. There are no exceptions stated.

[105] [1994] 1 WLR 161.

[106] On the other hand, it has been argued that the debtor had a reasonable expectation that the nature of the right assigned, a right to payment conditional on provision of the ship, would be respected by the assignee and so denial of that reasonable expectation without good cause was unconscionable: see G. Tolhurt 'Assignment, Equities, the Trident Beauty and Restitution' [1999] *CLJ* 546. For further discussion of the case see also K. Barker 'Restitution and Third Parties' [1994] *LMCLQ* 305.

The Article 9 filing obligation as applied to receivables

Article 9 applies broadly to any transaction, regardless of form, that creates a security interest in personal property. It also applies to a 'sale of accounts, chattel paper, payment intangibles or promissory notes'.[107] Why bring sale transactions within the scope of Article 9? One reason is that factoring is primarily a financing arrangement: 'In substance the factor is a supplier of working capital, not a joint venturer in a business enterprise. In that sense one may properly describe him as a financier, a "banker", a lender of money against security.'[108] On the other hand, factoring is not exclusively a financing arrangement and it has been pointed out that the drafters of personal property security legislation, including Article 9, did not see the interest of a buyer-assignee as being automatically included within their functional definition of 'security'. It was found to be necessary artificially to extend the definition.[109] One of the reasons given for broadening the definition centres on the fact that financing transactions are often carried out in a way which blurs the distinction between outright sales and security transfers of receivables.[110]

While Article 9 applies, generally speaking, to a sale of accounts there are a number of specific exclusions. The article does not apply, *inter alia*, to a sale of accounts as part of a sale of the business out of which they arose; an assignment of accounts which is for the purpose of collection only; or an assignment of a right to payment under a contract to an assignee that is also obligated to perform under the contract.[111] These exclusions reflect a belief that Article 9 should not encompass transactions

---

[107] Article 9-109.

[108] See Grant Gilmore *Security Interests in Personal Property* (Little Brown, 1965) at pp. 128–9; and see also M. Bridge, R. Macdonald, R. Simmonds and C. Walsh 'Formalism, Functionalism and Understanding the Law of Secured Transactions' (1999) 44 *McGill LJ* 567 at n. 38.

[109] That an extension of the ordinary definition of security is intended is clear from the wording of Article 9-109(a)(3) of UCC; and see also T. Plank 'Sacred Cows and Workhorses: The Sale of Accounts and Chattel Paper under the UCC and the Effects of Violating a Fundamental Drafting Principle' (1994) 26 *Conn L Rev* 397.

[110] The Official Comment to Article 9-109 refers to the 'difficult problems of distinguishing between transactions in which a receivable secures an obligation and those in which the receivable has been sold outright. In many commercial financing transactions the distinction is blurred.'

[111] Article 9-109(d). It should be noted that, pursuant to Article 9-309(2), an assignment of accounts which does not, by itself, or in conjunction with other assignments to the same assignee, transfer a significant part of the assignor's outstanding accounts is automatically perfected upon attachment. In other words, no filing is required for perfection purposes. According to the Official Comment, the purpose of this provision is to save from *ex post facto* invalidation casual or isolated assignments – assignments which no one would think of filing.

that have nothing to do with commercial financing operations and that would be swept up within a broad definition of sale of accounts.

Difficulties in characterisation alone, however, cannot sufficiently explain the assimilation in treatment of factoring and security transfer in Article 9. The distinction between factoring and security transfer retains its importance in other contexts such as accounting, tax and insolvency. Indeed, the distinction is vitally important in the context of the securitisation transaction which, as a form of financing, has assumed enormous practical importance. Basically, the term 'securitisation' refers to the process of collecting and pooling receivables; assigning them to a special-purpose vehicle (SPV) which in turn raises the finance to 'buy' the receivables by itself issuing commercial paper to investors. The originator of the securitisation transaction will continue to collect the receivables for which it receives a 'servicing' fee. If the originator is a financial institution subject to capital adequacy requirements, the securitisation process performs the valuable function of removing debt from the originator's balance sheet. In other words, the originator's capital adequacy ratio will be improved. Moreover, to make the commercial paper issued by the SPV attractive to potential investors, the SPV must be 'bankruptcy-remote', i.e. it should not be liable in any way for the debts of the originator. Ensuring that there is a 'true' sale of receivables from originator to SPV assists in establishing the bankruptcy-remoteness of the SPV. The characterisation exercise – distinguishing between a genuine sale and a security assignment of receivables – therefore still has to be undergone.[112] Article 9 has certainly not eliminated the distinction from American law. One US treatise states the position as follows:[113]

> The basic distinction between the sale and securing of accounts is seen in the fact that any surplus from collections goes to the buyer in the case of a sale and to the seller in the case of a security assignment. The limited purpose for which Article 9 applies to the sale of accounts is to avoid litigation on characterization and to notify third parties of the assignee's interest. But this limited purpose does not prevent characterization of absolute assignments as sales for other purposes albeit that Art. 9 does have a bankruptcy impact insofar as the failure of the buyer to file allows the trustee to grab the accounts.

The enormous continuing significance of characterisation issues is also illustrated by Canadian jurisprudence. It must be remembered that

---

[112] See P. Shupack 'Securitization under Revised Article 9' (1999) 73 *American Bankruptcy LJ* at 167. For a British perspective see A. Berg 'Recharacterisation after Enron' [2003] *JBL* 205.

[113] See B. Clark *The Law of Secured Transactions under the Uniform Commercial Code* (Warren, Gorham & Lamont, 1996; Cumulative Supplement) at S1.11–S1.12 cited by Bridge et al. 'Formalism, Functionalism and Understanding' at n. 64.

common-law Canada has followed the Article 9 model but the decision of the Supreme Court of Canada in *R* v. *Alberta (Treasury Branches)*[114] highlights the fact that the distinction between absolute assignments of debts and security assignments is still crucial in certain contexts. The issue in the case arose because of the provisions of section 224(1.2) of the Canadian Income Tax Code which stated that a secured creditor who had a right to receive a payment that, but for a security interest in favour of the secured creditor would be payable to a tax debtor, could be required to make direct payment to the Revenue. It was further provided that the money so required to be paid should, 'notwithstanding any security interest in those monies, become the property of Her Majesty and should be paid to the Receiver General, in priority to any such security interest'. 'Secured creditor' is defined as 'a person who has a security interest in the property of another person' and 'security interest' as 'any interest in property that secures payment or performance of an obligation'.

In a number of cases, tax debtors had executed assignments of debts in favour of lenders and, in each of these cases, the Revenue claimed priority over the lender. The assignments were specifically stated to be by way of 'continuing collateral security'. The key issue was whether the lender was a secured party within the meaning of the statutory provision. This question was answered in the affirmative by a majority of the Supreme Court of Canada, and the court distinguished between factoring – the outright transfer of debts – and the security transfer of debts. With factoring, no property remained in the hands of the assignor and those engaged in the business of factoring were protected from the tentacles of the tax code. In this particular case, though, the borrower retained the right to redeem the book debts once the debt had been paid off and this right of redemption demonstrated that the assignment was something less than absolute.

Chattel-paper financing and Article 9

Article 9 uses extensively the concept of 'chattel paper', but this concept is not recognised as a separate category of receivables financing under English law.[115] The term is defined basically as meaning a record or records that evidence both (a) a monetary obligation and (b) a security interest in specific goods or a lease of specific goods. One type of chattel paper is

---

[114] (1996) 133 DLR (4th) 609; on which see generally G. McCormack 'Personal Property Security Law Reform in England and Canada' [2002] *JBL* 113 at 130–2.

[115] See generally Law Commission *Registration of Security Interests* at p. 193, which expresses scepticism about the desirability of separate legislative recognition of the concept of chattel paper in the UK.

created when a written security agreement in specific goods is given by a debtor to a secured party. If, as will invariably be the case, the terms of the security agreement include the debtor's payment obligations, then the writing constitutes chattel paper. The secured party can itself secure financing by either borrowing on the security of the paper or alternatively by selling the paper. The same principle applies to written chattel leases which contain the payment obligations of the lessee. The lease constitutes chattel paper against which the lessor can borrow and the position is similar where the parties enter into a hire-purchase or conditional-sale agreement and the written agreement contains the hirer/buyer's payment obligations. Under the functional approach towards security adopted in Article 9, the hire-purchase or conditional-sale agreement is regarded as creating a security interest and therefore, in the circumstances, the documents represent chattel-paper in the hands of the owner/vendor of the goods. There are writings which evidence both a monetary obligation and a security interest in specific goods. In all of these instances, there is a payment obligation that is tied to specific goods against which the obligee can proceed in the event of there being some default in payment. Chattel-paper financing is essentially a device that enables a lessor or conditional seller of goods to obtain finance on the security of the lease or conditional-sale agreement.

In English law 'chattel paper' is not treated as a specific separate category of collateral. There is no special law applying to chattel-paper financing.[116] Rather, it is an undifferentiated aspect of the law pertaining to factoring and receivables financing more generally.[117] Many of the leading cases on receivables financing in England involve what, in the US, would be referred to as 'chattel-paper financing'. Cases in point include *Re Atlantic Computers plc*[118] and *Lloyds & Scottish Finance Ltd* v. *Cyril Lord Carpet Sales Ltd.*[119] In the latter case Lord Scarman explained the essence of such transactions, stating:[120]

---

[116] *Ibid.*

[117] See also the comments of the New Zealand Law Commission in Report No. 8 *A Personal Property Securities Act for New Zealand* (1989) at pp. 81–2 when proposing draft new legislation for New Zealand:

> The term chattel paper has no counterpart under current New Zealand law. It includes hire purchase agreements, finance leases and conditional sale contracts. Such writings serve primarily to document rights and obligations of the parties to the particular transaction. However, the bundle of rights arising under such an agreement comprises a distinct form of personal property. The proposed statute facilitates the use of this property as an independent source of credit. Parties who inject new value into the debtor's business by purchasing or lending against chattel paper enjoy priority over creditors who claim the paper as proceeds or after-acquired property.

[118] [1992] Ch 505.   [119] [1992] BCLC 609.   [120] *Ibid.* at 618–19.

Block discounting is a well-known service offered by certain finance houses to traders who do a substantial business by way of hire-purchase or credit-sale agreements with their customers. Though there are variations of detail, the essential feature of the service is that in return for an immediate advance the trader sells to the finance house at a discount his interest in the agreements he has with his customers. The trader gives the house his guarantee of the performance by his customers of their obligations. He includes a number, often a very large number, of hire-purchase or credit-sale agreements in each discounting transaction: hence the City's name 'block discounting' for this type of transactions.

Under Article 9 as well, in both the former and revised versions, the categories were sufficiently broad to encompass all rights to payment that were taken as collateral. The question arises why another separate category of collateral was recognised – namely, chattel paper. The answer seems to be because at the time that Article 9 was enacted 'written payment obligations that were secured by (or represented leases of) specific goods received special treatment by professional financiers'.[121] Chattel paper was frequently delivered to the purchaser and special rules were devised to protect the chattel-paper financier.[122] Under what is now Article 9-330(b), for example, a purchaser of chattel paper has priority over a security interest in the chattel paper, which is claimed merely as proceeds of inventory subject to a security interest, if the purchaser gives new value and takes possession of the chattel paper, or obtains control of the chattel paper, in good faith, in the ordinary course of the purchaser's business and the chattel paper does not indicate that it has been assigned to an identified assignee other than the purchaser. These special rules are continued and refined in the revised Article 9. Also, the new Article 9 recognises a concept of 'electronic chattel paper' which is defined as meaning chattel paper evidenced by a record or records consisting of information stored in an electronic medium.[123] In the main, control of 'electronic chattel paper' is equated with possession of tangible chattel paper.[124]

---

[121] See J. O. Honnold, S. L. Harris and C. W. Mooney *Security Interests in Personal Property* (Foundation Press, 3rd edn. 2001) at p. 403.

[122] For a criticism of the privileged treatment afforded chattel-paper financing see J. Zekan 'Chattel Paper Financing: Metaphysical Property and Real Money' (1992) 29 *Idaho LR* 723 at 744–6, who argues that the super-priority principle rewards ignorance on the part of chattel-paper financiers as well as undermining the more general policy underlying Article 9, which is based on the primacy of the filing system. In her view chattel paper no longer merits special treatment – if it ever did. For more standard accounts and justifications see J. Levie 'Security Interests in Chattel Paper' (1969) 78 *Yale LJ* 935; and D. Rapson 'Receivables Financing under Revised Article 9' (1999) 73 *American Bankruptcy Law Journal* 133.

[123] See Article 9-102(2).

[124] For a discussion of the rules pertaining to electronic chattel paper see J. Winn 'Electronic Chattel Paper under Revised Article 9: Updating the Concept of Embodied Rights for

The following example demonstrates how the Article 9 priority rules work in the context of chattel-paper financing. A secured party has a perfected security interest in the borrower's inventory. The borrower then sells items of inventory under a conditional-sale agreement. The security interest will extend to payments due under the conditional-sale agreement as these payments represent proceeds of the inventory and, under Article 9, a security interest in proceeds is automatically perfected.[125] The borrower then hands the conditional-sale agreement over to a perfected chattel-paper financier and obtains finance from the latter. The chattel-paper financier prevails over the holder of the other security interest even though a different result is dictated by the normal temporal priority rules of Article 9. According to the Official Comment, this 'special' priority rule, 'under which the chattel paper purchaser who gives new value in ordinary course can rely on possession of unlegended, tangible chattel paper without any concern for other facts that it may know, comports with the expectations of both inventory and chattel paper financiers'.

The statutory protection afforded chattel-paper financiers is slightly less generous when the competing secured party is claiming the collateral not simply 'as proceeds of inventory subject to a security interest', for example where the competing secured party is claiming the chattel paper as original collateral. In these circumstances the chattel-paper financier loses out not only where there is a legend on the chattel paper that it has been assigned to somebody else but also where the chattel-paper financier has 'knowledge that the purchase violates the rights of the secured party'. As the Official Comment makes clear, if a purchaser sees a statement in a financing statement to the effect that a purchase of chattel paper from the debtor would violate the rights of the filed secured party, the purchaser would have such knowledge.

Priority issues and the Article 9 treatment of receivables

As a general proposition, Article 9 assimilates the treatment of outright sales and security transfers of receivables in so far as priority and perfection rules are concerned.[126] To facilitate achievement of this objective,

---

Electronic Commerce' (1999) 74 *Chicago-Kent L Rev* 1055; R. Gross and C. Jones 'The Treatment of Electronic "Chattel Paper" under Revised Article 9' (1998) 31 *UCC LJ* 47.

[125] According to Article 9-315(a)(2) a security interest attaches to any identifiable proceeds of collateral. The security interest in proceeds is declared to be a perfected security interest if the security interest in the original collateral was perfected; but the security interest becomes unperfected on the twenty-first day after the security interest attaches to the proceeds, in certain circumstances.

[126] See generally Plank 'Sacred Cows and Workhorses'.

Article 9-318 provides that a debtor that has sold an account does not retain a legal or equitable interest in the collateral sold. The provision, however, goes on to state that for the purpose of determining the rights of creditors of, and purchasers for value of an account or chattel paper from, a debtor that has sold an account or chattel paper, while the buyer's security interest is unperfected, the debtor is deemed to have rights and title to the account or chattel paper identical to those the debtor sold. This means that so long as the buyer's security interest is unperfected, the seller can transfer and the creditors of the seller can reach the account or chattel paper as if it had not been sold. If the position were otherwise, it would mean that somebody who had sold his accounts or chattel paper would have no property interest left to support a second assignment. Therefore, the central purpose of including outright assignments within the perfection and priority scheme of Article 9 would be defeated.

The new Article 9-318 really makes explicit what was supposed all along to be implicit in Article 9. Some uncertainty, however, was introduced by the decision of the Tenth Circuit Court of Appeals in *Octagon Gas Systems Inc. v. Rimmer*.[127] In this case it was held that royalties sold outright to a third party prior to bankruptcy remained the property of the debtor and thus formed part of the bankruptcy estate. The decision engendered widespread criticism, not least from the UCC Permanent Editorial Board.[128] One critical comment read as follows:[129]

The application of Article 9 to the sale of accounts does not prevent the transfer of ownership from seller to buyer for bankruptcy purposes. The UCC was not intended to take away the right of an owner of property to transfer ownership to another. The basic distinction between the sale and securing of accounts is seen in the fact that any surplus from collections goes to the buyer in the case of a sale and to the seller in the case of a security assignment. The limited purpose for which Article 9 applies to the sale of accounts is to avoid litigation on characterisation and to notify third parties of the assignee's interest. But this limited purpose does not prevent characterisation of absolute assignments as sales for other purposes albeit that Art. 9 does have a bankruptcy impact insofar as the failure of the buyer to file allows the trustee to grab the accounts under the 'strong-arm clause' . . . But that impact does not affect the transfer of ownership between seller and buyer.

---

[127] (1993) 995 F 2d 948.
[128] According to the Permanent Editorial Board Commentary No. 14 *Transfer of Accounts or Chattel Paper* (1994) the court in *Rimmer* erroneously stated that 'the impact of applying Article 9 to [the buyer's] account is that Article 9's treatment of accounts sold as collateral would place [the buyer's] account within the property of [the seller's] bankruptcy estate'.
[129] Clark *Law of Secured Transactions* at S1.11–S1.12; and see generally Bridge et al. 'Formalism, Functionalism and Understanding' at n. 64.

It is submitted that the imposition of a requirement of registration in relation to assignments of debts has a valuable role to play in sorting out the issue of priorities if there are competing assignments of the same debt.[130] Priority should be determined by the timing of registration.[131] In many respects, the 'first-to-perfect' priority rule of Article 9 is a more satisfactory method of determining priorities in receivables financing than the somewhat uncertain application of the rule in *Dearle* v. *Hall*[132] in England.[133] The rule in *Dearle* v. *Hall* states that if a second or subsequent assignee has no notice of a prior assignment, at the time of the second or subsequent assignment,[134] then the subsequent assignee can gain priority by being the first to notify the debtor of the assignment.[135] Two rationales have been stated for the rule, both of which derive a measure of support from the case itself. One view sees the giving of notice as tantamount to taking possession of a tangible asset. Another view sees the rule as being based on the prevention of fraud. In *Dearle* v. *Hall* Plumer MR suggested that the omission to give notice enabled the assignor to

---

[130] See C. Walsh 'Registration, Constructive Notice and the Rule in Dearle v Hall' (1997) 12 *Banking and Finance Law Review* 129; and see also Bridge et al. 'Formalism, Functionalism and Understanding' at nn. 49–56; and D. Baird 'Security Interests Reconsidered' (1994) 80 *Va L Rev* 2249 at 2267–9.

[131] For a discussion of priority principles where there are two charges over a debt rather than two assignments see Smith *Law of Tracing* at p. 359. Even if the rule in *Dearle* v. *Hall* applies in this context – as was held to be the case by the Privy Council in *Colonial Mutual Central Insurance Co. Ltd* v. *ANZ Banking Group* [1995] 1 WLR 1140 – the fact of registration will give the second chargee constructive notice of the earlier charge and thus determine the priority question.

[132] (1828) 3 Russ 1.

[133] See Goode *Commercial Law* at p. 705:

> It is high time that the rule in *Dearle* v. *Hall* was abolished. . . . [It] is quite impracticable when applied to a continuous flow of dealings in receivables involving a substantial number of debtors . . . The rule is effectively displaced where the previous security or assignment is registrable and is duly registered, for the second assignee is then fixed with notice of the previous assignment, and if registration were to be extended to cover all assignments of pure intangibles, whether outright or by way of security, *Dearle* v. *Hall* would de facto become obsolete.

[134] According to Cotton LJ in *Mutual Life Assurance Society* v. *Langley* (1886) 32 Ch D 460 at 468: 'It is not a question of what a man knows, when he does that which will better or perfect his security, but what he knows at the time when he took his security and paid his money.'

[135] J. De Lacy, however, argues in 'Reflections on the Ambit of the Rule in *Dearle* v. *Hall* and the Priority of Personal Property Assignments – 1' (1999) 28 *Anglo-American Law Review* 87 at 130 that

> the courts should now reject the existence of the second limb to the rule in *Dearle* v. *Hall*. There is neither principle, nor substantive precedent, in the way of acting on this conclusion. Although it is possible that a court of first instance might not find this recommendation at all palatable, given the long history of the second limb, the Appeal Courts should not entertain similar reservations. In future *Dearle* v. *Hall* should be confined to a simple priority rule according to the dates upon which notice of assignments is received by a fund holder.

'carry the same security repeatedly into the market' and thereby to induce 'third persons to advance money upon it in the erroneous belief that it continues to belong to him absolutely, free from encumbrance'. The rule has been widely condemned as an unsatisfactory determinant of priorities in the context of receivables financing.[136] Non-notification factoring is quite common and the priority principle in *Dearle* v. *Hall* works to the disadvantage of this form of business arrangement. Moreover, the rule transforms notice of the assignment to the debtor into a priority point, but the debtor is not a publicly commissioned official charged with the task of receiving and tracking notices.[137] It may be argued that requiring notice to be filed in a public register is a more logically coherent way of sorting out priorities.[138] Determining the rank of assignments according to the order in which each is publicised by registration would enable the later assignees to work out more efficiently a fair purchase price for the receivables, or the legal and operational risks of the transaction, as the case may be.

Complexities in the Article 9 treatment of receivables and criticism thereof

The first criticism of the Article 9 treatment of receivables centres on the fact that the provision does not set out rules for distinguishing between straightforward sales of receivables and security transfers. As we have seen, the sale/security distinction continues to be of fundamental importance in many contexts in the US, not least bankruptcy. If anything, the advent of new financing techniques such as securitisation have accentuated the importance of the distinction. In a securitisation the originator

---

[136] See the report of the Crowther Committee on Consumer Credit (1971) Cmnd. 4596, vol. 2 at p. 579; J. Ziegel 'The Legal Problems of Wholesale Financing of Durable Goods in Canada' (1963) 41 *Canadian Bar Review* 54 at 109–10; R. Goode 'The Right to Trace and its Impact in Commercial Transactions – 11' (1976) 92 *LQR* 528 at 566; F. Oditah 'Priorities: Equitable versus Legal Assignments of Book Debts' (1989) 9 *OJLS* 521 at 525–7.

[137] Oditah 'Priorities' at 525–7 advances eight considerations in support of the proposition that the rule is harsh, hard to justify and decidedly inconvenient.

[138] J. De Lacy comments in 'Reflections on the Ambit of the Rule in *Dearle* v. *Hall* and the Priority of Personal Property Assignments – 11' (1999) 28 *Anglo-American Law Review* 197 at 214 that

> the rule in *Dearle* v. *Hall* is no longer suitable to meet the requirements of information and priority in an efficient or satisfactory manner. The only effective solution to this problem is to replace the fundholder with a centralised public register onto which information regarding assignments could be stored. This would solve the problem relating to the quality and objectivity of a fundholder that, at present, besets the operation of the rule. The establishment of a centralised register should also be coupled with a priority rule according to the date that assignments are registered. This would produce a simple and readily ascertainable priority point free of any issue relating to the doctrine of notice.

transfers receivables to a separate legal entity – referred to as a special-purchase vehicle (SPV). The SPV raises the finance to pay for the transferred receivables by itself issuing bonds to investors. The marketability and price paid for the bonds depends on the investors' assessment of the value of the transferred assets and also on the degree of legal and other risk attached to the transaction. To ensure the marketability of the bonds it is important to ensure that the SPV is bankruptcy-remote, i.e. that the bankruptcy of the originator does not impinge on the investors. Securitisation is said to reduce the net financing costs for the business by eliminating the risk of bankruptcy to the bankruptcy-remote entity's investors. As Professor Schwarcz points out:[139]

> Because the SPV (and no longer the originator) owns the assets, their investment decision often can be made without concern for the originator's financial condition. Thus, viable companies that otherwise cannot obtain financing because of a weakened financial condition now can do so. Even companies that otherwise could obtain financing now will be able to obtain lower-cost capital market financing.

The success of any securitisation operation depends partly on achieving a true sale of the accounts, and this requires the originator to limit or to forgo any residual beneficial interest in the receivables. The legal opinions on this 'true-sale' issue in a securitisation are likely to be detailed and complex and Article 9 has not simplified the process of determination.

Secondly, Article 9 is complex in its individualisation and categorisation of collateral. One could say that, by maintaining a separate category of collateral in 'chattel paper', Article 9 is more complex than the present English position. Moreover, the revision of Article 9 has added to this complexity by increasing the categories of collateral. Also, while the revised Article 9 broadens the definition of 'account' so as to include many rights to payment other than for services provided or goods sold or leased, there are still many payment rights that fall outside the definition of 'account'. 'General intangible' is the residual category of personal property and is defined to mean any personal property but excluding various things such as accounts, chattel paper, deposit accounts etc.[140] A 'payment intangible' is defined as a general intangible under which the account debtor's principal obligation is a monetary obligation. Subject to specified exclusions Article 9 applies to a sale of accounts, chattel paper,

---

[139] S. Schwarcz 'The Impact on Securitization of Revised UCC Article 9' (1999) 74 *Chicago-Kent L Rev* 947 at 948; and for a general discussion of this whole area see the symposium on Cross-Border Securitisation and Structured Finance in (1998) 8 *Duke Journal of Comparative and International Law*.

[140] Article 9-102.

payment intangibles or promissory notes but, depending on the nature of the collateral, slightly different rules operate. For instance, according to Article 9-309, certain security interests are automatically perfected upon attachment, including the sale of a payment intangible. In other words, no filing is required to perfect the sale of a payment intangible.[141] The automatic-perfection provision was included to avoid causing any disruption in the market for loan participations, which is a very intense, high-volume business.[142] Loan participations are created when the originator of a loan sells part of it, i.e. an undivided interest in the loan and any security given in respect of the loan to a third party, which would normally be another financial institution. The loan-participation business is a way in which banks may reduce their exposure to particular borrowers or get loans off their balance sheet for capital-adequacy purposes. In some instances, however, the distinction between a 'general intangible' and other types of payment right may not be entirely clear-cut. As the Article 9 reporters, Harris and Mooney, point out:[143]

In some cases, doubt may arise concerning whether the collateral is a payment intangible or an account or, if the collateral is a payment intangible, whether the transaction is a sale or an assignment that secures an obligation. The parties most likely to engage in the assignment of rights to payment are likely to be sophisticated and to file in doubtful cases. By doing so, for very little cost they can protect against the possibility that the collateral is an account or that the transaction is the assignment of a payment intangible to secure an obligation.

Thirdly, it should also be noted that the rules governing default and enforcement in Part 6 of Article 9 do not apply to buyers of accounts. In a sense, the equation of outright sales and security transfers that appears to have been effected by Article 9 suggests more than it actually delivers. While, in the main, the perfection and priority rules of Article 9 apply to outright sales, the enforcement rules of Article 9 do not.

Conclusion

It is strongly arguable that Article 9 contains provisions that represent an improvement on the present English position. For example, the article

---

[141] See generally S. L. Harris and C. W. Mooney 'The Article 9 Study Committee Report: Strong Signals and Hard Choices' (1993) 29 *Idaho LR* 561 at 571–2; S. L. Harris and C. W. Mooney 'How Successful was the Revision of UCC Article 9?: Reflections of the Reporters' (1999) 74 *Chicago-Kent L Rev* 1357 at 1369–73.

[142] For an explanation of the provision see Bjerre 'Secured Transactions Inside Out' at 392, who suggests that the imposition of a filing requirement would impose a large and needless burden on the loan-participation market.

[143] 'Reflections' at 1372–3.

clarifies and makes explicit rules governing the effect of assignment on the account debtor and third parties that arguably are implicit in England. Moreover, in making priorities between competing assignments of the same debt turn on the first assignee to file notice of the assignment, it may be that Article 9 contains a clearer and more logically coherent rule for determining priorities than the first-to-give-notice-to-the-debtor principle encapsulated in English law. The Law Commission in their consultation paper on *Registration of Security Interests* followed the broad contours of the Article 9 approach, though without addressing some of the details. The Law Commission recommended that sales of receivables, for example under a factoring or block-discounting agreement or as part of a securitisation, should be registrable but that there should be an exception to the requirement to register when book debts are sold as part of a larger transaction such as the overall sale of the business.[144] The overall approach of Article 9 is to prefer substance over form, reflecting commercial reality. On the other hand, in apparently assimilating the treatment of outright sales and security transfers of receivables, it may be that Article 9 goes more to obscure reality rather than to reflect it. Far from being obliterated, the distinction remains of profound significance, particularly in the settings of bankruptcy and securitisation.

[144] Law Commission *Registration of Security Interests* para. 7.45.

8   Security interests in deposit accounts, investment property and insurance policies

The revised Article 9 makes it possible to create an Article 9 security interest in deposit accounts as original collateral. The revision to Article 9 followed a long debate. At about the same time, across the Atlantic, the House of Lords in *Re BCCI (No. 8)* also addressed the issue of security interests in deposit accounts, holding that there was no conceptual barrier at common law to the creation of such an interest. Equally the decision of the House of Lords followed a long period of debate. What is remarkable is that the debate proceeded on each side of the Atlantic almost oblivious to what was happening on the other side. This chapter attempts partly to repair the omission. It also addresses the issue of security interests in investment property and insurance policies where the legislative response to the issue of registration requirements has followed a similarly pragmatic path.

Security interests over deposit accounts in England

In *Re BCCI (No. 8)* the House of Lords upheld the legal effectiveness of 'charge-backs'.[1] In other words, the court held that it is possible for a debtor to take a charge over its own indebtedness to a creditor as security for the discharge of some reciprocal obligation, for example, there is no conceptual impossibility in a bank having a charge over a cash deposit made with it by a customer that serves as security for a loan advanced to the customer. In reaching this conclusion the House of Lords rejected the conceptual impossibility argument that had found favour with the Court of Appeal in *Re BCCI (No. 8)*[2] and also with Millett J in

---

[1] [1998] AC 214. See generally G. McCormack 'Charge Books and Commercial Certainty in the House of Lords' [1998] *Company, Financial and Insolvency Law Review* 111.

[2] The Court of Appeal decision is variously reported as *Morris* v. *Agrichemicals Ltd* [1996] BCC 204 and *Re Bank of Credit and Commerce International SA (No. 8)* [1996] Ch 245; [1996] 2 WLR 631; [1996] 2 All ER 121. For commentary on the case see Richard Millett 'Liquidation Set-Off: The Mutuality Principle and Security over Bank Balances' (1996) 112 *LQR* 524; and A. Berg 'Pleasing Paradoxes' [1996] *LMCLQ* 177.

Re Charge Card Services Ltd.[3] Reciprocal indebtedness of this kind is a feature of many commercial transactions, and the House of Lords decision has been welcomed by many in the commercial community as removing uncertainty and facilitating a form of transaction that is seen as highly beneficial, notwithstanding the probable availability of efficacious, legally acceptable alternatives. These alternatives encompass contractual rights of set-off[4] and making the deposit a 'flawed asset' which the depositor or third parties standing in the shoes of the depositor are not at liberty to withdraw.

These alternatives were accepted by Millett J in *Re Charge Card Services*,[5] the leading English decision prior to *Re BCCI (No. 8)*, but, at the same time, the judge denied that a charge could be created in a situation of reciprocal indebtedness. Millett J said:

It is true . . . that no conveyance or assignment is involved in the creation of an equitable charge, but in my judgment the benefit of a debt can no more be appropriated or made available to the debtor than it can be conveyed or assigned to him. The objection to a charge in these circumstances is not to the process by which it is created, but to the result. A debt is a chose in action, it is the right to sue the debtor. This can be assigned or made available to a third party, but not to the debtor, who cannot sue himself. Once any assignment or appropriation to the debtor becomes unconditional, the debt is wholly or partially released. The debtor cannot and does not need to, resort to the creditor's claim against him in order to obtain the benefit of the security; his own liability to the creditor is automatically discharged or reduced.

The judge also said:[6]

It does not, of course, follow that an attempt to create an express mortgage or charge of a debt in favour of the debtor would be ineffective to create a security. Equity looks to the substance not the form, and while in my judgment this would not create a mortgage or charge, it would no doubt give a right of set off which would be effective against the creditor's liquidator or trustee in bankruptcy.

---

[3] [1987] Ch 150. This case has generated an enormous literature. For discussion of the case see generally R. Goode *Legal Problems of Credit and Security* (Sweet & Maxwell, 2nd edn. 1988) at pp. 124–9. See also W. Blair *Butterworths' Banking and Financial Law Review 1987* (Butterworths, 1987) at pp. 173–6; F. Neate [1981] *Int Bus Lawyer* 247; D. Pollard [1988] *JBL* 127 and 219; T. Shea [1986] 3 *JIBL* 192; P. Wood 'Three Problems of Set-Off' (1987) 8 *Co Law* 262.

[4] In other words, the secured party would have the right to apply the balance of the account towards the discharge of the secured obligations. The overall effect of a charge-back, a set-off and a flawed asset arrangement operating in tandem is referred to as a 'triple cocktail'.

[5] [1987] Ch 150 at 176. Reference is made to the definition of an equitable charge given by Atkin LJ in *National Provincial and Union Bank of England* v. *Charnley* [1924] 1 KB 431 at 449.

[6] [1987] Ch 150 at 177.

The *Charge Card* holding that there can be no charge in favour of oneself of one's own indebtedness to another has been subjected to strong criticism, particularly those arguing the toss from the point of view of the banking community. The anti-*Charge Card* contingent argue that in some cases rights of set-off may not be available, such as with respect to a purely contingent liability and, in any event, a charge-back of the debt may be desirable to improve the priority of the set-off against assignees, garnishers, undisclosed principals and the like.[7] The legal objections to *Charge Card* could be summarised as follows:[8]

(1) In one category of cases the protection afforded to a counterparty by set-off as judicially recognised and validated in *Charge Card* requires complex contractual provisions which may be either unnecessarily cumbersome or which are not feasible in the commercial world.

(2) In the second set of cases, set-off may be prohibited or legally risky.

Moreover, on the conceptual level, it is claimed that the property in the deposit is held by the customer as the beneficial owner, and the depositor may create security rights over this property in favour of anybody as over its other property.[9] The Court of Appeal in *Re BCCI (No. 8)* was very conscious of practical realities and the criticisms of *Charge Card*. The court said:[10]

It is important that . . . routine financing arrangements should not be put at risk. If the reasoning in *Re Charge Card Services Ltd* led to the conclusion that charge-backs were invalid or ineffective to give security in the event of the chargor's insolvency, then that reasoning would be suspect and if it could not be faulted then we would be willing to sacrifice doctrinal purity on the altar of commercial necessity. But we are satisfied that neither conclusion would be justified.

In other words, the court was prepared to dismiss as of no practical significance the fact that a charge-back cannot confer rights of property on the chargee because a chargee has powerful rights and remedies under a charge-back through the contractual set-off and flawed asset techniques. The Court of Appeal decision[11] led to a practice recommendation by the Financial Law Panel and a strengthening of resolve that the existing legal dispensation could be made to work satisfactorily without the need for

---

[7] See Wood 'Three Problems of Set-Off' at 266. Wood also argued that the methods of getting around *Re Charge Card Ltd* are sometimes commercially or legally unattractive; sometimes they are vitiated for regulatory or tax reasons; always they are a nuisance. Moreover, he suggests that there is no reason why the law should insist that business should adopt these contrivances when there is a perfectly acceptable alternative: see *ibid.* at 269.

[8] Final Report of the Legal Risk Review Committee at p. 42.

[9] See Blair *Banking and Financial Law Review* at pp. 173–4.

[10] [1996] BCC 204 at 214.   [11] [1996] 2 All ER 121; [1996] BCC 204.

legislative interventions.[12] The supplemental recommendation read as follows:

1. The use of a charge-back will be effective to confer on the chargee security over cash deposited with it, or otherwise over indebtedness which it owes.
2. Appropriate restrictions should be included in the charge document to regulate the terms on which the deposit will be held and will become repayable. Although basic restrictions and contingencies may be implied merely by the use of the term 'charge-back' or 'charge' to describe the contract between the depositor and the lender, it will almost always be preferable to set them out expressly.

Notwithstanding the element of practical reassurance introduced by the Court of Appeal in *Re BCCI (No. 8)*, the views of the court on charge-backs were rejected when the case went on appeal to the House of Lords. Lord Hoffmann, who spoke for a unanimous House of Lords, categorically rejected the proposition that it was conceptually impossible to create a charge in circumstances of reciprocal indebtedness.[13] His reasons for arriving at this decision may be summarised thus:

1. The doctrine appeared to date from the judgment of Millett J in *Re Charge Card Services Ltd.*[14] The Legal Risk Review Committee had expressed disquiet about this ruling as a potential cause of obscurity and uncertainty in the law affecting financial markets.[15]
2. Documents purporting to create charge-backs have been used by banks for many years.
3. In many nineteenth-century cases the possibility of a charge over a debt owed by the chargee caused no judicial surprise.
4. The depositor's right to claim payment of his deposit is a chose in action which the law has always recognised as property. A charge over such a chose in action could validly be granted to a third party. A charge is a security interest created without any transfer of title or possession to the beneficiary. The fact that the beneficiary of the charge was the debtor himself was not inconsistent with the transaction having some or all of the traditional features of a charge. It would be a proprietary interest because subject to questions of registration and purchaser for value without notice it would be binding upon assignees and a liquidator or trustee in bankruptcy. The depositor would retain

---

[12] Financial Law Panel *Security over Cash Deposits: A Supplemental Practice Recommendation* (March 1996).
[13] [1998] AC 214 at 225–8.   [14] [1987] Ch 150.
[15] The Legal Risk Review Committee was appointed by the Governor of the Bank of England in April 1991 to ascertain the correct approach in tackling legal uncertainties that affected the UK's wholesale financial markets. The committee was chaired by Lord Alexander of Weedon, chairman of NatWest Bank and former practising QC.

an equity of redemption. There would be no merger of interests. The depositor would retain title to the deposit subject only to the bank's charge.[16]

5. A bank could obtain effective security in other ways, such as contractual rights of set-off or combining accounts where the deposit was made by the principal debtor. Alternatively, it could make the deposit a 'flawed asset' by imposing contractual limitations on the right to withdraw the deposit. Nevertheless, these were not good reasons for preventing banks and their customers from creating charges over deposits if, for reasons of their own, they wanted to do so.

6. Legislation reversing the effect of *Charge Card* had been passed in many offshore banking jurisdictions such as Hong Kong, Singapore and the Cayman Islands.[17] In none of these jurisdictions did the statutes amend or repeal any rule of common law which would be inconsistent with the existence of a charge over a debt owed by the charge holder. The legislation simply said that such a charge could be created. If legislative simplicity of this kind was possible then it was difficult, if not impossible, to detect conceptual impossibility.

7. The law should be slow to declare a practice of the commercial community to be commercially impossible given the fact that the law was fashioned to suit the practicalities of life.

Registration of charges over cash deposits

It is not entirely clear whether charges over cash deposits created by companies require registration under Part 12 Companies Act 1985.[18] Lord Hoffmann said on this issue in *Re BCCI (No. 8)*:[19]

There is a suggestion in the judgment of the Court of Appeal that the banking community has been insufficiently grateful for being spared the necessity of registering such charges. In my view, this is a matter on which banks are entitled to make up their own minds and take their own advice on whether the deposit charged is a 'book debt' or not.

---

[16] The House of Lords considered that there was a slight difference between charge-backs and other charges in the manner of enforcement of the charge. According to Lord Hoffmann ([1998] AC 214 at 226–7), 'the method by which the property would be realised would differ slightly: instead of the beneficiary of the charge having to claim payment from the debtor, the realisation would take the form of a book entry'.

[17] The Singapore legislation – now section 13 Civil Law Act – declares that it is possible, and always has been possible, for an obligor under a chose in action to take a mortgage or charge over that chose in action. Cap. 43, 1994 Rev. Ed. Sing. p. 265 n55.

[18] See the comments by Sir Peter Millett at (1991) 107 *LQR* 679, reviewing Dr Fidelis Oditah's work *Legal Aspects of Receivables Financing* (Sweet & Maxwell, 1991).

[19] [1998] AC 214 at 227.

Reference was made by Lord Hoffmann to the judgment of Lord Hutton in the Northern Ireland Court of Appeal in *Northern Bank Ltd* v. *Ross*[20] which suggests that, in the case of deposits with banks, an obligation to register is unlikely to arise. Lord Hoffmann could equally have invoked his own observations in *Re Brightlife Ltd*,[21] which in fact formed the cornerstone of the decision in *Northern Bank Ltd* v. *Ross*.

In *Re Brightlife Ltd*[22] Hoffmann J, as he then was, made the point that the relationship between banker and customer was one of debtor and creditor so that it would not be legally inaccurate to describe a credit balance with a banker as a debt. It would not be normal usage, however, for an accountant or businessperson to describe a bank account in credit as a debt. Instead, it would be referred to as 'cash at bank'. It should be noted, however, that Hoffmann J's decision that the expression 'debts' in one commercial debenture did not capture a bank account in credit is not conclusive as to the meaning of the phrase 'book debts' in the companies legislation. In particular, the wording in the debenture was inappropriate to cover credit balances. The chargor was prohibited from dealing with its 'books or other debts' without the prior consent in writing of the charge holder 'otherwise than in the ordinary course of getting in and realising the same'. A credit balance at the bank could not sensibly be 'got in' or 'realised'.

In *Northern Bank Ltd* v. *Ross*[23] the question arose whether a sum of money paid into an account with Allied Irish Banks by the company before it went into liquidation was subject to a fixed charge over 'all book debts and other debts' previously executed by the company in favour of Northern Bank. Lord Hutton LCJ decided that 'cash at bank' was excluded from the expression 'book debts and other debts' and that 'cash at bank' meant money in a bank account whether or not the account was used as a trading account. There were three pillars to this conclusion. Firstly, the wording of the specific debenture which referred to getting in or realising the debts; secondly, business and accountancy practice; and thirdly, Hoffmann J's observations in *Re Brightlife Ltd* and two poorly reported earlier cases. One of these cases is *Re Stevens*,[24] where North J held that the balance at the bankers of a firm did not come within the term 'book debts'.

---

[20] [1990] BCC 883.   [21] [1987] Ch 200.   [22] *Ibid.* at 209.

[23] [1990] BCC 883. The first-instance judge had drawn a distinction between a trading account and a so-called special account, and held that cash deposited in a special account came within the expression 'book debts and other debts'.

[24] [1888] WN 110 and 116. The second case, even more obscure, is referred to in *Dawson* v. *Isle* [1906] 1 Ch 633.

It should be remembered that again *Northern Bank Ltd* v. *Ross* is tailored to the wording of a particular debenture and does not purport to provide a definitive interpretation of the phrase 'book debts' as used in the company-charge legislation. In this connection, it should be noted that in *Re Permanent Houses (Holdings) Ltd* [25] Hoffmann J took the opportunity to say that *Re Brightlife Ltd* did not decide that a credit balance at a bank could not in any context be a 'book debt' or 'other debt'. No opinion was expressed on whether a credit balance was a 'book debt' for the purposes of the company-charge-registration system. [26]

The potential registration problems are even more acute where the cash deposit is made with an institution or person other than a bank. The example has been given of a situation where a client pays a margin deposit to his broker or to a clearing house in a securities or financial market to cover price swings, and his broker or clearing house becomes a debtor to the client in respect of the margin deposit. [27] Is the margin deposit made by a corporate customer registrable as a charge over book debts? The same question arises with a factor's right of retention, which question involves a reconsideration of *Re Charge Card Services Ltd*. [28] In that case Millett J said that if the right of retention constitutes a charge, there was no doubt that it was a charge on book debts and so registrable. His reasons for concluding that the right of retention did not constitute a charge were twofold. Firstly, there was the conceptual impossibility argument, i.e. that it was logically impossible to have a charge in favour of X over a debt owed by X. Secondly, however, he took the view that there was no relevant property capable of forming the subject matter of a charge. The only asset which the company could charge was its chose in action, i.e. the right to sue the factor for the sum due under the agreement, but this already contained within it the liability to suffer a retention. Under standard condition 3B of the factoring agreement the factor was to remit

---

[25] [1988] BCLC 563 at 566–7.
[26] See also *M. O'Donnell & Sons (Huddersfield) Ltd* v. *Midland Bank plc* 2001 WL 1676963 where it was held that a sum arising from the sale of all the company's assets was not a 'book debt' but came within the expression 'other debts' as used in a bank debenture. The Court of Appeal applied the general principles of interpretation set out by the House of Lords in *Investors Compensation Scheme Ltd* v. *West Bromwich Building Society* [1998] 1 WLR 896 that interpretation is the ascertainment of the meaning that the document would convey to a reasonable person having all the background knowledge which would reasonably have been available to the parties in the situation in which they were at the time of the contract. The background included absolutely anything that would have affected the way in which the language of the document would have been understood by a reasonable man.
[27] See Philip Wood *Comparative Law of Security and Guarantees* (Sweet & Maxwell, 1995) at p. 50.
[28] [1987] Ch 150 at 175.

to the company or its order any balance for the time being standing to the credit of the current account less any amount which the factor in its absolute discretion decided to retain as security for, *inter alia*, any claims or defences against the company or any risk of non-payment by a debtor.

The consequences of non-registration from the point of view of the chargee are draconian. An unregistered but registrable charge is void, and the charge holder deprived of secured status, if the company granting the charge goes into liquidation. In the circumstances the only safe advice would appear to be to submit details of the charge-back to the registrar of companies for registration. In this way the sanction of voidness is avoided if the charge is in fact held to be registrable and the corporate customer goes into liquidation. Under Part 12 Companies Act 1985 avoidance consequences are eliminated if prescribed particulars of a registered charge were in fact delivered for registration within twenty-one days of the date of creation of the charge irrespective of whether the registrar declined to register the particulars.[29] In fact, the policy of the registrar over accepting for registration details of purported charge-backs to the debtor has vacillated considerably.[30] At the moment it seems that registration will not be rejected merely because the chargee is a bank with which the credit balance is held. This is part of a more general policy to accept details of charges over credit balances for registration notwithstanding the hesitation over registrability manifested by Hoffmann J in *Re Brightlife Ltd.*

The Legal Risk Review Committee, while recommending that *Re Charge Card Services Ltd* should be reversed by statute, also argued that charge-backs of bank deposits should not become registrable. There were three grounds for this contention. Firstly, charge-backs usually mirror the effect of a set-off, and the latter did not require registration. Secondly, other creditors would not be caught by surprise if bank deposits were subject to a secret lien. Finally, registration of charges over quickly moving transactions and ephemeral or evanescent assets made registration too burdensome and also impeded commercial activity.[31] In the *Review of Security Interests in Property* conducted by Professor Diamond for the Department of Trade and Industry it was argued similarly that charges over cash deposits should not require registration. Diamond reasoned that prospective creditors of a company are not misled by the absence of any public acknowledgement of charges over bank balances. Bank accounts were generally conducted in secrecy and the amount a company was in credit was not visible to an outside creditor. In many cases the assumption

---

[29] *NV Slavenburg's Bank* v. *Intercontinental Natural Resources Ltd* [1980] 1 WLR 1076.
[30] See generally Goode *Legal Problems* at pp. 130–1.
[31] For an analysis of the Legal Risk Review Committee's report see D. Capper 'Final Report of the Legal Risk Review Committee' (1993) 44 *NILQ* 71.

was that the company, far from being in credit, had an overdraft.[32] Similarly, the Law Commission in the consultation paper *Registration of Security Interests* endorsed the viewpoint that registration of a security interest in a bank account was unnecessary to warn potential secured creditors and was equally unnecessary to warn potential investors.[33]

On the other hand, it has been argued that since intangibles of all types are such an important and growing form of collateral, one should be slow to dispense with registration requirements. Moreover, if there is little difference between charges strictly so-called and rights of set-off, why have banks agitated so vociferously in favour of being able to create charges in such circumstances? It should be noted, however, that security interests in cash deposits are not subject to any filing requirements under the revised Article 9 in the US. Such security interests, to use the language of Article 9, are perfected by control rather than by filing. The US position will now be examined.

Deposit accounts under Article 9 UCC

Prior to the 1998 revision, Article 9 excluded from its ambit original security interests in deposit accounts. While the original drafters of Article 9 recognised the fact that deposit accounts were often used as collateral in financing transactions, they suggested that such transactions 'are often quite special, do not fit easily under a general commercial statute and are adequately covered by existing law'.[34] Nevertheless, the 'old' Article 9 did cover security interests in bank deposits that served as the proceeds of other collateral. The limitation on the application of Article 9 attracted criticism, and the issue of security interests in deposit accounts was considered by the UCC Permanent Editorial Board Study Group. This analysis led to a detailed report, *Use of Deposit Accounts as Original Collateral*,[35] which recommended revision of Article 9 so as to embrace original security interests in deposit accounts. The following reasons were given:[36]

(1) since depositories would retain their rights of set-off, their position would be strengthened, not weakened, by allowing them to hold a security interest;

(2) it would allow depository institutions to avoid the cumbersome and complex set off rules in s. 553 of the United States Bankruptcy Code;

(3) it would avoid mutuality problems for depositories arising out of 'special deposits' and parent/subsidiary relationships;

---

[32] A. Diamond *A Review of Security Interests in Property* (HMSO, 1989) at p. 112.

[33] Law Commission Consultation Paper No. 164 *Registration of Security Interests* (July 2002), at pp. 142–3.

[34] See the Official Comment to the former Article 9-104.

[35] (American Law Institute, 1992).   [36] *Ibid.* at pp. 333–4.

(4) it would avoid mutuality problems where the deposit is in a foreign currency; and

(5) it would give depository institutions stronger priority vis-à-vis federal tax liens.

The recommendations of the Study Group were substantially adopted by the drafters of the revised Article 9. In so far as deposit accounts as original collateral are concerned, the revised Article 9 departs fairly radically from the traditional perfection and priority rules.[37] The only permissible method of perfecting such a security interest is by 'control' rather than by filing. According to Article 9-104 a secured party has control of a deposit account if

(1) the secured party is the bank with which the deposit account is maintained; (2) the debtor, secured party, and bank have agreed in an authenticated record that the bank will comply with instructions originated by the secured party directing disposition of the funds in the deposit account without further consent by the debtor; or (3) the secured party becomes the bank's customer with respect to the deposit account.

Article 9-327 deals with the priority of security interests in deposit accounts and once again reinforces the primacy of control. The basic principle is that a security interest held by a secured party having control of the deposit account has priority over a conflicting security interest held by a secured party that does not have control. The deposit account could represent the proceeds of non-cash collateral over which a security interest has been perfected by filing and which security interest automatically extends into the proceeds. Be that as it may, the secured party having control of the collateral will prevail in any priority conflict. Moreover, a depositary bank with a security interest, in the generality of cases, takes priority over competing security interests in the same deposit account, regardless of whether these other secured parties are relying on the deposit account as original collateral or the proceeds of other collateral.[38]

---

[37] 'Deposit account' is defined in Article 9-102(a)(29) as meaning a 'demand, time, savings, passbook, or similar account maintained with a bank. The term does not include investment property or accounts evidenced by an instrument.'

[38] See the comment by Bruce Markell in 'From Property to Contract and Back: An Examination of Deposit Accounts and Revised Article 9' (1999) 74 *Chicago-Kent L Rev* 963 at 1027:

> Revised Article 9's provisions on deposit accounts do have complexities that bear more than one reading. The more one reads, the more one confirms that these complexities do indeed fit together, and snugly. More often than not, however, the result of these re-readings will confirm what one initially suspected: the depositary bank always wins, or at least starts out the game far ahead. This can be seen not only in rules respecting perfection by and only by, control, but also in the reversal of current law regarding the victor in contests between proceeds claims and offset rights.

The Official Comment rationalises this rule as follows: 'A rule of this kind enables banks to extend credit to their depositors without the need to examine either the public record or their own records to determine whether another party might have a security interest in the deposit account.' A competing secured party could escape from the clutches of this rule by negotiating an express subordination agreement with the depositary bank. This would be effective according to Article 9-339. The second possibility is to take control of the deposit account by becoming the bank's customer in respect of the same. The effect of Article 9-327 is that such an arrangement trumps the bank's security interest. It is also worth pointing out that a transferee of funds from a deposit account takes the funds free of a security interest in the deposit account unless the transferee acts in collusion with the debtor in violating the rights of the secured party.[39]

Notwithstanding this effort to protect the transferee of funds, Article 9 clearly privileges the position of the depositary bank in the secured-transactions game. There are complexities in the provisions, but the depositary bank invariably wins a priority conflict. Moreover, there is no requirement of writing to authenticate a security agreement in favour of a depositary bank. Generally speaking, there are three requirements which must be satisfied before a security interest attaches.[40] Firstly, value must have been given; secondly, the debtor must have rights in the collateral; and thirdly, either the secured party must be granted possession of the items used as collateral or there must be a written security agreement. The third requirement is modified in the case of deposit accounts as original collateral with attachment is deemed to have taken place if 'the secured party has control . . . pursuant to the debtor's security agreement'. Working through the various definitions, a security interest in favour of a bank in the case of a deposit account can arise by oral agreement – or, indeed, by implication, from circumstances. A security agreement is defined simply as 'an agreement that creates or provides for a security interest' while 'agreement' is in turn defined as 'the bargain of the parties in fact as found in their language or by implication from other circumstances including course of dealing or usage of trade or course of performance'. The position of the depositary bank is further strengthened by Articles 9-340 and 9-341. The latter provision entitles the bank to refuse

---

[39] This provision was designed to allay fears expressed by the Federal Reserve Bank of New York that security interests in deposit accounts would impede the free flow of funds through the payment system: see S. L. Harris and C. W. Mooney 'How Successful was the Revision of UCC Article 9?: Reflections of the Reporters' (1999) 74 *Chicago-Kent L Rev* 1357 at 1365.

[40] Article 9-203.

to enter into a control agreement with another potential secured party even if the customer so requests. Moreover, a bank that has made such an agreement is not obliged to disclose the existence of the agreement to another person unless requested so to do by the customer. Article 9-341 preserves the position of the depositary bank under existing banking law, with the bank being entitled to ignore notices from a third party with a security interest, unless it has agreed otherwise in an authenticated record. The bank's rights and duties with respect to the deposit account are not affected at all by (1) the creation, attachment or perfection of a security interest in the deposit account; (2) the bank's knowledge of the security interest; or (3) the bank's receipt of instructions from the secured party.

A fundamental feature underlying the Article 9 rules on deposit accounts is that of 'control'. This concept did not spring unheralded from the head of the drafters of the revised Article 9. Rather, it was borrowed from Article 8 of the UCC on investment securities, which developed the concept in response to the fact that securities were often bought and sold without the transfer of physical possession. In some respects, control over an intangible may be regarded as equivalent to possession of tangible collateral. The functional equivalence of the two concepts having regard to the different types of collateral might justify the absence of any perfection-through-filing requirement in the case of bank accounts. According to the Article 9 reporters, the control-only perfection rule of the revised Article 9 is partly a response to those who argued that it should not be overly easy to acquire a security interest in a deposit account. As far as third parties are concerned, the control-only perfection rule actually makes it more difficult to perfect a security interest in a deposit account as original collateral than under the non-uniform versions of the former Article 9 that were in force in some jurisdictions such as California.[41] The reporters suggest:[42]

For some participants in the drafting process control served as a proxy for the secured party's having relied on the deposit account as collateral when deciding whether and to what extent to extend credit to the debtor. Perhaps more accurately, lack of control served as a proxy for lack of reliance. A secured party who does not even take the steps necessary to enable itself to reach the funds on the debtor's default is unlikely to rely on the deposit account as original collateral in any meaningful way.

---

[41] The matter is discussed by Harris and Mooney 'Reflections' at 1366–7. Californian law provided that perfection was achieved merely by giving written notice of the security interest to the bank at which the deposit account is maintained: California Commercial Code Article 9-302(1)(g)(ii).

[42] Harris and Mooney 'Reflections' at 1366.

The new Article 9 rules have, however, been heavily criticised by Canadian commentators who point out that the depositary bank is given a veto over whether or not the debtor can give a security interest in its bank account.[43] The bank is allowed to play 'dog-in-the-manger' and this state of affairs is considered to be unhealthy. Moreover, the relevant provisions permit what is supposed to be completely anaethema to the general scheme of Article 9: secret security interests. A bank that has a security interest through control over a deposit account is not obliged to inform anybody unless it is requested to do so by its customer. It is argued that the control approach of Article 9 would impose additional requirements and transaction costs for both third-party inquirer and account debtor by obliging someone who proposes to take a security interest in the account to make inquiries as to the bank where the account is held. In general, security interests under Article 9 are registrable in a system that is easily and efficiently accessible. Taking deposit accounts outside this system adds an unnecessary layer of complication to the perfection process, it is argued.

Perhaps the most vehement Canadian critics of the revised Article 9 approach to deposit accounts have been Professors Cuming and Walsh. In a paper for the Canadian Uniform Law Commissioners on the implications of the revised Article 9 for the Canadian Personal Property Security Acts they argue that there is no commercial justification in a Canadian context for giving to deposit-taking institutions a veto over the right of a debtor to grant a security interest in his or her account to someone other than the bank with whom the account is maintained.[44] In their view:

If a bank or credit union wants to have a perfected security interest in an account under which it is an account debtor, it can register a financing statement. The Canadian registry systems are efficient, easily accessible and relied upon by third parties. The control approach of Article 9 would simply add an additional step (and transaction costs for both the inquiring party and the account debtor) by requiring someone who proposes to acquire a security interest in the account to make inquiries from the bank where the account is held. There is no commercial justification for giving a special priority to deposit-taking institutions that are also account debtors. They do not occupy a position equivalent to a purchase money financier. The mere fact that a bank or credit union 'holds' the account in the capacity of an account debtor should not give it a special status superior to that of another security party who has a prior registered security interest in

[43] See, e.g., J. Ziegel 'Canadian Perspectives on the Law Lords' Rejection of the Objection to Charge-Backs' (1999) 14 *Banking and Finance Law Review* 131.

[44] The paper is available on the Canadian Uniform Law Commissioners website: at www.chlc.ca.

the account and should certainly not give priority over the interest of a supplier who has a proceeds purchase money security interest in case proceeds are deposited in the account.

It is somewhat unfortunate that the Law Commission did not refer to these Canadian criticisms when recommending the enactment of provisions in relation to deposit accounts that closely parallel the US Article 9. Under current English law a lender can take a general security interest, i.e. a floating charge, in all the debtor's property including bank accounts held at other lending institutions; but under the new dispensation proposed by the Law Commission this would no longer be possible. The only permissible method of perfecting a security interest in a deposit account would be by 'control', and obtaining the consent of the depositary bank is necessary to obtain 'control' in the sense envisaged by the Law Commission.[45]

Security over shares and other investment property

Where a prospective lender wishes to take a security interest over shares held by the debtor a number of security possibilities present themselves.[46] The first is the pledge, but this can only be used in relation to bearer shares, which are most uncommon in England.[47] The second is the floating charge, which may be – and is – employed with facility and ease. On the other hand, the floating-charge holder is in a weaker priority position than other secured creditors with fixed security interests. For this reason, lenders may wish to take either a legal mortgage or an equitable charge over shares. A legal mortgage is possible only in relation to existing shares whereas an equitable charge may extend over after-acquired shares. With a legal mortgage the lender becomes the legal owner of the shares and is registered as such in the books of the relevant company, and there is a covenant to reconvey the shares to the borrower once the loan is repaid. Lenders, however, may be reluctant to go on the register of members – and this leaves the equitable charge as the alternative security option.

---

[45] See Law Commission *Registration of Security Interests* at para. 5.52: 'We provisionally propose that a charge over a bank account in favour of a party other than the bank itself should also be possible only if the third party takes "control" of the account; and that it too should be exempt from registration.'

[46] See generally, for a brief discussion of the process involved in the taking of security over shares, Richard Calnan 'Taking Security in England' in Michael Bridge and Robert Stevens eds. *Cross-Border Security and Insolvency* (Oxford University Press, 2001) p. 17 at pp. 40–1; and for a discussion of the impact of 'dematerialisation' see Joanna Benjamin *Interests in Securities* (Oxford University Press, 2000); and Jacqueline Lipton *Security over Intangible Property* (LBC Information Services, 2000) at pp. 69–84.

[47] *Harrold v. Plenty* [1901] 2 Ch 314.

The equitable charge, though, can be trumped by subsequent registered holders of the shares who acquire the shares bona fide, for value, and without notice of the earlier equitable interest. Because of the absence of any registration requirement pertaining to shares the status of a bona fide purchaser may be relatively easy to establish. For this reason equitable chargees may wish to obtain possession of the relevant share certificates but, of course, this is not possible where the shares exist in so-called 'dematerialised' or uncertificated form.[48] The securities-settlement system operating in London for dematerialised shares is known as Crest. The mechanics for creating an equitable charge over uncertificated shares are discussed by Dr Joanna Benjamin in her book *Interests in Securities*. Basically, where a Crest member wishes to grant a security interest over uncertificated securities to another Crest member it may do this by transferring the securities to a sub-account known as the escrow balance within its general securities account. As Dr Benjamin explains:[49]

Here the securities are blocked from the control of collateral giver and subject to the control of the collateral taker. The collateral taker may instruct Crest to release the securities back into the general account of the collateral giver (which it will do on discharge of the secured obligation) or alternatively instruct Crest to transfer them to its own account (which it will do on the default of the collateral giver, in order to enforce its security interest). Crest does not monitor whether such enforcement action is authorised under the terms of the collateral agreement.

A fixed charge over a corporate debtor's portfolio of shares does not have to be registered under Part 12 Companies Act 1985 though a similar floating charge, like all floating charges, would have to be registered. The presence or absence of registration requirements has occasionally provoked lively debate, and a security taker runs the risk that what purports to be a fixed charge will be recharacterised as a floating charge and hence require registration.[50] The non-registrability of charges over shares is

---

[48] The practical steps a lender might take to protect itself in this situation are discussed in Lipton *Intangible Property* at pp. 69–84.

[49] *Interests in Securities* at p. 209; and see also J. Coiley 'New Protections for Cross-Border Collateral Arrangements' [2001] *JIBL* 119 at 121.

[50] A Singaporean case in point is *Dresdner Bank* v. *Ho Mun-Tuke Don* [1993] 1 SLR 114. Here as security for financial facilities, a stockbroking company, City Securities, executed letters of hypothecation in favour of various banks charging shares listed in periodical securities to be issued to the banks. There was, however, no actual physical delivery of the shares listed in the periodical certificates to the banks and City Securities dealt with the shares in their trading. The Singapore Court of Appeal held that despite the terms of the letters of hypothecation and the periodical certificates, the freedom which the banks allowed the stockbroking firm to deal with the shares listed in the periodical certificates resulted in the creation of floating charges and not fixed charges. L.P. Thean J said that the shares charged to the banks in the ordinary course of business of the stockbroking

perhaps the most significant gap in the existing registration regime, in that a relatively easy way to circumvent the registration requirements is for a company to transfer its assets to a subsidiary and then to charge the shares in the subsidiary. The loophole was successfully used in *Arthur D. Little* v. *Ableco Finance*[51] where a company purported to create, *inter alia*, a 'first fixed charge' on shares in a subsidiary together with 'distribution rights'. The judge noted that the description of the security was not de-terminative of the issue of categorisation and that the characterisation question was to be resolved by looking at the effect of the terms and pro-visions of the debenture in the light of the circumstances prevailing when the charge was created. The totality of the circumstances indicated that a fixed-charge construction was appropriate. The chargor was not free to dispose of or deal with the shares which were not to be substituted. The judge added that the fact that certain clauses in the lending agreement also charged the 'distribution rights' did not alter the characterisation over the shares as fixed:[52]

The use of the words 'together with' show that the intention of the parties was to include the shares as charged and everything that went with them. What was being charged was the entire bundle of rights making up the shares, including the right to receive dividends and to exploit the shares. True it is . . . that the 'distribution rights' are merely ancillary to and a composite part of the bundle of rights making up the shares so that it is not possible to sever these rights from the shares.

The court was unperturbed by the fact that, after the granting of the charge, the company continued to have the right to receive dividends. That mere fact did not render the charge over the shares and all the ancillary rights thereto a floating charge. An analogy was drawn with a charge over land, and as Nichols LJ remarked in *Re Atlantic Computer Systems plc*:[53] 'A mortgage of land does not become a floating charge by reason of a mortgagor being permitted to remain in possession and enjoy the fruits of the property charged from time to time.' Reference was also made to the observations of Lord Millett in the *Brumark* case that a fixed charge could allow the security taker to exploit the characteristics inherent in the nature of the asset itself.[54]

---

firm changed from time to time, and, until some steps were taken by the banks to enforce the charges, the stockbrokers were at liberty to carry on business in the ordinary way as far as concerned the shares charged. In essence, the security giver and not the security taker had control over the assets in question. See on this point the later comments of Millett LJ in *Re Coslett (Contractors) Ltd* [1998] Ch 495 at 510.
[51] [2002] 3 WLR 1387.   [52] *Ibid.* at para. 31.
[53] [1992] Ch 505 at 534.   [54] [2001] 2 AC 710 at 727.

Reforming registration requirements with respect to shares

There have been various suggestions over the years that the loophole should be plugged.[55] As the Law Commission has pointed out, the Jenkins Committee on Company Law Reform, which reported in 1962, considered that charges on shares in a subsidiary should become registrable.[56] Jenkins adopted the analogy of a company carrying on business through branches. If the company raised a loan on the security of assets used by one of the branches then the charge was registrable, whereas if a company conducted business through subsidiary companies, charges on shares in the subsidiaries were not registrable. This analogy was, however, not accepted by the Diamond report[57] or by Parliament when considering the provisions that became Part 4 Companies Act 1989. At that time an amendment to the legislation was rejected that would have made registrable charges on shares in subsidiaries.[58] The main objection to registration raised in the Diamond report rests on the fact that a company's portfolio of shares may be changing all the time. If each purchase or sale of shares were accompanied by an obligation to file details of a charge thereon, or to file a memorandum of satisfaction, as the case may be, a great deal of paperwork would be generated[59] and lenders might become reluctant to accept shares as security.[60] One commentator has concluded that, if expediency is to be preferred over general principles, then Diamond is probably correct in his assessment, but it does seem somewhat anomalous to exclude a common and often major asset from public disclosure.[61]

Moreover, in Australia, section 262(1)(g) Corporations Act 2001 makes registrable a charge on a marketable security, not being (i) a charge created in whole or in part by the deposit of a document of title to the marketable security or (ii) a mortgage under which the marketable security is registered in the name of the chargee or a person nominated by the chargee. The Diamond report commented, however, that the Australian

---

[55] For an example of such plugging see section 131(3) Singapore Companies Act. Cap. 150, 2000 Rev. Ed. Sing

[56] Cmnd 1749, para. 301.   [57] *A Review of Security Interests in Property* at pp. 115–18.

[58] HL debates vol. 504, cols. 121–3 (14 February 1989).

[59] Diamond report at p. 117.

[60] Diamond also considered that it was inadvisable to make registrable charges on shares in subsidiaries but not on other shares, because of the risk that a searcher might be misled into thinking that there is no such charge, whereas the reality is that the charge was created before the relationship of holding and subsidiary company existed. Further, there were difficulties for a charge holder in determining whether a particular company was a subsidiary: see generally on these points *ibid.* at pp. 116–17.

[61] See M. Lawson 'The Reform of the Law Relating to Security Interests in Property' [1989] *JBL* 287 at 303.

exclusions would probably exclude the vast majority of charges on shares in England.[62] The first exclusion is the equivalent of a pledge or deposit of negotiable instruments or documents of title to goods. The second exclusion seems premised on the assumption that there is no fear of persons being misled as to the creditworthiness of the person creating the charge since that person no longer appears as the registered owner of the shares.

Under a notice-filing system the reasons traditionally given for excluding shares from the category of registrable securities no longer seem to be valid. By virtue of a single filing, it would be possible to create a valid security interest fully enforceable against third parties over a changing portfolio of shares. Nevertheless, the Law Commission in the consultation paper *Registration of Security Interests* did not recommend the extension of the notice-filing system to shares. In its view, there were good reasons of principle for making registration of charges over shares and investment securities unnecessary under a notice-filing regime. In arriving at this conclusion the Law Commission referred back to the public-notice function that the registration system was designed to serve. The rationale disappeared where relevant information was readily available elsewhere. Consequently, the register need not duplicate information from other sources or warn about securities that would be obvious to third parties. The Law Commission stated:[63]

A mortgage or charge over shares may be created by a simple agreement, but in practice the mortgagee or chargee will wish to protect the security interest against third parties. There are two ways of what amounts to perfecting a charge over shares. One is to take custody of any share certificates, usually together with a transfer form signed in blank by the share owner. The other is to have the shares registered in the name of the mortgagee or chargee . . . In either case, the position will be clear to third party enquirers; and Article 9 treats securities that are under the control of the secured party as perfected, just as it does possessory securities once the collateral is in the possession of the creditor.

The proposals made by the Law Commission depart somewhat, however, from the Article 9 (and indeed Article 8 UCC) framework. Article 9 permits the perfection of security interests over investment property (including shares) by filing as well as 'control', though 'control' is recognised as a superior method of perfection.[64] In other words, a secured

---

[62] See Diamond report at p. 116.   [63] *Registration of Security Interests* at para. 5.24.
[64] For a definition of 'control' see Article 9-106. Control over a securities account is defined in terms of obtaining control over the security entitlement. As the Official Comment explains:

An agreement that provides that (without further consent of the debtor) the securities intermediary or commodity intermediary will honor instructions from the secured party concerning a securities account . . . described as such is sufficient. Such an

party who is perfected by control will have priority over an earlier secured party who is perfected by filing.[65] The approach envisaged by the Law Commission is even more restrictive in that 'control' would be become the sole permissible method of perfecting a security interest in shares and investment securities. In its view, to permit the perfection of such security interests by filing seemed like an unnecessary refinement.[66]

The Law Commission proposals have been severely criticised for their restrictive nature.[67] In effect, lenders are denied recourse to a form of security – namely, the floating charge over shares or a functional equivalent – that is well established under the current law of security interests. The taking of security is forced into a relatively tight straitjacket and this seems to contradict the goals of a new system, which is supposed to be facilitative and enabling. The Law Commission cites the fact that its proposals should be compatible with the EU Financial Collateral Directive[68] but it is submitted that the Collateral Directive does not serve as a justification for the Law Commission's restrictive prescriptions.[69] The Financial Collateral Directive is part of the Financial Services Action Plan[70] and is designed to contribute to the creation and maintenance of more efficient and competitive financial markets in Europe. It contains a number of provisions that may impact on the English law of security interests, and warrants closer examination.

The EU Financial Collateral Directive

The Directive makes provision for the establishment of a Community Regime under which financial instruments (securities) and cash may

> agreement necessarily implies that the intermediary will honor instructions concerning all security entitlements . . . carried in the account and thus affords the secured party control of all the security entitlements.

[65] Article 9-328. The Official Comment explains the rationale of the control-priority rule on the basis that parties who deal in securities never developed a practice of searching the UCC files before conducting securities transactions. The primacy afforded control is designed to take account of the circumstances of the securities markets.

[66] It should be noted too that under Article 9-309(10) security interests in investment property that have been created by a broker or securities intermediary are automatically perfected. The Official Comment explains that this provision is designed to facilitate current secured-financing arrangements for securities firms as well as to provide sufficient flexibility to accommodate new arrangements that develop in the future.

[67] 'A Practitioner's Perspective on Registration of Security Interests', paper by Richard Calnan, partner in Norton Rose, delivered to the QMW conference on the Reform of the Law of Security Interests, 2 September 2002.

[68] Directive 2002/47/EC on financial collateral arrangements, OJL 168 27.06.2002.

[69] The Law Commission recognises (*Registration of Security Interests* para. 5. 31 n. 52) that the Collateral Directive does not seem to preclude registration as an alternative method of perfecting a charge.

[70] COM (1999) 232.

be used as collateral under both security-interest and title-transfer structures.[71] According to the somewhat long-winded preamble this will aid in the 'integration and cost-efficiency of the financial market as well as to the stability of the financial system in the Community, thereby supporting the freedom to provide services and the free movement of capital in the single market in financial services'.[72] The preamble also refers to the need to achieve a balance between market efficiency and the safety of the parties to the arrangement and of third parties. Consequently, the Directive is limited in its application to those financial collateral arrangements that provide for some form of dispossession, i.e. 'the provision of the financial collateral, and where the provision of the financial collateral can be evidenced in writing or in a durable medium, ensuring thereby the traceability of the collateral'.[73] Moreover, member states may exclude the application of the Directive where either the collateral giver or the collateral taker is other than a public authority or financial institution, provided that the other party to the transaction is one of the aforementioned.[74]

Essentially, the Financial Collateral Directive seeks to resolve the main problems affecting cross-border use of collateral in wholesale financial markets. The scale of these transactions is enormous, with one EU estimate being that at the beginning of 2000 the value of collateral-backing transactions in the 'over-the-counter' (OTC) derivatives market amounted to approximately $250,000m. in over 12,000 collateral arrangements.[75] The Directive attempts to create a clear framework that brings about legal certainty in the sphere of collateral. It does this by ensuring that an effective and simple community-wide regime exists for the creation of collateral under both security-interest and title-transfer collateral arrangements. Such title-transfer arrangements are required to be recognised in all member states and freed from the risk of being recharacterised as invalidly created security interests. 'Title transfer' is directive-speak for sale-and-repurchase agreements in respect of securities (or 'repos'). The Directive also seeks to restrict the imposition of

---

[71] For a definition of cash and financial instruments see Directive 2002/47/EC Article 2.

[72] *Ibid.*, para. 3 of the preamble.   [73] *Ibid.*, para. 10 of the preamble.

[74] *Ibid.*, Article 1(3). In other words, member states may limit the application of the Directive to transactions among public authorities and financial institutions. It may be that if member states exercise this option they will restrict significantly the usefulness of the Directive and the degree of harmonisation and simplification achieved by it.

[75] See 'Financial Services: Commission Proposes Simplified EU Legal Framework for Collateral' document of 30 March 2001, available on the EU website: www.europa.eu.int; and for further details contact MARKT-CI@cec.eu.int/.

onerous formalities on either the creation or enforcement of collateral arrangements.[76] According to the Commission:[77]

Collateral takers today must comply with impractical publicity requirements, sometimes dating back many centuries, to ensure that third parties are aware that the assets being provided as collateral would not be generally available in an insolvency situation. In today's fast-moving securities market the application of these rules can be difficult and inconvenient, but failure to comply can result in the invalidity of the collateral.

All this is explained in the preamble,[78] but unfortunately, however, like some other emanations from Brussels,[79] the length of the preamble does not necessarily mean greater clarity and there may be a discordance between the substantive provisions of the Directive and the provisions of the preamble. It is stated in Article 3 that member states shall not require that the creation, validity, perfection, enforceability or admissibility in evidence of a financial collateral arrangement or the provision of financial collateral under a financial collateral arrangement be dependent on the performance of any formal act. But does this provision preclude filing or registration as an alternative method of perfection?[80] If this were the case, perfection, in the words of paragraph 10 of the preamble, would not be made dependent on the performance of any formal act such as the

---

[76] Furthermore, the Directive permits the re-pledging of collateral; provides limited protection of collateral arrangements from some rules of insolvency law that might inhibit the use of top-up or substitute collateral; and endeavours to create legal certainty in respect of book-entry securities by extending the principles enshrined in the Settlement Finality Directive (98/26/EC) so as to determine where such securities are located (place of the relevant intermediary account).

[77] 'Proposed Directive on Financial Collateral Arrangements – Frequently Asked Questions' document of 30 March 2001 at p. 2; available at www.europa.eu.int.

[78] Directive 2002/47/EC paras. 9 and 10 of the preamble.

[79] See the European Insolvency Regulation 1346/2000, OJ 2000 L160/1 where the preamble has been criticised by H. Rajak 'The Harmonisation of Insolvency Proceedings in the European Union' [2000] *CFILR* 180 at 187 in the following terms:

> This preamble . . . is unstructured, overlong and unnecessarily complex. It goes well beyond the generally accepted role of a preamble – to provide a context for the substance of the Regulation and thereby to assist in its interpretation. It will be left to judges to decide which provisions in the preamble are of substantive effect and to be treated as within the body of the Regulation and which are simply precatory and providing a context. With the likelihood that hundreds, possibly thousands of courts in the EC will be required to interpret and apply provisions of this Regulation, the present state of the preamble will be likely to be the cause of growing uncertainty and disharmony.

Professor Rajak adds (at 189) that the provision comes close to contradicting provisions in the body of the Regulation.

[80] The Law Commission seemed to think not: see *Registration of Security Interests* p. 136 n. 52. It may be, however, that the Law Commission had a previous draft of the Directive in mind when framing this comment.

execution of any document in a specific form or in a particular manner, the making of any filing with an official or public body or registration in a public register. Perfection is not dependent on filing; but filing is, nevertheless, one of the ways in which perfection may be achieved, the other way being control. It is not clear, however, whether this is a correct interpretation of the Directive, and the matter will ultimately be solved only by the intervention of the European Court of Justice on an interpretative question.

A second area of doubt concerns the status of the floating charge over securities which, like all floating charges created by companies, is registrable under Part 12 Companies Act 1985. Can this state of affairs continue post-implementation of the Directive? The argument for exempting floating charges over securities from registration requirements goes as follows: – one of the objectives of the Directive is to permit collateral substitution. In other words, substitution of collateral is to be permitted without throwing into doubt the validity of the collateral arrangements or making it subject to 'onerous' formality requirements such as registration.[81] Provision for collateral substitution may mean that the collateral arrangement would be categorised in England as a floating charge[82] though the recharacterisation risk is reduced, if not entirely eliminated, by standard market documentation which provides that the ability of the collateral giver to substitute assets is subject to the consent of the collateral taker.[83] Certainty would only be achieved by disapplying registration requirements from all types of financial collateral. It would be a rather strained and strong reading of the Directive, however, to say that this result is actually prescribed. One of the main concerns of the Directive appears to be to disallow certain provisions of insolvency law, such as the preference-avoidance mechanism contained in section 239 Insolvency Act 1986, that might cast doubt on the provision of top-up collateral and the substitution of collateral.[84] In the words of paragraph 16 of the preamble: 'The intention is merely that the provision of top-up or substitution of financial collateral cannot be questioned on the sole basis

---

[81] See generally D. Turing 'The EU Collateral Directive' [2002] *Financial Regulation International* 4.

[82] See Coiley 'New Protections' at 121–2: 'Collateral providers are also required to register floating charges, and this head of charge would be potentially applicable where the security created is deemed to constitute a floating charge by virtue of a collateral provider's right of substitution.'

[83] As Benjamin explains in *Interests in Securities* at p. 108, substitution provisions are customary but 'if they are so drafted that the collateral taker can withdraw (interests in) securities from the collateral pool without restriction, this may render the security interest a floating charge, particularly in the light of the Court of Appeal judgment in *Re Cosslett (Contractors) Ltd* [1988] Ch.'

[84] Directive 2002/47/EC para. 5 of the preamble and Article 8(3).

that the relevant financial obligations existed before that financial collateral was provided, or that the financial collateral was provided during a prescribed period.'[85]

The Directive, however, does introduce a welcome reform by permitting, to use the jargon of the financial markets, the rehypothecation or repledging of charged assets.[86] In other words, where financial collateral is provided under a traditional security-interest-type collateral arrangement, the 'collateral taker is entitled to exercise a right of use' in relation to the financial collateral. Article 5 lays down that where a collateral taker exercises a right of use, he thereby incurs an obligation to transfer equivalent collateral to replace the original financial collateral. The objective is that this proposal should increase liquidity in the market, with collateral, takers being able to generate income from the reuse of collateral and, consequently, enabled to offer better financing terms to the collateral giver.[87]

Under current English law there are significant legal problems associated with the reuse by the collateral taker of charged assets, and it has been suggested that where B wishes to use the collateral assets it receives from A to collateralise its own exposures to C, the transaction between A and B should be structured as an outright collateral transfer.[88] The legal objection to rehypothecation centres on the principle that 'once a mortgage, always a mortgage and the accompanying principles that there should be no clogs on the equity of redemption and that no side benefits should be provided to the collateral taker'.[89] On the other hand, some

---

[85] For the position under current English law see Benjamin *Interests in Securities* at pp. 92–3, who argues that the provision of top-up or substitute collateral should generally be safe from challenge as an improper preference or a transaction at an undervalue, though the avoidance (subject to validation by the court) of dispositions of property after the commencement of winding-up proceedings under section 127 Insolvency Act 1986 may pose more problems; and see also Turing 'The EU Collateral Directive'.

[86] But only 'if and to the extent that the terms of a security financial collateral arrangement so provide'; see Directive 2002/47/EC Article 5.

[87] See International Swaps and Derivatives Association 'Collateral Arrangements in the European Financial Markets: The Need for Law Reform' (1999) at p. 3.

> Most financial institutions holding collateral in the form of securities in fungible form consider it a commercial imperative that they be able to deal freely with the securities until they are required to re-deliver securities under the collateral arrangement. Freedom to deal would include the freedom to sell, lend or repo the securities or to re-pledge (rehypothecate) them to a third party, subject always to an obligation to return equivalent fungible securities to the collateral provider assuming that it performs its obligations in full. By dealing freely with the securities, the financial institution holding the collateral is able to use it most efficiently, lowering its own costs and therefore the cost of financial services provided to the collateral provider.

[88] See Benjamin *Interests in Securities* at p. 111.

[89] See the classic cases *Noakes* v. *Rice* [1902] AC 24; *Bradley* v. *Carritt* [1903] AC 253; and *Kreglinger* v. *New Patagonia Meat and Cold Storage Co.* [1914] AC 25.

authorities suggest that rehypothecation in the context of the securities markets may be compatible with the 'once a mortgage, always a mortgage' principle. For example, in *Ellis & Co.'s Trustee* v. *Dixon-Johnson* Sargant LJ said:[90]

> It would be absurd to insist on a retransfer of the identical shares mortgaged when other shares of the same nature are available . . . in a case like the present, where the security that has been wrongly disposed of in part by the mortgagees consisted of freely marketable shares which can readily be replaced by others of precisely similar value, there is no necessity for insisting on the restoration of the particular shares charged.

In other common-law jurisdictions the doctrine of clogs and fetters on the equity of redemption has been cut down by judicial decision. Singapore is a case in point. In *Citicorp Investment Bank (Singapore) Ltd* v. *Wee Ah Kee*[91] Yong Pung How CJ said:

> We recognise that innovations in methods of financing have resulted in a wide range of loan and security arrangements. Some of these arrangements tie a lender's return on the money loaned to increases in the value of the secured property or the profits earned on that property. The lender often shares some of the risks in return for sharing some of the benefits. Since such parties are businessmen capable of protecting their own interests, the doctrine of clogs on the equity of redemption should arguably have no application. Indeed, for our part, we accept that there is no compelling reason that commercial parties should not ordinarily be free to seek and pursue their legitimate expectations through flexible and innovative financing schemes. The courts, in such instances, would be most chary and slow in applying the doctrine to interfere with the freedom of contract.

Moreover, the problems with rehypothecation can be circumvented by making use of outright collateral transfers and utilising insolvency set-off. Be that as it may, the consensus of opinion seems to be that law reform permitting hypothecation would assist the competitive position of London as an international financial market.[92] It should be noted that Article 9-207(c) permits the free reuse of collateral by the collateral taker.[93] Implementation of the EU Directive might bring about the same result in terms of English law, though this result is not actually required by the terms of the Directive. Article 5 merely requires that a right to reuse collateral should be available if, and to the extent that, the terms of a security financial collateral arrangement so provide. As one commentator

---

[90] [1924] 2 Ch 451 at 469–71.   [91] [1997] 2 SLR 759 at 770.

[92] See, e.g., Benjamin *Interests in Securities* at p. 118; K. Summe 'The European Union's Collateral Reform Initiatives' (2001) 22 *Co Law* 186.

[93] The Official Comment to the revised Article 9-207 provides a valuable example of how 'repledges' of investment property might work in practice.

has noted,[94] the intention of the directive in this respect appears rather to be to set down a uniform mechanism for the exercise and recognition of rights of reuse in the context of security financial-collateral arrangements by stipulating that:

- where a collateral taker exercises such rights, it comes under an obligation to retransfer equivalent collateral to be held subject to the security agreements;
- collateral retransferred in this fashion is deemed to have been transferred at the time of the original transfer to the collateral taker thereby avoiding the application of insolvency rules that might invalidate transfers occurring during a cut-off period prior to insolvency;
- if collateral is enforced while assets are being reused, the collateral taker's obligations to redeliver equivalent securities may be brought into the reckoning in a close-out netting arrangement.

Security interests over insurance policies

Charges on insurance policies are not registrable under current English law. The leading case is *Paul & Frank Ltd* v. *Discount Bank (Overseas) Ltd*,[95] where a letter of authority authorised the payment of the proceeds of an insurance policy to the defendant and it was contended, unsuccessfully, that this letter amounted to a charge on book debts. There are two bases to the decision. Firstly, Pennycuick J said that, in order to ascertain whether a particular charge constituted a charge on book debts, one had to scrutinise the units of property which formed the subject matter of the charge at the date of its creation and to see whether any of those items represented a book debt. In a situation where the unit of property was the benefit of a contract and, at the date of the charge, the benefit of the contract did not encompass any book debt, the contract was not within the section merely by reason of the fact that it might ultimately result in a book debt. In common parlance, one would not depict as a 'book debt' a right under a contingency contract before the contingency occurs. Secondly, the test for book debts was whether they would be entered in the books of a company as an ordinary principle of accountancy.[96] The accountancy evidence indicated that an insurance policy would not be so entered even after admission of the claim and ascertainment of the amount.

In the Diamond report it was suggested that, subject to an exception wide enough to cover certain policies of marine insurance and other policies on goods, charges on insurance policies should become registrable.[97] Moreover, the grounds advanced for the general recommendation

---

[94] See Coiley 'New Protections' at 122.   [95] [1967] Ch 348.
[96] *Ibid.* at 362.   [97] Diamond report at p. 112.

seem fairly convincing, for, as Diamond points out, a life policy might well be a significant asset and persons dealing with a company might be interested to know whether it had charged the benefit of such a policy. So too with a policy over property. Likewise, the Law Commission saw no reason why charges over insurance policies should be exempt from registration, and suggested that the existing exclusion of insurance policies seemed to be based on political rather than reasoned legal or practical reasons.[98]

In general, security interests over insurance policies are not covered by Article 9. Article 9-109(d)(8) renders the article inapplicable to the transfer of an interest in or an assignment of a claim under a policy on insurance. This does not mean that it is impossible to create security interests or the functional equivalent of the same in insurance policies, but merely that the relevant law is not contained in Article 9. The Article 9 reporters, Professors Harris and Mooney, strove to bring insurance policies within the Article 9 framework but their efforts were frustrated by opposition from within the insurance industry.[99] Insurers wanted to make certain determinations about whom to pay to discharge their obligations under insurance policies and they did not wish to alter or change existing practices in making these determinations. Revised Article 9 narrows the exclusion somewhat by bringing health-care insurance receivables within the scope of the UCC.[100] The inclusion of the latter is intended to facilitate health-care providers such as hospitals in obtaining financing. The latter often finance themselves by assigning to financiers monies owing to them under insurance policies for health-care goods and services provided, and it was felt that bringing health-care insurance within the Article 9 framework would provide a more stable foundation for this form of financing. Nevertheless, the incorporation of health-care insurance within the Article 9 framework is only partial, and in particular Article 9 does not override contractual and legal restrictions with respect to the rights and duties of the account debtor.[101] Consequently, other law, and not Article 9, must be consulted to ascertain to whom an account debtor under a health-care insurance policy must pay before obtaining the discharge of its obligations under an insurance policy.[102]

[98] Law Commission *Registration of Security Interests* paras. 5.38–5.39.
[99] See generally Harris and Mooney 'Reflections' at 1374–6.
[100] See also J. O. Honnold, S. L. Harris and C. W. Mooney *Security Interests in Personal Property: Cases, Problems and Materials* (Foundation Press, 3rd edn. 2001) at p. 342.
[101] Article 9-408(d). Article 9-408 does, however, override restrictions on the assignment of heath-care-insurance receivables.
[102] Article 9-406, which applies generally to the discharge of account debtors, states in para. (i) that the provision does not apply to an assignment of a health-care-insurance receivable.

Conclusion

There are some similarities in the law pertaining to security interests in deposit accounts in England and the US in the wake of the revisions to Article 9. On both sides of the Atlantic, security interests in deposit accounts can be created – even in favour of the deposit-taking body. The relevant authorities in both countries adopted a pragmatic approach and had no truck with the view that such a security interest was a conceptual impossibility. Moreover, there is a corresponding absence of publicity. In the US it is not permissible to perfect such a security interest by filing, but only by control. Thus one of the most basic features of Article 9, at least in its original guise, namely a comprehensive registration obligation, has been set aside. In England, charges on bank accounts appear to be outside the scope of the company-charge-registration system since a bank account in credit is not considered to be a 'book debt' in terms of accountancy practice, even though legally speaking the banker–customer relationship is a debtor–creditor one. In their detailed nuances, however, there are differences between the two systems. In particular, in the US, the depositary bank can veto the grant of a security interest over the deposit account in favour of anybody else. This provision seems to be at variance with a fundamental feature of Article 9, i.e. the facilitation of secured credit, and has no counterpart in England. In this jurisdiction, a person that has a cash account with bank X could create a charge over this account in favour of bank Y without having to seek the permission of bank X. If the customer in the contract providing for security with bank Y continues to have an unfettered right to deal with the account then the charge is a floating charge. If, on the other hand, the customer has to get the permission of bank Y to deal with the account with bank X, then the charge is a fixed charge. Admittedly, the latter situation is somewhat unusual but theoretically possible. The important point is that bank X has no power of veto over the creation of security interests in the account. This is an aspect of the American system and, in my view, an unhealthy one.

On the other hand, there are certain features of the Article 9 scheme in relation to intangible property that warrant serious consideration for incorporation in a reformed English law of security interests. Article 9 permits perfection of a security interest in investment property (including shares) by filing as well as by control, whereas the Law Commission proposals are more restrictive, designating 'control' as the sole permissible method of perfection. 'Control' would equate with the existing methods of taking security over shares save for the fact that a floating charge over shares would no longer be possible, for a floating-charge holder would not be regarded as having 'control'. If the goal of the law is not to put hurdles and hindrances in the way of the creation of security interests then the Article 9 approach would seem to be preferable. Moreover, Article 9-207 permits the reuse by the collateral taker of charged assets, whereas this mechanism is questionable under current English law – though implementation of the reforms contained in the EU Financial Collateral Directive may lead to legislative change.

Article 9 and the current English company-charge-registration provisions are more or less at one, however, in the treatment of security interests over insurance policies. Broadly speaking, security interests in insurance contracts are not subject to filing or registration requirements under Article 9 or under Part 12 Companies Act 1985. The exclusion seems more a result of lobbying from the insurance industry and the maintenance of standard commercial practices than any great conceptual design. All in all, in this whole area of security over intangible property such as deposit accounts, shares and insurance policies, there are more similarities between English law and Article 9 than is first apparent.

Appendix
Article 9 of the Uniform Commercial Code

NATIONAL CONFERENCE OF COMMISSIONERS
ON UNIFORM STATE LAWS

REVISED ARTICLE 9. SECURED TRANSACTIONS
(With Conforming Amendments to Articles 1, 2, 2a, 4, 5, 6, 7, and 8)

WITH 1999 AMENDMENTS TO
§§ 9-102, 9-210, 9-317, 9-323, 9-406, 9-407, 9-408, 9-409, 9-504

APPROVED AND RECOMMENDED FOR ENACTMENT IN ALL
THE STATES
at its
ANNUAL CONFERENCE
MEETING IN ITS ONE-HUNDRED-AND-SEVENTH YEAR
CLEVELAND, OHIO
JULY 24–31, 1998

REVISION OF UNIFORM COMMERCIAL CODE
ARTICLE 9 – SECURED TRANSACTIONS

PART 1 – GENERAL PROVISIONS

SECTION 9-107. CONTROL OF LETTER-OF-CREDIT RIGHT
SECTION 9-108. SUFFICIENCY OF DESCRIPTION

[SUBPART 2. APPLICABILITY OF ARTICLE]

SECTION 9-109. SCOPE
SECTION 9-110. SECURITY INTERESTS ARISING UNDER ARTICLE 2 OR 2A

PART 2 – EFFECTIVENESS OF SECURITY AGREEMENT; ATTACHMENT OF SECURITY INTEREST; RIGHTS OF PARTIES TO SECURITY AGREEMENT

[SUBPART 1. EFFECTIVENESS AND ATTACHMENT]

SECTION 9-201. GENERAL EFFECTIVENESS OF SECURITY AGREEMENT
SECTION 9-202. TITLE TO COLLATERAL IMMATERIAL
SECTION 9-203. ATTACHMENT AND ENFORCEABILITY OF SECURITY INTEREST; PROCEEDS; SUPPORTING OBLIGATIONS; FORMAL REQUISITES
SECTION 9-204. AFTER-ACQUIRED PROPERTY; FUTURE ADVANCES
SECTION 9-205. USE OR DISPOSITION OF COLLATERAL PERMISSIBLE
SECTION 9-206. SECURITY INTEREST ARISING IN PURCHASE OR DELIVERY OF FINANCIAL ASSET

[SUBPART 2. RIGHTS AND DUTIES]

SECTION 9-207. RIGHTS AND DUTIES OF SECURED PARTY HAVING POSSESSION OR CONTROL OF COLLATERAL
SECTION 9-208. ADDITIONAL DUTIES OF SECURED PARTY HAVING CONTROL OF COLLATERAL
SECTION 9-209. DUTIES OF SECURED PARTY IF ACCOUNT DEBTOR HAS BEEN NOTIFIED OF ASSIGNMENT
SECTION 9-210. REQUEST FOR ACCOUNTING; REQUEST REGARDING LIST OF COLLATERAL OR STATEMENT OF ACCOUNT

PART 3 – PERFECTION AND PRIORITY

[SUBPART 1. LAW GOVERNING PERFECTION AND PRIORITY]

[SUBPART 2. PERFECTION]

SECTION 9-316. CONTINUED PERFECTION OF SECURITY INTEREST FOLLOWING CHANGE IN GOVERNING LAW

[SUBPART 3. PRIORITY]

PART 4 – RIGHTS OF THIRD PARTIES

[SUBPART 2. DUTIES AND OPERATION OF FILING OFFICE]

PART 6. DEFAULT

[SUBPART 1. DEFAULT AND ENFORCEMENT OF SECURITY
INTEREST]

REVISION OF UNIFORM COMMERCIAL CODE
ARTICLE 9 - SECURED TRANSACTIONS

PART 1 GENERAL PROVISIONS

[SUBPART 1. SHORT TITLE, DEFINITIONS, AND GENERAL CONCEPTS]

SECTION 9-101. SHORT TITLE.
This article may be cited as Uniform Commercial Code-Secured Transactions.

SECTION 9-102. DEFINITIONS AND INDEX OF DEFINITIONS.

(a) **[Article 9 definitions.]** In this article:
  (1) "Accession" means goods that are physically united with other goods in such a manner that the identity of the original goods is not lost.
  (2) "Account," except as used in "account for," means a right to payment of a monetary obligation, whether or not earned by performance, (i) for property that has been or is to be sold, leased, licensed, assigned, or otherwise disposed of, (ii) for services rendered or to be rendered, (iii) for a policy of insurance issued or to be issued, (iv) for a secondary obligation incurred or to be incurred, (v) for energy provided or to be provided, (vi) for the use or hire of a vessel under a charter or other contract, (vii) arising out of the use of a credit or charge card or information contained on or for use with the card, or (viii) as winnings in a lottery or other game of chance operated or sponsored by a State, governmental unit of a State, or person licensed or authorized to operate the game by a State or governmental unit of a State. The term includes health-care-insurance receivables. The term does not include (i) rights to payment evidenced by chattel paper or an instrument, (ii) commercial tort claims, (iii) deposit accounts, (iv) investment property, (v) letter-of-credit rights or letters of credit, or (vi) rights to payment for money or funds advanced or sold, other than rights arising out of the use of a credit or charge card or information contained on or for use with the card.
  (3) "Account debtor" means a person obligated on an account, chattel paper, or general intangible. The term does not include persons obligated to pay a negotiable instrument, even if the instrument constitutes part of chattel paper.

(4) "Accounting," except as used in "accounting for," means a record:
   (A) authenticated by a secured party;
   (B) indicating the aggregate unpaid secured obligations as of a date not more than 35 days earlier or 35 days later than the date of the record; and
   (C) identifying the components of the obligations in reasonable detail.
(5) "Agricultural lien" means an interest, other than a security interest, in farm products:
   (A) which secures payment or performance of an obligation for:
      (i) goods or services furnished in connection with a debtor's farming operation; or
      (ii) rent on real property leased by a debtor in connection with its farming operation;
   (B) which is created by statute in favor of a person that:
      (i) in the ordinary course of its business furnished goods or services to a debtor in connection with a debtor's farming operation; or
      (ii) leased real property to a debtor in connection with the debtor's farming operation; and
   (C) whose effectiveness does not depend on the person's possession of the personal property.
(6) "As-extracted collateral" means:
   (A) oil, gas, or other minerals that are subject to a security interest that:
      (i) is created by a debtor having an interest in the minerals before extraction; and
      (ii) attaches to the minerals as extracted; or
   (B) accounts arising out of the sale at the wellhead or minehead of oil, gas, or other minerals in which the debtor had an interest before extraction.
(7) "Authenticate" means:
   (A) to sign; or
   (B) to execute or otherwise adopt a symbol, or encrypt or similarly process a record in whole or in part, with the present intent of the authenticating person to identify the person and adopt or accept a record.
(8) "Bank" means an organization that is engaged in the business of banking. The term includes savings banks, savings and loan associations, credit unions, and trust companies.

(9) "Cash proceeds" means proceeds that are money, checks, deposit accounts, or the like.

(10) "Certificate of title" means a certificate of title with respect to which a statute provides for the security interest in question to be indicated on the certificate as a condition or result of the security interest's obtaining priority over the rights of a lien creditor with respect to the collateral.

(11) "Chattel paper" means a record or records that evidence both a monetary obligation and a security interest in specific goods, a security interest in specific goods and software used in the goods, a security interest in specific goods and license of software used in the goods, a lease of specific goods, or a lease of specific goods and license of software used in the goods. In this paragraph, "monetary obligation" means a monetary obligation secured by the goods or owed under a lease of the goods and includes a monetary obligation with respect to software used in the goods. The term does not include (i) charters or other contracts involving the use or hire of a vessel or (ii) records that evidence a right to payment arising out of the use of a credit or charge card or information contained on or for use with the card. If a transaction is evidenced by records that include an instrument or series of instruments, the group of records taken together constitutes chattel paper.

(12) "Collateral" means the property subject to a security interest or agricultural lien. The term includes:
 (A) proceeds to which a security interest attaches;
 (B) accounts, chattel paper, payment intangibles, and promissory notes that have been sold; and
 (C) goods that are the subject of a consignment.

(13) "Commercial tort claim" means a claim arising in tort with respect to which:
 (A) the claimant is an organization; or
 (B) the claimant is an individual and the claim:
  (i) arose in the course of the claimant's business or profession; and
  (ii) does not include damages arising out of personal injury to or the death of an individual.

(14) "Commodity account" means an account maintained by a commodity intermediary in which a commodity contract is carried for a commodity customer.

(15) "Commodity contract" means a commodity futures contract, an option on a commodity futures contract, a commodity option, or another contract if the contract or option is:

    (A) traded on or subject to the rules of a board of trade that has been designated as a contract market for such a contract pursuant to federal commodities laws; or

    (B) traded on a foreign commodity board of trade, exchange, or market, and is carried on the books of a commodity intermediary for a commodity customer.

(16) "Commodity customer" means a person for which a commodity intermediary carries a commodity contract on its books.

(17) "Commodity intermediary" means a person that:

    (A) is registered as a futures commission merchant under federal commodities law; or

    (B) in the ordinary course of its business provides clearance or settlement services for a board of trade that has been designated as a contract market pursuant to federal commodities law.

(18) "Communicate" means:

    (A) to send a written or other tangible record;

    (B) to transmit a record by any means agreed upon by the persons sending and receiving the record; or

    (C) in the case of transmission of a record to or by a filing office, to transmit a record by any means prescribed by filing-office rule.

(19) "Consignee" means a merchant to which goods are delivered in a consignment.

(20) "Consignment" means a transaction, regardless of its form, in which a person delivers goods to a merchant for the purpose of sale and:

    (A) the merchant:

        (i) deals in goods of that kind under a name other than the name of the person making delivery;

        (ii) is not an auctioneer; and

        (iii) is not generally known by its creditors to be substantially engaged in selling the goods of others;

    (B) with respect to each delivery, the aggregate value of the goods is $1,000 or more at the time of delivery;

    (C) the goods are not consumer goods immediately before delivery; and

    (D) the transaction does not create a security interest that secures an obligation.

(21) "Consignor" means a person that delivers goods to a consignee in a consignment.

(22) "Consumer debtor" means a debtor in a consumer transaction.

(23) "Consumer goods" means goods that are used or bought for use primarily for personal, family, or household purposes.

(24) "Consumer-goods transaction" means a consumer transaction in which:

(A) an individual incurs an obligation primarily for personal, family, or household purposes; and

(B) a security interest in consumer goods secures the obligation.

(25) "Consumer obligor" means an obligor who is an individual and who incurred the obligation as part of a transaction entered into primarily for personal, family, or household purposes.

(26) "Consumer transaction" means a transaction in which (i) an individual incurs an obligation primarily for personal, family, or household purposes, (ii) a security interest secures the obligation, and (iii) the collateral is held or acquired primarily for personal, family, or household purposes. The term includes consumer-goods transactions.

(27) "Continuation statement" means an amendment of a financing statement which:

(A) identifies, by its file number, the initial financing statement to which it relates; and

(B) indicates that it is a continuation statement for, or that it is filed to continue the effectiveness of, the identified financing statement.

(28) "Debtor" means:

(A) a person having an interest, other than a security interest or other lien, in the collateral, whether or not the person is an obligor;

(B) a seller of accounts, chattel paper, payment intangibles, or promissory notes; or

(C) a consignee.

(29) "Deposit account" means a demand, time, savings, passbook, or similar account maintained with a bank. The term does not include investment property or accounts evidenced by an instrument.

(30) "Document" means a document of title or a receipt of the type described in Section 7-201(2).

(31) "Electronic chattel paper" means chattel paper evidenced by a record or records consisting of information stored in an electronic medium.

(32) "Encumbrance" means a right, other than an ownership interest, in real property. The term includes mortgages and other liens on real property.

(33) "Equipment" means goods other than inventory, farm products, or consumer goods.

(34) "Farm products" means goods, other than standing timber, with respect to which the debtor is engaged in a farming operation and which are:
   (A) crops grown, growing, or to be grown, including:
      (i) crops produced on trees, vines, and bushes; and
      (ii) aquatic goods produced in aquacultural operations;
   (B) livestock, born or unborn, including aquatic goods produced in aquacultural operations;
   (C) supplies used or produced in a farming operation; or
   (D) products of crops or livestock in their unmanufactured states.

(35) "Farming operation" means raising, cultivating, propagating, fattening, grazing, or any other farming, livestock, or aquacultural operation.

(36) "File number" means the number assigned to an initial financing statement pursuant to Section 9-519(a).

(37) "Filing office" means an office designated in Section 9-501 as the place to file a financing statement.

(38) "Filing-office rule" means a rule adopted pursuant to Section 9-526.

(39) "Financing statement" means a record or records composed of an initial financing statement and any filed record relating to the initial financing statement.

(40) "Fixture filing" means the filing of a financing statement covering goods that are or are to become fixtures and satisfying Section 9-502(a) and (b). The term includes the filing of a financing statement covering goods of a transmitting utility which are or are to become fixtures.

(41) "Fixtures" means goods that have become so related to particular real property that an interest in them arises under real property law.

(42) "General intangible" means any personal property, including things in action, other than accounts, chattel paper, commercial tort claims, deposit accounts, documents, goods, instruments, investment property, letter-of-credit rights, letters of credit, money, and oil, gas, or other minerals before extraction. The term includes payment intangibles and software.

(43) "Good faith" means honesty in fact and the observance of reasonable commercial standards of fair dealing.

(44) "Goods" means all things that are movable when a security interest attaches. The term includes (i) fixtures, (ii) standing timber that is to be cut and removed under a conveyance or contract for sale, (iii) the unborn young of animals, (iv) crops grown, growing, or to be grown, even if the crops are produced on trees, vines, or bushes, and (v) manufactured homes. The term also includes a computer program embedded in goods and any supporting information provided in connection with a transaction relating to the program if (i) the program is associated with the goods in such a manner that it customarily is considered part of the goods, or (ii) by becoming the owner of the goods, a person acquires a right to use the program in connection with the goods. The term does not include a computer program embedded in goods that consist solely of the medium in which the program is embedded. The term also does not include accounts, chattel paper, commercial tort claims, deposit accounts, documents, general intangibles, instruments, investment property, letter-of-credit rights, letters of credit, money, or oil, gas, or other minerals before extraction.

(45) "Governmental unit" means a subdivision, agency, department, county, parish, municipality, or other unit of the government of the United States, a State, or a foreign country. The term includes an organization having a separate corporate existence if the organization is eligible to issue debt on which interest is exempt from income taxation under the laws of the United States.

(46) "Health-care-insurance receivable" means an interest in or claim under a policy of insurance which is a right to payment of a monetary obligation for health-care goods or services provided.

(47) "Instrument" means a negotiable instrument or any other writing that evidences a right to the payment of a monetary obligation, is not itself a security agreement or lease, and is of a type that in ordinary course of business is transferred by delivery with any necessary indorsement or assignment. The term does not include (i) investment property, (ii) letters of credit, or (iii) writings that evidence a right to payment arising out of the use of a credit or charge card or information contained on or for use with the card.

(48) "Inventory" means goods, other than farm products, which:
    (A) are leased by a person as lessor;
    (B) are held by a person for sale or lease or to be furnished under a contract of service;

      (C) are furnished by a person under a contract of service; or

      (D) consist of raw materials, work in process, or materials used or consumed in a business.

(49) "Investment property" means a security, whether certificated or uncertificated, security entitlement, securities account, commodity contract, or commodity account.

(50) "Jurisdiction of organization," with respect to a registered organization, means the jurisdiction under whose law the organization is organized.

(51) "Letter-of-credit right" means a right to payment or performance under a letter of credit, whether or not the beneficiary has demanded or is at the time entitled to demand payment or performance. The term does not include the right of a beneficiary to demand payment or performance under a letter of credit.

(52) "Lien creditor" means:

      (A) a creditor that has acquired a lien on the property involved by attachment, levy, or the like;

      (B) an assignee for benefit of creditors from the time of assignment;

      (C) a trustee in bankruptcy from the date of the filing of the petition; or

      (D) a receiver in equity from the time of appointment.

(53) "Manufactured home" means a structure, transportable in one or more sections, which, in the traveling mode, is eight body feet or more in width or 40 body feet or more in length, or, when erected on site, is 320 or more square feet, and which is built on a permanent chassis and designed to be used as a dwelling with or without a permanent foundation when connected to the required utilities, and includes the plumbing, heating, air-conditioning, and electrical systems contained therein. The term includes any structure that meets all of the requirements of this paragraph except the size requirements and with respect to which the manufacturer voluntarily files a certification required by the United States Secretary of Housing and Urban Development and complies with the standards established under Title 42 of the United States Code.

(54) "Manufactured-home transaction" means a secured transaction:

      (A) that creates a purchase-money security interest in a manufactured home, other than a manufactured home held as inventory; or

(B) in which a manufactured home, other than a manufactured home held as inventory, is the primary collateral.

(55) "Mortgage" means a consensual interest in real property, including fixtures, which secures payment or performance of an obligation.

(56) "New debtor" means a person that becomes bound as debtor under Section 9-203(d) by a security agreement previously entered into by another person.

(57) "New value" means (i) money, (ii) money's worth in property, services, or new credit, or (iii) release by a transferee of an interest in property previously transferred to the transferee. The term does not include an obligation substituted for another obligation.

(58) "Noncash proceeds" means proceeds other than cash proceeds.

(59) "Obligor" means a person that, with respect to an obligation secured by a security interest in or an agricultural lien on the collateral, (i) owes payment or other performance of the obligation, (ii) has provided property other than the collateral to secure payment or other performance of the obligation, or (iii) is otherwise accountable in whole or in part for payment or other performance of the obligation. The term does not include issuers or nominated persons under a letter of credit.

(60) "Original debtor," except as used in Section 9-310(c), means a person that, as debtor, entered into a security agreement to which a new debtor has become bound under Section 9-203(d).

(61) "Payment intangible" means a general intangible under which the account debtor's principal obligation is a monetary obligation.

(62) "Person related to," with respect to an individual, means:
  (A) the spouse of the individual;
  (B) a brother, brother-in-law, sister, or sister-in-law of the individual;
  (C) an ancestor or lineal descendant of the individual or the individual's spouse; or
  (D) any other relative, by blood or marriage, of the individual or the individual's spouse who shares the same home with the individual.

(63) "Person related to," with respect to an organization, means:
  (A) a person directly or indirectly controlling, controlled by, or under common control with the organization;
  (B) an officer or director of, or a person performing similar functions with respect to, the organization;

   (C) an officer or director of, or a person performing similar functions with respect to, a person described in subparagraph (A);

   (D) the spouse of an individual described in subparagraph (A), (B), or (C); or

   (E) an individual who is related by blood or marriage to an individual described in subparagraph (A), (B), (C), or (D) and shares the same home with the individual.

(64) "Proceeds," except as used in Section 9-609(b), means the following property:

   (A) whatever is acquired upon the sale, lease, license, exchange, or other disposition of collateral;

   (B) whatever is collected on, or distributed on account of, collateral;

   (C) rights arising out of collateral;

   (D) to the extent of the value of collateral, claims arising out of the loss, nonconformity, or interference with the use of, defects or infringement of rights in, or damage to, the collateral; or

   (E) to the extent of the value of collateral and to the extent payable to the debtor or the secured party, insurance payable by reason of the loss or nonconformity of, defects or infringement of rights in, or damage to, the collateral.

(65) "Promissory note" means an instrument that evidences a promise to pay a monetary obligation, does not evidence an order to pay, and does not contain an acknowledgment by a bank that the bank has received for deposit a sum of money or funds.

(66) "Proposal" means a record authenticated by a secured party which includes the terms on which the secured party is willing to accept collateral in full or partial satisfaction of the obligation it secures pursuant to Sections 9-620, 9-621, and 9-622.

(67) "Public-finance transaction" means a secured transaction in connection with which:

   (A) debt securities are issued;

   (B) all or a portion of the securities issued have an initial stated maturity of at least 20 years; and

   (C) the debtor, obligor, secured party, account debtor or other person obligated on collateral, assignor or assignee of a secured obligation, or assignor or assignee of a security interest is a State or a governmental unit of a State.

(68) "Pursuant to commitment," with respect to an advance made or other value given by a secured party, means pursuant to the secured party's obligation, whether or not a subsequent event of default or other event not within the secured party's control has relieved or may relieve the secured party from its obligation.

(69) "Record," except as used in "for record," "of record," "record or legal title," and "record owner," means information that is inscribed on a tangible medium or which is stored in an electronic or other medium and is retrievable in perceivable form.

(70) "Registered organization" means an organization organized solely under the law of a single State or the United States and as to which the State or the United States must maintain a public record showing the organization to have been organized.

(71) "Secondary obligor" means an obligor to the extent that:
  (A) the obligor's obligation is secondary; or
  (B) the obligor has a right of recourse with respect to an obligation secured by collateral against the debtor, another obligor, or property of either.

(72) "Secured party" means:
  (A) a person in whose favor a security interest is created or provided for under a security agreement, whether or not any obligation to be secured is outstanding;
  (B) a person that holds an agricultural lien;
  (C) a consignor;
  (D) a person to which accounts, chattel paper, payment intangibles, or promissory notes have been sold;
  (E) a trustee, indenture trustee, agent, collateral agent, or other representative in whose favor a security interest or agricultural lien is created or provided for; or
  (F) a person that holds a security interest arising under Section 2-401, 2-505, 2-711(3), 2A-508(5), 4-210, or 5-118.

(73) "Security agreement" means an agreement that creates or provides for a security interest.

(74) "Send," in connection with a record or notification, means:
  (A) to deposit in the mail, deliver for transmission, or transmit by any other usual means of communication, with postage or cost of transmission provided for, addressed to any address reasonable under the circumstances; or
  (B) to cause the record or notification to be received within the time that it would have been received if properly sent under subparagraph (A).

(75) "Software" means a computer program and any supporting information provided in connection with a transaction relating to the program. The term does not include a computer program that is included in the definition of goods.

(76) "State" means a State of the United States, the District of Columbia, Puerto Rico, the United States Virgin Islands, or any territory or insular possession subject to the jurisdiction of the United States.

(77) "Supporting obligation" means a letter-of-credit right or secondary obligation that supports the payment or performance of an account, chattel paper, a document, a general intangible, an instrument, or investment property.

(78) "Tangible chattel paper" means chattel paper evidenced by a record or records consisting of information that is inscribed on a tangible medium.

(79) "Termination statement" means an amendment of a financing statement which:

(A) identifies, by its file number, the initial financing statement to which it relates; and

(B) indicates either that it is a termination statement or that the identified financing statement is no longer effective.

(80) "Transmitting utility" means a person primarily engaged in the business of:

(A) operating a railroad, subway, street railway, or trolley bus;

(B) transmitting communications electrically, electromagnetically, or by light;

(C) transmitting goods by pipeline or sewer; or

(D) transmitting or producing and transmitting electricity, steam, gas, or water.

(b) **[Definitions in other articles.]** The following definitions in other articles apply to this article:

"Applicant"	Section 5-102.
"Beneficiary"	Section 5-102.
"Broker"	Section 8-102.
"Certificated security"	Section 8-102.
"Check"	Section 3-104.
"Clearing corporation"	Section 8-102.
"Contract for sale"	Section 2-106.
"Customer"	Section 4-104.
"Entitlement holder"	Section 8-102.
"Financial asset"	Section 8-102.

"Holder in due course"	Section 3-302.
"Issuer" (with respect to a letter of credit or letter-of-credit right)	Section 5-102.
"Issuer" (with respect to a security)	Section 8-201.
"Lease"	Section 2A-103.
"Lease agreement"	Section 2A-103.
"Lease contract"	Section 2A-103.
"Leasehold interest"	Section 2A-103.
"Lessee"	Section 2A-103.
"Lessee in ordinary course of business"	Section 2A-103.
"Lessor"	Section 2A-103.
"Lessor's residual interest"	Section 2A-103.
"Letter of credit"	Section 5-102.
"Merchant"	Section 2-104.
"Negotiable instrument"	Section 3-104.
"Nominated person"	Section 5-102.
"Note"	Section 3-104.
"Proceeds of a letter of credit"	Section 5-114.
"Prove"	Section 3-103.
"Sale"	Section 2-106.
"Securities account"	Section 8-501.
"Securities intermediary"	Section 8-102.
"Security"	Section 8-102.
"Security certificate"	Section 8-102.
"Security entitlement"	Section 8-102.
"Uncertificated security"	Section 8-102.

(c) **[Article 1 definitions and principles.]** Article 1 contains general definitions and principles of construction and interpretation applicable throughout this article.

SECTION 9-103. PURCHASE-MONEY SECURITY INTEREST; APPLICATION OF PAYMENTS; BURDEN OF ESTABLISHING.

(a) **[Definitions.]** In this section:

(1) "purchase-money collateral" means goods or software that secures a purchase-money obligation incurred with respect to that collateral; and

(2) "purchase-money obligation" means an obligation of an obligor incurred as all or part of the price of the collateral or for value given to enable the debtor to acquire rights in or the use of the collateral if the value is in fact so used.

(b) **[Purchase-money security interest in goods.]** A security interest in goods is a purchase-money security interest:

(1) to the extent that the goods are purchase-money collateral with respect to that security interest;

(2) if the security interest is in inventory that is or was purchase-money collateral, also to the extent that the security interest secures a purchase-money obligation incurred with respect to other inventory in which the secured party holds or held a purchase-money security interest; and

(3) also to the extent that the security interest secures a purchase-money obligation incurred with respect to software in which the secured party holds or held a purchase-money security interest.

(c) **[Purchase-money security interest in software.]** A security interest in software is a purchase-money security interest to the extent that the security interest also secures a purchase-money obligation incurred with respect to goods in which the secured party holds or held a purchase-money security interest if:

(1) the debtor acquired its interest in the software in an integrated transaction in which it acquired an interest in the goods; and

(2) the debtor acquired its interest in the software for the principal purpose of using the software in the goods.

(d) **[Consignor's inventory purchase-money security interest.]** The security interest of a consignor in goods that are the subject of a consignment is a purchase-money security interest in inventory.

(e) **[Application of payment in non-consumer-goods transaction.]** In a transaction other than a consumer-goods transaction, if the extent to which a security interest is a purchase-money security interest depends on the application of a payment to a particular obligation, the payment must be applied:

(1) in accordance with any reasonable method of application to which the parties agree;

(2) in the absence of the parties' agreement to a reasonable method, in accordance with any intention of the obligor manifested at or before the time of payment; or

(3) in the absence of an agreement to a reasonable method and a timely manifestation of the obligor's intention, in the following order:

(A) to obligations that are not secured; and

(B) if more than one obligation is secured, to obligations secured by purchase-money security interests in the order in which those obligations were incurred.

(f) **[No loss of status of purchase-money security interest in non-consumer-goods transaction.]** In a transaction other than a consumer-goods transaction, a purchase-money security interest does not lose its status as such, even if:

(1) the purchase-money collateral also secures an obligation that is not a purchase-money obligation;

(2) collateral that is not purchase-money collateral also secures the purchase-money obligation; or

(3) the purchase-money obligation has been renewed, refinanced, consolidated, or restructured.

(g) **[Burden of proof in non-consumer-goods transaction.]** In a transaction other than a consumer-goods transaction, a secured party claiming a purchase-money security interest has the burden of establishing the extent to which the security interest is a purchase-money security interest.

(h) **[Non-consumer-goods transactions; no inference.]** The limitation of the rules in subsections (e), (f), and (g) to transactions other than consumer-goods transactions is intended to leave to the court the determination of the proper rules in consumer-goods transactions. The court may not infer from that limitation the nature of the proper rule in consumer-goods transactions and may continue to apply established approaches.

SECTION 9-104. CONTROL OF DEPOSIT ACCOUNT.

(a) **[Requirements for control.]** A secured party has control of a deposit account if:

(1) the secured party is the bank with which the deposit account is maintained;

(2) the debtor, secured party, and bank have agreed in an authenticated record that the bank will comply with instructions originated by the secured party directing disposition of the funds in the deposit account without further consent by the debtor; or

(3) the secured party becomes the bank's customer with respect to the deposit account.

(b) **[Debtor's right to direct disposition.]** A secured party that has satisfied subsection (a) has control, even if the debtor retains the right to direct the disposition of funds from the deposit account.

SECTION 9-105. CONTROL OF ELECTRONIC CHATTEL PAPER.

A secured party has control of electronic chattel paper if the record or records comprising the chattel paper are created, stored, and assigned in such a manner that:

(1) a single authoritative copy of the record or records exists which is unique, identifiable and, except as otherwise provided in paragraphs (4), (5), and (6), unalterable;

(2) the authoritative copy identifies the secured party as the assignee of the record or records;

(3) the authoritative copy is communicated to and maintained by the secured party or its designated custodian;

(4) copies or revisions that add or change an identified assignee of the authoritative copy can be made only with the participation of the secured party;

(5) each copy of the authoritative copy and any copy of a copy is readily identifiable as a copy that is not the authoritative copy; and

(6) any revision of the authoritative copy is readily identifiable as an authorized or unauthorized revision.

SECTION 9-106. CONTROL OF INVESTMENT PROPERTY.

(a) **[Control under Section 8-106.]** A person has control of a certificated security, uncertificated security, or security entitlement as provided in Section 8-106.

(b) **[Control of commodity contract.]** A secured party has control of a commodity contract if:

    (1) the secured party is the commodity intermediary with which the commodity contract is carried; or

    (2) the commodity customer, secured party, and commodity intermediary have agreed that the commodity intermediary will apply any value distributed on account of the commodity contract as directed by the secured party without further consent by the commodity customer.

(c) **[Effect of control of securities account or commodity account.]** A secured party having control of all security entitlements or commodity contracts carried in a securities account or commodity account has control over the securities account or commodity account.

SECTION 9-107. CONTROL OF LETTER-OF-CREDIT RIGHT.

A secured party has control of a letter-of-credit right to the extent of any right to payment or performance by the issuer or any nominated person if the issuer or nominated person has consented to an assignment of proceeds of the letter of credit under Section 5-114(c) or otherwise applicable law or practice.

SECTION 9-108. SUFFICIENCY OF DESCRIPTION.

(a) **[Sufficiency of description.]** Except as otherwise provided in subsections (c), (d), and (e), a description of personal or real property is sufficient, whether or not it is specific, if it reasonably identifies what is described.

(b) **[Examples of reasonable identification.]** Except as otherwise provided in subsection (d), a description of collateral reasonably identifies the collateral if it identifies the collateral by:

(1) specific listing;

(2) category;

(3) except as otherwise provided in subsection (e), a type of collateral defined in [the Uniform Commercial Code];

(4) quantity;

(5) computational or allocational formula or procedure; or

(6) except as otherwise provided in subsection (c), any other method, if the identity of the collateral is objectively determinable.

(c) **[Supergeneric description not sufficient.]** A description of collateral as "all the debtor's assets" or "all the debtor's personal property" or using words of similar import does not reasonably identify the collateral.

(d) **[Investment property.]** Except as otherwise provided in subsection (e), a description of a security entitlement, securities account, or commodity account is sufficient if it describes:

(1) the collateral by those terms or as investment property; or

(2) the underlying financial asset or commodity contract.

(e) **[When description by type insufficient.]** A description only by type of collateral defined in [the Uniform Commercial Code] is an insufficient description of:

(1) a commercial tort claim; or

(2) in a consumer transaction, consumer goods, a security entitlement, a securities account, or a commodity account.

[SUBPART 2. APPLICABILITY OF ARTICLE]

SECTION 9-109. SCOPE.

(a) **[General scope of article.]** Except as otherwise provided in subsections (c) and (d), this article applies to:

(1) a transaction, regardless of its form, that creates a security interest in personal property or fixtures by contract;

(2) an agricultural lien;

(3) a sale of accounts, chattel paper, payment intangibles, or promissory notes;

(4) a consignment;

(5) a security interest arising under Section 2-401, 2-505, 2-711(3), or 2A-508(5), as provided in Section 9-110; and

(6) a security interest arising under Section 4-210 or 5-118.

(b) **[Security interest in secured obligation.]** The application of this article to a security interest in a secured obligation is not affected by the fact that the obligation is itself secured by a transaction or interest to which this article does not apply.

(c) **[Extent to which article does not apply.]** This article does not apply to the extent that:

(1) a statute, regulation, or treaty of the United States preempts this article;

(2) another statute of this State expressly governs the creation, perfection, priority, or enforcement of a security interest created by this State or a governmental unit of this State;

(3) a statute of another State, a foreign country, or a governmental unit of another State or a foreign country, other than a statute generally applicable to security interests, expressly governs creation, perfection, priority, or enforcement of a security interest created by the State, country, or governmental unit; or

(4) the rights of a transferee beneficiary or nominated person under a letter of credit are independent and superior under Section 5-114.

(d) **[Inapplicability of article.]** This article does not apply to:

(1) a landlord's lien, other than an agricultural lien;

(2) a lien, other than an agricultural lien, given by statute or other rule of law for services or materials, but Section 9-333 applies with respect to priority of the lien;

(3) an assignment of a claim for wages, salary, or other compensation of an employee;

(4) a sale of accounts, chattel paper, payment intangibles, or promissory notes as part of a sale of the business out of which they arose;

(5) an assignment of accounts, chattel paper, payment intangibles, or promissory notes which is for the purpose of collection only;

(6) an assignment of a right to payment under a contract to an assignee that is also obligated to perform under the contract;

(7) an assignment of a single account, payment intangible, or promissory note to an assignee in full or partial satisfaction of a preexisting indebtedness;

(8) a transfer of an interest in or an assignment of a claim under a policy of insurance, other than an assignment by or to a health-care provider of a health-care-insurance receivable and any subsequent assignment of the right to payment, but Sections 9-315 and 9-322 apply with respect to proceeds and priorities in proceeds;

(9) an assignment of a right represented by a judgment, other than a judgment taken on a right to payment that was collateral;

(10) a right of recoupment or set-off, but:

   (A) Section 9-340 applies with respect to the effectiveness of rights of recoupment or set-off against deposit accounts; and

   (B) Section 9-404 applies with respect to defenses or claims of an account debtor;

(11) the creation or transfer of an interest in or lien on real property, including a lease or rents thereunder, except to the extent that provision is made for:

   (A) liens on real property in Sections 9-203 and 9-308;

   (B) fixtures in Section 9-334;

   (C) fixture filings in Sections 9-501, 9-502, 9-512, 9-516, and 9-519; and

   (D) security agreements covering personal and real property in Section 9-604;

(12) an assignment of a claim arising in tort, other than a commercial tort claim, but Sections 9-315 and 9-322 apply with respect to proceeds and priorities in proceeds; or

(13) an assignment of a deposit account in a consumer transaction, but Sections 9-315 and 9-322 apply with respect to proceeds and priorities in proceeds.

SECTION 9-110. SECURITY INTERESTS ARISING UNDER ARTICLE 2 OR 2A.

A security interest arising under Section 2-401, 2-505, 2-711(3), or 2A-508(5) is subject to this article. However, until the debtor obtains possession of the goods:

(1) the security interest is enforceable, even if Section 9-203(b)(3) has not been satisfied;

(2) filing is not required to perfect the security interest;

(3) the rights of the secured party after default by the debtor are governed by Article 2 or 2A; and

(4) the security interest has priority over a conflicting security interest created by the debtor.

PART 2 – EFFECTIVENESS OF SECURITY AGREEMENT; ATTACHMENT OF SECURITY INTEREST; RIGHTS OF PARTIES TO SECURITY AGREEMENT

[SUBPART 1. EFFECTIVENESS AND ATTACHMENT]

SECTION 9-201. GENERAL EFFECTIVENESS OF SECURITY AGREEMENT.

(a) **[General effectiveness.]** Except as otherwise provided in [the Uniform Commercial Code], a security agreement is effective according to its terms between the parties, against purchasers of the collateral, and against creditors.

(b) **[Applicable consumer laws and other law.]** A transaction subject to this article is subject to any applicable rule of law which establishes a different rule for consumers and [insert reference to (i) any other statute or regulation that regulates the rates, charges, agreements, and practices for loans, credit sales, or other extensions of credit and (ii) any consumer-protection statute or regulation].

(c) **[Other applicable law controls.]** In case of conflict between this article and a rule of law, statute, or regulation described in subsection (b), the rule of law, statute, or regulation controls. Failure to comply with a statute or regulation described in subsection (b) has only the effect the statute or regulation specifies.

(d) **[Further deference to other applicable law.]** This article does not:

(1) validate any rate, charge, agreement, or practice that violates a rule of law, statute, or regulation described in subsection (b); or

(2) extend the application of the rule of law, statute, or regulation to a transaction not otherwise subject to it.

SECTION 9-202. TITLE TO COLLATERAL IMMATERIAL.

Except as otherwise provided with respect to consignments or sales of accounts, chattel paper, payment intangibles, or promissory notes, the provisions of this article with regard to rights and obligations apply whether title to collateral is in the secured party or the debtor.

SECTION 9-203. ATTACHMENT AND ENFORCEABILITY OF SECURITY INTEREST; PROCEEDS; SUPPORTING OBLIGATIONS; FORMAL REQUISITES.

(a) **[Attachment.]** A security interest attaches to collateral when it becomes enforceable against the debtor with respect to the collateral, unless an agreement expressly postpones the time of attachment.

(b) **[Enforceability.]** Except as otherwise provided in subsections (c) through (i), a security interest is enforceable against the debtor and third parties with respect to the collateral only if :

(1) value has been given;

(2) the debtor has rights in the collateral or the power to transfer rights in the collateral to a secured party; and

(3) one of the following conditions is met:

(A) the debtor has authenticated a security agreement that provides a description of the collateral and, if the security interest covers timber to be cut, a description of the land concerned;

(B) the collateral is not a certificated security and is in the possession of the secured party under Section 9-313 pursuant to the debtor's security agreement;

(C) the collateral is a certificated security in registered form and the security certificate has been delivered to the secured party under Section 8-301 pursuant to the debtor's security agreement; or

(D) the collateral is deposit accounts, electronic chattel paper, investment property, or letter-of-credit rights, and the secured party has control under Section 9-104, 9-105, 9-106, or 9-107 pursuant to the debtor's security agreement.

(c) **[Other UCC provisions.]** Subsection (b) is subject to Section 4-210 on the security interest of a collecting bank, Section 5-118 on the security interest of a letter-of-credit issuer or nominated person, Section 9-110 on a security interest arising under Article 2 or 2A, and Section 9-206 on security interests in investment property.

(d) **[When a person becomes bound by another person's security agreement.]** A person becomes bound as debtor by a security agreement entered into by another person if, by operation of law other than this article or by contract:

(1) the security agreement becomes effective to create a security interest in the person's property; or

(2) the person becomes generally obligated for the obligations of the other person, including the obligation secured under the security agreement, and acquires or succeeds to all or substantially all of the assets of the other person.

(e) **[Effect of new debtor becoming bound.]** If a new debtor becomes bound as debtor by a security agreement entered into by another person:

    (1) the agreement satisfies subsection (b)(3) with respect to existing or after-acquired property of the new debtor to the extent the property is described in the agreement; and

    (2) another agreement is not necessary to make a security interest in the property enforceable.

(f) **[Proceeds and supporting obligations.]** The attachment of a security interest in collateral gives the secured party the rights to proceeds provided by Section 9-315 and is also attachment of a security interest in a supporting obligation for the collateral.

(g) **[Lien securing right to payment.]** The attachment of a security interest in a right to payment or performance secured by a security interest or other lien on personal or real property is also attachment of a security interest in the security interest, mortgage, or other lien.

(h) **[Security entitlement carried in securities account.]** The attachment of a security interest in a securities account is also attachment of a security interest in the security entitlements carried in the securities account.

(i) **[Commodity contracts carried in commodity account.]** The attachment of a security interest in a commodity account is also attachment of a security interest in the commodity contracts carried in the commodity account.

SECTION 9-204. AFTER-ACQUIRED PROPERTY; FUTURE ADVANCES.

(a) **[After-acquired collateral.]** Except as otherwise provided in subsection (b), a security agreement may create or provide for a security interest in after-acquired collateral.

(b) **[When after-acquired property clause not effective.]** A security interest does not attach under a term constituting an after-acquired property clause to:

    (1) consumer goods, other than an accession when given as additional security, unless the debtor acquires rights in them within 10 days after the secured party gives value; or

    (2) a commercial tort claim.

(c) **[Future advances and other value.]** A security agreement may provide that collateral secures, or that accounts, chattel paper, payment intangibles, or promissory notes are sold in connection with, future advances or other value, whether or not the advances or value are given pursuant to commitment.

SECTION 9-205. USE OR DISPOSITION OF COLLATERAL PERMISSIBLE.

(a) **[When security interest not invalid or fraudulent.]** A security interest is not invalid or fraudulent against creditors solely because:

    (1) the debtor has the right or ability to:

        (A) use, commingle, or dispose of all or part of the collateral, including returned or repossessed goods;

        (B) collect, compromise, enforce, or otherwise deal with collateral;

        (C) accept the return of collateral or make repossessions; or

        (D) use, commingle, or dispose of proceeds; or

    (2) the secured party fails to require the debtor to account for proceeds or replace collateral.

(b) **[Requirements of possession not relaxed.]** This section does not relax the requirements of possession if attachment, perfection, or enforcement of a security interest depends upon possession of the collateral by the secured party.

SECTION 9-206. SECURITY INTEREST ARISING IN PURCHASE OR DELIVERY OF FINANCIAL ASSET.

(a) **[Security interest when person buys through securities intermediary.]** A security interest in favor of a securities intermediary attaches to a person's security entitlement if:

    (1) the person buys a financial asset through the securities intermediary in a transaction in which the person is obligated to pay the purchase price to the securities intermediary at the time of the purchase; and

    (2) the securities intermediary credits the financial asset to the buyer's securities account before the buyer pays the securities intermediary.

(b) **[Security interest secures obligation to pay for financial asset.]** The security interest described in subsection (a) secures the person's obligation to pay for the financial asset.

(c) **[Security interest in payment against delivery transaction.]** A security interest in favor of a person that delivers a certificated security or other financial asset represented by a writing attaches to the security or other financial asset if:

    (1) the security or other financial asset:

(A) in the ordinary course of business is transferred by delivery with any necessary indorsement or assignment;
and

(B) is delivered under an agreement between persons in the
business of dealing with such securities or financial assets;
and

(2) the agreement calls for delivery against payment.

(d) **[Security interest secures obligation to pay for delivery.]** The
security interest described in subsection (c) secures the obligation to
make payment for the delivery.

[SUBPART 2. RIGHTS AND DUTIES]

SECTION 9-207. RIGHTS AND DUTIES OF SECURED PARTY HAVING POSSESSION OR CONTROL OF COLLATERAL.

(a) **[Duty of care when secured party in possession.]** Except as otherwise provided in subsection (d), a secured party shall use reasonable
care in the custody and preservation of collateral in the secured party's
possession. In the case of chattel paper or an instrument, reasonable
care includes taking necessary steps to preserve rights against prior
parties unless otherwise agreed.

(b) **[Expenses, risks, duties, and rights when secured party in
possession.]** Except as otherwise provided in subsection (d), if a
secured party has possession of collateral:

(1) reasonable expenses, including the cost of insurance and payment
of taxes or other charges, incurred in the custody, preservation,
use, or operation of the collateral are chargeable to the debtor
and are secured by the collateral;

(2) the risk of accidental loss or damage is on the debtor to the extent
of a deficiency in any effective insurance coverage;

(3) the secured party shall keep the collateral identifiable, but fungi-
ble collateral may be commingled; and

(4) the secured party may use or operate the collateral:

(A) for the purpose of preserving the collateral or its value;

(B) as permitted by an order of a court having competent jurisdiction; or

(C) except in the case of consumer goods, in the manner and to
the extent agreed by the debtor.

(c) **[Duties and rights when secured party in possession or
control.]** Except as otherwise provided in subsection (d), a secured
party having possession of collateral or control of collateral under
Section 9-104, 9-105, 9-106, or 9-107:

(1) may hold as additional security any proceeds, except money or funds, received from the collateral;

(2) shall apply money or funds received from the collateral to reduce the secured obligation, unless remitted to the debtor; and

(3) may create a security interest in the collateral.

(d) **[Buyer of certain rights to payment.]** If the secured party is a buyer of accounts, chattel paper, payment intangibles, or promissory notes or a consignor:

(1) subsection (a) does not apply unless the secured party is entitled under an agreement:

(A) to charge back uncollected collateral; or

(B) otherwise to full or limited recourse against the debtor or a secondary obligor based on the nonpayment or other default of an account debtor or other obligor on the collateral; and

(2) subsections (b) and (c) do not apply.

SECTION 9-208. ADDITIONAL DUTIES OF SECURED PARTY HAVING CONTROL OF COLLATERAL.

(a) **[Applicability of section.]** This section applies to cases in which there is no outstanding secured obligation and the secured party is not committed to make advances, incur obligations, or otherwise give value.

(b) **[Duties of secured party after receiving demand from debtor.]** Within 10 days after receiving an authenticated demand by the debtor:

(1) a secured party having control of a deposit account under Section 9-104(a)(2) shall send to the bank with which the deposit account is maintained an authenticated statement that releases the bank from any further obligation to comply with instructions originated by the secured party;

(2) a secured party having control of a deposit account under Section 9-104(a)(3) shall:

(A) pay the debtor the balance on deposit in the deposit account; or

(B) transfer the balance on deposit into a deposit account in the debtor's name;

(3) a secured party, other than a buyer, having control of electronic chattel paper under Section 9-105 shall:

(A) communicate the authoritative copy of the electronic chattel paper to the debtor or its designated custodian;

(B) if the debtor designates a custodian that is the designated custodian with which the authoritative copy of the electronic chattel paper is maintained for the secured party, communicate to the custodian an authenticated record releasing the designated custodian from any further obligation to comply with instructions originated by the secured party and instructing the custodian to comply with instructions originated by the debtor; and

(C) take appropriate action to enable the debtor or its designated custodian to make copies of or revisions to the authoritative copy which add or change an identified assignee of the authoritative copy without the consent of the secured party;

(4) a secured party having control of investment property under Section 8-106(d)(2) or 9-106(b) shall send to the securities intermediary or commodity intermediary with which the security entitlement or commodity contract is maintained an authenticated record that releases the securities intermediary or commodity intermediary from any further obligation to comply with entitlement orders or directions originated by the secured party; and

(5) a secured party having control of a letter-of-credit right under Section 9-107 shall send to each person having an unfulfilled obligation to pay or deliver proceeds of the letter of credit to the secured party an authenticated release from any further obligation to pay or deliver proceeds of the letter of credit to the secured party.

SECTION 9-209. DUTIES OF SECURED PARTY IF ACCOUNT DEBTOR HAS BEEN NOTIFIED OF ASSIGNMENT.

(a) **[Applicability of section.]** Except as otherwise provided in subsection (c), this section applies if:

(1) there is no outstanding secured obligation; and

(2) the secured party is not committed to make advances, incur obligations, or otherwise give value.

(b) **[Duties of secured party after receiving demand from debtor.]** Within 10 days after receiving an authenticated demand by the debtor, a secured party shall send to an account debtor that has received notification of an assignment to the secured party as assignee under Section 9-406(a) an authenticated record that releases the account debtor from any further obligation to the secured party.

(c) **[Inapplicability to sales.]** This section does not apply to an assignment constituting the sale of an account, chattel paper, or payment intangible.

SECTION 9-210. REQUEST FOR ACCOUNTING; REQUEST REGARDING LIST OF COLLATERAL OR STATEMENT OF ACCOUNT.

(a) **[Definitions.]** In this section:

    (1) "Request" means a record of a type described in paragraph (2), (3), or (4).

    (2) "Request for an accounting" means a record authenticated by a debtor requesting that the recipient provide an accounting of the unpaid obligations secured by collateral and reasonably identifying the transaction or relationship that is the subject of the request.

    (3) "Request regarding a list of collateral" means a record authenticated by a debtor requesting that the recipient approve or correct a list of what the debtor believes to be the collateral securing an obligation and reasonably identifying the transaction or relationship that is the subject of the request.

    (4) "Request regarding a statement of account" means a record authenticated by a debtor requesting that the recipient approve or correct a statement indicating what the debtor believes to be the aggregate amount of unpaid obligations secured by collateral as of a specified date and reasonably identifying the transaction or relationship that is the subject of the request.

(b) **[Duty to respond to requests.]** Subject to subsections (c), (d), (e), and (f), a secured party, other than a buyer of accounts, chattel paper, payment intangibles, or promissory notes or a consignor, shall comply with a request within 14 days after receipt:

    (1) in the case of a request for an accounting, by authenticating and sending to the debtor an accounting; and

    (2) in the case of a request regarding a list of collateral or a request regarding a statement of account, by authenticating and sending to the debtor an approval or correction.

(c) **[Request regarding list of collateral; statement concerning type of collateral.]** A secured party that claims a security interest in all of a particular type of collateral owned by the debtor may comply with a request regarding a list of collateral by sending to the debtor an authenticated record including a statement to that effect within 14 days after receipt.

(d) **[Request regarding list of collateral; no interest claimed.]** A person that receives a request regarding a list of collateral, claims no interest in the collateral when it receives the request, and claimed an interest in the collateral at an earlier time shall comply with the request within 14 days after receipt by sending to the debtor an authenticated record:

    (1) disclaiming any interest in the collateral; and

    (2) if known to the recipient, providing the name and mailing address of any assignee of or successor to the recipient's interest in the collateral.

(e) **[Request for accounting or regarding statement of account; no interest in obligation claimed.]** A person that receives a request for an accounting or a request regarding a statement of account, claims no interest in the obligations when it receives the request, and claimed an interest in the obligations at an earlier time shall comply with the request within 14 days after receipt by sending to the debtor an authenticated record:

    (1) disclaiming any interest in the obligations; and

    (2) if known to the recipient, providing the name and mailing address of any assignee of or successor to the recipient's interest in the obligations.

(f) **[Charges for responses.]** A debtor is entitled without charge to one response to a request under this section during any six-month period. The secured party may require payment of a charge not exceeding $25 for each additional response.

PART 3 – PERFECTION AND PRIORITY

[SUBPART 1. LAW GOVERNING PERFECTION AND PRIORITY]

SECTION 9-301. LAW GOVERNING PERFECTION AND PRIORITY OF SECURITY INTERESTS.

Except as otherwise provided in Sections 9-303 through 9-306, the following rules determine the law governing perfection, the effect of perfection or nonperfection, and the priority of a security interest in collateral:

(1) Except as otherwise provided in this section, while a debtor is located in a jurisdiction, the local law of that jurisdiction governs perfection, the effect of perfection or nonperfection, and the priority of a security interest in collateral.

(2) While collateral is located in a jurisdiction, the local law of that jurisdiction governs perfection, the effect of perfection or

nonperfection, and the priority of a possessory security interest in that collateral.

(3) Except as otherwise provided in paragraph (4), while negotiable documents, goods, instruments, money, or tangible chattel paper is located in a jurisdiction, the local law of that jurisdiction governs:

(A) perfection of a security interest in the goods by filing a fixture filing;

(B) perfection of a security interest in timber to be cut; and

(C) the effect of perfection or nonperfection and the priority of a nonpossessory security interest in the collateral.

(4) The local law of the jurisdiction in which the wellhead or minehead is located governs perfection, the effect of perfection or nonperfection, and the priority of a security interest in as-extracted collateral.

SECTION 9-302. LAW GOVERNING PERFECTION AND PRIORITY OF AGRICULTURAL LIENS.

While farm products are located in a jurisdiction, the local law of that jurisdiction governs perfection, the effect of perfection or nonperfection, and the priority of an agricultural lien on the farm products.

SECTION 9-303. LAW GOVERNING PERFECTION AND PRIORITY OF SECURITY INTERESTS IN GOODS COVERED BY A CERTIFICATE OF TITLE.

(a) **[Applicability of section.]** This section applies to goods covered by a certificate of title, even if there is no other relationship between the jurisdiction under whose certificate of title the goods are covered and the goods or the debtor.

(b) **[When goods covered by certificate of title.]** Goods become covered by a certificate of title when a valid application for the certificate of title and the applicable fee are delivered to the appropriate authority. Goods cease to be covered by a certificate of title at the earlier of the time the certificate of title ceases to be effective under the law of the issuing jurisdiction or the time the goods become covered subsequently by a certificate of title issued by another jurisdiction.

(c) **[Applicable law.]** The local law of the jurisdiction under whose certificate of title the goods are covered governs perfection, the effect of perfection or nonperfection, and the priority of a security interest in goods covered by a certificate of title from the time the goods become covered by the certificate of title until the goods cease to be covered by the certificate of title.

SECTION 9-304. LAW GOVERNING PERFECTION AND PRIORITY OF SECURITY INTERESTS IN DEPOSIT ACCOUNTS.

(a) **[Law of bank's jurisdiction governs.]** The local law of a bank's jurisdiction governs perfection, the effect of perfection or nonperfection, and the priority of a security interest in a deposit account maintained with that bank.

(b) **[Bank's jurisdiction.]** The following rules determine a bank's jurisdiction for purposes of this part:

    (1) If an agreement between the bank and the debtor governing the deposit account expressly provides that a particular jurisdiction is the bank's jurisdiction for purposes of this part, this article, or [the Uniform Commercial Code], that jurisdiction is the bank's jurisdiction.

    (2) If paragraph (1) does not apply and an agreement between the bank and its customer governing the deposit account expressly provides that the agreement is governed by the law of a particular jurisdiction, that jurisdiction is the bank's jurisdiction.

    (3) If neither paragraph (1) nor paragraph (2) applies and an agreement between the bank and its customer governing the deposit account expressly provides that the deposit account is maintained at an office in a particular jurisdiction, that jurisdiction is the bank's jurisdiction.

    (4) If none of the preceding paragraphs applies, the bank's jurisdiction is the jurisdiction in which the office identified in an account statement as the office serving the customer's account is located.

    (5) If none of the preceding paragraphs applies, the bank's jurisdiction is the jurisdiction in which the chief executive office of the bank is located.

SECTION 9-305. LAW GOVERNING PERFECTION AND PRIORITY OF SECURITY INTERESTS IN INVESTMENT PROPERTY.

(a) **[Governing law: general rules.]** Except as otherwise provided in subsection (c), the following rules apply:

    (1) While a security certificate is located in a jurisdiction, the local law of that jurisdiction governs perfection, the effect of perfection or nonperfection, and the priority of a security interest in the certificated security represented thereby.

    (2) The local law of the issuer's jurisdiction as specified in Section 8-110(d) governs perfection, the effect of perfection or

nonperfection, and the priority of a security interest in an uncertificated security.

(3) The local law of the securities intermediary's jurisdiction as specified in Section 8-110(e) governs perfection, the effect of perfection or nonperfection, and the priority of a security interest in a security entitlement or securities account.

(4) The local law of the commodity intermediary's jurisdiction governs perfection, the effect of perfection or nonperfection, and the priority of a security interest in a commodity contract or commodity account.

(b) **[Commodity intermediary's jurisdiction.]** The following rules determine a commodity intermediary's jurisdiction for purposes of this part:

(1) If an agreement between the commodity intermediary and commodity customer governing the commodity account expressly provides that a particular jurisdiction is the commodity intermediary's jurisdiction for purposes of this part, this article, or [the Uniform Commercial Code], that jurisdiction is the commodity intermediary's jurisdiction.

(2) If paragraph (1) does not apply and an agreement between the commodity intermediary and commodity customer governing the commodity account expressly provides that the agreement is governed by the law of a particular jurisdiction, that jurisdiction is the commodity intermediary's jurisdiction.

(3) If neither paragraph (1) nor paragraph (2) applies and an agreement between the commodity intermediary and commodity customer governing the commodity account expressly provides that the commodity account is maintained at an office in a particular jurisdiction, that jurisdiction is the commodity intermediary's jurisdiction.

(4) If none of the preceding paragraphs applies, the commodity intermediary's jurisdiction is the jurisdiction in which the office identified in an account statement as the office serving the commodity customer's account is located.

(5) If none of the preceding paragraphs applies, the commodity intermediary's jurisdiction is the jurisdiction in which the chief executive office of the commodity intermediary is located.

(c) **[When perfection governed by law of jurisdiction where debtor located.]** The local law of the jurisdiction in which the debtor is located governs:

(1) perfection of a security interest in investment property by filing;

(2) automatic perfection of a security interest in investment property created by a broker or securities intermediary; and

(3) automatic perfection of a security interest in a commodity contract or commodity account created by a commodity intermediary.

SECTION 9-306. LAW GOVERNING PERFECTION AND PRIORITY OF SECURITY INTERESTS IN LETTER-OF-CREDIT RIGHTS.

(a) **[Governing law: issuer's or nominated person's jurisdiction.]** Subject to subsection (c), the local law of the issuer's jurisdiction or a nominated person's jurisdiction governs perfection, the effect of perfection or nonperfection, and the priority of a security interest in a letter-of-credit right if the issuer's jurisdiction or nominated person's jurisdiction is a State.

(b) **[Issuer's or nominated person's jurisdiction.]** For purposes of this part, an issuer's jurisdiction or nominated person's jurisdiction is the jurisdiction whose law governs the liability of the issuer or nominated person with respect to the letter-of-credit right as provided in Section 5-116.

(c) **[When section not applicable.]** This section does not apply to a security interest that is perfected only under Section 9-308(d).

SECTION 9-307. LOCATION OF DEBTOR.

(a) **["Place of business."]** In this section, "place of business" means a place where a debtor conducts its affairs.

(b) **[Debtor's location: general rules.]** Except as otherwise provided in this section, the following rules determine a debtor's location:

(1) A debtor who is an individual is located at the individual's principal residence.

(2) A debtor that is an organization and has only one place of business is located at its place of business.

(3) A debtor that is an organization and has more than one place of business is located at its chief executive office.

(c) **[Limitation of applicability of subsection (b).]** Subsection (b) applies only if a debtor's residence, place of business, or chief executive office, as applicable, is located in a jurisdiction whose law generally requires information concerning the existence of a nonpossessory security interest to be made generally available in a filing, recording, or registration system as a condition or result of the security interest's obtaining priority over the rights of a lien creditor with respect to the collateral. If subsection (b) does not apply, the debtor is located in the District of Columbia.

(d) **[Continuation of location: cessation of existence, etc.]** A person that ceases to exist, have a residence, or have a place of business continues to be located in the jurisdiction specified by subsections (b) and (c).

(e) **[Location of registered organization organized under State law.]** A registered organization that is organized under the law of a State is located in that State.

(f) **[Location of registered organization organized under federal law; bank branches and agencies.]** Except as otherwise provided in subsection (i), a registered organization that is organized under the law of the United States and a branch or agency of a bank that is not organized under the law of the United States or a State are located:
   (1) in the State that the law of the United States designates, if the law designates a State of location;
   (2) in the State that the registered organization, branch, or agency designates, if the law of the United States authorizes the registered organization, branch, or agency to designate its State of location; or
   (3) in the District of Columbia, if neither paragraph (1) nor paragraph (2) applies.

(g) **[Continuation of location: change in status of registered organization.]** A registered organization continues to be located in the jurisdiction specified by subsection (e) or (f) notwithstanding:
   (1) the suspension, revocation, forfeiture, or lapse of the registered organization's status as such in its jurisdiction of organization; or
   (2) the dissolution, winding up, or cancellation of the existence of the registered organization.

(h) **[Location of United States.]** The United States is located in the District of Columbia.

(i) **[Location of foreign bank branch or agency if licensed in only one state.]** A branch or agency of a bank that is not organized under the law of the United States or a State is located in the State in which the branch or agency is licensed, if all branches and agencies of the bank are licensed in only one State.

(j) **[Location of foreign air carrier.]** A foreign air carrier under the Federal Aviation Act of 1958, as amended, is located at the designated office of the agent upon which service of process may be made on behalf of the carrier.

(k) **[Section applies only to this part.]** This section applies only for purposes of this part.

[SUBPART 2. PERFECTION]

SECTION 9-308. WHEN SECURITY INTEREST OR AGRICULTURAL LIEN IS PERFECTED; CONTINUITY OF PERFECTION.

(a) **[Perfection of security interest.]** Except as otherwise provided in this section and Section 9-309, a security interest is perfected if it has attached and all of the applicable requirements for perfection in Sections 9-310 through 9-316 have been satisfied. A security interest is perfected when it attaches if the applicable requirements are satisfied before the security interest attaches.

(b) **[Perfection of agricultural lien.]** An agricultural lien is perfected if it has become effective and all of the applicable requirements for perfection in Section 9-310 have been satisfied. An agricultural lien is perfected when it becomes effective if the applicable requirements are satisfied before the agricultural lien becomes effective.

(c) **[Continuous perfection; perfection by different methods.]** A security interest or agricultural lien is perfected continuously if it is originally perfected by one method under this article and is later perfected by another method under this article, without an intermediate period when it was unperfected.

(d) **[Supporting obligation.]** Perfection of a security interest in collateral also perfects a security interest in a supporting obligation for the collateral.

(e) **[Lien securing right to payment.]** Perfection of a security interest in a right to payment or performance also perfects a security interest in a security interest, mortgage, or other lien on personal or real property securing the right.

(f) **[Security entitlement carried in securities account.]** Perfection of a security interest in a securities account also perfects a security interest in the security entitlements carried in the securities account.

(g) **[Commodity contract carried in commodity account.]** Perfection of a security interest in a commodity account also perfects a security interest in the commodity contracts carried in the commodity account.

Legislative Note: Any statute conflicting with subsection (e) must be made expressly subject to that subsection.

SECTION 9-309. SECURITY INTEREST PERFECTED UPON ATTACHMENT.

The following security interests are perfected when they attach:

(1) a purchase-money security interest in consumer goods, except as otherwise provided in Section 9-311(b) with respect to consumer goods that are subject to a statute or treaty described in Section 9-311(a);

(2) an assignment of accounts or payment intangibles which does not by itself or in conjunction with other assignments to the same assignee transfer a significant part of the assignor's outstanding accounts or payment intangibles;

(3) a sale of a payment intangible;

(4) a sale of a promissory note;

(5) a security interest created by the assignment of a health-care-insurance receivable to the provider of the health-care goods or services;

(6) a security interest arising under Section 2-401, 2-505, 2-711(3), or 2A-508(5), until the debtor obtains possession of the collateral;

(7) a security interest of a collecting bank arising under Section 4-210;

(8) a security interest of an issuer or nominated person arising under Section 5-118;

(9) a security interest arising in the delivery of a financial asset under Section 9-206(c);

(10) a security interest in investment property created by a broker or securities intermediary;

(11) a security interest in a commodity contract or a commodity account created by a commodity intermediary;

(12) an assignment for the benefit of all creditors of the transferor and subsequent transfers by the assignee thereunder; and

(13) a security interest created by an assignment of a beneficial interest in a decedent's estate.

SECTION 9-310. WHEN FILING REQUIRED TO PERFECT SECURITY INTEREST OR AGRICULTURAL LIEN; SECURITY INTERESTS AND AGRICULTURAL LIENS TO WHICH FILING PROVISIONS DO NOT APPLY.

(a) **[General rule: perfection by filing.]** Except as otherwise provided in subsection (b) and Section 9-312(b), a financing statement must be filed to perfect all security interests and agricultural liens.

(b) **[Exceptions: filing not necessary.]** The filing of a financing statement is not necessary to perfect a security interest:

(1) that is perfected under Section 9-308(d), (e), (f), or (g);

(2) that is perfected under Section 9-309 when it attaches;

(3) in property subject to a statute, regulation, or treaty described in Section 9-311(a);

(4) in goods in possession of a bailee which is perfected under Section 9-312(d)(1) or (2);

(5) in certificated securities, documents, goods, or instruments which is perfected without filing or possession under Section 9-312(e), (f), or (g);

(6) in collateral in the secured party's possession under Section 9-313;

(7) in a certificated security which is perfected by delivery of the security certificate to the secured party under Section 9-313;

(8) in deposit accounts, electronic chattel paper, investment property, or letter-of-credit rights which is perfected by control under Section 9-314;

(9) in proceeds which is perfected under Section 9-315; or

(10) that is perfected under Section 9-316.

(c) **[Assignment of perfected security interest.]** If a secured party assigns a perfected security interest or agricultural lien, a filing under this article is not required to continue the perfected status of the security interest against creditors of and transferees from the original debtor.

SECTION 9-311. PERFECTION OF SECURITY INTERESTS IN PROPERTY SUBJECT TO CERTAIN STATUTES, REGULATIONS, AND TREATIES.

(a) **[Security interest subject to other law.]** Except as otherwise provided in subsection (d), the filing of a financing statement is not necessary or effective to perfect a security interest in property subject to:

(1) a statute, regulation, or treaty of the United States whose requirements for a security interest's obtaining priority over the rights of a lien creditor with respect to the property preempt Section 9-310(a);

(2) [list any certificate-of-title statute covering automobiles, trailers, mobile homes, boats, farm tractors, or the like, which provides for a security interest to be indicated on the certificate as a condition or result of perfection, and any non-Uniform Commercial Code central filing statute]; or

(3) a certificate-of-title statute of another jurisdiction which provides for a security interest to be indicated on the certificate as a condition or result of the security interest's obtaining priority over the rights of a lien creditor with respect to the property.

(b) **[Compliance with other law.]** Compliance with the requirements of a statute, regulation, or treaty described in subsection (a) for obtaining priority over the rights of a lien creditor is equivalent to the filing of a financing statement under this article. Except as otherwise provided in subsection (d) and Sections 9-313 and 9-316(d) and (e) for goods covered by a certificate of title, a security interest in property subject to a statute, regulation, or treaty described in subsection (a) may be perfected only by compliance with those requirements, and a security interest so perfected remains perfected notwithstanding a change in the use or transfer of possession of the collateral.

(c) **[Duration and renewal of perfection.]** Except as otherwise provided in subsection (d) and Section 9-316(d) and (e), duration and renewal of perfection of a security interest perfected by compliance with the requirements prescribed by a statute, regulation, or treaty described in subsection (a) are governed by the statute, regulation, or treaty. In other respects, the security interest is subject to this article.

(d) **[Inapplicability to certain inventory.]** During any period in which collateral subject to a statute specified in subsection (a)(2) is inventory held for sale or lease by a person or leased by that person as lessor and that person is in the business of selling goods of that kind, this section does not apply to a security interest in that collateral created by that person.

Legislative Note: This Article contemplates that perfection of a security interest in goods covered by a certificate of title occurs upon receipt by appropriate State officials of a properly tendered application for a certificate of title on which the security interest is to be indicated, without a relation back to an earlier time. States whose certificate-of-title statutes provide for perfection at a different time or contain a relation-back provision should amend the statutes accordingly.

SECTION 9-312. PERFECTION OF SECURITY INTERESTS IN CHATTEL PAPER, DEPOSIT ACCOUNTS, DOCUMENTS, GOODS COVERED BY DOCUMENTS, INSTRUMENTS, INVESTMENT PROPERTY, LETTER-OF-CREDIT RIGHTS, AND MONEY; PERFECTION BY PERMISSIVE FILING; TEMPORARY PERFECTION WITHOUT FILING OR TRANSFER OF POSSESSION.

(a) **[Perfection by filing permitted.]** A security interest in chattel paper, negotiable documents, instruments, or investment property may be perfected by filing.

(b) **[Control or possession of certain collateral.]** Except as otherwise provided in Section 9-315(c) and (d) for proceeds:

(1) a security interest in a deposit account may be perfected only by control under Section 9-314;

(2) and except as otherwise provided in Section 9-308(d), a security interest in a letter-of-credit right may be perfected only by control under Section 9-314; and

(3) a security interest in money may be perfected only by the secured party's taking possession under Section 9-313.

(c) **[Goods covered by negotiable document.]** While goods are in the possession of a bailee that has issued a negotiable document covering the goods:

(1) a security interest in the goods may be perfected by perfecting a security interest in the document; and

(2) a security interest perfected in the document has priority over any security interest that becomes perfected in the goods by another method during that time.

(d) **[Goods covered by nonnegotiable document.]** While goods are in the possession of a bailee that has issued a nonnegotiable document covering the goods, a security interest in the goods may be perfected by:

(1) issuance of a document in the name of the secured party;

(2) the bailee's receipt of notification of the secured party's interest; or

(3) filing as to the goods.

(e) **[Temporary perfection: new value.]** A security interest in certificated securities, negotiable documents, or instruments is perfected without filing or the taking of possession for a period of 20 days from the time it attaches to the extent that it arises for new value given under an authenticated security agreement.

(f) **[Temporary perfection: goods or documents made available to debtor.]** A perfected security interest in a negotiable document or goods in possession of a bailee, other than one that has issued a negotiable document for the goods, remains perfected for 20 days without filing if the secured party makes available to the debtor the goods or documents representing the goods for the purpose of:

(1) ultimate sale or exchange; or

(2) loading, unloading, storing, shipping, transshipping, manufacturing, processing, or otherwise dealing with them in a manner preliminary to their sale or exchange.

(g) **[Temporary perfection: delivery of security certificate or instrument to debtor.]** A perfected security interest in a certificated security or instrument remains perfected for 20 days without filing if the secured party delivers the security certificate or instrument to the debtor for the purpose of:

(1) ultimate sale or exchange; or

(2) presentation, collection, enforcement, renewal, or registration of transfer.

(h) **[Expiration of temporary perfection.]** After the 20-day period specified in subsection (e), (f), or (g) expires, perfection depends upon compliance with this article.

SECTION 9-313. WHEN POSSESSION BY OR DELIVERY TO SECURED PARTY PERFECTS SECURITY INTEREST WITHOUT FILING.

(a) **[Perfection by possession or delivery.]** Except as otherwise provided in subsection (b), a secured party may perfect a security interest in negotiable documents, goods, instruments, money, or tangible chattel paper by taking possession of the collateral. A secured party may perfect a security interest in certificated securities by taking delivery of the certificated securities under Section 8-301.

(b) **[Goods covered by certificate of title.]** With respect to goods covered by a certificate of title issued by this State, a secured party may perfect a security interest in the goods by taking possession of the goods only in the circumstances described in Section 9-316(d).

(c) **[Collateral in possession of person other than debtor.]** With respect to collateral other than certificated securities and goods covered by a document, a secured party takes possession of collateral in the possession of a person other than the debtor, the secured party, or a lessee of the collateral from the debtor in the ordinary course of the debtor's business, when:

(1) the person in possession authenticates a record acknowledging that it holds possession of the collateral for the secured party's benefit; or

(2) the person takes possession of the collateral after having authenticated a record acknowledging that it will hold possession of collateral for the secured party's benefit.

(d) **[Time of perfection by possession; continuation of perfection.]** If perfection of a security interest depends upon possession of the collateral by a secured party, perfection occurs no earlier than the time the secured party takes possession and continues only while the secured party retains possession.

(e) **[Time of perfection by delivery; continuation of perfection.]** A security interest in a certificated security in registered form is perfected by delivery when delivery of the certificated security occurs under Section 8-301 and remains perfected by delivery until the debtor obtains possession of the security certificate.

(f) **[Acknowledgment not required.]** A person in possession of collateral is not required to acknowledge that it holds possession for a secured party's benefit.

(g) **[Effectiveness of acknowledgment; no duties or confirmation.]** If a person acknowledges that it holds possession for the secured party's benefit:

    (1) the acknowledgment is effective under subsection (c) or Section 8-301(a), even if the acknowledgment violates the rights of a debtor; and

    (2) unless the person otherwise agrees or law other than this article otherwise provides, the person does not owe any duty to the secured party and is not required to confirm the acknowledgment to another person.

(h) **[Secured party's delivery to person other than debtor.]** A secured party having possession of collateral does not relinquish possession by delivering the collateral to a person other than the debtor or a lessee of the collateral from the debtor in the ordinary course of the debtor's business if the person was instructed before the delivery or is instructed contemporaneously with the delivery:

    (1) to hold possession of the collateral for the secured party's benefit; or

    (2) to redeliver the collateral to the secured party.

(i) **[Effect of delivery under subsection (h); no duties or confirmation.]** A secured party does not relinquish possession, even if a delivery under subsection (h) violates the rights of a debtor. A person to which collateral is delivered under subsection (h) does not owe any duty to the secured party and is not required to confirm the delivery to another person unless the person otherwise agrees or law other than this article otherwise provides.

SECTION 9-314. PERFECTION BY CONTROL.

(a) **[Perfection by control.]** A security interest in investment property, deposit accounts, letter-of-credit rights, or electronic chattel paper may be perfected by control of the collateral under Section 9-104, 9-105, 9-106, or 9-107.

(b) **[Specified collateral: time of perfection by control; continuation of perfection.]** A security interest in deposit accounts, electronic chattel paper, or letter-of-credit rights is perfected by control under Section 9-104, 9-105, or 9-107 when the secured party obtains control and remains perfected by control only while the secured party retains control.

(c) **[Investment property: time of perfection by control; continuation of perfection.]** A security interest in investment property is perfected by control under Section 9-106 from the time the secured party obtains control and remains perfected by control until:

    (1) the secured party does not have control; and

    (2) one of the following occurs:

        (A) if the collateral is a certificated security, the debtor has or acquires possession of the security certificate;

        (B) if the collateral is an uncertificated security, the issuer has registered or registers the debtor as the registered owner; or

        (C) if the collateral is a security entitlement, the debtor is or becomes the entitlement holder.

SECTION 9-315. SECURED PARTY'S RIGHTS ON DISPOSITION OF COLLATERAL AND IN PROCEEDS.

(a) **[Disposition of collateral: continuation of security interest or agricultural lien; proceeds.]** Except as otherwise provided in this article and in Section 2-403(2):

    (1) a security interest or agricultural lien continues in collateral notwithstanding sale, lease, license, exchange, or other disposition thereof unless the secured party authorized the disposition free of the security interest or agricultural lien; and

    (2) a security interest attaches to any identifiable proceeds of collateral.

(b) **[When commingled proceeds identifiable.]** Proceeds that are commingled with other property are identifiable proceeds:

    (1) if the proceeds are goods, to the extent provided by Section 9-336; and

    (2) if the proceeds are not goods, to the extent that the secured party identifies the proceeds by a method of tracing, including application of equitable principles, that is permitted under law other than this article with respect to commingled property of the type involved.

(c) **[Perfection of security interest in proceeds.]** A security interest in proceeds is a perfected security interest if the security interest in the original collateral was perfected.

(d) **[Continuation of perfection.]** A perfected security interest in proceeds becomes unperfected on the 21st day after the security interest attaches to the proceeds unless:

(1) the following conditions are satisfied:
  (A) a filed financing statement covers the original collateral;
  (B) the proceeds are collateral in which a security interest may be perfected by filing in the office in which the financing statement has been filed; and
  (C) the proceeds are not acquired with cash proceeds;
(2) the proceeds are identifiable cash proceeds; or
(3) the security interest in the proceeds is perfected other than under subsection (c) when the security interest attaches to the proceeds or within 20 days thereafter.

(e) **[When perfected security interest in proceeds becomes unperfected.]** If a filed financing statement covers the original collateral, a security interest in proceeds which remains perfected under subsection (d)(1) becomes unperfected at the later of:
  (1) when the effectiveness of the filed financing statement lapses under Section 9-515 or is terminated under Section 9-513; or
  (2) the 21st day after the security interest attaches to the proceeds.

SECTION 9-316. CONTINUED PERFECTION OF SECURITY INTEREST FOLLOWING CHANGE IN GOVERNING LAW.

(a) **[General rule: effect on perfection of change in governing law.]** A security interest perfected pursuant to the law of the jurisdiction designated in Section 9-301(1) or 9-305(c) remains perfected until the earliest of:
  (1) the time perfection would have ceased under the law of that jurisdiction;
  (2) the expiration of four months after a change of the debtor's location to another jurisdiction; or
  (3) the expiration of one year after a transfer of collateral to a person that thereby becomes a debtor and is located in another jurisdiction.

(b) **[Security interest perfected or unperfected under law of new jurisdiction.]** If a security interest described in subsection (a) becomes perfected under the law of the other jurisdiction before the earliest time or event described in that subsection, it remains perfected thereafter. If the security interest does not become perfected under the law of the other jurisdiction before the earliest time or event, it becomes unperfected and is deemed never to have been perfected as against a purchaser of the collateral for value.

(c) **[Possessory security interest in collateral moved to new jurisdiction.]** A possessory security interest in collateral, other than goods covered by a certificate of title and as-extracted collateral consisting of goods, remains continuously perfected if:

(1) the collateral is located in one jurisdiction and subject to a security interest perfected under the law of that jurisdiction;

(2) thereafter the collateral is brought into another jurisdiction; and

(3) upon entry into the other jurisdiction, the security interest is perfected under the law of the other jurisdiction.

(d) **[Goods covered by certificate of title from this state.]** Except as otherwise provided in subsection (e), a security interest in goods covered by a certificate of title which is perfected by any method under the law of another jurisdiction when the goods become covered by a certificate of title from this State remains perfected until the security interest would have become unperfected under the law of the other jurisdiction had the goods not become so covered.

(e) **[When subsection (d) security interest becomes unperfected against purchasers.]** A security interest described in subsection (d) becomes unperfected as against a purchaser of the goods for value and is deemed never to have been perfected as against a purchaser of the goods for value if the applicable requirements for perfection under Section 9-311(b) or 9-313 are not satisfied before the earlier of:

(1) the time the security interest would have become unperfected under the law of the other jurisdiction had the goods not become covered by a certificate of title from this State; or

(2) the expiration of four months after the goods had become so covered.

(f) **[Change in jurisdiction of bank, issuer, nominated person, securities intermediary, or commodity intermediary.]** A security interest in deposit accounts, letter-of-credit rights, or investment property which is perfected under the law of the bank's jurisdiction, the issuer's jurisdiction, a nominated person's jurisdiction, the securities intermediary's jurisdiction, or the commodity intermediary's jurisdiction, as applicable, remains perfected until the earlier of:

(1) the time the security interest would have become unperfected under the law of that jurisdiction; or

(2) the expiration of four months after a change of the applicable jurisdiction to another jurisdiction.

(g) **[Subsection (f) security interest perfected or unperfected under law of new jurisdiction.]** If a security interest described in subsection (f) becomes perfected under the law of the other jurisdiction before the earlier of the time or the end of the period described in that subsection, it remains perfected thereafter. If the security interest does not become perfected under the law of the other jurisdiction before the earlier of that time or the end of that period, it becomes unperfected and is deemed never to have been perfected as against a purchaser of the collateral for value.

[SUBPART 3. PRIORITY]

SECTION 9-317. INTERESTS THAT TAKE PRIORITY OVER OR TAKE FREE OF SECURITY INTEREST OR AGRICULTURAL LIEN.

(a) **[Conflicting security interests and rights of lien creditors.]** A security interest or agricultural lien is subordinate to the rights of:
  (1) a person entitled to priority under Section 9-322; and
  (2) except as otherwise provided in subsection (e), a person that becomes a lien creditor before the earlier of the time:
      (A) the security interest or agricultural lien is perfected; or
      (B) one of the conditions specified in Section 9-203(b)(3) is met and a financing statement covering the collateral is filed.

(b) **[Buyers that receive delivery.]** Except as otherwise provided in subsection (e), a buyer, other than a secured party, of tangible chattel paper, documents, goods, instruments, or a security certificate takes free of a security interest or agricultural lien if the buyer gives value and receives delivery of the collateral without knowledge of the security interest or agricultural lien and before it is perfected.

(c) **[Lessees that receive delivery.]** Except as otherwise provided in subsection (e), a lessee of goods takes free of a security interest or agricultural lien if the lessee gives value and receives delivery of the collateral without knowledge of the security interest or agricultural lien and before it is perfected.

(d) **[Licensees and buyers of certain collateral.]** A licensee of a general intangible or a buyer, other than a secured party, of accounts, electronic chattel paper, general intangibles, or investment property other than a certificated security takes free of a security interest if the licensee or buyer gives value without knowledge of the security interest and before it is perfected.

(e) **[Purchase-money security interest.]** Except as otherwise provided in Sections 9-320 and 9-321, if a person files a financing statement with respect to a purchase-money security interest before or within 20 days after the debtor receives delivery of the collateral, the security interest takes priority over the rights of a buyer, lessee, or lien creditor which arise between the time the security interest attaches and the time of filing.

SECTION 9-318. NO INTEREST RETAINED IN RIGHT TO PAYMENT THAT IS SOLD; RIGHTS AND TITLE OF SELLER OF ACCOUNT OR CHATTEL PAPER WITH RESPECT TO CREDITORS AND PURCHASERS.

(a) **[Seller retains no interest.]** A debtor that has sold an account, chattel paper, payment intangible, or promissory note does not retain a legal or equitable interest in the collateral sold.

(b) **[Deemed rights of debtor if buyer's security interest unperfected.]** For purposes of determining the rights of creditors of, and purchasers for value of an account or chattel paper from, a debtor that has sold an account or chattel paper, while the buyer's security interest is unperfected, the debtor is deemed to have rights and title to the account or chattel paper identical to those the debtor sold.

SECTION 9-319. RIGHTS AND TITLE OF CONSIGNEE WITH RESPECT TO CREDITORS AND PURCHASERS.

(a) **[Consignee has consignor's rights.]** Except as otherwise provided in subsection (b), for purposes of determining the rights of creditors of, and purchasers for value of goods from, a consignee, while the goods are in the possession of the consignee, the consignee is deemed to have rights and title to the goods identical to those the consignor had or had power to transfer.

(b) **[Applicability of other law.]** For purposes of determining the rights of a creditor of a consignee, law other than this article determines the rights and title of a consignee while goods are in the consignee's possession if, under this part, a perfected security interest held by the consignor would have priority over the rights of the creditor.

SECTION 9-320. BUYER OF GOODS.

(a) **[Buyer in ordinary course of business.]** Except as otherwise provided in subsection (e), a buyer in ordinary course of business, other than a person buying farm products from a person engaged in farming operations, takes free of a security interest created by the buyer's seller, even if the security interest is perfected and the buyer knows of its existence.

(b) **[Buyer of consumer goods.]** Except as otherwise provided in subsection (e), a buyer of goods from a person who used or bought the goods for use primarily for personal, family, or household purposes takes free of a security interest, even if perfected, if the buyer buys:

(1) without knowledge of the security interest;

(2) for value;

(3) primarily for the buyer's personal, family, or household purposes; and

(4) before the filing of a financing statement covering the goods.

(c) **[Effectiveness of filing for subsection (b).]** To the extent that it affects the priority of a security interest over a buyer of goods under subsection (b), the period of effectiveness of a filing made in the jurisdiction in which the seller is located is governed by Section 9-316(a) and (b).

(d) **[Buyer in ordinary course of business at wellhead or minehead.]** A buyer in ordinary course of business buying oil, gas, or other minerals at the wellhead or minehead or after extraction takes free of an interest arising out of an encumbrance.

(e) **[Possessory security interest not affected.]** Subsections (a) and (b) do not affect a security interest in goods in the possession of the secured party under Section 9-313.

SECTION 9-321. LICENSEE OF GENERAL INTANGIBLE AND LESSEE OF GOODS IN ORDINARY COURSE OF BUSINESS.

(a) **["Licensee in ordinary course of business."]** In this section, "licensee in ordinary course of business" means a person that becomes a licensee of a general intangible in good faith, without knowledge that the license violates the rights of another person in the general intangible, and in the ordinary course from a person in the business of licensing general intangibles of that kind. A person becomes a licensee in the ordinary course if the license to the person comports with the usual or customary practices in the kind of business in which the licensor is engaged or with the licensor's own usual or customary practices.

(b) **[Rights of licensee in ordinary course of business.]** A licensee in ordinary course of business takes its rights under a nonexclusive license free of a security interest in the general intangible created by the licensor, even if the security interest is perfected and the licensee knows of its existence.

(c) **[Rights of lessee in ordinary course of business.]** A lessee in ordinary course of business takes its leasehold interest free of a security interest in the goods created by the lessor, even if the security interest is perfected and the lessee knows of its existence.

SECTION 9-322. PRIORITIES AMONG CONFLICTING
SECURITY INTERESTS IN AND AGRICULTURAL LIENS ON
SAME COLLATERAL.

(a) **[General priority rules.]** Except as otherwise provided in this section, priority among conflicting security interests and agricultural
liens in the same collateral is determined according to the following
rules:

   (1) Conflicting perfected security interests and agricultural liens rank
according to priority in time of filing or perfection. Priority dates
from the earlier of the time a filing covering the collateral is first
made or the security interest or agricultural lien is first perfected,
if there is no period thereafter when there is neither filing nor
perfection.

   (2) A perfected security interest or agricultural lien has priority
over a conflicting unperfected security interest or agricultural
lien.

   (3) The first security interest or agricultural lien to attach or become
effective has priority if conflicting security interests and agricultural liens are unperfected.

(b) **[Time of perfection: proceeds and supporting obligations.]** For
the purposes of subsection (a)(1):

   (1) the time of filing or perfection as to a security interest in collateral
is also the time of filing or perfection as to a security interest in
proceeds; and

   (2) the time of filing or perfection as to a security interest in collateral
supported by a supporting obligation is also the time of filing
or perfection as to a security interest in the supporting obligation.

(c) **[Special priority rules: proceeds and supporting obligations.]**
Except as otherwise provided in subsection (f), a security interest
in collateral which qualifies for priority over a conflicting security
interest under Section 9-327, 9-328, 9-329, 9-330, or 9-331 also has
priority over a conflicting security interest in:

   (1) any supporting obligation for the collateral; and

   (2) proceeds of the collateral if:

      (A) the security interest in proceeds is perfected;

      (B) the proceeds are cash proceeds or of the same type as the
collateral; and

      (C) in the case of proceeds that are proceeds of proceeds, all in-
tervening proceeds are cash proceeds, proceeds of the same
type as the collateral, or an account relating to the collateral.

(d) **[First-to-file priority rule for certain collateral.]** Subject to subsection (e) and except as otherwise provided in subsection (f), if a security interest in chattel paper, deposit accounts, negotiable documents, instruments, investment property, or letter-of-credit rights is perfected by a method other than filing, conflicting perfected security interests in proceeds of the collateral rank according to priority in time of filing.

(e) **[Applicability of subsection (d).]** Subsection (d) applies only if the proceeds of the collateral are not cash proceeds, chattel paper, negotiable documents, instruments, investment property, or letter-of-credit rights.

(f) **[Limitations on subsections (a) through (e).]** Subsections (a) through (e) are subject to:

(1) subsection (g) and the other provisions of this part;

(2) Section 4-210 with respect to a security interest of a collecting bank;

(3) Section 5-118 with respect to a security interest of an issuer or nominated person; and

(4) Section 9-110 with respect to a security interest arising under Article 2 or 2A.

(g) **[Priority under agricultural lien statute.]** A perfected agricultural lien on collateral has priority over a conflicting security interest in or agricultural lien on the same collateral if the statute creating the agricultural lien so provides.

SECTION 9-323. FUTURE ADVANCES.

(a) **[When priority based on time of advance.]** Except as otherwise provided in subsection (c), for purposes of determining the priority of a perfected security interest under Section 9-322(a)(1), perfection of the security interest dates from the time an advance is made to the extent that the security interest secures an advance that:

(1) is made while the security interest is perfected only:

(A) under Section 9-309 when it attaches; or

(B) temporarily under Section 9-312(e), (f), or (g); and

(2) is not made pursuant to a commitment entered into before or while the security interest is perfected by a method other than under Section 9-309 or 9-312(e), (f), or (g).

(b) **[Lien creditor.]** Except as otherwise provided in subsection (c), a security interest is subordinate to the rights of a person that becomes a lien creditor to the extent that the security interest secures an advance made more than 45 days after the person becomes a lien creditor unless the advance is made:

(1) without knowledge of the lien; or

(2) pursuant to a commitment entered into without knowledge of the lien.

(c) **[Buyer of receivables.]** Subsections (a) and (b) do not apply to a security interest held by a secured party that is a buyer of accounts, chattel paper, payment intangibles, or promissory notes or a consignor.

(d) **[Buyer of goods.]** Except as otherwise provided in subsection (e), a buyer of goods other than a buyer in ordinary course of business takes free of a security interest to the extent that it secures advances made after the earlier of:

(1) the time the secured party acquires knowledge of the buyer's purchase; or

(2) 45 days after the purchase.

(e) **[Advances made pursuant to commitment: priority of buyer of goods.]** Subsection (d) does not apply if the advance is made pursuant to a commitment entered into without knowledge of the buyer's purchase and before the expiration of the 45-day period.

(f) **[Lessee of goods.]** Except as otherwise provided in subsection (g), a lessee of goods, other than a lessee in ordinary course of business, takes the leasehold interest free of a security interest to the extent that it secures advances made after the earlier of:

(1) the time the secured party acquires knowledge of the lease; or

(2) 45 days after the lease contract becomes enforceable.

(g) **[Advances made pursuant to commitment: priority of lessee of goods.]** Subsection (f) does not apply if the advance is made pursuant to a commitment entered into without knowledge of the lease and before the expiration of the 45-day period.

SECTION 9-324. PRIORITY OF PURCHASE-MONEY SECURITY INTERESTS.

(a) **[General rule: purchase-money priority.]** Except as otherwise provided in subsection (g), a perfected purchase-money security interest in goods other than inventory or livestock has priority over a conflicting security interest in the same goods, and, except as otherwise provided in Section 9-327, a perfected security interest in its identifiable proceeds also has priority, if the purchase-money security interest is perfected when the debtor receives possession of the collateral or within 20 days thereafter.

(b) **[Inventory purchase-money priority.]** Subject to subsection (c) and except as otherwise provided in subsection (g), a perfected purchase-money security interest in inventory has priority over a conflicting security interest in the same inventory, has priority over a conflicting security interest in chattel paper or an instrument constituting proceeds of the inventory and in proceeds of the chattel paper, if so provided in Section 9-330, and, except as otherwise provided in Section 9-327, also has priority in identifiable cash proceeds of the inventory to the extent the identifiable cash proceeds are received on or before the delivery of the inventory to a buyer, if:

(1) the purchase-money security interest is perfected when the debtor receives possession of the inventory;

(2) the purchase-money secured party sends an authenticated notification to the holder of the conflicting security interest;

(3) the holder of the conflicting security interest receives the notification within five years before the debtor receives possession of the inventory; and

(4) the notification states that the person sending the notification has or expects to acquire a purchase-money security interest in inventory of the debtor and describes the inventory.

(c) **[Holders of conflicting inventory security interests to be notified.]** Subsections (b)(2) through (4) apply only if the holder of the conflicting security interest had filed a financing statement covering the same types of inventory:

(1) if the purchase-money security interest is perfected by filing, before the date of the filing; or

(2) if the purchase-money security interest is temporarily perfected without filing or possession under Section 9-312(f), before the beginning of the 20-day period thereunder.

(d) **[Livestock purchase-money priority.]** Subject to subsection (e) and except as otherwise provided in subsection (g), a perfected purchase-money security interest in livestock that are farm products has priority over a conflicting security interest in the same livestock, and, except as otherwise provided in Section 9-327, a perfected security interest in their identifiable proceeds and identifiable products in their unmanufactured states also has priority, if:

(1) the purchase-money security interest is perfected when the debtor receives possession of the livestock;

(2) the purchase-money secured party sends an authenticated notification to the holder of the conflicting security interest;

(3) the holder of the conflicting security interest receives the notification within six months before the debtor receives possession of the livestock; and

(4) the notification states that the person sending the notification has or expects to acquire a purchase-money security interest in livestock of the debtor and describes the livestock.

(e) **[Holders of conflicting livestock security interests to be notified.]** Subsections (d)(2) through (4) apply only if the holder of the conflicting security interest had filed a financing statement covering the same types of livestock:

(1) if the purchase-money security interest is perfected by filing, before the date of the filing; or

(2) if the purchase-money security interest is temporarily perfected without filing or possession under Section 9-312(f), before the beginning of the 20-day period thereunder.

(f) **[Software purchase-money priority.]** Except as otherwise provided in subsection (g), a perfected purchase-money security interest in software has priority over a conflicting security interest in the same collateral, and, except as otherwise provided in Section 9-327, a perfected security interest in its identifiable proceeds also has priority, to the extent that the purchase-money security interest in the goods in which the software was acquired for use has priority in the goods and proceeds of the goods under this section.

(g) **[Conflicting purchase-money security interests.]** If more than one security interest qualifies for priority in the same collateral under subsection (a), (b), (d), or (f):

(1) a security interest securing an obligation incurred as all or part of the price of the collateral has priority over a security interest securing an obligation incurred for value given to enable the debtor to acquire rights in or the use of collateral; and

(2) in all other cases, Section 9-322(a) applies to the qualifying security interests.

SECTION 9-325. PRIORITY OF SECURITY INTERESTS IN TRANSFERRED COLLATERAL.

(a) **[Subordination of security interest in transferred collateral.]** Except as otherwise provided in subsection (b), a security interest created by a debtor is subordinate to a security interest in the same collateral created by another person if:

(1) the debtor acquired the collateral subject to the security interest created by the other person;

(2) the security interest created by the other person was perfected when the debtor acquired the collateral; and

(3) there is no period thereafter when the security interest is unperfected.

(b) **[Limitation of subsection (a) subordination.]** Subsection (a) subordinates a security interest only if the security interest:

(1) otherwise would have priority solely under Section 9-322(a) or 9-324; or

(2) arose solely under Section 2-711(3) or 2A-508(5).

SECTION 9-326. PRIORITY OF SECURITY INTERESTS CREATED BY NEW DEBTOR.

(a) **[Subordination of security interest created by new debtor.]** Subject to subsection (b), a security interest created by a new debtor which is perfected by a filed financing statement that is effective solely under Section 9-508 in collateral in which a new debtor has or acquires rights is subordinate to a security interest in the same collateral which is perfected other than by a filed financing statement that is effective solely under Section 9-508.

(b) **[Priority under other provisions; multiple original debtors.]** The other provisions of this part determine the priority among conflicting security interests in the same collateral perfected by filed financing statements that are effective solely under Section 9-508. However, if the security agreements to which a new debtor became bound as debtor were not entered into by the same original debtor, the conflicting security interests rank according to priority in time of the new debtor's having become bound.

SECTION 9-327. PRIORITY OF SECURITY INTERESTS IN DEPOSIT ACCOUNT.

The following rules govern priority among conflicting security interests in the same deposit account:

(1) A security interest held by a secured party having control of the deposit account under Section 9-104 has priority over a conflicting security interest held by a secured party that does not have control.

(2) Except as otherwise provided in paragraphs (3) and (4), security interests perfected by control under Section 9-314 rank according to priority in time of obtaining control.

(3) Except as otherwise provided in paragraph (4), a security interest held by the bank with which the deposit account is maintained has priority over a conflicting security interest held by another secured party.

(4) A security interest perfected by control under Section 9-104(a)(3) has priority over a security interest held by the bank with which the deposit account is maintained.

SECTION 9-328. PRIORITY OF SECURITY INTERESTS IN INVESTMENT PROPERTY.
The following rules govern priority among conflicting security interests in the same investment property:
(1) A security interest held by a secured party having control of investment property under Section 9-106 has priority over a security interest held by a secured party that does not have control of the investment property.
(2) Except as otherwise provided in paragraphs (3) and (4), conflicting security interests held by secured parties each of which has control under Section 9-106 rank according to priority in time of:
   (A) if the collateral is a security, obtaining control;
   (B) if the collateral is a security entitlement carried in a securities account and:
      (i) if the secured party obtained control under Section 8-106(d)(1), the secured party's becoming the person for which the securities account is maintained;
      (ii) if the secured party obtained control under Section 8-106(d)(2), the securities intermediary's agreement to comply with the secured party's entitlement orders with respect to security entitlements carried or to be carried in the securities account; or
      (iii) if the secured party obtained control through another person under Section 8-106(d)(3), the time on which priority would be based under this paragraph if the other person were the secured party; or
   (C) if the collateral is a commodity contract carried with a commodity intermediary, the satisfaction of the requirement for control specified in Section 9-106(b)(2) with respect to commodity contracts carried or to be carried with the commodity intermediary.
(3) A security interest held by a securities intermediary in a security entitlement or a securities account maintained with the securities intermediary has priority over a conflicting security interest held by another secured party.
(4) A security interest held by a commodity intermediary in a commodity contract or a commodity account maintained with the commodity intermediary has priority over a conflicting security interest held by another secured party.

(5) A security interest in a certificated security in registered form which is perfected by taking delivery under Section 9-313(a) and not by control under Section 9-314 has priority over a conflicting security interest perfected by a method other than control.

(6) Conflicting security interests created by a broker, securities intermediary, or commodity intermediary which are perfected without control under Section 9-106 rank equally.

(7) In all other cases, priority among conflicting security interests in investment property is governed by Sections 9-322 and 9-323.

SECTION 9-329. PRIORITY OF SECURITY INTERESTS IN LETTER-OF-CREDIT RIGHT.

The following rules govern priority among conflicting security interests in the same letter-of-credit right:

(1) A security interest held by a secured party having control of the letter-of-credit right under Section 9-107 has priority to the extent of its control over a conflicting security interest held by a secured party that does not have control.

(2) Security interests perfected by control under Section 9-314 rank according to priority in time of obtaining control.

SECTION 9-330. PRIORITY OF PURCHASER OF CHATTEL PAPER OR INSTRUMENT.

(a) **[Purchaser's priority: security interest claimed merely as proceeds.]** A purchaser of chattel paper has priority over a security interest in the chattel paper which is claimed merely as proceeds of inventory subject to a security interest if:

(1) in good faith and in the ordinary course of the purchaser's business, the purchaser gives new value and takes possession of the chattel paper or obtains control of the chattel paper under Section 9-105; and

(2) the chattel paper does not indicate that it has been assigned to an identified assignee other than the purchaser.

(b) **[Purchaser's priority: other security interests.]** A purchaser of chattel paper has priority over a security interest in the chattel paper which is claimed other than merely as proceeds of inventory subject to a security interest if the purchaser gives new value and takes possession of the chattel paper or obtains control of the chattel paper under Section 9-105 in good faith, in the ordinary course of the purchaser's business, and without knowledge that the purchase violates the rights of the secured party.

(c) **[Chattel paper purchaser's priority in proceeds.]** Except as otherwise provided in Section 9-327, a purchaser having priority in chattel paper under subsection (a) or (b) also has priority in proceeds of the chattel paper to the extent that:

(1) Section 9-322 provides for priority in the proceeds; or

(2) the proceeds consist of the specific goods covered by the chattel paper or cash proceeds of the specific goods, even if the purchaser's security interest in the proceeds is unperfected.

(d) **[Instrument purchaser's priority.]** Except as otherwise provided in Section 9-331(a), a purchaser of an instrument has priority over a security interest in the instrument perfected by a method other than possession if the purchaser gives value and takes possession of the instrument in good faith and without knowledge that the purchase violates the rights of the secured party.

(e) **[Holder of purchase-money security interest gives new value.]** For purposes of subsections (a) and (b), the holder of a purchase-money security interest in inventory gives new value for chattel paper constituting proceeds of the inventory.

(f) **[Indication of assignment gives knowledge.]** For purposes of subsections (b) and (d), if chattel paper or an instrument indicates that it has been assigned to an identified secured party other than the purchaser, a purchaser of the chattel paper or instrument has knowledge that the purchase violates the rights of the secured party.

SECTION 9-331. PRIORITY OF RIGHTS OF PURCHASERS OF INSTRUMENTS, DOCUMENTS, AND SECURITIES UNDER OTHER ARTICLES; PRIORITY OF INTERESTS IN FINANCIAL ASSETS AND SECURITY ENTITLEMENTS UNDER ARTICLE 8.

(a) **[Rights under Articles 3, 7, and 8 not limited.]** This article does not limit the rights of a holder in due course of a negotiable instrument, a holder to which a negotiable document of title has been duly negotiated, or a protected purchaser of a security. These holders or purchasers take priority over an earlier security interest, even if perfected, to the extent provided in Articles 3, 7, and 8.

(b) **[Protection under Article 8.]** This article does not limit the rights of or impose liability on a person to the extent that the person is protected against the assertion of a claim under Article 8.

(c) **[Filing not notice.]** Filing under this article does not constitute notice of a claim or defense to the holders, or purchasers, or persons described in subsections (a) and (b).

SECTION 9-332. TRANSFER OF MONEY; TRANSFER OF FUNDS FROM DEPOSIT ACCOUNT.

(a) **[Transferee of money.]** A transferee of money takes the money free of a security interest unless the transferee acts in collusion with the debtor in violating the rights of the secured party.

(b) **[Transferee of funds from deposit account.]** A transferee of funds from a deposit account takes the funds free of a security interest in the deposit account unless the transferee acts in collusion with the debtor in violating the rights of the secured party.

SECTION 9-333. PRIORITY OF CERTAIN LIENS ARISING BY OPERATION OF LAW.

(a) **["Possessory lien."]** In this section, "possessory lien" means an interest, other than a security interest or an agricultural lien:

    (1) which secures payment or performance of an obligation for services or materials furnished with respect to goods by a person in the ordinary course of the person's business;

    (2) which is created by statute or rule of law in favor of the person; and

    (3) whose effectiveness depends on the person's possession of the goods.

(b) **[Priority of possessory lien.]** A possessory lien on goods has priority over a security interest in the goods unless the lien is created by a statute that expressly provides otherwise.

SECTION 9-334. PRIORITY OF SECURITY INTERESTS IN FIXTURES AND CROPS.

(a) **[Security interest in fixtures under this article.]** A security interest under this article may be created in goods that are fixtures or may continue in goods that become fixtures. A security interest does not exist under this article in ordinary building materials incorporated into an improvement on land.

(b) **[Security interest in fixtures under real-property law.]** This article does not prevent creation of an encumbrance upon fixtures under real-property law.

(c) **[General rule: subordination of security interest in fixtures.]** In cases not governed by subsections (d) through (h), a security interest in fixtures is subordinate to a conflicting interest of an encumbrancer or owner of the related real property other than the debtor.

(d) **[Fixtures purchase-money priority.]** Except as otherwise provided in subsection (h), a perfected security interest in fixtures has priority over a conflicting interest of an encumbrancer or owner of the real property if the debtor has an interest of record in or is in possession of the real property and:

(1) the security interest is a purchase-money security interest;

(2) the interest of the encumbrancer or owner arises before the goods become fixtures; and

(3) the security interest is perfected by a fixture filing before the goods become fixtures or within 20 days thereafter.

(e) **[Priority of security interest in fixtures over interests in real property.]** A perfected security interest in fixtures has priority over a conflicting interest of an encumbrancer or owner of the real property if:

(1) the debtor has an interest of record in the real property or is in possession of the real property and the security interest:

    (A) is perfected by a fixture filing before the interest of the encumbrancer or owner is of record; and

    (B) has priority over any conflicting interest of a predecessor in title of the encumbrancer or owner;

(2) before the goods become fixtures, the security interest is perfected by any method permitted by this article and the fixtures are readily removable:

    (A) factory or office machines;

    (B) equipment that is not primarily used or leased for use in the operation of the real property; or

    (C) replacements of domestic appliances that are consumer goods;

(3) the conflicting interest is a lien on the real property obtained by legal or equitable proceedings after the security interest was perfected by any method permitted by this article; or

(4) the security interest is:

    (A) created in a manufactured home in a manufactured-home transaction; and

    (B) perfected pursuant to a statute described in Section 9-311(a)(2).

(f) **[Priority based on consent, disclaimer, or right to remove.]** A security interest in fixtures, whether or not perfected, has priority over a conflicting interest of an encumbrancer or owner of the real property if:

(1) the encumbrancer or owner has, in an authenticated record, consented to the security interest or disclaimed an interest in the goods as fixtures; or

(2) the debtor has a right to remove the goods as against the encumbrancer or owner.

(g) **[Continuation of paragraph (f)(2) priority.]** The priority of the security interest under paragraph (f)(2) continues for a reasonable time if the debtor's right to remove the goods as against the encumbrancer or owner terminates.

(h) **[Priority of construction mortgage.]** A mortgage is a construction mortgage to the extent that it secures an obligation incurred for the construction of an improvement on land, including the acquisition cost of the land, if a recorded record of the mortgage so indicates. Except as otherwise provided in subsections (e) and (f), a security interest in fixtures is subordinate to a construction mortgage if a record of the mortgage is recorded before the goods become fixtures and the goods become fixtures before the completion of the construction. A mortgage has this priority to the same extent as a construction mortgage to the extent that it is given to refinance a construction mortgage.

(i) **[Priority of security interest in crops.]** A perfected security interest in crops growing on real property has priority over a conflicting interest of an encumbrancer or owner of the real property if the debtor has an interest of record in or is in possession of the real property.

(j) **[Subsection (i) prevails.]** Subsection (i) prevails over any inconsistent provisions of the following statutes:

[List here any statutes containing provisions inconsistent with subsection (i).]

Legislative Note: States that amend statutes to remove provisions inconsistent with subsection (i) need not enact subsection (j).

SECTION 9-335. ACCESSIONS.

(a) **[Creation of security interest in accession.]** A security interest may be created in an accession and continues in collateral that becomes an accession.

(b) **[Perfection of security interest.]** If a security interest is perfected when the collateral becomes an accession, the security interest remains perfected in the collateral.

(c) **[Priority of security interest.]** Except as otherwise provided in subsection (d), the other provisions of this part determine the priority of a security interest in an accession.

(d) **[Compliance with certificate-of-title statute.]** A security interest in an accession is subordinate to a security interest in the whole which is perfected by compliance with the requirements of a certificate-of-title statute under Section 9-311(b).

(e) **[Removal of accession after default.]** After default, subject to Part 6, a secured party may remove an accession from other goods if the security interest in the accession has priority over the claims of every person having an interest in the whole.

(f) **[Reimbursement following removal.]** A secured party that removes an accession from other goods under subsection (e) shall promptly reimburse any holder of a security interest or other lien on, or owner of, the whole or of the other goods, other than the debtor, for the cost of repair of any physical injury to the whole or the other goods. The secured party need not reimburse the holder or owner for any diminution in value of the whole or the other goods caused by the absence of the accession removed or by any necessity for replacing it. A person entitled to reimbursement may refuse permission to remove until the secured party gives adequate assurance for the performance of the obligation to reimburse.

SECTION 9-336. COMMINGLED GOODS.

(a) **["Commingled goods."]** In this section, "commingled goods" means goods that are physically united with other goods in such a manner that their identity is lost in a product or mass.

(b) **[No security interest in commingled goods as such.]** A security interest does not exist in commingled goods as such. However, a security interest may attach to a product or mass that results when goods become commingled goods.

(c) **[Attachment of security interest to product or mass.]** If collateral becomes commingled goods, a security interest attaches to the product or mass.

(d) **[Perfection of security interest.]** If a security interest in collateral is perfected before the collateral becomes commingled goods, the security interest that attaches to the product or mass under subsection (c) is perfected.

(e) **[Priority of security interest.]** Except as otherwise provided in subsection (f), the other provisions of this part determine the priority of a security interest that attaches to the product or mass under subsection (c).

(f) **[Conflicting security interests in product or mass.]** If more than one security interest attaches to the product or mass under subsection (c), the following rules determine priority:

   (1) A security interest that is perfected under subsection (d) has priority over a security interest that is unperfected at the time the collateral becomes commingled goods.

(2) If more than one security interest is perfected under subsection (d), the security interests rank equally in proportion to the value of the collateral at the time it became commingled goods.

SECTION 9-337. PRIORITY OF SECURITY INTERESTS IN GOODS COVERED BY CERTIFICATE OF TITLE.

If, while a security interest in goods is perfected by any method under the law of another jurisdiction, this State issues a certificate of title that does not show that the goods are subject to the security interest or contain a statement that they may be subject to security interests not shown on the certificate:

(1) a buyer of the goods, other than a person in the business of selling goods of that kind, takes free of the security interest if the buyer gives value and receives delivery of the goods after issuance of the certificate and without knowledge of the security interest; and

(2) the security interest is subordinate to a conflicting security interest in the goods that attaches, and is perfected under Section 9-311(b), after issuance of the certificate and without the conflicting secured party's knowledge of the security interest.

SECTION 9-338. PRIORITY OF SECURITY INTEREST OR AGRICULTURAL LIEN PERFECTED BY FILED FINANCING STATEMENT PROVIDING CERTAIN INCORRECT INFORMATION.

If a security interest or agricultural lien is perfected by a filed financing statement providing information described in Section 9-516(b)(5) which is incorrect at the time the financing statement is filed:

(1) the security interest or agricultural lien is subordinate to a conflicting perfected security interest in the collateral to the extent that the holder of the conflicting security interest gives value in reasonable reliance upon the incorrect information; and

(2) a purchaser, other than a secured party, of the collateral takes free of the security interest or agricultural lien to the extent that, in reasonable reliance upon the incorrect information, the purchaser gives value and, in the case of chattel paper, documents, goods, instruments, or a security certificate, receives delivery of the collateral.

SECTION 9-339. PRIORITY SUBJECT TO SUBORDINATION.

This article does not preclude subordination by agreement by a person entitled to priority.

[SUBPART 4. RIGHTS OF BANK]

SECTION 9-340. EFFECTIVENESS OF RIGHT OF RECOUPMENT OR SET-OFF AGAINST DEPOSIT ACCOUNT.

(a) **[Exercise of recoupment or set-off.]** Except as otherwise provided in subsection (c), a bank with which a deposit account is maintained may exercise any right of recoupment or set-off against a secured party that holds a security interest in the deposit account.

(b) **[Recoupment or set-off not affected by security interest.]** Except as otherwise provided in subsection (c), the application of this article to a security interest in a deposit account does not affect a right of recoupment or set-off of the secured party as to a deposit account maintained with the secured party.

(c) **[When set-off ineffective.]** The exercise by a bank of a set-off against a deposit account is ineffective against a secured party that holds a security interest in the deposit account which is perfected by control under Section 9-104(a)(3), if the set-off is based on a claim against the debtor.

SECTION 9-341. BANK'S RIGHTS AND DUTIES WITH RESPECT TO DEPOSIT ACCOUNT.

Except as otherwise provided in Section 9-340(c), and unless the bank otherwise agrees in an authenticated record, a bank's rights and duties with respect to a deposit account maintained with the bank are not terminated, suspended, or modified by:

(1) the creation, attachment, or perfection of a security interest in the deposit account;

(2) the bank's knowledge of the security interest; or

(3) the bank's receipt of instructions from the secured party.

SECTION 9-342. BANK'S RIGHT TO REFUSE TO ENTER INTO OR DISCLOSE EXISTENCE OF CONTROL AGREEMENT.

This article does not require a bank to enter into an agreement of the kind described in Section 9-104(a)(2), even if its customer so requests or directs. A bank that has entered into such an agreement is not required to confirm the existence of the agreement to another person unless requested to do so by its customer.

PART 4 – RIGHTS OF THIRD PARTIES

SECTION 9-401. ALIENABILITY OF DEBTOR'S RIGHTS.

(a) **[Other law governs alienability; exceptions.]** Except as otherwise provided in subsection (b) and Sections 9-406, 9-407, 9-408, and

9-409, whether a debtor's rights in collateral may be voluntarily or involuntarily transferred is governed by law other than this article.

(b) **[Agreement does not prevent transfer.]** An agreement between the debtor and secured party which prohibits a transfer of the debtor's rights in collateral or makes the transfer a default does not prevent the transfer from taking effect.

SECTION 9-402. SECURED PARTY NOT OBLIGATED ON CONTRACT OF DEBTOR OR IN TORT.

The existence of a security interest, agricultural lien, or authority given to a debtor to dispose of or use collateral, without more, does not subject a secured party to liability in contract or tort for the debtor's acts or omissions.

SECTION 9-403. AGREEMENT NOT TO ASSERT DEFENSES AGAINST ASSIGNEE.

(a) **["Value."]** In this section, "value" has the meaning provided in Section 3-303(a).

(b) **[Agreement not to assert claim or defense.]** Except as otherwise provided in this section, an agreement between an account debtor and an assignor not to assert against an assignee any claim or defense that the account debtor may have against the assignor is enforceable by an assignee that takes an assignment:

(1) for value;

(2) in good faith;

(3) without notice of a claim of a property or possessory right to the property assigned; and

(4) without notice of a defense or claim in recoupment of the type that may be asserted against a person entitled to enforce a negotiable instrument under Section 3-305(a).

(c) **[When subsection (b) not applicable.]** Subsection (b) does not apply to defenses of a type that may be asserted against a holder in due course of a negotiable instrument under Section 3-305(b).

(d) **[Omission of required statement in consumer transaction.]** In a consumer transaction, if a record evidences the account debtor's obligation, law other than this article requires that the record include a statement to the effect that the rights of an assignee are subject to claims or defenses that the account debtor could assert against the original obligee, and the record does not include such a statement:

(1) the record has the same effect as if the record included such a statement; and

(2) the account debtor may assert against an assignee those claims and defenses that would have been available if the record included such a statement.

(e) **[Rule for individual under other law.]** This section is subject to law other than this article which establishes a different rule for an account debtor who is an individual and who incurred the obligation primarily for personal, family, or household purposes.

(f) **[Other law not displaced.]** Except as otherwise provided in subsection (d), this section does not displace law other than this article which gives effect to an agreement by an account debtor not to assert a claim or defense against an assignee.

SECTION 9-404. RIGHTS ACQUIRED BY ASSIGNEE; CLAIMS AND DEFENSES AGAINST ASSIGNEE.

(a) **[Assignee's rights subject to terms, claims, and defenses; exceptions.]** Unless an account debtor has made an enforceable agreement not to assert defenses or claims, and subject to subsections (b) through (e), the rights of an assignee are subject to:

(1) all terms of the agreement between the account debtor and assignor and any defense or claim in recoupment arising from the transaction that gave rise to the contract; and

(2) any other defense or claim of the account debtor against the assignor which accrues before the account debtor receives a notification of the assignment authenticated by the assignor or the assignee.

(b) **[Account debtor's claim reduces amount owed to assignee.]** Subject to subsection (c) and except as otherwise provided in subsection (d), the claim of an account debtor against an assignor may be asserted against an assignee under subsection (a) only to reduce the amount the account debtor owes.

(c) **[Rule for individual under other law.]** This section is subject to law other than this article which establishes a different rule for an account debtor who is an individual and who incurred the obligation primarily for personal, family, or household purposes.

(d) **[Omission of required statement in consumer transaction.]** In a consumer transaction, if a record evidences the account debtor's obligation, law other than this article requires that the record include a statement to the effect that the account debtor's recovery against an assignee with respect to claims and defenses against the assignor may not exceed amounts paid by the account debtor under the record, and the record does not include such a statement, the extent to which a claim of an account debtor against the assignor may be asserted against an assignee is determined as if the record included such a statement.

(e) **[Inapplicability to health-care-insurance receivable.]** This section does not apply to an assignment of a health-care-insurance receivable.

SECTION 9-405. MODIFICATION OF ASSIGNED CONTRACT.

(a) **[Effect of modification on assignee.]** A modification of or substitution for an assigned contract is effective against an assignee if made in good faith. The assignee acquires corresponding rights under the modified or substituted contract. The assignment may provide that the modification or substitution is a breach of contract by the assignor. This subsection is subject to subsections (b) through (d).

(b) **[Applicability of subsection (a).]** Subsection (a) applies to the extent that:

(1) the right to payment or a part thereof under an assigned contract has not been fully earned by performance; or

(2) the right to payment or a part thereof has been fully earned by performance and the account debtor has not received notification of the assignment under Section 9-406(a).

(c) **[Rule for individual under other law.]** This section is subject to law other than this article which establishes a different rule for an account debtor who is an individual and who incurred the obligation primarily for personal, family, or household purposes.

(d) **[Inapplicability to health-care-insurance receivable.]** This section does not apply to an assignment of a health-care-insurance receivable.

SECTION 9-406. DISCHARGE OF ACCOUNT DEBTOR; NOTIFICATION OF ASSIGNMENT; IDENTIFICATION AND PROOF OF ASSIGNMENT; RESTRICTIONS ON ASSIGNMENT OF ACCOUNTS, CHATTEL PAPER, PAYMENT INTANGIBLES, AND PROMISSORY NOTES INEFFECTIVE.

(a) **[Discharge of account debtor; effect of notification.]** Subject to subsections (b) through (i), an account debtor on an account, chattel paper, or a payment intangible may discharge its obligation by paying the assignor until, but not after, the account debtor receives a notification, authenticated by the assignor or the assignee, that the amount due or to become due has been assigned and that payment is to be made to the assignee. After receipt of the notification, the account debtor may discharge its obligation by paying the assignee and may not discharge the obligation by paying the assignor.

(b) **[When notification ineffective.]** Subject to subsection (h), notification is ineffective under subsection (a):

    (1) if it does not reasonably identify the rights assigned;

    (2) to the extent that an agreement between an account debtor and a seller of a payment intangible limits the account debtor's duty to pay a person other than the seller and the limitation is effective under law other than this article; or

    (3) at the option of an account debtor, if the notification notifies the account debtor to make less than the full amount of any installment or other periodic payment to the assignee, even if:

        (A) only a portion of the account, chattel paper, or payment intangible has been assigned to that assignee;

        (B) a portion has been assigned to another assignee; or

        (C) the account debtor knows that the assignment to that assignee is limited.

(c) **[Proof of assignment.]** Subject to subsection (h), if requested by the account debtor, an assignee shall seasonably furnish reasonable proof that the assignment has been made. Unless the assignee complies, the account debtor may discharge its obligation by paying the assignor, even if the account debtor has received a notification under subsection (a).

(d) **[Term restricting assignment generally ineffective.]** Except as otherwise provided in subsection (e) and Sections 2A-303 and 9-407, and subject to subsection (h), a term in an agreement between an account debtor and an assignor or in a promissory note is ineffective to the extent that it:

    (1) prohibits, restricts, or requires the consent of the account debtor or person obligated on the promissory note to the assignment or transfer of, or the creation, attachment, perfection, or enforcement of a security interest in, the account, chattel paper, payment intangible, or promissory note; or

    (2) provides that the assignment or transfer or the creation, attachment, perfection, or enforcement of the security interest may give rise to a default, breach, right of recoupment, claim, defense, termination, right of termination, or remedy under the account, chattel paper, payment intangible, or promissory note.

(e) **[Inapplicability of subsection (d) to certain sales.]** Subsection (d) does not apply to the sale of a payment intangible or promissory note.

(f) **[Legal restrictions on assignment generally ineffective.]** Except as otherwise provided in Sections 2A-303 and 9-407 and subject to subsections (h) and (i), a rule of law, statute, or regulation that prohibits, restricts, or requires the consent of a government, governmental body or official, or account debtor to the assignment or transfer of, or creation of a security interest in, an account or chattel paper is ineffective to the extent that the rule of law, statute, or regulation:

(1) prohibits, restricts, or requires the consent of the government, governmental body or official, or account debtor to the assignment or transfer of, or the creation, attachment, perfection, or enforcement of a security interest in the account or chattel paper; or

(2) provides that the assignment or transfer or the creation, attachment, perfection, or enforcement of the security interest may give rise to a default, breach, right of recoupment, claim, defense, termination, right of termination, or remedy under the account or chattel paper.

(g) **[Subsection (b)(3) not waivable.]** Subject to subsection (h), an account debtor may not waive or vary its option under subsection (b)(3).

(h) **[Rule for individual under other law.]** This section is subject to law other than this article which establishes a different rule for an account debtor who is an individual and who incurred the obligation primarily for personal, family, or household purposes.

(i) **[Inapplicability to health-care-insurance receivable.]** This section does not apply to an assignment of a health-care-insurance receivable.

(j) **[Section prevails over specified inconsistent law.]** This section prevails over any inconsistent provisions of the following statutes, rules, and regulations:

[List here any statutes, rules, and regulations containing provisions inconsistent with this section.]

Legislative Note: States that amend statutes, rules, and regulations to remove provisions inconsistent with this section need not enact subsection (j).

SECTION 9-407. RESTRICTIONS ON CREATION OR ENFORCEMENT OF SECURITY INTEREST IN LEASEHOLD INTEREST OR IN LESSOR'S RESIDUAL INTEREST.

(a) **[Term restricting assignment generally ineffective.]** Except as otherwise provided in subsection (b), a term in a lease agreement is ineffective to the extent that it:

(1) prohibits, restricts, or requires the consent of a party to the lease to the assignment or transfer of, or the creation, attachment, perfection, or enforcement of a security interest in, an interest of

a party under the lease contract or in the lessor's residual interest
in the goods; or

(2) provides that the assignment or transfer or the creation, attachment, perfection, or enforcement of the security interest may
give rise to a default, breach, right of recoupment, claim, defense, termination, right of termination, or remedy under the
lease.

(b) **[Effectiveness of certain terms.]** Except as otherwise provided in
Section 2A-303(7), a term described in subsection (a)(2) is effective
to the extent that there is:

(1) a transfer by the lessee of the lessee's right of possession or use
of the goods in violation of the term; or

(2) a delegation of a material performance of either party to the lease
contract in violation of the term.

(c) **[Security interest not material impairment.]** The creation, attachment, perfection, or enforcement of a security interest in the
lessor's interest under the lease contract or the lessor's residual interest in the goods is not a transfer that materially impairs the lessee's
prospect of obtaining return performance or materially changes the
duty of or materially increases the burden or risk imposed on the lessee
within the purview of Section 2A-303(4) unless, and then only to the
extent that, enforcement actually results in a delegation of material
performance of the lessor.

SECTION 9-408. RESTRICTIONS ON ASSIGNMENT OF PROMISSORY NOTES, HEALTH-CARE-INSURANCE RECEIVABLES, AND CERTAIN GENERAL INTANGIBLES INEFFECTIVE.

(a) **[Term restricting assignment generally ineffective.]** Except as
otherwise provided in subsection (b), a term in a promissory note
or in an agreement between an account debtor and a debtor which
relates to a health-care-insurance receivable or a general intangible,
including a contract, permit, license, or franchise, and which term
prohibits, restricts, or requires the consent of the person obligated
on the promissory note or the account debtor to, the assignment or
transfer of, or creation, attachment, or perfection of a security interest
in, the promissory note, health-care-insurance receivable, or general
intangible, is ineffective to the extent that the term:

(1) would impair the creation, attachment, or perfection of a security
interest; or

(2) provides that the assignment or transfer or the creation, attachment, or perfection of the security interest may give rise to a

default, breach, right of recoupment, claim, defense, termination, right of termination, or remedy under the promissory note, health-care-insurance receivable, or general intangible.

(b) **[Applicability of subsection (a) to sales of certain rights to payment.]** Subsection (a) applies to a security interest in a payment intangible or promissory note only if the security interest arises out of a sale of the payment intangible or promissory note.

(c) **[Legal restrictions on assignment generally ineffective.]** A rule of law, statute, or regulation that prohibits, restricts, or requires the consent of a government, governmental body or official, person obligated on a promissory note, or account debtor to the assignment or transfer of, or creation of a security interest in, a promissory note, health-care-insurance receivable, or general intangible, including a contract, permit, license, or franchise between an account debtor and a debtor, is ineffective to the extent that the rule of law, statute, or regulation:

(1) would impair the creation, attachment, or perfection of a security interest; or

(2) provides that the assignment or transfer or the creation, attachment, or perfection of the security interest may give rise to a default, breach, right of recoupment, claim, defense, termination, right of termination, or remedy under the promissory note, health-care-insurance receivable, or general intangible.

(d) **[Limitation on ineffectiveness under subsections (a) and (c).]** To the extent that a term in a promissory note or in an agreement between an account debtor and a debtor which relates to a health-care-insurance receivable or general intangible or a rule of law, statute, or regulation described in subsection (c) would be effective under law other than this article but is ineffective under subsection (a) or (c), the creation, attachment, or perfection of a security interest in the promissory note, health-care-insurance receivable, or general intangible:

(1) is not enforceable against the person obligated on the promissory note or the account debtor;

(2) does not impose a duty or obligation on the person obligated on the promissory note or the account debtor;

(3) does not require the person obligated on the promissory note or the account debtor to recognize the security interest, pay or render performance to the secured party, or accept payment or performance from the secured party;

(4) does not entitle the secured party to use or assign the debtor's rights under the promissory note, health-care-insurance

receivable, or general intangible, including any related information or materials furnished to the debtor in the transaction giving rise to the promissory note, health-care-insurance receivable, or general intangible;

(5) does not entitle the secured party to use, assign, possess, or have access to any trade secrets or confidential information of the person obligated on the promissory note or the account debtor; and

(6) does not entitle the secured party to enforce the security interest in the promissory note, health-care-insurance receivable, or general intangible.

(e) **[Section prevails over specified inconsistent law.]** This section prevails over any inconsistent provisions of the following statutes, rules, and regulations:

[List here any statutes, rules, and regulations containing provisions inconsistent with this section.]

Legislative Note: States that amend statutes, rules, and regulations to remove provisions inconsistent with this section need not enact subsection (e).

SECTION 9-409. RESTRICTIONS ON ASSIGNMENT OF LETTER-OF-CREDIT RIGHTS INEFFECTIVE.

(a) **[Term or law restricting assignment generally ineffective.]** A term in a letter of credit or a rule of law, statute, regulation, custom, or practice applicable to the letter of credit which prohibits, restricts, or requires the consent of an applicant, issuer, or nominated person to a beneficiary's assignment of or creation of a security interest in a letter-of-credit right is ineffective to the extent that the term or rule of law, statute, regulation, custom, or practice:

(1) would impair the creation, attachment, or perfection of a security interest in the letter-of-credit right; or

(2) provides that the assignment or the creation, attachment, or perfection of the security interest may give rise to a default, breach, right of recoupment, claim, defense, termination, right of termination, or remedy under the letter-of-credit right.

(b) **[Limitation on ineffectiveness under subsection (a).]** To the extent that a term in a letter of credit is ineffective under subsection (a) but would be effective under law other than this article or a custom or practice applicable to the letter of credit, to the transfer of a right to draw or otherwise demand performance under the letter of credit, or to the assignment of a right to proceeds of the letter of credit, the creation, attachment, or perfection of a security interest in the letter-of-credit right:

(1) is not enforceable against the applicant, issuer, nominated person, or transferee beneficiary;

(2) imposes no duties or obligations on the applicant, issuer, nominated person, or transferee beneficiary; and

(3) does not require the applicant, issuer, nominated person, or transferee beneficiary to recognize the security interest, pay or render performance to the secured party, or accept payment or other performance from the secured party.

PART 5 – FILING

[SUBPART 1. FILING OFFICE; CONTENTS AND EFFECTIVENESS OF FINANCING STATEMENT]

SECTION 9-501. FILING OFFICE.

(a) **[Filing offices.]** Except as otherwise provided in subsection (b), if the local law of this State governs perfection of a security interest or agricultural lien, the office in which to file a financing statement to perfect the security interest or agricultural lien is:

(1) the office designated for the filing or recording of a record of a mortgage on the related real property, if:

(A) the collateral is as-extracted collateral or timber to be cut; or

(B) the financing statement is filed as a fixture filing and the collateral is goods that are or are to become fixtures; or

(2) the office of [ ] [or any office duly authorized by [ ]], in all other cases, including a case in which the collateral is goods that are or are to become fixtures and the financing statement is not filed as a fixture filing.

(b) **[Filing office for transmitting utilities.]** The office in which to file a financing statement to perfect a security interest in collateral, including fixtures, of a transmitting utility is the office of [ ]. The financing statement also constitutes a fixture filing as to the collateral indicated in the financing statement which is or is to become fixtures.

Legislative Note: The State should designate the filing office where the brackets appear. The filing office may be that of a governmental official (e.g., the Secretary of State) or a private party that maintains the State's filing system.

SECTION 9-502. CONTENTS OF FINANCING STATEMENT; RECORD OF MORTGAGE AS FINANCING STATEMENT; TIME OF FILING FINANCING STATEMENT.

(a) **[Sufficiency of financing statement.]** Subject to subsection (b), a financing statement is sufficient only if it:

(1) provides the name of the debtor;

(2) provides the name of the secured party or a representative of the secured party; and

(3) indicates the collateral covered by the financing statement.

(b) **[Real-property-related financing statements.]** Except as otherwise provided in Section 9-501(b), to be sufficient, a financing statement that covers as-extracted collateral or timber to be cut, or which is filed as a fixture filing and covers goods that are or are to become fixtures, must satisfy subsection (a) and also:

(1) indicate that it covers this type of collateral;

(2) indicate that it is to be filed [for record] in the real-property records;

(3) provide a description of the real property to which the collateral is related [sufficient to give constructive notice of a mortgage under the law of this State if the description were contained in a record of the mortgage of the real property]; and

(4) if the debtor does not have an interest of record in the real property, provide the name of a record owner.

(c) **[Record of mortgage as financing statement.]** A record of a mortgage is effective, from the date of recording, as a financing statement filed as a fixture filing or as a financing statement covering as-extracted collateral or timber to be cut only if:

(1) the record indicates the goods or accounts that it covers;

(2) the goods are or are to become fixtures related to the real property described in the record or the collateral is related to the real property described in the record and is as-extracted collateral or timber to be cut;

(3) the record satisfies the requirements for a financing statement in this section other than an indication that it is to be filed in the real-property records; and

(4) the record is [duly] recorded.

(d) **[Filing before security agreement or attachment.]** A financing statement may be filed before a security agreement is made or a security interest otherwise attaches.

Legislative Note: Language in brackets is optional. Where the State has any special recording system for real property other than the usual grantor–grantee index (as, for instance, a tract system or a title registration or Torrens system) local adaptations of subsection (b) and Section 9-519(d) and (e) may be necessary. See, e.g., Mass. Gen. Laws Chapter 106, Section 9-410.

SECTION 9-503. NAME OF DEBTOR AND SECURED PARTY.

(a) **[Sufficiency of debtor's name.]** A financing statement sufficiently provides the name of the debtor:

(1) if the debtor is a registered organization, only if the financing statement provides the name of the debtor indicated on the public record of the debtor's jurisdiction of organization which shows the debtor to have been organized;

(2) if the debtor is a decedent's estate, only if the financing statement provides the name of the decedent and indicates that the debtor is an estate;

(3) if the debtor is a trust or a trustee acting with respect to property held in trust, only if the financing statement:

   (A) provides the name specified for the trust in its organic documents or, if no name is specified, provides the name of the settlor and additional information sufficient to distinguish the debtor from other trusts having one or more of the same settlors; and

   (B) indicates, in the debtor's name or otherwise, that the debtor is a trust or is a trustee acting with respect to property held in trust; and

(4) in other cases:

   (A) if the debtor has a name, only if it provides the individual or organizational name of the debtor; and

   (B) if the debtor does not have a name, only if it provides the names of the partners, members, associates, or other persons comprising the debtor.

(b) **[Additional debtor-related information.]** A financing statement that provides the name of the debtor in accordance with subsection (a) is not rendered ineffective by the absence of:

(1) a trade name or other name of the debtor; or

(2) unless required under subsection (a)(4)(B), names of partners, members, associates, or other persons comprising the debtor.

(c) **[Debtor's trade name insufficient.]** A financing statement that provides only the debtor's trade name does not sufficiently provide the name of the debtor.

(d) **[Representative capacity.]** Failure to indicate the representative capacity of a secured party or representative of a secured party does not affect the sufficiency of a financing statement.

(e) **[Multiple debtors and secured parties.]** A financing statement may provide the name of more than one debtor and the name of more than one secured party.

SECTION 9-504. INDICATION OF COLLATERAL.

A financing statement sufficiently indicates the collateral that it covers if the financing statement provides:

(1) a description of the collateral pursuant to Section 9-108; or

(2) an indication that the financing statement covers all assets or all personal property.

SECTION 9-505. FILING AND COMPLIANCE WITH OTHER STATUTES AND TREATIES FOR CONSIGNMENTS, LEASES, OTHER BAILMENTS, AND OTHER TRANSACTIONS.

(a) **[Use of terms other than "debtor" and "secured party."]** A consignor, lessor, or other bailor of goods, a licensor, or a buyer of a payment intangible or promissory note may file a financing statement, or may comply with a statute or treaty described in Section 9-311(a), using the terms "consignor," "consignee," "lessor," "lessee," "bailor," "bailee," "licensor," "licensee," "owner," "registered owner," "buyer," "seller," or words of similar import, instead of the terms "secured party" and "debtor."

(b) **[Effect of financing statement under subsection (a).]** This part applies to the filing of a financing statement under subsection (a) and, as appropriate, to compliance that is equivalent to filing a financing statement under Section 9-311(b), but the filing or compliance is not of itself a factor in determining whether the collateral secures an obligation. If it is determined for another reason that the collateral secures an obligation, a security interest held by the consignor, lessor, bailor, licensor, owner, or buyer which attaches to the collateral is perfected by the filing or compliance.

SECTION 9-506. EFFECT OF ERRORS OR OMISSIONS.

(a) **[Minor errors and omissions.]** A financing statement substantially satisfying the requirements of this part is effective, even if it has minor errors or omissions, unless the errors or omissions make the financing statement seriously misleading.

(b) **[Financing statement seriously misleading.]** Except as otherwise provided in subsection (c), a financing statement that fails sufficiently to provide the name of the debtor in accordance with Section 9-503(a) is seriously misleading.

(c) **[Financing statement not seriously misleading.]** If a search of the records of the filing office under the debtor's correct name, using the filing office's standard search logic, if any, would disclose a financing statement that fails sufficiently to provide the name of the debtor in accordance with Section 9-503(a), the name provided does not make the financing statement seriously misleading.

(d) **["Debtor's correct name."]** For purposes of Section 9-508(b), the "debtor's correct name" in subsection (c) means the correct name of the new debtor.

SECTION 9-507. EFFECT OF CERTAIN EVENTS ON
EFFECTIVENESS OF FINANCING STATEMENT.

(a) **[Disposition.]** A filed financing statement remains effective with respect to collateral that is sold, exchanged, leased, licensed, or otherwise disposed of and in which a security interest or agricultural
lien continues, even if the secured party knows of or consents to the
disposition.

(b) **[Information becoming seriously misleading.]** Except as otherwise provided in subsection (c) and Section 9-508, a financing statement is not rendered ineffective if, after the financing statement is
filed, the information provided in the financing statement becomes
seriously misleading under Section 9-506.

(c) **[Change in debtor's name.]** If a debtor so changes its name that a
filed financing statement becomes seriously misleading under Section
9-506:

   (1) the financing statement is effective to perfect a security interest
   in collateral acquired by the debtor before, or within four months
   after, the change; and

   (2) the financing statement is not effective to perfect a security interest in collateral acquired by the debtor more than four months
   after the change, unless an amendment to the financing statement
   which renders the financing statement not seriously misleading
   is filed within four months after the change.

SECTION 9-508. EFFECTIVENESS OF FINANCING
STATEMENT IF NEW DEBTOR BECOMES BOUND BY
SECURITY AGREEMENT.

(a) **[Financing statement naming original debtor.]** Except as otherwise provided in this section, a filed financing statement naming an
original debtor is effective to perfect a security interest in collateral
in which a new debtor has or acquires rights to the extent that the
financing statement would have been effective had the original debtor
acquired rights in the collateral.

(b) **[Financing statement becoming seriously misleading.]** If the
difference between the name of the original debtor and that of the
new debtor causes a filed financing statement that is effective under
subsection (a) to be seriously misleading under Section 9-506:

   (1) the financing statement is effective to perfect a security interest
   in collateral acquired by the new debtor before, and within four
   months after, the new debtor becomes bound under Section 9-
   203(d); and

(2) the financing statement is not effective to perfect a security interest in collateral acquired by the new debtor more than four months after the new debtor becomes bound under Section 9-203(d) unless an initial financing statement providing the name of the new debtor is filed before the expiration of that time.

(c) **[When section not applicable.]** This section does not apply to collateral as to which a filed financing statement remains effective against the new debtor under Section 9-507(a).

SECTION 9-509. PERSONS ENTITLED TO FILE A RECORD.

(a) **[Person entitled to file record.]** A person may file an initial financing statement, amendment that adds collateral covered by a financing statement, or amendment that adds a debtor to a financing statement only if:

   (1) the debtor authorizes the filing in an authenticated record or pursuant to subsection (b) or (c); or

   (2) the person holds an agricultural lien that has become effective at the time of filing and the financing statement covers only collateral in which the person holds an agricultural lien.

(b) **[Security agreement as authorization.]** By authenticating or becoming bound as debtor by a security agreement, a debtor or new debtor authorizes the filing of an initial financing statement, and an amendment, covering:

   (1) the collateral described in the security agreement; and

   (2) property that becomes collateral under Section 9-315(a)(2), whether or not the security agreement expressly covers proceeds.

(c) **[Acquisition of collateral as authorization.]** By acquiring collateral in which a security interest or agricultural lien continues under Section 9-315(a)(1), a debtor authorizes the filing of an initial financing statement, and an amendment, covering the collateral and property that becomes collateral under Section 9-315(a)(2).

(d) **[Person entitled to file certain amendments.]** A person may file an amendment other than an amendment that adds collateral covered by a financing statement or an amendment that adds a debtor to a financing statement only if:

   (1) the secured party of record authorizes the filing; or

   (2) the amendment is a termination statement for a financing statement as to which the secured party of record has failed to file or send a termination statement as required by Section 9-513(a) or

(c), the debtor authorizes the filing, and the termination statement indicates that the debtor authorized it to be filed.

(e) **[Multiple secured parties of record.]** If there is more than one secured party of record for a financing statement, each secured party of record may authorize the filing of an amendment under subsection (d).

SECTION 9-510. EFFECTIVENESS OF FILED RECORD.

(a) **[Filed record effective if authorized.]** A filed record is effective only to the extent that it was filed by a person that may file it under Section 9-509.

(b) **[Authorization by one secured party of record.]** A record authorized by one secured party of record does not affect the financing statement with respect to another secured party of record.

(c) **[Continuation statement not timely filed.]** A continuation statement that is not filed within the six-month period prescribed by Section 9-515(d) is ineffective.

SECTION 9-511. SECURED PARTY OF RECORD.

(a) **[Secured party of record.]** A secured party of record with respect to a financing statement is a person whose name is provided as the name of the secured party or a representative of the secured party in an initial financing statement that has been filed. If an initial financing statement is filed under Section 9-514(a), the assignee named in the initial financing statement is the secured party of record with respect to the financing statement.

(b) **[Amendment naming secured party of record.]** If an amendment of a financing statement which provides the name of a person as a secured party or a representative of a secured party is filed, the person named in the amendment is a secured party of record. If an amendment is filed under Section 9-514(b), the assignee named in the amendment is a secured party of record.

(c) **[Amendment deleting secured party of record.]** A person remains a secured party of record until the filing of an amendment of the financing statement which deletes the person.

SECTION 9-512. AMENDMENT OF FINANCING STATEMENT.

[Alternative A]

(a) **[Amendment of information in financing statement.]** Subject to Section 9-509, a person may add or delete collateral covered by, continue or terminate the effectiveness of, or, subject to subsection (e), otherwise amend the information provided in, a financing statement by filing an amendment that:

(1) identifies, by its file number, the initial financing statement to which the amendment relates; and

(2) if the amendment relates to an initial financing statement filed [or recorded] in a filing office described in Section 9-501(a)(1), provides the information specified in Section 9-502(b).

[Alternative B]

(a) **[Amendment of information in financing statement.]** Subject to Section 9-509, a person may add or delete collateral covered by, continue or terminate the effectiveness of, or, subject to subsection (e), otherwise amend the information provided in, a financing statement by filing an amendment that:

(1) identifies, by its file number, the initial financing statement to which the amendment relates; and

(2) if the amendment relates to an initial financing statement filed [or recorded] in a filing office described in Section 9-501(a)(1), provides the date [and time] that the initial financing statement was filed [or recorded] and the information specified in Section 9-502(b).

[End of Alternatives]

(b) **[Period of effectiveness not affected.]** Except as otherwise provided in Section 9-515, the filing of an amendment does not extend the period of effectiveness of the financing statement.

(c) **[Effectiveness of amendment adding collateral.]** A financing statement that is amended by an amendment that adds collateral is effective as to the added collateral only from the date of the filing of the amendment.

(d) **[Effectiveness of amendment adding debtor.]** A financing statement that is amended by an amendment that adds a debtor is effective as to the added debtor only from the date of the filing of the amendment.

(e) **[Certain amendments ineffective.]** An amendment is ineffective to the extent it:

(1) purports to delete all debtors and fails to provide the name of a debtor to be covered by the financing statement; or

(2) purports to delete all secured parties of record and fails to provide the name of a new secured party of record.

Legislative Note: States whose real-estate filing offices require additional information in amendments and cannot search their records by both the name of the debtor and the file number should enact Alternative B to Sections 9-512(a), 9-518(b), 9-519(f) and 9-522(a).

SECTION 9-513. TERMINATION STATEMENT.

(a) **[Consumer goods.]** A secured party shall cause the secured party of record for a financing statement to file a termination statement for the financing statement if the financing statement covers consumer goods and:

    (1) there is no obligation secured by the collateral covered by the financing statement and no commitment to make an advance, incur an obligation, or otherwise give value; or

    (2) the debtor did not authorize the filing of the initial financing statement.

(b) **[Time for compliance with subsection (a).]** To comply with subsection (a), a secured party shall cause the secured party of record to file the termination statement:

    (1) within one month after there is no obligation secured by the collateral covered by the financing statement and no commitment to make an advance, incur an obligation, or otherwise give value; or

    (2) if earlier, within 20 days after the secured party receives an authenticated demand from a debtor.

(c) **[Other collateral.]** In cases not governed by subsection (a), within 20 days after a secured party receives an authenticated demand from a debtor, the secured party shall cause the secured party of record for a financing statement to send to the debtor a termination statement for the financing statement or file the termination statement in the filing office if:

    (1) except in the case of a financing statement covering accounts or chattel paper that has been sold or goods that are the subject of a consignment, there is no obligation secured by the collateral covered by the financing statement and no commitment to make an advance, incur an obligation, or otherwise give value;

    (2) the financing statement covers accounts or chattel paper that has been sold but as to which the account debtor or other person obligated has discharged its obligation;

    (3) the financing statement covers goods that were the subject of a consignment to the debtor but are not in the debtor's possession; or

    (4) the debtor did not authorize the filing of the initial financing statement.

(d) **[Effect of filing termination statement.]** Except as otherwise provided in Section 9-510, upon the filing of a termination statement with the filing office, the financing statement to which the termination statement relates ceases to be effective. Except as otherwise provided in Section 9-510, for purposes of Sections 9-519(g), 9-522(a), and 9-523(c), the filing with the filing office of a termination statement relating to a financing statement that indicates that the debtor is a transmitting utility also causes the effectiveness of the financing statement to lapse.

SECTION 9-514. ASSIGNMENT OF POWERS OF SECURED PARTY OF RECORD.

(a) **[Assignment reflected on initial financing statement.]** Except as otherwise provided in subsection (c), an initial financing statement may reflect an assignment of all of the secured party's power to authorize an amendment to the financing statement by providing the name and mailing address of the assignee as the name and address of the secured party.

(b) **[Assignment of filed financing statement.]** Except as otherwise provided in subsection (c), a secured party of record may assign of record all or part of its power to authorize an amendment to a financing statement by filing in the filing office an amendment of the financing statement which:

   (1) identifies, by its file number, the initial financing statement to which it relates;

   (2) provides the name of the assignor; and

   (3) provides the name and mailing address of the assignee.

(c) **[Assignment of record of mortgage.]** An assignment of record of a security interest in a fixture covered by a record of a mortgage which is effective as a financing statement filed as a fixture filing under Section 9-502(c) may be made only by an assignment of record of the mortgage in the manner provided by law of this State other than [the Uniform Commercial Code].

SECTION 9-515. DURATION AND EFFECTIVENESS OF FINANCING STATEMENT; EFFECT OF LAPSED FINANCING STATEMENT.

(a) **[Five-year effectiveness.]** Except as otherwise provided in subsections (b), (e), (f), and (g), a filed financing statement is effective for a period of five years after the date of filing.

(b) **[Public-finance or manufactured-home transaction.]** Except as otherwise provided in subsections (e), (f), and (g), an initial financing statement filed in connection with a public-finance transaction or manufactured-home transaction is effective for a period of 30 years after the date of filing if it indicates that it is filed in connection with a public-finance transaction or manufactured-home transaction.

(c) **[Lapse and continuation of financing statement.]** The effectiveness of a filed financing statement lapses on the expiration of the period of its effectiveness unless before the lapse a continuation statement is filed pursuant to subsection (d). Upon lapse, a financing statement ceases to be effective and any security interest or agricultural lien that was perfected by the financing statement becomes unperfected, unless the security interest is perfected otherwise. If the security interest or agricultural lien becomes unperfected upon lapse, it is deemed never to have been perfected as against a purchaser of the collateral for value.

(d) **[When continuation statement may be filed.]** A continuation statement may be filed only within six months before the expiration of the five-year period specified in subsection (a) or the 30-year period specified in subsection (b), whichever is applicable.

(e) **[Effect of filing continuation statement.]** Except as otherwise provided in Section 9-510, upon timely filing of a continuation statement, the effectiveness of the initial financing statement continues for a period of five years commencing on the day on which the financing statement would have become ineffective in the absence of the filing. Upon the expiration of the five-year period, the financing statement lapses in the same manner as provided in subsection (c), unless, before the lapse, another continuation statement is filed pursuant to subsection (d). Succeeding continuation statements may be filed in the same manner to continue the effectiveness of the initial financing statement.

(f) **[Transmitting utility financing statement.]** If a debtor is a transmitting utility and a filed financing statement so indicates, the financing statement is effective until a termination statement is filed.

(g) **[Record of mortgage as financing statement.]** A record of a mortgage that is effective as a financing statement filed as a fixture filing under Section 9-502(c) remains effective as a financing statement filed as a fixture filing until the mortgage is released or satisfied of record or its effectiveness otherwise terminates as to the real property.

SECTION 9-516. WHAT CONSTITUTES FILING;
EFFECTIVENESS OF FILING.

(a) **[What constitutes filing.]** Except as otherwise provided in subsection (b), communication of a record to a filing office and tender of the filing fee or acceptance of the record by the filing office constitutes filing.

(b) **[Refusal to accept record; filing does not occur.]** Filing does not occur with respect to a record that a filing office refuses to accept because:

(1) the record is not communicated by a method or medium of communication authorized by the filing office;

(2) an amount equal to or greater than the applicable filing fee is not tendered;

(3) the filing office is unable to index the record because:

    (A) in the case of an initial financing statement, the record does not provide a name for the debtor;

    (B) in the case of an amendment or correction statement, the record:

        (i) does not identify the initial financing statement, as required by Section 9-512 or 9-518, as applicable; or

        (ii) identifies an initial financing statement whose effectiveness has lapsed under Section 9-515;

    (C) in the case of an initial financing statement that provides the name of a debtor identified as an individual or an amendment that provides a name of a debtor identified as an individual which was not previously provided in the financing statement to which the record relates, the record does not identify the debtor's last name; or

    (D) in the case of a record filed [or recorded] in the filing office described in Section 9-501(a)(1), the record does not provide a sufficient description of the real property to which it relates;

(4) in the case of an initial financing statement or an amendment that adds a secured party of record, the record does not provide a name and mailing address for the secured party of record;

(5) in the case of an initial financing statement or an amendment that provides a name of a debtor which was not previously provided in the financing statement to which the amendment relates, the record does not:

    (A) provide a mailing address for the debtor;

    (B) indicate whether the debtor is an individual or an organization; or

    (C) if the financing statement indicates that the debtor is an organization, provide:

        (i) a type of organization for the debtor;

        (ii) a jurisdiction of organization for the debtor; or

        (iii) an organizational identification number for the debtor or indicate that the debtor has none;

(6) in the case of an assignment reflected in an initial financing statement under Section 9-514(a) or an amendment filed under Section 9-514(b), the record does not provide a name and mailing address for the assignee; or

(7) in the case of a continuation statement, the record is not filed within the six-month period prescribed by Section 9-515(d).

(c) **[Rules applicable to subsection (b).]** For purposes of subsection (b):

(1) a record does not provide information if the filing office is unable to read or decipher the information; and

(2) a record that does not indicate that it is an amendment or identify an initial financing statement to which it relates, as required by Section 9-512, 9-514, or 9-518, is an initial financing statement.

(d) **[Refusal to accept record; record effective as filed record.]** A record that is communicated to the filing office with tender of the filing fee, but which the filing office refuses to accept for a reason other than one set forth in subsection (b), is effective as a filed record except as against a purchaser of the collateral which gives value in reasonable reliance upon the absence of the record from the files.

SECTION 9-517. EFFECT OF INDEXING ERRORS.

The failure of the filing office to index a record correctly does not affect the effectiveness of the filed record.

SECTION 9-518. CLAIM CONCERNING INACCURATE OR WRONGFULLY FILED RECORD.

(a) **[Correction statement.]** A person may file in the filing office a correction statement with respect to a record indexed there under the person's name if the person believes that the record is inaccurate or was wrongfully filed.

[Alternative A]

(b) **[Sufficiency of correction statement.]** A correction statement must:

(1) identify the record to which it relates by the file number assigned to the initial financing statement to which the record relates;

(2) indicate that it is a correction statement; and

(3) provide the basis for the person's belief that the record is inaccurate and indicate the manner in which the person believes the record should be amended to cure any inaccuracy or provide the basis for the person's belief that the record was wrongfully filed.

[Alternative B]

(b) **[Sufficiency of correction statement.**] A correction statement must:

    (1) identify the record to which it relates by:

        (A) the file number assigned to the initial financing statement to which the record relates; and

        (B) if the correction statement relates to a record filed [or recorded] in a filing office described in Section 9-501(a)(1), the date [and time] that the initial financing statement was filed [or recorded] and the information specified in Section 9-502(b);

    (2) indicate that it is a correction statement; and

    (3) provide the basis for the person's belief that the record is inaccurate and indicate the manner in which the person believes the record should be amended to cure any inaccuracy or provide the basis for the person's belief that the record was wrongfully filed.

[End of Alternatives]

(c) **[Record not affected by correction statement.**] The filing of a correction statement does not affect the effectiveness of an initial financing statement or other filed record.

Legislative Note: States whose real-estate filing offices require additional information in amendments and cannot search their records by both the name of the debtor and the file number should enact Alternative B to Sections 9-512(a), 9-518(b), 9-519(f) and 9-522(a).

[SUBPART 2. DUTIES AND OPERATION OF FILING OFFICE]

SECTION 9-519. NUMBERING, MAINTAINING, AND INDEXING RECORDS; COMMUNICATING INFORMATION PROVIDED IN RECORDS.

(a) **[Filing-office duties.**] For each record filed in a filing office, the filing office shall:

    (1) assign a unique number to the filed record;

    (2) create a record that bears the number assigned to the filed record and the date and time of filing;

    (3) maintain the filed record for public inspection; and

    (4) index the filed record in accordance with subsections (c), (d), and (e).

(b) **[File number.**] A file number [assigned after January 1, 2002,] must include a digit that:

    (1) is mathematically derived from or related to the other digits of the file number; and

(2) aids the filing office in determining whether a number communicated as the file number includes a single-digit or transpositional error.

(c) **[Indexing: general.]** Except as otherwise provided in subsections (d) and (e), the filing office shall:

    (1) index an initial financing statement according to the name of the debtor and index all filed records relating to the initial financing statement in a manner that associates with one another an initial financing statement and all filed records relating to the initial financing statement; and

    (2) index a record that provides a name of a debtor which was not previously provided in the financing statement to which the record relates also according to the name that was not previously provided.

(d) **[Indexing: real-property-related financing statement.]** If a financing statement is filed as a fixture filing or covers as-extracted collateral or timber to be cut, [it must be filed for record and] the filing office shall index it:

    (1) under the names of the debtor and of each owner of record shown on the financing statement as if they were the mortgagors under a mortgage of the real property described; and

    (2) to the extent that the law of this State provides for indexing of records of mortgages under the name of the mortgagee, under the name of the secured party as if the secured party were the mortgagee thereunder, or, if indexing is by description, as if the financing statement were a record of a mortgage of the real property described.

(e) **[Indexing: real-property-related assignment.]** If a financing statement is filed as a fixture filing or covers as-extracted collateral or timber to be cut, the filing office shall index an assignment filed under Section 9-514(a) or an amendment filed under Section 9-514(b):

    (1) under the name of the assignor as grantor; and

    (2) to the extent that the law of this State provides for indexing a record of the assignment of a mortgage under the name of the assignee, under the name of the assignee.

[Alternative A]

(f) **[Retrieval and association capability.]** The filing office shall maintain a capability:

    (1) to retrieve a record by the name of the debtor and by the file number assigned to the initial financing statement to which the record relates; and

(2) to associate and retrieve with one another an initial financing statement and each filed record relating to the initial financing statement.

[Alternative B]

(f) **[Retrieval and association capability.]** The filing office shall maintain a capability:

   (1) to retrieve a record by the name of the debtor and:

      (A) if the filing office is described in Section 9-501(a)(1), by the file number assigned to the initial financing statement to which the record relates and the date [and time] that the record was filed [or recorded]; or

      (B) if the filing office is described in Section 9-501(a)(2), by the file number assigned to the initial financing statement to which the record relates; and

   (2) to associate and retrieve with one another an initial financing statement and each filed record relating to the initial financing statement.

[End of Alternatives]

(g) **[Removal of debtor's name.]** The filing office may not remove a debtor's name from the index until one year after the effectiveness of a financing statement naming the debtor lapses under Section 9-515 with respect to all secured parties of record.

(h) **[Timeliness of filing office performance.]** The filing office shall perform the acts required by subsections (a) through (e) at the time and in the manner prescribed by filing-office rule, but not later than two business days after the filing office receives the record in question.

[(i) **[Inapplicability to real-property-related filing office.]** Subsection[s] [(b)] [and] [(h)] do[es] not apply to a filing office described in Section 9-501(a)(1).]

Legislative Notes:

1. *States whose filing offices currently assign file numbers that include a verification number, commonly known as a "check digit," or can implement this requirement before the effective date of this Article should omit the bracketed language in subsection (b).*

2. *In States in which writings will not appear in the real-property records and indices unless actually recorded the bracketed language in subsection (d) should be used.*

3. *States whose real-estate filing offices require additional information in amendments and cannot search their records by both the name of the debtor and the file number should enact Alternative B to Sections 9-512(a), 9-518(b), 9-519(f) and 9-522(a).*

4. *A State that elects not to require real-estate filing offices to comply with either or both of subsections (b) and (h) may adopt an applicable variation of subsection (i) and add "Except as otherwise provided in subsection (i)," to the appropriate subsection or subsections.*

SECTION 9-520. ACCEPTANCE AND REFUSAL TO ACCEPT RECORD.

(a) **[Mandatory refusal to accept record.]** A filing office shall refuse to accept a record for filing for a reason set forth in Section 9-516(b) and may refuse to accept a record for filing only for a reason set forth in Section 9-516(b).

(b) **[Communication concerning refusal.]** If a filing office refuses to accept a record for filing, it shall communicate to the person that presented the record the fact of and reason for the refusal and the date and time the record would have been filed had the filing office accepted it. The communication must be made at the time and in the manner prescribed by filing-office rule but [, in the case of a filing office described in Section 9-501(a)(2),] in no event more than two business days after the filing office receives the record.

(c) **[When filed financing statement effective.]** A filed financing statement satisfying Section 9-502(a) and (b) is effective, even if the filing office is required to refuse to accept it for filing under subsection (a). However, Section 9-338 applies to a filed financing statement providing information described in Section 9-516(b)(5) which is incorrect at the time the financing statement is filed.

(d) **[Separate application to multiple debtors.]** If a record communicated to a filing office provides information that relates to more than one debtor, this part applies as to each debtor separately.

Legislative Note: A State that elects not to require real-property filing offices to comply with subsection (b) should include the bracketed language.

SECTION 9-521. UNIFORM FORM OF WRITTEN FINANCING STATEMENT AND AMENDMENT.

(a) **[Initial financing statement form.]** A filing office that accepts written records may not refuse to accept a written initial financing statement in the following form and format except for a reason set forth in Section 9-516(b):

(b) **[Amendment form.]** A filing office that accepts written records may not refuse to accept a written record in the following form and format except for a reason set forth in Section 9-516(b):

UCC FINANCING STATEMENT

FOLLOW INSTRUCTIONS (front and back) CAREFULLY

A. NAME & PHONE OF CONTACT AT FILER [optional]

B. SEND ACKNOWLEDGMENT TO: (Name and Address)

THE ABOVE SPACE IS FOR FILING OFFICE USE ONLY

1. DEBTOR'S EXACT FULL LEGAL NAME - insert only one debtor name (1a or 1b) - do not abbreviate or combine names

1a. ORGANIZATION'S NAME			
OR 1b. INDIVIDUAL'S LAST NAME	FIRST NAME	MIDDLE NAME	SUFFIX
1c. MAILING ADDRESS	CITY	STATE	POSTAL CODE	COUNTRY

1d. TAX ID #: SSN OR EIN	ADD'L INFO RE ORGANIZATION DEBTOR	1e. TYPE OF ORGANIZATION	1f. JURISDICTION OF ORGANIZATION	1g. ORGANIZATIONAL ID #, if any
				□ NONE

2. ADDITIONAL DEBTOR'S EXACT FULL LEGAL NAME - insert only one debtor name (2a or 2b) - do not abbreviate or combine names

2a. ORGANIZATION'S NAME			
OR 2b. INDIVIDUAL'S LAST NAME	FIRST NAME	MIDDLE NAME	SUFFIX
2c. MAILING ADDRESS	CITY	STATE	POSTAL CODE	COUNTRY

2d. TAX ID #: SSN OR EIN	ADD'L INFO RE ORGANIZATION DEBTOR	2e. TYPE OF ORGANIZATION	2f. JURISDICTION OF ORGANIZATION	2g. ORGANIZATIONAL ID #, if any
				□ NONE

3. SECURED PARTY'S NAME (or NAME of TOTAL ASSIGNEE of ASSIGNOR S/P) - insert only one secured party name (3a or 3b)

3a. ORGANIZATION'S NAME			
OR 3b. INDIVIDUAL'S LAST NAME	FIRST NAME	MIDDLE NAME	SUFFIX
3c. MAILING ADDRESS	CITY	STATE	POSTAL CODE	COUNTRY

4. This FINANCING STATEMENT covers the following collateral:

5. ALTERNATIVE DESIGNATION [if applicable]:	LESSEE/LESSOR	CONSIGNEE/CONSIGNOR	BAILEE/BAILOR	SELLER/BUYER	AG. LIEN	NON-UCC FILING

6. □ This FINANCING STATEMENT is to be filed [for record] (or recorded) in the REAL ESTATE RECORDS. Attach Addendum [if applicable]	7. Check to REQUEST SEARCH REPORT(S) on Debtor(s) [ADDITIONAL FEE] [optional]	All Debtors	Debtor 1	Debtor 2

8. OPTIONAL FILER REFERENCE DATA

NATIONAL UCC FINANCING STATEMENT (FORM UCC1) (REV. 07/29/98)

UCC FINANCING STATEMENT ADDENDUM

FOLLOW INSTRUCTIONS (front and back) CAREFULLY

9. NAME OF FIRST DEBTOR (1a or 1b) ON RELATED FINANCING STATEMENT

9a. ORGANIZATION'S NAME		

OR

9b. INDIVIDUAL'S LAST NAME	FIRST NAME	MIDDLE NAME,SUFFIX

10. MISCELLANEOUS:

THE ABOVE SPACE IS FOR FILING OFFICE USE ONLY

11. ADDITIONAL DEBTOR'S EXACT FULL LEGAL NAME - insert only one name (11a or 11b) - do not abbreviate or combine names

11a. ORGANIZATION'S NAME			

OR

11b. INDIVIDUAL'S LAST NAME	FIRST NAME	MIDDLE NAME	SUFFIX

11c. MAILING ADDRESS	CITY	STATE	POSTAL CODE	COUNTRY

11d. TAX ID #: SSN OR EIN	ADD'L INFO RE ORGANIZATION DEBTOR	11e. TYPE OF ORGANIZATION	11f. JURISDICTION OF ORGANIZATION	11g. ORGANIZATIONAL ID #, if any ☐ NONE

12. ☐ ADDITIONAL SECURED PARTY'S or ☐ ASSIGNOR S/P'S NAME - insert only one name (12a or 12b)

12a. ORGANIZATION'S NAME			

OR

12b. INDIVIDUAL'S LAST NAME	FIRST NAME	MIDDLE NAME	SUFFIX

12c. MAILING ADDRESS	CITY	STATE	POSTAL CODE	COUNTRY

13. This FINANCING STATEMENT covers ☐ timber to be cut or ☐ as-extracted collateral, or is filed as a ☐ fixture filing.

14. Description of real estate:

16. Additional collateral description:

15. Name and address of a RECORD OWNER of above-described real estate (if Debtor does not have a record interest):

17. Check only if applicable and check only one box.

Debtor is a ☐ Trust or ☐ Trustee acting with respect to property held in trust or ☐ Decedent's Estate

18. Check only if applicable and check only one box.

☐ Debtor is a TRANSMITTING UTILITY

☐ Filed in connection with a Manufactured-Home Transaction — effective 30 years

☐ Filed in connection with a Public-Finance Transaction — effective 30 years

NATIONAL UCC FINANCING STATEMENT ADDENDUM (FORM UCC1Ad) (REV. 07/29/98)

UCC FINANCING STATEMENT AMENDMENT

FOLLOW INSTRUCTIONS (front and back) CAREFULLY

A. NAME & PHONE OF CONTACT AT FILER [optional]

B. SEND ACKNOWLEDGMENT TO: (Name and Address)

THE ABOVE SPACE IS FOR FILING OFFICE USE ONLY

1a. INITIAL FINANCING STATEMENT FILE #	1b. This FINANCING STATEMENT AMENDMENT is to be filed [for record] (or recorded) in the ☐ REAL ESTATE RECORDS.

2. ☐ **TERMINATION:** Effectiveness of the Financing Statement identified above is terminated with respect to security interest(s) of the Secured Party authorizing this Termination Statement.

3. ☐ **CONTINUATION:** Effectiveness of the Financing Statement identified above with respect to security interest(s) of the Secured Party authorizing this Continuation Statement is continued for the additional period provided by applicable law.

4. ☐ **ASSIGNMENT** (full or partial): Give name of assignee in item 7a or 7b and address of assignee in item 7c; and also give name of assignor in item 9.

5. AMENDMENT (PARTY INFORMATION): This Amendment affects ☐ Debtor or ☐ Secured Party of record. Check only one of these two boxes.

Also check one of the following three boxes and provide appropriate information in items 6 and/or 7.

☐ CHANGE name and/or address: Give current record name in item 6a or 6b; also give new name (if name change) in item 7a or 7b and/or new address (if address change) in item 7c.   ☐ DELETE name: Give record name to be deleted in item 6a or 6b.   ☐ ADD name: Complete item 7a or 7b, and also item 7c; also complete items 7d-7g (if applicable).

6. CURRENT RECORD INFORMATION:

6a. ORGANIZATION'S NAME			
OR 6b. INDIVIDUAL'S LAST NAME	FIRST NAME	MIDDLE NAME	SUFFIX

7. CHANGED (NEW) OR ADDED INFORMATION:

7a. ORGANIZATION'S NAME			
OR 7b. INDIVIDUAL'S LAST NAME	FIRST NAME	MIDDLE NAME	SUFFIX
7c. MAILING ADDRESS	CITY	STATE POSTAL CODE	COUNTRY

7d. TAX ID #: SSN OR EIN	ADD'L INFO RE ORGANIZATION DEBTOR	7e. TYPE OF ORGANIZATION	7f. JURISDICTION OF ORGANIZATION	7g. ORGANIZATIONAL ID #, if any ☐ NONE

8. AMENDMENT (COLLATERAL CHANGE): check only one box.

Describe collateral ☐ deleted or ☐ added, or give entire ☐ restated collateral description, or describe collateral ☐ assigned.

9. NAME OF SECURED PARTY OF RECORD AUTHORIZING THIS AMENDMENT (name of assignor, if this is an Assignment). If this is an Amendment authorized by a Debtor which adds collateral or adds the authorizing Debtor, or if this is a Termination authorized by a Debtor, check here ☐ and enter name of DEBTOR authorizing this Amendment.

9a. ORGANIZATION'S NAME			
OR 9b. INDIVIDUAL'S LAST NAME	FIRST NAME	MIDDLE NAME	SUFFIX

10. OPTIONAL FILER REFERENCE DATA

NATIONAL UCC FINANCING STATEMENT AMENDMENT (FORM UCC3) (REV. 07/29/98)

UCC FINANCING STATEMENT AMENDMENT ADDENDUM

FOLLOW INSTRUCTIONS (front and back) CAREFULLY

11. INITIAL FINANCING STATEMENT FILE # (same as Item 1a on Amendment form)

12. NAME OF PARTY AUTHORIZING THIS AMENDMENT (same as Item 9 on Amendment form)

12a. ORGANIZATION'S NAME

OR

12b. INDIVIDUAL'S LAST NAME	FIRST NAME	MIDDLE NAME,SUFFIX

13. Use this space for additional information

THE ABOVE SPACE IS FOR FILING OFFICE USE ONLY

SECTION 9-522. MAINTENANCE AND DESTRUCTION OF RECORDS.

[Alternative A]

(a) **[Post-lapse maintenance and retrieval of information.]** The filing office shall maintain a record of the information provided in a filed financing statement for at least one year after the effectiveness of the financing statement has lapsed under Section 9-515 with respect to all secured parties of record. The record must be retrievable by using the name of the debtor and by using the file number assigned to the initial financing statement to which the record relates.

[Alternative B]

(a) **[Post-lapse maintenance and retrieval of information.]** The filing office shall maintain a record of the information provided in a filed financing statement for at least one year after the effectiveness of the financing statement has lapsed under Section 9-515 with respect to all secured parties of record. The record must be retrievable by using the name of the debtor and:

(1) if the record was filed [or recorded] in the filing office described in Section 9-501(a)(1), by using the file number assigned to the initial financing statement to which the record relates and the date [and time] that the record was filed [or recorded]; or

(2) if the record was filed in the filing office described in Section 9-501(a)(2), by using the file number assigned to the initial financing statement to which the record relates.

[End of Alternatives]

(b) **[Destruction of written records.]** Except to the extent that a statute governing disposition of public records provides otherwise, the filing office immediately may destroy any written record evidencing a financing statement. However, if the filing office destroys a written record, it shall maintain another record of the financing statement which complies with subsection (a).

Legislative Note: States whose real-estate filing offices require additional information in amendments and cannot search their records by both the name of the debtor and the file number should enact Alternative B to Sections 9-512(a), 9-518(b), 9-519(f) and 9-522(a).

SECTION 9-523. INFORMATION FROM FILING OFFICE; SALE OR LICENSE OF RECORDS.

(a) **[Acknowledgment of filing written record.]** If a person that files a written record requests an acknowledgment of the filing, the filing office shall send to the person an image of the record showing the number assigned to the record pursuant to Section 9-519(a)(1) and the date and time of the filing of the record. However, if the person furnishes a copy of the record to the filing office, the filing office may instead:

(1) note upon the copy the number assigned to the record pursuant to Section 9-519(a)(1) and the date and time of the filing of the record; and

(2) send the copy to the person.

(b) **[Acknowledgment of filing other record.]** If a person files a record other than a written record, the filing office shall communicate to the person an acknowledgment that provides:

(1) the information in the record;

(2) the number assigned to the record pursuant to Section 9-519(a)(1); and

(3) the date and time of the filing of the record.

(c) **[Communication of requested information.]** The filing office shall communicate or otherwise make available in a record the following information to any person that requests it:

(1) whether there is on file on a date and time specified by the filing office, but not a date earlier than three business days before the filing office receives the request, any financing statement that:

(A) designates a particular debtor [or, if the request so states, designates a particular debtor at the address specified in the request];

(B) has not lapsed under Section 9-515 with respect to all secured parties of record; and

(C) if the request so states, has lapsed under Section 9-515 and a record of which is maintained by the filing office under Section 9-522(a);

(2) the date and time of filing of each financing statement; and

(3) the information provided in each financing statement.

(d) **[Medium for communicating information.]** In complying with its duty under subsection (c), the filing office may communicate information in any medium. However, if requested, the filing office shall communicate information by issuing [its written certificate] [a record that can be admitted into evidence in the courts of this State without extrinsic evidence of its authenticity].

(e) **[Timeliness of filing office performance.]** The filing office shall perform the acts required by subsections (a) through (d) at the time and in the manner prescribed by filing-office rule, but not later than two business days after the filing office receives the request.

(f) **[Public availability of records.]** At least weekly, the [insert appropriate official or governmental agency] [filing office] shall offer to sell or license to the public on a nonexclusive basis, in bulk, copies of all records filed in it under this part, in every medium from time to time available to the filing office.

Legislative Notes:

1. *States whose filing office does not offer the additional service of responding to search requests limited to a particular address should omit the bracketed language in subsection (c)(1)(A).*

2. *A State that elects not to require real-estate filing offices to comply with either or both of subsections (e) and (f) should specify in the appropriate subsection(s) only the filing office described in Section 9-501(a)(2).*

SECTION 9-524. DELAY BY FILING OFFICE.

Delay by the filing office beyond a time limit prescribed by this part is excused if:

(1) the delay is caused by interruption of communication or computer facilities, war, emergency conditions, failure of equipment, or other circumstances beyond control of the filing office; and

(2) the filing office exercises reasonable diligence under the circumstances.

SECTION 9-525. FEES.

(a) **[Initial financing statement or other record: general rule.]** Except as otherwise provided in subsection (e), the fee for filing and indexing a record under this part, other than an initial financing statement of the kind described in subsection (b), is [the amount specified in subsection (c), if applicable, plus]:

   (1) $ __[X]_____ if the record is communicated in writing and consists of one or two pages;

   (2) $ __[2X]_____ if the record is communicated in writing and consists of more than two pages; and

   (3) $ __[1/2X]_____ if the record is communicated by another medium authorized by filing-office rule.

(b) **[Initial financing statement: public-finance and manufactured-housing transactions.]** Except as otherwise provided in subsection (e), the fee for filing and indexing an initial financing statement of the following kind is [the amount specified in subsection (c), if applicable, plus]:

   (1) $ _____ if the financing statement indicates that it is filed in connection with a public-finance transaction;

(2) $ _____ if the financing statement indicates that it is filed in connection with a manufactured-home transaction.

[Alternative A]

(c) **[Number of names.]** The number of names required to be indexed does not affect the amount of the fee in subsections (a) and (b).

[Alternative B]

(c) **[Number of names.]** Except as otherwise provided in subsection (e), if a record is communicated in writing, the fee for each name more than two required to be indexed is $ _____.

[End of Alternatives]

(d) **[Response to information request.]** The fee for responding to a request for information from the filing office, including for [issuing a certificate showing] [communicating] whether there is on file any financing statement naming a particular debtor, is:

(1) $ ____ if the request is communicated in writing; and

(e) $ ____ if the request is communicated by another medium authorized by filing-office rule.

(e) **[Record of mortgage.]** This section does not require a fee with respect to a record of a mortgage which is effective as a financing statement filed as a fixture filing or as a financing statement covering as-extracted collateral or timber to be cut under Section 9-502(c). However, the recording and satisfaction fees that otherwise would be applicable to the record of the mortgage apply.

Legislative Notes:

1. *To preserve uniformity, a State that places the provisions of this section together with statutes setting fees for other services should do so without modification.*

2. *A State should enact subsection (c), Alternative A, and omit the bracketed language in subsections (a) and (b) unless its indexing system entails a substantial additional cost when indexing additional names.*

SECTION 9-526. FILING-OFFICE RULES.

(a) **[Adoption of filing-office rules.]** The [insert appropriate governmental official or agency] shall adopt and publish rules to implement this article. The filing-office rules must be[:

(1)]consistent with this article[; and

(2) adopted and published in accordance with the [insert any applicable state administrative procedure act]].

(b) **[Harmonization of rules.]** To keep the filing-office rules and practices of the filing office in harmony with the rules and practices of filing offices in other jurisdictions that enact substantially this part, and to keep the technology used by the filing office compatible with the technology used by filing offices in other jurisdictions that enact substantially this part, the [insert appropriate governmental official or agency], so far as is consistent with the purposes, policies, and provisions of this article, in adopting, amending, and repealing filing-office rules, shall:

(1) consult with filing offices in other jurisdictions that enact substantially this part; and

(2) consult the most recent version of the Model Rules promulgated by the International Association of Corporate Administrators or any successor organization; and

(3) take into consideration the rules and practices of, and the technology used by, filing offices in other jurisdictions that enact substantially this part.

SECTION 9-527. DUTY TO REPORT.

The [insert appropriate governmental official or agency] shall report [annually on or before _____] to the [Governor and Legislature] on the operation of the filing office. The report must contain a statement of the extent to which:

(1) the filing-office rules are not in harmony with the rules of filing offices in other jurisdictions that enact substantially this part and the reasons for these variations; and

(2) the filing-office rules are not in harmony with the most recent version of the Model Rules promulgated by the International Association of Corporate Administrators, or any successor organization, and the reasons for these variations.

PART 6 – DEFAULT

[SUBPART 1. DEFAULT AND ENFORCEMENT OF SECURITY INTEREST]

SECTION 9-601. RIGHTS AFTER DEFAULT; JUDICIAL ENFORCEMENT; CONSIGNOR OR BUYER OF ACCOUNTS, CHATTEL PAPER, PAYMENT INTANGIBLES, OR PROMISSORY NOTES.

(a) **[Rights of secured party after default.]** After default, a secured party has the rights provided in this part and, except as otherwise provided in Section 9-602, those provided by agreement of the parties. A secured party:

(1) may reduce a claim to judgment, foreclose, or otherwise enforce the claim, security interest, or agricultural lien by any available judicial procedure; and

(2) if the collateral is documents, may proceed either as to the documents or as to the goods they cover.

(b) **[Rights and duties of secured party in possession or control.]** A secured party in possession of collateral or control of collateral under Section 9-104, 9-105, 9-106, or 9-107 has the rights and duties provided in Section 9-207.

(c) **[Rights cumulative; simultaneous exercise.]** The rights under subsections (a) and (b) are cumulative and may be exercised simultaneously.

(d) **[Rights of debtor and obligor.]** Except as otherwise provided in subsection (g) and Section 9-605, after default, a debtor and an obligor have the rights provided in this part and by agreement of the parties.

(e) **[Lien of levy after judgment.]** If a secured party has reduced its claim to judgment, the lien of any levy that may be made upon the collateral by virtue of an execution based upon the judgment relates back to the earliest of:

(1) the date of perfection of the security interest or agricultural lien in the collateral;

(2) the date of filing a financing statement covering the collateral; or

(3) any date specified in a statute under which the agricultural lien was created.

(f) **[Execution sale.]** A sale pursuant to an execution is a foreclosure of the security interest or agricultural lien by judicial procedure within the meaning of this section. A secured party may purchase at the sale and thereafter hold the collateral free of any other requirements of this article.

(g) **[Consignor or buyer of certain rights to payment.]** Except as otherwise provided in Section 9-607(c), this part imposes no duties upon a secured party that is a consignor or is a buyer of accounts, chattel paper, payment intangibles, or promissory notes.

SECTION 9-602. WAIVER AND VARIANCE OF RIGHTS AND DUTIES.

Except as otherwise provided in Section 9-624, to the extent that they give rights to a debtor or obligor and impose duties on a secured party, the debtor or obligor may not waive or vary the rules stated in the following listed sections:

(1) Section 9-207(b)(4)(C), which deals with use and operation of the collateral by the secured party;

(2) Section 9-210, which deals with requests for an accounting and requests concerning a list of collateral and statement of account;

(3) Section 9-607(c), which deals with collection and enforcement of collateral;

(4) Sections 9-608(a) and 9-615(c) to the extent that they deal with application or payment of noncash proceeds of collection, enforcement, or disposition;

(5) Sections 9-608(a) and 9-615(d) to the extent that they require accounting for or payment of surplus proceeds of collateral;

(6) Section 9-609 to the extent that it imposes upon a secured party that takes possession of collateral without judicial process the duty to do so without breach of the peace;

(7) Sections 9-610(b), 9-611, 9-613, and 9-614, which deal with disposition of collateral;

(8) Section 9-615(f), which deals with calculation of a deficiency or surplus when a disposition is made to the secured party, a person related to the secured party, or a secondary obligor;

(9) Section 9-616, which deals with explanation of the calculation of a surplus or deficiency;

(10) Sections 9-620, 9-621, and 9-622, which deal with acceptance of collateral in satisfaction of obligation;

(11) Section 9-623, which deals with redemption of collateral;

(12) Section 9-624, which deals with permissible waivers; and

(13) Sections 9-625 and 9-626, which deal with the secured party's liability for failure to comply with this article.

SECTION 9-603. AGREEMENT ON STANDARDS CONCERNING RIGHTS AND DUTIES.

(a) **[Agreed standards.]** The parties may determine by agreement the standards measuring the fulfillment of the rights of a debtor or obligor and the duties of a secured party under a rule stated in Section 9-602 if the standards are not manifestly unreasonable.

(b) **[Agreed standards inapplicable to breach of peace.]** Subsection (a) does not apply to the duty under Section 9-609 to refrain from breaching the peace.

SECTION 9-604. PROCEDURE IF SECURITY AGREEMENT COVERS REAL PROPERTY OR FIXTURES.

(a) **[Enforcement: personal and real property.]** If a security agreement covers both personal and real property, a secured party may proceed:

    (1) under this part as to the personal property without prejudicing any rights with respect to the real property; or

    (2) as to both the personal property and the real property in accordance with the rights with respect to the real property, in which case the other provisions of this part do not apply.

(b) **[Enforcement: fixtures.]** Subject to subsection (c), if a security agreement covers goods that are or become fixtures, a secured party may proceed:

    (1) under this part; or

    (2) in accordance with the rights with respect to real property, in which case the other provisions of this part do not apply.

(c) **[Removal of fixtures.]** Subject to the other provisions of this part, if a secured party holding a security interest in fixtures has priority over all owners and encumbrancers of the real property, the secured party, after default, may remove the collateral from the real property.

(d) **[Injury caused by removal.]** A secured party that removes collateral shall promptly reimburse any encumbrancer or owner of the real property, other than the debtor, for the cost of repair of any physical injury caused by the removal. The secured party need not reimburse the encumbrancer or owner for any diminution in value of the real property caused by the absence of the goods removed or by any necessity of replacing them. A person entitled to reimbursement may refuse permission to remove until the secured party gives adequate assurance for the performance of the obligation to reimburse.

SECTION 9-605. UNKNOWN DEBTOR OR SECONDARY OBLIGOR.

A secured party does not owe a duty based on its status as secured party:

(1) to a person that is a debtor or obligor, unless the secured party knows:

    (A) that the person is a debtor or obligor;

    (B) the identity of the person; and

    (C) how to communicate with the person; or

(2) to a secured party or lienholder that has filed a financing statement against a person, unless the secured party knows:

    (A) that the person is a debtor; and

    (B) the identity of the person.

SECTION 9-606. TIME OF DEFAULT FOR AGRICULTURAL LIEN.

For purposes of this part, a default occurs in connection with an agricultural lien at the time the secured party becomes entitled to enforce the lien in accordance with the statute under which it was created.

SECTION 9-607. COLLECTION AND ENFORCEMENT BY SECURED PARTY.

(a) **[Collection and enforcement generally.]** If so agreed, and in any event after default, a secured party:

   (1) may notify an account debtor or other person obligated on collateral to make payment or otherwise render performance to or for the benefit of the secured party;

   (2) may take any proceeds to which the secured party is entitled under Section 9-315;

   (3) may enforce the obligations of an account debtor or other person obligated on collateral and exercise the rights of the debtor with respect to the obligation of the account debtor or other person obligated on collateral to make payment or otherwise render performance to the debtor, and with respect to any property that secures the obligations of the account debtor or other person obligated on the collateral;

   (4) if it holds a security interest in a deposit account perfected by control under Section 9-104(a)(1), may apply the balance of the deposit account to the obligation secured by the deposit account; and

   (5) if it holds a security interest in a deposit account perfected by control under Section 9-104(a)(2) or (3), may instruct the bank to pay the balance of the deposit account to or for the benefit of the secured party.

(b) **[Nonjudicial enforcement of mortgage.]** If necessary to enable a secured party to exercise under subsection (a)(3) the right of a debtor to enforce a mortgage nonjudicially, the secured party may record in the office in which a record of the mortgage is recorded:

   (1) a copy of the security agreement that creates or provides for a security interest in the obligation secured by the mortgage; and

   (2) the secured party's sworn affidavit in recordable form stating that:

      (A) a default has occurred; and

      (B) the secured party is entitled to enforce the mortgage nonjudicially.

(c) **[Commercially reasonable collection and enforcement.]** A secured party shall proceed in a commercially reasonable manner if the secured party:

(1) undertakes to collect from or enforce an obligation of an account debtor or other person obligated on collateral; and

(2) is entitled to charge back uncollected collateral or otherwise to full or limited recourse against the debtor or a secondary obligor.

(d) **[Expenses of collection and enforcement.]** A secured party may deduct from the collections made pursuant to subsection (c) reasonable expenses of collection and enforcement, including reasonable attorney's fees and legal expenses incurred by the secured party.

(e) **[Duties to secured party not affected.]** This section does not determine whether an account debtor, bank, or other person obligated on collateral owes a duty to a secured party.

SECTION 9-608. APPLICATION OF PROCEEDS OF
COLLECTION OR ENFORCEMENT; LIABILITY FOR
DEFICIENCY AND RIGHT TO SURPLUS.

(a) **[Application of proceeds, surplus, and deficiency if obligation secured.]** If a security interest or agricultural lien secures payment or performance of an obligation, the following rules apply:

(1) A secured party shall apply or pay over for application the cash proceeds of collection or enforcement under Section 9-607 in the following order to:

(A) the reasonable expenses of collection and enforcement and, to the extent provided for by agreement and not prohibited by law, reasonable attorney's fees and legal expenses incurred by the secured party;

(B) the satisfaction of obligations secured by the security interest or agricultural lien under which the collection or enforcement is made; and

(C) the satisfaction of obligations secured by any subordinate security interest in or other lien on the collateral subject to the security interest or agricultural lien under which the collection or enforcement is made if the secured party receives an authenticated demand for proceeds before distribution of the proceeds is completed.

(2) If requested by a secured party, a holder of a subordinate security interest or other lien shall furnish reasonable proof of the interest or lien within a reasonable time. Unless the holder complies, the secured party need not comply with the holder's demand under paragraph (1)(C).

(3) A secured party need not apply or pay over for application non-cash proceeds of collection and enforcement under Section 9-607 unless the failure to do so would be commercially unreasonable. A secured party that applies or pays over for application noncash proceeds shall do so in a commercially reasonable manner.

(4) A secured party shall account to and pay a debtor for any surplus, and the obligor is liable for any deficiency.

(b) **[No surplus or deficiency in sales of certain rights to payment.]** If the underlying transaction is a sale of accounts, chattel paper, payment intangibles, or promissory notes, the debtor is not entitled to any surplus, and the obligor is not liable for any deficiency.

SECTION 9-609. SECURED PARTY'S RIGHT TO TAKE POSSESSION AFTER DEFAULT.

(a) **[Possession; rendering equipment unusable; disposition on debtor's premises.]** After default, a secured party:
  (1) may take possession of the collateral; and
  (2) without removal, may render equipment unusable and dispose of collateral on a debtor's premises under Section 9-610.

(b) **[Judicial and nonjudicial process.]** A secured party may proceed under subsection (a):
  (1) pursuant to judicial process; or
  (2) without judicial process, if it proceeds without breach of the peace.

(c) **[Assembly of collateral.]** If so agreed, and in any event after default, a secured party may require the debtor to assemble the collateral and make it available to the secured party at a place to be designated by the secured party which is reasonably convenient to both parties.

SECTION 9-610. DISPOSITION OF COLLATERAL AFTER DEFAULT.

(a) **[Disposition after default.]** After default, a secured party may sell, lease, license, or otherwise dispose of any or all of the collateral in its present condition or following any commercially reasonable preparation or processing.

(b) **[Commercially reasonable disposition.]** Every aspect of a disposition of collateral, including the method, manner, time, place, and other terms, must be commercially reasonable. If commercially reasonable, a secured party may dispose of collateral by public or private proceedings, by one or more contracts, as a unit or in parcels, and at any time and place and on any terms.

(c) **[Purchase by secured party.]** A secured party may purchase collateral:

    (1) at a public disposition; or

    (2) at a private disposition only if the collateral is of a kind that is customarily sold on a recognized market or the subject of widely distributed standard price quotations.

(d) **[Warranties on disposition.]** A contract for sale, lease, license, or other disposition includes the warranties relating to title, possession, quiet enjoyment, and the like which by operation of law accompany a voluntary disposition of property of the kind subject to the contract.

(e) **[Disclaimer of warranties.]** A secured party may disclaim or modify warranties under subsection (d):

    (1) in a manner that would be effective to disclaim or modify the warranties in a voluntary disposition of property of the kind subject to the contract of disposition; or

    (2) by communicating to the purchaser a record evidencing the contract for disposition and including an express disclaimer or modification of the warranties.

(f) **[Record sufficient to disclaim warranties.]** A record is sufficient to disclaim warranties under subsection (e) if it indicates "There is no warranty relating to title, possession, quiet enjoyment, or the like in this disposition" or uses words of similar import.

SECTION 9-611. NOTIFICATION BEFORE DISPOSITION OF COLLATERAL.

(a) **["Notification date."]** In this section, "notification date" means the earlier of the date on which:

    (1) a secured party sends to the debtor and any secondary obligor an authenticated notification of disposition; or

    (2) the debtor and any secondary obligor waive the right to notification.

(b) **[Notification of disposition required.]** Except as otherwise provided in subsection (d), a secured party that disposes of collateral under Section 9-610 shall send to the persons specified in subsection (c) a reasonable authenticated notification of disposition.

(c) **[Persons to be notified.]** To comply with subsection (b), the secured party shall send an authenticated notification of disposition to:

    (1) the debtor;

    (2) any secondary obligor; and

    (3) if the collateral is other than consumer goods:

(A) any other person from which the secured party has received, before the notification date, an authenticated notification of a claim of an interest in the collateral;

(B) any other secured party or lienholder that, 10 days before the notification date, held a security interest in or other lien on the collateral perfected by the filing of a financing statement that:

　(i) identified the collateral;

　(ii) was indexed under the debtor's name as of that date; and

　(iii) was filed in the office in which to file a financing statement against the debtor covering the collateral as of that date; and

(C) any other secured party that, 10 days before the notification date, held a security interest in the collateral perfected by compliance with a statute, regulation, or treaty described in Section 9-311(a).

(d) **[Subsection (b) inapplicable: perishable collateral; recognized market.]** Subsection (b) does not apply if the collateral is perishable or threatens to decline speedily in value or is of a type customarily sold on a recognized market.

(e) **[Compliance with subsection (c)(3)(B).]** A secured party complies with the requirement for notification prescribed by subsection (c)(3)(B) if:

(1) not later than 20 days or earlier than 30 days before the notification date, the secured party requests, in a commercially reasonable manner, information concerning financing statements indexed under the debtor's name in the office indicated in subsection (c)(3)(B); and

(2) before the notification date, the secured party:

(A) did not receive a response to the request for information; or

(B) received a response to the request for information and sent an authenticated notification of disposition to each secured party or other lienholder named in that response whose financing statement covered the collateral.

SECTION 9-612. TIMELINESS OF NOTIFICATION BEFORE DISPOSITION OF COLLATERAL.

(a) **[Reasonable time is question of fact.]** Except as otherwise provided in subsection (b), whether a notification is sent within a reasonable time is a question of fact.

(b) **[10-day period sufficient in non-consumer transaction.]** In a transaction other than a consumer transaction, a notification of disposition sent after default and 10 days or more before the earliest time of disposition set forth in the notification is sent within a reasonable time before the disposition.

SECTION 9-613. CONTENTS AND FORM OF NOTIFICATION BEFORE DISPOSITION OF COLLATERAL: GENERAL.

Except in a consumer-goods transaction, the following rules apply:

(1) The contents of a notification of disposition are sufficient if the notification:

    (A) describes the debtor and the secured party;

    (B) describes the collateral that is the subject of the intended disposition;

    (C) states the method of intended disposition;

    (D) states that the debtor is entitled to an accounting of the unpaid indebtedness and states the charge, if any, for an accounting; and

    (E) states the time and place of a public disposition or the time after which any other disposition is to be made.

(2) Whether the contents of a notification that lacks any of the information specified in paragraph (1) are nevertheless sufficient is a question of fact.

(3) The contents of a notification providing substantially the information specified in paragraph (1) are sufficient, even if the notification includes:

    (A) information not specified by that paragraph; or

    (B) minor errors that are not seriously misleading.

(4) A particular phrasing of the notification is not required.

(5) The following form of notification and the form appearing in Section 9-614(3), when completed, each provides sufficient information:

NOTIFICATION OF DISPOSITION OF COLLATERAL

To: *[Name of debtor, obligor, or other person to which]*
                        [the notification is sent]

From: *[Name, address, and telephone number of secured]*
                        [party]

Name of Debtor(s):   *[Include only if debtor(s) are not an addressee]*

[For a public disposition:]

We will sell [or lease or license, *as applicable*] the [*describe collateral*] [to the highest qualified bidder] in public as follows:

Day and Date: _____
Time: _____
Place: _____

[*For a private disposition:*]

We will sell [or lease or license, *as applicable*] the [*describe collateral*] privately sometime after [*day and date*].

You are entitled to an accounting of the unpaid indebtedness secured by the property that we intend to sell [or lease or license, *as applicable*] [for a charge of $_____]. You may request an accounting by calling us at [*telephone number*].

[End of Form]

SECTION 9-614. CONTENTS AND FORM OF NOTIFICATION BEFORE DISPOSITION OF COLLATERAL: CONSUMER-GOODS TRANSACTION.

In a consumer-goods transaction, the following rules apply:

(1) A notification of disposition must provide the following information:

   (A) the information specified in Section 9-613(1);

   (B) a description of any liability for a deficiency of the person to which the notification is sent;

   (C) a telephone number from which the amount that must be paid to the secured party to redeem the collateral under Section 9-623 is available; and

   (D) a telephone number or mailing address from which additional information concerning the disposition and the obligation secured is available.

(2) A particular phrasing of the notification is not required.

(3) The following form of notification, when completed, provides sufficient information:

[*Name and address of secured party*]

[*Date*]

NOTICE OF OUR PLAN TO SELL PROPERTY

[*Name and address of any obligor who is also a debtor*]

Subject: [*Identification of Transaction*]

We have your [*describe collateral*], because you broke promises in our agreement.

[*For a public disposition:*]

We will sell [*describe collateral*] at public sale. A sale could include a lease or license. The sale will be held as follows:

Date: _____
Time: _____
Place: _____

You may attend the sale and bring bidders if you want.
[*For a private disposition:*]

We will sell [*describe collateral*] at private sale sometime after [*date*]. A sale could include a lease or license.

The money that we get from the sale (after paying our costs) will reduce the amount you owe. If we get less money than you owe, you [*will or will not, as applicable*] still owe us the difference. If we get more money than you owe, you will get the extra money, unless we must pay it to someone else.

You can get the property back at any time before we sell it by paying us the full amount you owe (not just the past due payments), including our expenses. To learn the exact amount you must pay, call us at [*telephone number*].

If you want us to explain to you in writing how we have figured the amount that you owe us, you may call us at [*telephone number*] [or write us at [*secured party's address*]] and request a written explanation. [We will charge you $ _____ for the explanation if we sent you another written explanation of the amount you owe us within the last six months.]

If you need more information about the sale call us at [*telephone number*]] [or write us at [*secured party's address*]].

We are sending this notice to the following other people who have an interest in [*describe collateral*] or who owe money under your agreement:
    [*Names of all other debtors and obligors, if any*]

[End of Form]

(4) A notification in the form of paragraph (3) is sufficient, even if additional information appears at the end of the form.

(5) A notification in the form of paragraph (3) is sufficient, even if it includes errors in information not required by paragraph (1), unless the error is misleading with respect to rights arising under this article.

(6) If a notification under this section is not in the form of paragraph (3), law other than this article determines the effect of including information not required by paragraph (1).

SECTION 9-615. APPLICATION OF PROCEEDS OF DISPOSITION; LIABILITY FOR DEFICIENCY AND RIGHT TO SURPLUS.

(a) **[Application of proceeds.]** A secured party shall apply or pay over for application the cash proceeds of disposition under Section 9-610 in the following order to:

    (1) the reasonable expenses of retaking, holding, preparing for disposition, processing, and disposing, and, to the extent provided for by agreement and not prohibited by law, reasonable attorney's fees and legal expenses incurred by the secured party;

    (2) the satisfaction of obligations secured by the security interest or agricultural lien under which the disposition is made;

    (3) the satisfaction of obligations secured by any subordinate security interest in or other subordinate lien on the collateral if:

        (A) the secured party receives from the holder of the subordinate security interest or other lien an authenticated demand for proceeds before distribution of the proceeds is completed; and

        (B) in a case in which a consignor has an interest in the collateral, the subordinate security interest or other lien is senior to the interest of the consignor; and

    (4) a secured party that is a consignor of the collateral if the secured party receives from the consignor an authenticated demand for proceeds before distribution of the proceeds is completed.

(b) **[Proof of subordinate interest.]** If requested by a secured party, a holder of a subordinate security interest or other lien shall furnish reasonable proof of the interest or lien within a reasonable time. Unless the holder does so, the secured party need not comply with the holder's demand under subsection (a)(3).

(c) **[Application of noncash proceeds.]** A secured party need not apply or pay over for application noncash proceeds of disposition under Section 9-610 unless the failure to do so would be commercially unreasonable. A secured party that applies or pays over for application noncash proceeds shall do so in a commercially reasonable manner.

(d) **[Surplus or deficiency if obligation secured.]** If the security interest under which a disposition is made secures payment or performance of an obligation, after making the payments and applications required by subsection (a) and permitted by subsection (c):

(1) unless subsection (a)(4) requires the secured party to apply or pay over cash proceeds to a consignor, the secured party shall account to and pay a debtor for any surplus; and

(2) the obligor is liable for any deficiency.

(e) **[No surplus or deficiency in sales of certain rights to payment.]** If the underlying transaction is a sale of accounts, chattel paper, payment intangibles, or promissory notes:

(1) the debtor is not entitled to any surplus; and

(2) the obligor is not liable for any deficiency.

(f) **[Calculation of surplus or deficiency in disposition to person related to secured party.]** The surplus or deficiency following a disposition is calculated based on the amount of proceeds that would have been realized in a disposition complying with this part to a transferee other than the secured party, a person related to the secured party, or a secondary obligor if:

(1) the transferee in the disposition is the secured party, a person related to the secured party, or a secondary obligor; and

(2) the amount of proceeds of the disposition is significantly below the range of proceeds that a complying disposition to a person other than the secured party, a person related to the secured party, or a secondary obligor would have brought.

(g) **[Cash proceeds received by junior secured party.]** A secured party that receives cash proceeds of a disposition in good faith and without knowledge that the receipt violates the rights of the holder of a security interest or other lien that is not subordinate to the security interest or agricultural lien under which the disposition is made:

(1) takes the cash proceeds free of the security interest or other lien;

(2) is not obligated to apply the proceeds of the disposition to the satisfaction of obligations secured by the security interest or other lien; and

(3) is not obligated to account to or pay the holder of the security interest or other lien for any surplus.

SECTION 9-616. EXPLANATION OF CALCULATION OF SURPLUS OR DEFICIENCY.

(a) **[Definitions.]** In this section:

(1) "Explanation" means a writing that:

(A) states the amount of the surplus or deficiency;

(B) provides an explanation in accordance with subsection (c) of how the secured party calculated the surplus or deficiency;

    (C) states, if applicable, that future debits, credits, charges, including additional credit service charges or interest, rebates, and expenses may affect the amount of the surplus or deficiency; and

    (D) provides a telephone number or mailing address from which additional information concerning the transaction is available.

  (2) "Request" means a record:

    (A) authenticated by a debtor or consumer obligor;

    (B) requesting that the recipient provide an explanation; and

    (C) sent after disposition of the collateral under Section 9-610.

(b) **[Explanation of calculation.]** In a consumer-goods transaction in which the debtor is entitled to a surplus or a consumer obligor is liable for a deficiency under Section 9-615, the secured party shall:

  (1) send an explanation to the debtor or consumer obligor, as applicable, after the disposition and:

    (A) before or when the secured party accounts to the debtor and pays any surplus or first makes written demand on the consumer obligor after the disposition for payment of the deficiency; and

    (B) within 14 days after receipt of a request; or

  (2) in the case of a consumer obligor who is liable for a deficiency, within 14 days after receipt of a request, send to the consumer obligor a record waiving the secured party's right to a deficiency.

(c) **[Required information.]** To comply with subsection (a)(1)(B), a writing must provide the following information in the following order:

  (1) the aggregate amount of obligations secured by the security interest under which the disposition was made, and, if the amount reflects a rebate of unearned interest or credit service charge, an indication of that fact, calculated as of a specified date:

    (A) if the secured party takes or receives possession of the collateral after default, not more than 35 days before the secured party takes or receives possession; or

    (B) if the secured party takes or receives possession of the collateral before default or does not take possession of the collateral, not more than 35 days before the disposition;

  (2) the amount of proceeds of the disposition;

  (3) the aggregate amount of the obligations after deducting the amount of proceeds;

  (4) the amount, in the aggregate or by type, and types of expenses, including expenses of retaking, holding, preparing for disposition,

processing, and disposing of the collateral, and attorney's fees secured by the collateral which are known to the secured party and relate to the current disposition;

(5) the amount, in the aggregate or by type, and types of credits, including rebates of interest or credit service charges, to which the obligor is known to be entitled and which are not reflected in the amount in paragraph (1); and

(6) the amount of the surplus or deficiency.

(d) **[Substantial compliance.]** A particular phrasing of the explanation is not required. An explanation complying substantially with the requirements of subsection (a) is sufficient, even if it includes minor errors that are not seriously misleading.

(e) **[Charges for responses.]** A debtor or consumer obligor is entitled without charge to one response to a request under this section during any six-month period in which the secured party did not send to the debtor or consumer obligor an explanation pursuant to subsection (b)(1). The secured party may require payment of a charge not exceeding $25 for each additional response.

SECTION 9-617. RIGHTS OF TRANSFEREE OF COLLATERAL.

(a) **[Effects of disposition.]** A secured party's disposition of collateral after default:

(1) transfers to a transferee for value all of the debtor's rights in the collateral;

(2) discharges the security interest under which the disposition is made; and

(3) discharges any subordinate security interest or other subordinate lien [other than liens created under [cite acts or statutes providing for liens, if any, that are not to be discharged]].

(b) **[Rights of good-faith transferee.]** A transferee that acts in good faith takes free of the rights and interests described in subsection (a), even if the secured party fails to comply with this article or the requirements of any judicial proceeding.

(c) **[Rights of other transferee.]** If a transferee does not take free of the rights and interests described in subsection (a), the transferee takes the collateral subject to:

(1) the debtor's rights in the collateral;

(2) the security interest or agricultural lien under which the disposition is made; and

(3) any other security interest or other lien.

SECTION 9-618. RIGHTS AND DUTIES OF CERTAIN
SECONDARY OBLIGORS.

(a) **[Rights and duties of secondary obligor.]** A secondary obligor
acquires the rights and becomes obligated to perform the duties of
the secured party after the secondary obligor:

    (1) receives an assignment of a secured obligation from the secured
party;

    (2) receives a transfer of collateral from the secured party and agrees
to accept the rights and assume the duties of the secured party;
or

    (3) is subrogated to the rights of a secured party with respect to
collateral.

(b) **[Effect of assignment, transfer, or subrogation.]** An assignment,
transfer, or subrogation described in subsection (a):

    (1) is not a disposition of collateral under Section 9-610; and

    (2) relieves the secured party of further duties under this article.

SECTION 9-619. TRANSFER OF RECORD OR LEGAL TITLE.

(a) **["Transfer statement."]** In this section, "transfer statement"
means a record authenticated by a secured party stating:

    (1) that the debtor has defaulted in connection with an obligation
secured by specified collateral;

    (2) that the secured party has exercised its post-default remedies with
respect to the collateral;

    (3) that, by reason of the exercise, a transferee has acquired the rights
of the debtor in the collateral; and

    (4) the name and mailing address of the secured party, debtor, and
transferee.

(b) **[Effect of transfer statement.]** A transfer statement entitles the
transferee to the transfer of record of all rights of the debtor in the
collateral specified in the statement in any official filing, recording,
registration, or certificate-of-title system covering the collateral. If a
transfer statement is presented with the applicable fee and request
form to the official or office responsible for maintaining the system,
the official or office shall:

    (1) accept the transfer statement;

    (2) promptly amend its records to reflect the transfer; and

    (3) if applicable, issue a new appropriate certificate of title in the
name of the transferee.

(c) **[Transfer not a disposition; no relief of secured party's duties.]**
A transfer of the record or legal title to collateral to a secured party
under subsection (b) or otherwise is not of itself a disposition of

collateral under this article and does not of itself relieve the secured party of its duties under this article.

SECTION 9-620. ACCEPTANCE OF COLLATERAL IN FULL OR PARTIAL SATISFACTION OF OBLIGATION; COMPULSORY DISPOSITION OF COLLATERAL.

(a) **[Conditions to acceptance in satisfaction.]** Except as otherwise provided in subsection (g), a secured party may accept collateral in full or partial satisfaction of the obligation it secures only if:

  (1) the debtor consents to the acceptance under subsection (c);

  (2) the secured party does not receive, within the time set forth in subsection (d), a notification of objection to the proposal authenticated by:

    (A) a person to which the secured party was required to send a proposal under Section 9-621; or

    (B) any other person, other than the debtor, holding an interest in the collateral subordinate to the security interest that is the subject of the proposal;

  (3) if the collateral is consumer goods, the collateral is not in the possession of the debtor when the debtor consents to the acceptance; and

  (4) subsection (e) does not require the secured party to dispose of the collateral or the debtor waives the requirement pursuant to Section 9-624.

(b) **[Purported acceptance ineffective.]** A purported or apparent acceptance of collateral under this section is ineffective unless:

  (1) the secured party consents to the acceptance in an authenticated record or sends a proposal to the debtor; and

  (2) the conditions of subsection (a) are met.

(c) **[Debtor's consent.]** For purposes of this section:

  (1) a debtor consents to an acceptance of collateral in partial satisfaction of the obligation it secures only if the debtor agrees to the terms of the acceptance in a record authenticated after default; and

  (2) a debtor consents to an acceptance of collateral in full satisfaction of the obligation it secures only if the debtor agrees to the terms of the acceptance in a record authenticated after default or the secured party:

    (A) sends to the debtor after default a proposal that is unconditional or subject only to a condition that collateral not in the possession of the secured party be preserved or maintained;

  (B) in the proposal, proposes to accept collateral in full satisfac-
    tion of the obligation it secures; and

  (C) does not receive a notification of objection authenti-
    cated by the debtor within 20 days after the proposal is
    sent.

(d) **[Effectiveness of notification.]** To be effective under subsection
(a)(2), a notification of objection must be received by the secured
party:

  (1) in the case of a person to which the proposal was sent pursuant to
    Section 9-621, within 20 days after notification was sent to that
    person; and

  (2) in other cases:

    (A) within 20 days after the last notification was sent pursuant
      to Section 9-621; or

    (B) if a notification was not sent, before the debtor consents to
      the acceptance under subsection (c).

(e) **[Mandatory disposition of consumer goods.]** A secured party
that has taken possession of collateral shall dispose of the collateral
pursuant to Section 9-610 within the time specified in subsection (f)
if:

  (1) 60 percent of the cash price has been paid in the case of a
    purchase-money security interest in consumer goods; or

  (2) 60 percent of the principal amount of the obligation secured has
    been paid in the case of a non-purchase-money security interest
    in consumer goods.

(f) **[Compliance with mandatory disposition requirement.]** To
comply with subsection (e), the secured party shall dispose of the
collateral:

  (1) within 90 days after taking possession; or

  (2) within any longer period to which the debtor and all secondary
    obligors have agreed in an agreement to that effect entered into
    and authenticated after default.

(g) **[No partial satisfaction in consumer transaction.]** In a consumer transaction, a secured party may not accept collateral in partial
satisfaction of the obligation it secures.

SECTION 9-621. NOTIFICATION OF PROPOSAL TO ACCEPT
COLLATERAL.

(a) **[Persons to which proposal to be sent.]** A secured party that desires to accept collateral in full or partial satisfaction of the obligation
it secures shall send its proposal to:

(1) any person from which the secured party has received, before the debtor consented to the acceptance, an authenticated notification of a claim of an interest in the collateral;

(2) any other secured party or lienholder that, 10 days before the debtor consented to the acceptance, held a security interest in or other lien on the collateral perfected by the filing of a financing statement that:

   (A) identified the collateral;

   (B) was indexed under the debtor's name as of that date; and

   (C) was filed in the office or offices in which to file a financing statement against the debtor covering the collateral as of that date; and

(3) any other secured party that, 10 days before the debtor consented to the acceptance, held a security interest in the collateral perfected by compliance with a statute, regulation, or treaty described in Section 9-311(a).

(b) **[Proposal to be sent to secondary obligor in partial satisfaction.]** A secured party that desires to accept collateral in partial satisfaction of the obligation it secures shall send its proposal to any secondary obligor in addition to the persons described in subsection (a).

SECTION 9-622. EFFECT OF ACCEPTANCE OF COLLATERAL.

(a) **[Effect of acceptance.]** A secured party's acceptance of collateral in full or partial satisfaction of the obligation it secures:

(1) discharges the obligation to the extent consented to by the debtor;

(2) transfers to the secured party all of a debtor's rights in the collateral;

(3) discharges the security interest or agricultural lien that is the subject of the debtor's consent and any subordinate security interest or other subordinate lien; and

(4) terminates any other subordinate interest.

(b) **[Discharge of subordinate interest notwithstanding noncompliance.]** A subordinate interest is discharged or terminated under subsection (a), even if the secured party fails to comply with this article.

SECTION 9-623. RIGHT TO REDEEM COLLATERAL.

(a) **[Persons that may redeem.]** A debtor, any secondary obligor, or any other secured party or lienholder may redeem collateral.

(b) **[Requirements for redemption.]** To redeem collateral, a person shall tender:

(1) fulfillment of all obligations secured by the collateral; and

(2) the reasonable expenses and attorney's fees described in Section 9-615(a)(1).

(c) **[When redemption may occur.]** A redemption may occur at any time before a secured party:

(1) has collected collateral under Section 9-607;

(2) has disposed of collateral or entered into a contract for its disposition under Section 9-610; or

(3) has accepted collateral in full or partial satisfaction of the obligation it secures under Section 9-622.

SECTION 9-624. WAIVER.

(a) **[Waiver of disposition notification.]** A debtor or secondary obligor may waive the right to notification of disposition of collateral under Section 9-611 only by an agreement to that effect entered into and authenticated after default.

(b) **[Waiver of mandatory disposition.]** A debtor may waive the right to require disposition of collateral under Section 9-620(e) only by an agreement to that effect entered into and authenticated after default.

(c) **[Waiver of redemption right.]** Except in a consumer-goods transaction, a debtor or secondary obligor may waive the right to redeem collateral under Section 9-623 only by an agreement to that effect entered into and authenticated after default.

[SUBPART 2. NONCOMPLIANCE WITH ARTICLE]

SECTION 9-625. REMEDIES FOR SECURED PARTY'S FAILURE TO COMPLY WITH ARTICLE.

(a) **[Judicial orders concerning noncompliance.]** If it is established that a secured party is not proceeding in accordance with this article, a court may order or restrain collection, enforcement, or disposition of collateral on appropriate terms and conditions.

(b) **[Damages for noncompliance.]** Subject to subsections (c), (d), and (f), a person is liable for damages in the amount of any loss caused by a failure to comply with this article. Loss caused by a failure to comply may include loss resulting from the debtor's inability to obtain, or increased costs of, alternative financing.

(c) **[Persons entitled to recover damages; statutory damages in consumer-goods transaction.]** Except as otherwise provided in Section 9-628:

(1) a person that, at the time of the failure, was a debtor, was an obligor, or held a security interest in or other lien on the collateral may recover damages under subsection (b) for its loss; and

(2) if the collateral is consumer goods, a person that was a debtor or a secondary obligor at the time a secured party failed to comply with this part may recover for that failure in any event an amount not less than the credit service charge plus 10 percent of the principal amount of the obligation or the time-price differential plus 10 percent of the cash price.

(d) **[Recovery when deficiency eliminated or reduced.]** A debtor whose deficiency is eliminated under Section 9-626 may recover damages for the loss of any surplus. However, a debtor or secondary obligor whose deficiency is eliminated or reduced under Section 9-626 may not otherwise recover under subsection (b) for noncompliance with the provisions of this part relating to collection, enforcement, disposition, or acceptance.

(e) **[Statutory damages: noncompliance with specified provisions.]** In addition to any damages recoverable under subsection (b), the debtor, consumer obligor, or person named as a debtor in a filed record, as applicable, may recover $500 in each case from a person that:

(1) fails to comply with Section 9-208;

(2) fails to comply with Section 9-209;

(3) files a record that the person is not entitled to file under Section 9-509(a);

(4) fails to cause the secured party of record to file or send a termination statement as required by Section 9-513(a) or (c);

(5) fails to comply with Section 9-616(b)(1) and whose failure is part of a pattern, or consistent with a practice, of noncompliance; or

(6) fails to comply with Section 9-616(b)(2).

(f) **[Statutory damages: noncompliance with Section 9-210.]** A debtor or consumer obligor may recover damages under subsection (b) and, in addition, $500 in each case from a person that, without reasonable cause, fails to comply with a request under Section 9-210. A recipient of a request under Section 9-210 which never claimed an interest in the collateral or obligations that are the subject of a request under that section has a reasonable excuse for failure to comply with the request within the meaning of this subsection.

(g) **[Limitation of security interest: noncompliance with Section 9-210.]** If a secured party fails to comply with a request regarding a list of collateral or a statement of account under Section 9-210, the secured party may claim a security interest only as shown in the list or statement included in the request as against a person that is reasonably misled by the failure.

SECTION 9-626. ACTION IN WHICH DEFICIENCY OR SURPLUS IS IN ISSUE.

(a) **[Applicable rules if amount of deficiency or surplus in issue.]** In an action arising from a transaction, other than a consumer transaction, in which the amount of a deficiency or surplus is in issue, the following rules apply:

(1) A secured party need not prove compliance with the provisions of this part relating to collection, enforcement, disposition, or acceptance unless the debtor or a secondary obligor places the secured party's compliance in issue.

(2) If the secured party's compliance is placed in issue, the secured party has the burden of establishing that the collection, enforcement, disposition, or acceptance was conducted in accordance with this part.

(3) Except as otherwise provided in Section 9-628, if a secured party fails to prove that the collection, enforcement, disposition, or acceptance was conducted in accordance with the provisions of this part relating to collection, enforcement, disposition, or acceptance, the liability of a debtor or a secondary obligor for a deficiency is limited to an amount by which the sum of the secured obligation, expenses, and attorney's fees exceeds the greater of:

(A) the proceeds of the collection, enforcement, disposition, or acceptance; or

(B) the amount of proceeds that would have been realized had the noncomplying secured party proceeded in accordance with the provisions of this part relating to collection, enforcement, disposition, or acceptance.

(4) For purposes of paragraph (3)(B), the amount of proceeds that would have been realized is equal to the sum of the secured obligation, expenses, and attorney's fees unless the secured party proves that the amount is less than that sum.

(5) If a deficiency or surplus is calculated under Section 9-615(f), the debtor or obligor has the burden of establishing that the amount of proceeds of the disposition is significantly below the range of prices that a complying disposition to a person other than the secured party, a person related to the secured party, or a secondary obligor would have brought.

(b) **[Non-consumer transactions; no inference.]** The limitation of the rules in subsection (a) to transactions other than consumer transactions is intended to leave to the court the determination of the proper rules in consumer transactions. The court may not infer from that limitation the nature of the proper rule in consumer transactions and may continue to apply established approaches.

SECTION 9-627. DETERMINATION OF WHETHER CONDUCT WAS COMMERCIALLY REASONABLE.

(a) **[Greater amount obtainable under other circumstances; no preclusion of commercial reasonableness.]** The fact that a greater amount could have been obtained by a collection, enforcement, disposition, or acceptance at a different time or in a different method from that selected by the secured party is not of itself sufficient to preclude the secured party from establishing that the collection, enforcement, disposition, or acceptance was made in a commercially reasonable manner.

(b) **[Dispositions that are commercially reasonable.]** A disposition of collateral is made in a commercially reasonable manner if the disposition is made:

(1) in the usual manner on any recognized market;

(2) at the price current in any recognized market at the time of the disposition; or

(3) otherwise in conformity with reasonable commercial practices among dealers in the type of property that was the subject of the disposition.

(c) **[Approval by court or on behalf of creditors.]** A collection, enforcement, disposition, or acceptance is commercially reasonable if it has been approved:

(1) in a judicial proceeding;

(2) by a bona fide creditors' committee;

(3) by a representative of creditors; or

(4) by an assignee for the benefit of creditors.

(d) **[Approval under subsection (c) not necessary; absence of approval has no effect.]** Approval under subsection (c) need not be obtained, and lack of approval does not mean that the collection, enforcement, disposition, or acceptance is not commercially reasonable.

SECTION 9-628. NONLIABILITY AND LIMITATION ON LIABILITY OF SECURED PARTY; LIABILITY OF SECONDARY OBLIGOR.

(a) **[Limitation of liability of secured party for noncompliance with article.]** Unless a secured party knows that a person is a debtor or obligor, knows the identity of the person, and knows how to communicate with the person:

(1) the secured party is not liable to the person, or to a secured party or lienholder that has filed a financing statement against the person, for failure to comply with this article; and

(2) the secured party's failure to comply with this article does not affect the liability of the person for a deficiency.

(b) **[Limitation of liability based on status as secured party.]** A secured party is not liable because of its status as secured party:

(1) to a person that is a debtor or obligor, unless the secured party knows:

(A) that the person is a debtor or obligor;

(B) the identity of the person; and

(C) how to communicate with the person; or

(2) to a secured party or lienholder that has filed a financing statement against a person, unless the secured party knows:

(A) that the person is a debtor; and

(B) the identity of the person.

(c) **[Limitation of liability if reasonable belief that transaction not a consumer-goods transaction or consumer transaction.]** A secured party is not liable to any person, and a person's liability for a deficiency is not affected, because of any act or omission arising out of the secured party's reasonable belief that a transaction is not a consumer-goods transaction or a consumer transaction or that goods are not consumer goods, if the secured party's belief is based on its reasonable reliance on:

(1) a debtor's representation concerning the purpose for which collateral was to be used, acquired, or held; or

(2) an obligor's representation concerning the purpose for which a secured obligation was incurred.

(d) **[Limitation of liability for statutory damages.]** A secured party is not liable to any person under Section 9-625(c)(2) for its failure to comply with Section 9-616.

(e) **[Limitation of multiple liability for statutory damages.]** A secured party is not liable under Section 9-625(c)(2) more than once with respect to any one secured obligation.

Index